THE GOTTSCHALK ANTIPHONARY

Music and Liturgy in Twelfth-Century Lambach

This book by Lisa Fagin Davis offers the first photographic reconstruction of the extant leaves of the Gottschalk Antiphonary, an important twelfth-century manuscript from the Austrian monastery in Lambach. The Gottschalk Antiphonary, which was dismantled for binding scrap in the fifteenth century, is examined from various angles – art historical, liturgical and musical – and its contributions to the study of medieval drama and the long-term ramifications of the investiture controversy are explored. The manuscript is studied within the historical and political context in which it was created, in order to better understand the decisions which went into its production. In addition to a black-and-white facsimile of the recovered portion of the manuscript, the book includes a survey of the twelfth-century Lambach scriptorium and a detailed codicological reconstruction of the codex. Appendices of charts and tables demonstrate how the Gottschalk Antiphonary compares with other liturgical manuscripts from the same period.

LISA FAGIN DAVIS is an independent scholar and has worked as a manuscript cataloguer for a number of institutions, including the Beinecke Rare Book and Manuscript Library, Yale University. She is a co-author of Volume IV of the Beinecke Rare Book and Manuscript Library manuscript catalogue and has published articles in *Codices Manuscripti* and *Plainsong and Medieval Music*.

Cambridge Studies in Palaeography and Codicology

This new series has been established to further the study of manuscripts from the Middle Ages to the Renaissance. It includes books devoted to particular types of manuscripts, their production and circulation, to individual codices of outstanding importance, and to regions, periods and scripts of especial interest to scholars. Certain volumes will be specially designed to provide students in the field with reliable introductions to central topics, and occasionally a classic originally published in another language will be translated into English. The series will be of interest not only to scholars and students of medieval literature and history, but also to theologians, art historians and others working with manuscript sources.

THE GOTTSCHALK
ANTIPHONARY

Music and Liturgy in Twelfth-Century Lambach

LISA FAGIN DAVIS

CAMBRIDGE
UNIVERSITY PRESS

PUBLISHED BY THE PRESS SYNDICATE OF THE UNIVERSITY OF CAMBRIDGE
The Pitt Building, Trumpington Street, Cambridge, United Kingdom

CAMBRIDGE UNIVERSITY PRESS
The Edinburgh Building, Cambridge CB2 2RU, UK   http:www.//cup.cam.ac.uk
40 West 20th Street, New York NY 10011-4211, USA   http://www.cup.org
10 Stamford Road, Oakleigh, Melbourne 3166, Australia
Ruiz de Alarcón 13, 28014 Madrid, Spain

© Lisa Fagin Davis 2000

First published 2000

Printed in the United Kingdom at the University Press, Cambridge

Typeset in 11.5/13.5 pt. Adobe Garamond in QuarkXPress™   [SE]

A catalogue record for this book is available from the British Library

Library of Congress cataloguing in publication data

ISBN 0 521 59249 6 hardback

Contents

Contents

Figures

Tables

Acknowledgements

This project would not have been possible without the encouragement, guidance, enthusiasm and expertise of Robert G. Babcock. For their time and assistance, I am also indebted to: the staff of the Beinecke Rare Book and Manuscript Library at Yale University; Eric Hollas, Julian Plante, Diane Warne Anderson, and the staff of the Hill Monastic Manuscript Library; Rodney Dennis, Laura Light, and the reading room staff of the Houghton Library at Harvard University; Jean E. Meeh Gosebrink at the St Louis Public Library; Otto Mazal, Eva Irblich and the reading room staff of the Österreichische Nationalbibliothek; Karl Hafner at the Studienbibliothek in Linz; Werner Telesko at the Stiftsbibliothek Göttweig; Hauke Fill at the Stiftsbibliothek Kremsmünster; Father Laurentius Kull at the Stiftsbibliothek St Paul; Abbot Berchtold Müller of the Stift Engelberg; former Lambach librarian Walter Wastl(†) for his help and enthusiasm during my stay at the abbey; and the current Lambach librarian Benedikt Weingartner. I am grateful to all of the above institutions and to the Preussischer Staatsbibliothek in Berlin for permission to reproduce photographs of manuscripts in their collections. In addition, I would like to thank the abbot of Lambach, Gotthard Schafelner, for allowing me access to the Lambach abbey library.

Many individuals were consulted during the process of researching and writing this book. For their musicological advice, I am indebted to Professors Andrew Hughes, Michel Huglo, Alejandro Planchart, Craig Wright, James Grier, and especially Ruth Steiner. Professor Ingeborg Glier served as my adviser on issues pertaining to liturgical drama. Professors Walter Cahn and Paul Binski advised me on the art historical aspects of my project. Professor Barbara Shailor offered invaluable advice on several codicological issues. Dr Kurt Holter spent many hours with me in the Lambach library sharing his insights into the scriptorium and particular manuscripts; this work would not have been possible without the foundation laid by his work on the Lambach library. Martin Czernin devoted many schillings' worth of postage to sharing with me his work on the Kremsmünster breviary. Charles Downey of the CANTUS project at Catholic University devoted countless hours to refining the database files of the Gottschalk Antiphonary, and his contributions to the identification of incomplete chants are considerable. I owe a special debt of gratitude to Hugh Feiss, OSB, and to Dr Melissa Conway. While I am grateful to all of the above individuals for their advice, I acknowledge any errors as my own.

Support for this project was generously provided by: Yale University, in the form of a Graduate Fellowship and an Enders Research Assistance Grant; the Austrian Cultural Institute; the American Bibliographical Society; and the Mrs Giles F. Whiting Foundation. I am particularly grateful to the Beinecke Rare Book and Manuscript Library, and to its director, Ralph Franklin, for financial support made possible by the H. P. Kraus Fellowship in Early Books and Manuscripts.

Finally, but at the top of the list, I send unending thanks and love to my husband for his support, encouragement, faith, enthusiasm, and undying patience. This work is dedicated to you, Dan, with love.

Abbreviations

AH	*Analecta Hymnica*
BRBL	Beinecke Rare Book and Manuscript Library, New Haven, CT
CAO	*Corpus Antiphonalium Officii*
CC	Codex Cremifarensis
Ccl	Codex chartaceus lambacensis
Clm	Bayerische Staatsbibliothek, Codex latinus monacensis
Cml	Codex membranaceus lambacensis
CSF	Codex sanflorianensis
CT	*Corpus Troporum*
Cvp	Codex vindobonensis palatinus
MGH	*Monumenta Germaniae Historica*
MGH Necr.	*MGH, Necrologia Germanica*
MGH SS	*MGH, Scriptores rerum Germanicarum*
MIÖG	*Mitteilungen des Instituts für Österreichische Geschichtsforschung*
O-ö	Oberösterreich
ÖNB	Österreichische Nationalbibliothek, Vienna
ÖKT	*Österreichische Kunsttopographie*
PL	*Patrologia Latina*
ser. n.	series nova

Manuscripts

Aug60:	Karlsruhe, Badische Landesbibliothek Aug. LX, saec. XII
Berl40047:	Berlin, Staatsbibliothek Preussischer Kulturbesitz, Mus. ms. 40047, saec. XI
BL19768:	London, British Library, Add. 19768, saec. XI
BN17296:	Paris, Bibliothèque Nationale, Lat. 17296, saec. XII
Bodl287:	Oxford, Bodleian Library, MS Canon Liturg. 287, saec. XII[ex]
Clm14845:	Munich, Bayerische Staatsbibliothek, Clm 14845, *c.* 1106–25

Clm14965b:	Munich, Bayerische Staatsbibliothek, Clm 14965b (the tonary of Frutolf von Bamberg), saec. XII
Clm18955:	Munich, Bayerische Staatsbibliothek, Clm 18955, saec. XI
Ein83:	Einsiedeln, Stiftsbibliothek, MS 83, saec. XII^med
Eng102:	Engelberg, Stiftsbibliothek, MS 102, saec. XII^med
Eng299:	Engelberg, Stiftsbibliothek, L 299 (printed breviary, saec. XVII)
GA:	The Gottschalk Antiphonary (New Haven, BRBL MS 481.51 etc.)
Gr29/30:	Graz, Universitätsbibliothek, No. 29/30, saec. XIV
Gr211:	Graz, Universitätsbibliothek, No. 211, saec. XII
Gr258:	Graz, Universitätsbibliothek, No. 258, saec. XII
Lc601:	Lucca, Biblioteca Capitolare, Cod. 601, saec. XII
Lei70:	Leiden, Bibliotheek der Rijksuniversiteit, Gronov. 70, saec. XI
Lm:	Lambach 2 (Beinecke MS 481.52; binding fragments in Lambach, Stiftsbibliothek Cml V and Leutkirch, Fürstlich Waldburgschen Gesamtarchiv, MS 5), saec. XII^ex
Lz290:	Linz, Studienbibliothek, MS 290, saec. XII^ex
Pas:	Passau Breviary, a conflation of various manuscripts from the thirteenth to the fifteenth centuries (see G. H. Karnowka, *Breviarium Passaviense*, Münchener Theologische Studien, 44) (Munich, 1983).
Pr:	Prague, Knihovna Kapitoly, Cap. P. VI, saec. XIV
SG388:	St Gall, Stiftsbibliothek, MS 388, saec. XII
SG389:	St Gall, Stiftsbibliothek, MS 389, *c.* 1265–71
SG390:	St Gall, Stiftsbibliothek, MS 390–391, *c.* 996–1006
SG390a:	fragmentary tonary of manuscript *SG390*
SG413:	St Gall, Stiftsbibliothek, MS 413 and MS 387, *c.* 1034–47
SG414:	St Gall, Stiftsbibliothek, MS 414, *c.* 1030
V2700:	Vienna, Österreichische Nationalbibliothek, ser. n. 2700 (a XII.7), saec. XII
Zü28:	Zürich, Zentralbibliothek, Rh. 28, saec. XII
Zü59:	Zürich, Zentralbibliothek, Rh. 59, saec. XII^ex
Zü80:	Zürich, Zentralbibliothek, Rh. 80, saec. XII

Folios of the Gottschalk Antiphonary

56	I.95.3	Lambach, Stiftsbibliothek, Ink. I.95, no. 3
57	I.95.4 + B10	Lambach, Stiftsbibliothek, Ink. I.95, no. 4 and New Haven, Beinecke Rare Book and Manuscript Library, MS 481.51.10
61	B11	New Haven, Beinecke Rare Book and Manuscript Library, MS 481.51.11
72	B12	New Haven, Beinecke Rare Book and Manuscript Library, MS 481.51.12
77	B13	New Haven, Beinecke Rare Book and Manuscript Library, MS 481.51.13
81	B14	New Haven, Beinecke Rare Book and Manuscript Library, MS 481.51.14
91	St1	St Louis, St Louis Public Library, Rare Books and Special Collections, Grolier #44
101	II.36.2	Lambach, Stiftsbibliothek, Ink. II.36, no. 2
102	B15	New Haven, Beinecke Rare Book and Manuscript Library, MS 481.51.15
111	B16	New Haven, Beinecke Rare Book and Manuscript Library, MS 481.51.16
121	B17	New Haven, Beinecke Rare Book and Manuscript Library, MS 481.51.17
131	H6	Cambridge, Mass., Houghton Library, Pf MS Typ 704 6
?	II.36.1	Lambach, Stiftsbibliothek, Ink. II.36, no. 1

I

Introduction

In the late twelfth century, a monk at the Austrian Benedictine abbey of Lambach created an antiphonary that was a musical masterpiece, combining beautifully historiated penwork initials with the newest developments in music theory and local styles of notation. Gottschalk of Lambach wrote, illustrated and notated this beautiful manuscript, and it was used and prized by the monks until the liturgy became outdated in the fifteenth century. At that time, the Gottschalk Antiphonary was dismantled for use as binding scrap, and its pages are currently scattered in collections around the world. This volume presents a reconstruction of the extant portion of the manuscript, an examination of the liturgy therein, and a detailed study of the context within which the codex was created.

The physical reconstruction of the extant portion of the manuscript functions not merely as a codicological exercise, but as a model of how the study of codicology and provenance can reflect on 'The History of the Book' in general. As a result of its long and complex journey, the manuscript has become much more than text, neumes and historiated initials. During its first three centuries of use, pertinent marginal annotations were added. In the late fifteenth century, the manuscript was dismantled and used for binding scrap. At this stage, the leaves were trimmed, the original binding holes became visible, and annotations were added pertaining to the books in which the fragments were bound. Four hundred and fifty years later, many of the fragments were pulled out of the bindings and sold. The bindings left scars on the leaves; additional binding holes, worm tracks and rodent holes, creases and glue stains became part of the fragments' topography. Some of the fragments then made the journey from Lambach to Switzerland to New York to New Haven. Others travelled from Lambach to Germany to Berkeley, California, from there to a private collector, and finally to Cambridge, Massachusetts. Two wandered from Lambach to St-Paul-im-Lavanttal, and one from the abbey to a Lambach book dealer to a private collector at an exclusive Alpine resort. One leaf made the strangest journey of all – from Lambach through an intermediary to a private collector in Cleveland to a travelling exhibit housed in an aluminium trailer (the leaf visited several dozen midwestern US cities and small towns, and was viewed by hundreds of schoolchildren and adults) to settle finally at the St Louis Public Library. During this phase, the fragments became prized as treasures in their own right, were given shelf numbers and were catalogued as individual items. It is only after painstaking research and study that they can be reunited, in facsimile if not in fact, with their cohorts, and something of their long and fascinating journey reconstructed.

The reconstructed, albeit incomplete, Gottschalk Antiphonary is worthy of study for many reasons, not the least of which is the mere fact of its existence. The importance of the study of liturgy in understanding monastic life cannot be overestimated. Every aspect of medieval monastic life was profoundly influenced by the liturgical cycle, especially the daily schedule, weekly and annual cycles, the choice of saints to commemorate, and the study and development of music and poetry. The Gottschalk Antiphonary represents the largest known body of Office liturgy from the medieval abbey at Lambach, which is located on the northern bank of the Traun river, ten miles south-west of Wels, in the Passau diocese. In addition, the manuscript was written, notated and illustrated by Gottschalk of Lambach, a monk whose artistic products have been studied and analysed for many years. The codex thus also sheds light on the art historical development of the abbey. The Antiphonary preserves an apparently unique method of musical classification wherein the tonary-letter system of antiphonal modal identification is adapted for use with responsories and invitatories, a fascinating footnote to the musical history of the monastery and of the region. The liturgy in the manuscript shows the clear influence of the twelfth-century monastic reform movements with which Lambach was associated. Finally, the discovery, reconstruction and study of the Gottschalk Antiphonary provide the first clear liturgical context for the performance of the eleventh-century Lambach Magi play in the context of the Romanesque frescoes in the Lambach abbey church, and allow for a more complete reconstruction of the celebration of Epiphany there. The antiphonary provides unequivocal evidence of the palpable impact of the historical and political context within which it was created.

The Gottschalk Antiphonary is particularly extraordinary for its clear use of multiple sources. Gottschalk drew not only upon earlier local sources, but on sources from the mother abbey, from the source of the reform movement with which Lambach was associated in the twelfth century, and from a distant, and as yet unexplained, French influence. The manuscript reflects these sources in its use of particular chants, the assignment of tonary-letters to antiphons, and in Gottschalk's inclusion of liturgical alternatives, some of which are from one tradition and some from another.

The manuscript is a product of the historical context within which Gottschalk lived and worked. In particular, the use of the chant 'Quem non praevalent' as a responsory trope at Epiphany Matins falls neatly into a political context, corresponding as it does with the political themes of the frescoes in the Lambach abbey church as well as with the Lambach Magi play. The abbey was founded in 1056 by Adalbero, Bishop of Würzburg, who was a key player in the power struggle between the papacy and the Holy Roman Emperor. We shall see how Gottschalk used the Antiphonary to promulgate the political propaganda planted by Adalbero and handed down by successive generations of monks.

After an introduction to the history of Lambach and its library (Chapters 1 and 2), Chapter 3 will examine the physical structure of the manuscript, culminating in a facsimile reconstruction of its various parts. Chapter 4 will examine the contents of the manuscript. Chapter 5 will present the political and historical context within which the Gottschalk Antiphonary was created, and will explore the implications of particular choices made by Gottschalk in the creation of the manuscript.

The Gottschalk Antiphonary is described in detail in Chapter 3 – the physical object as well as its provenance, script, music and decoration – in order to place the manuscript in an appropriate context within the history of book production in both the abbey and the region. Its fragments are reunited in facsimile, the reconstruction proceeding according to traditional rules of codicology. The leaves are organized in codicological groups, presented not only in manuscript order but according to their original quires. In many cases, it has been possible to reunite pairs of conjugate leaves and to reconstruct entire signatures. The contents of the manuscript are here presented in summary form, and in more detail when such data have implications for the relation of one leaf to another.

The core methodology of Chapter 4 is the comparison of the liturgical contents of the Gottschalk Antiphonary with other coeval manuscripts. These comparisons have resulted in various tables and charts, designed to summarize and aid in the interpretation of the vast amounts of data so accumulated. Such comparisons allow for an understanding of the sources of and influences on the manuscript, and lead to a clearer sense of Gottschalk's own contributions to the liturgical design.

In medieval Lambach, the celebration of Epiphany attained an uncommon resonance, for reasons which have never before been carefully explored. In the fifth and final chapter of this work, the liturgy for the celebration of Epiphany will be examined within the historical, political and art historical contexts presented in previous chapters in order to demonstrate how Gottschalk used and elaborated inherited traditions of monastic and institutional memory. This final chapter will demonstrate the importance of this manuscript as a historical document by demonstrating how, in combination with other elements, the Gottschalk Antiphonary helps to illuminate the celebration, and the layers of meaning behind the celebration, of Epiphany at Lambach.

Throughout this study, spelling of medieval Latin has been normalized according to the standards used by the CANTUS project (which are themselves based on Hesbert's practices in *Corpus Antiphonalium Officii*), except where Gottschalk's orthography is relevant to the specific argument. Translations of Latin are provided when the content is relevant.

This examination of the Gottschalk Antiphonary will touch upon many areas of study: art history and imperial politics, musicology and liturgy, palaeography and codicology, medieval drama, monastic book production, and the vagaries of early twentieth-century bibliophiles and book merchants. The Gottschalk Antiphonary is not alone among medieval manuscripts in its relation to these various subjects, although it illuminates them more clearly than some. Liturgical manuscripts in particular can be best understood by examining them within the different contexts in which they were produced. This may seem self-evident, but it bears repeating – every decision which went into the production of this manuscript was made for a reason, and these reasons merit examination. What were Gottschalk's liturgical sources? Why did he assign tonary-letters to responsories and invitatories instead of just antiphons? Why choose 'Quem non praevalent' as the Epiphany responsory trope? Why include a trope during Epiphany at all? These are some of the questions the Gottschalk Antiphonary poses, and which this study will attempt to answer.

I. THE POPE AND THE EMPEROR

The eleventh century was a time of great political strife and religious change for the papacy and for the Holy Roman Empire. One of the many issues dividing the secular and ecclesiastical authorities during this period was the ability to invest bishops. Emperor Henry IV declared this to be his right, hence giving himself the immense tactical advantage of selecting the bishops to his own liking, men of royal blood and courtly connections whose loyalty to the emperor was assured, bishops who during this period were endowed not only with ecclesiastical authority but also with tremendous power over local economic and legal affairs. Pope Gregory VII declared bishops vested by Henry to be falsely enthroned. During the 1070s and 1080s, the German bishops, whose episcopal authority and very lives were at stake, were forced to take sides. In general, the bishops of the southern dioceses were not men with royal connections. Mostly, they were former monks and abbots. Along with the majority of his fellows, Adalbero, the Bishop of Würzburg (1045–90), was an avid supporter of the pope.

It is important to understand the political and ecclesiastical climate of the latter half of the eleventh century in order to grasp something of the traditions Gottschalk was working with. The life of Bishop Adalbero, the founder of the Lambach abbey, is woven throughout these events, which have been studied by others in great detail – it is certainly not necessary to review the so-called 'Investiture Controversy' in depth here. A brief summary of the basic issues and events will suffice.

Pope Leo IX set the reform of the church in motion in the 1050s with his crusades against simony (the purchase of ecclesiastical office or benefices) and clerical marriage (commonplace during this period), and his support for a return to the acceptance of canon law as the ultimate rule and the necessity of the canonical election of bishops. The latter was not yet a strike against the powers of the emperor, rather a plea for the papacy and the royal court to work together for the purification and unity of the church. These programmes set in motion a series of events that would later lead to a full-scale crisis of church and state between Pope Gregory VII and Emperor Henry IV.

The next pope, Victor II, was also a relative and supporter of Henry III, and when he died in 1057 he brought an end a long line of German popes. His death, coming as it did on top of Henry's death in 1056, also brought to an end to the co-operation between papal reformers and the imperial court. Empress Agnes, assisted by Bishop Henry of Augsburg, was left as a feeble regent for her young son, Henry IV. Henry's lengthy minority left the door wide open for Italian and other noble families to regain control of the papacy. When the next pope was elected (Frederick of Lorraine, also known as Stephen X), the German court was not consulted, in opposition to the accepted custom. This was the first of a series of perceived insults to the Empire that would escalate the conflict over the next several decades.

Stephen was the first pope in many years to have come to the papacy from a monk's cell instead of a bishop's throne, and he immediately proceeded to strengthen the monastic position at the Lateran palace by surrounding himself with scholar-monks, appointing Peter Damian, respected monk, scholar and advisor, to the senior Cardinal-bishopric of Ostia, and Humbert of Moyenmoutier to the position of papal chancellor. When Stephen died, a schism ensued. John of Velletri was installed as Benedict X by the clergy and the laity, with the support of the emperor, but his election was challenged. The triumphal entry into Rome of the opposition, the Tuscan bishop Gerard of Florence (later Nicholas II), escorted by the military forces of Duke Godfrey of Tuscany, signalled the emperor's complete loss of control over the papacy.

The emperor's loss of control was made complete by the Papal Election Decree of 1059, which excluded the Holy Roman Empire entirely from the process of selecting the new pope. At this point, the German bishops, many of whom were imperial appointments, began to be divided in their support for the two centres of power as the conflict became increasingly divisive. The three men behind the papal throne were Peter Damian, Humbert and a respected monk named Hildebrand, who had been a clerk to Pope Gregory VI and lived with him in German exile after his deposition under charges of simony. Hildebrand was brought back to Rome by Nicholas, where he wielded great influence over the pope. In 1061, when Nicholas died and Alexander II was elected, not only was Henry IV (still in his minority) not consulted regarding the selection of the new pope, he was not even informed. In response, he nominated his own candidate, Bishop Cadalus of Parma, who would have been Honorius II had the emperor not retracted this nomination under pressure from Archbishop Anno of Cologne, who supported Alexander.

Hildebrand became the sole power behind the pope, with Humbert having died in 1061 and Peter Damian considering a return to his hermitage. Of Hildebrand's influence, Damian once wrote, 'If you want to live at Rome, obey the pope's lord rather than the lord pope'.[1] Though no great friend of Hildebrand (he once nicknamed him 'Holy Satan'),[2] Peter Damian would be united with the future Pope Gregory VII in their campaigns for church reform. As for the pope, Alexander was particularly worried about any charges of bribery or violence that might taint episcopal selections in Germany, and began to examine such cases carefully. By the time Henry IV assumed power in 1066, the pope had begun to actively interfere in the selection of bishops, and by 1073 the papacy was on the verge of a major confrontation with the authority of the emperor.

Hildebrand ascended to the papacy as Gregory VII in 1073. His papacy was clouded by controversy before it had even really begun – in his election, the cardinals had completely ignored the old tradition of at least consulting the emperor. Some considered this papacy tainted from the very beginning, and Hildebrand to be a false Christian and anti-pope. Others thought of him as a great reformer and defender of the faith, a defender not just in the figurative sense, but one willing to take up arms to defend his cause. From the start, the pope and the Holy Roman Emperor Henry IV were at odds, locked in a desperate power struggle. When Henry declared Gregory to be 'no longer pope, but a false monk', two of the German bishops opposed the proclamation: Hermann of Metz and Adalbero of Würzburg.[3] Adalbero, who was the emperor's godfather, had been a staunch supporter of Henry but now was forced to make the first of a number of choices between ecclesiastical and secular authority.

Gregory declared Henry excommunicate at the Synod of Worms in January 1076, whereupon several of the German bishops who had supported Henry against Gregory returned their support to the pope. Adalbero met the next month with Hermann and his friends Archbishop Gebhard of Salzburg and Bishop Altmann of Passau to discuss the situation. Adalbero was still not committed to either side – when the bishops met with the German princes in Mainz in June to publicly

---

[1] 'Vivere vis Romae, clara depromito voce: Plus Domino papae quam domno pareo papae.' *Carmen* CXLIX (*PL* 145:961D).

[2] *Opuscula* 20, 1 (*PL* 145:444AB). As Collin Morris cautions, however, this reference probably should not be taken out of context, and may in fact be Peter 'complaining about the pressure put on him by Hildebrand to involve himself in the affairs of the world rather than withdraw to his hermitage' (C. Morris, *The Papal Monarchy: The Western Church from 1050 to 1250*, Oxford History of the Christian Church (Oxford, 1989), p. 91 and n. 12).

[3] P. Scheele, *Die Herrlichkeit des Herrn: Die Lambacher Fresken aus der Zeit des heiligen Adalbero* (Würzburg, 1990), p. 16.

discuss their opposition to Henry, Adalbero was not among them.[4] But, according to Meyer von Knonau, when the bishops and nobles met in Tribur in October to throw their weight behind the pope's declaration, Adalbero had fully committed to the pope; one result of the assembly at Tribur was 'the anti-imperialist Adalbero turning his back to the king'.[5]

The relationship between church and state seemed to improve somewhat after Henry's penance and absolution at Canossa in January of 1077, although things became more complicated when the southern German princes threatened rebellion against Henry. When Gregory was unable to reach Augsburg to mediate a planned meeting with the German princes that same month, the princes elected their own king, Rudolf of Swabia. By this time, Adalbero had decided where his loyalties lay; shortly before Rudolf's coronation in Mainz on 26 March, he was Adalbero's guest in Würzburg. The coronation of Rudolf led to a bitter and brutal civil war. Würzburg was besieged in August, and Adalbero was forced to flee to his hometown of Lambach.

Support for the pope began to erode in 1080, after Gregory deposed and excommunicated Henry again. The Lombard bishops, sensing an opening, elected their own imperialist pope at the Synod of Mainz: Archbishop Wibert of Ravenna as Clement III. The civil war came to an end soon after Rudolf's death in 1080, because his successor was no match for Henry's forces. In 1081, because Adalbero had refused Henry's call to attend the Mainz synod, he was unseated, excommunicated and banished, along with fourteen other bishops who had opposed the emperor.[6] By 1084, Clement had garnered increasing support, even taking the step of crowning Henry and Empress Bertha himself. Gregory was forced to withdraw, and he died in exile in 1085. Henry had finally managed to return an imperialist pope to the throne. The schism continued, however, with the Gregorian faction electing Odo of Ostia as Urban II. Urban's support extended to such influential reformers as William of Hirsau, and with him Gebhard of Salzburg, Altmann of Passau and Adalbero of Würzburg. Adalbero was able to return to Würzburg briefly in 1086, but returned soon thereafter to Lambach, where he died in 1090. It is in the light of Adalbero's support of the pope and the shadow of his banishment that the early years of Lambach must be viewed.

2. THE FOUNDATION OF THE LAMBACH ABBEY

Previous to his dethronement, Bishop Adalbero was an active supporter of Gregorian reform and of the monastic reform movements, inheritors of the Cluniac tradition, that were sweeping across Germanic lands. To encourage the Gorze–Cluny reform

[4] *Ibid.*, p. 17.   [5] E. Wies, *Kaiser Heinrich IV* (Munich, 1996), p. 159.
[6] Scheele, *Die Herrlichkeit des Herrn*, p. 18.

movement in his bishopric, Adalbero brought a reform-minded monk named Ekkebert from Gorze to serve as abbot at Münsterschwarzach. In 1056, Adalbero founded a Benedictine monastery in his hometown and hereditary lordship of Lambach, on the northern bank of the Traun river in Upper Austria. In keeping with the trend towards what has been called the '"restitution" of local churches from lay to monastic control',[7] Adalbero's monastery took the place of the community of secular clerics founded by his father, Prince Arnold II, in the 1040s. The first monks came from Münsterschwarzach, and it was their Gorze abbot, Ekkebert, who served as Lambach's first abbot.

Other important monasteries were founded in the Passau diocese during this period, among them the abbeys in Göttweig and Admont. These two abbeys were established by Adalbero's close friends Altmann and Gebhard respectively. The relationship between the founders of these abbeys was to have profound implications in the region. It is no exaggeration to claim that Adalbero, Altmann and Gebhard forged bonds among their three 'lieblings' that had an impact on every aspect of monastic life in the region for centuries. The three men studied together in their youth in Paris before becoming a trio of the region's most powerful ecclesiastical authorities. A local legend is illustrated in Baroque murals on the walls of all three abbeys and is also recorded in a few early manuscripts of the founders' *vitae*. It is said that as young men the three once ate together on a riverbank. Some bread dropped into the river, and instead of sinking under the weight of the absorbed water, the bread floated. This miracle brought on a prophetic vision for each man of his future role as bishop and founder of an abbey.[8]

Cum adhuc scolares essent, et quadam die ad cuiusdam fontis fluenta forte panem comessuri, sed non saturandi, resedissent; ad invicem concludebant, et se episcopos futuros pronuntiabant. Gebehardus dixit, se in Salzburgensi ecclesia episcopum futurum; Adalbero Wirzeburgensis ecclesiae sedem se adepturum; Altmannus vero, Pataviense cathedram se possessurum; quod totum ita probavit eventus. Nam et Gebehardus in Salzburgensi ecclesia est pontifex infulatus, et Adalbero in Wirzeburgensi sede antistes sublimatus; Altmannus vero in Pataviensi cathedra praesul ordinatus. Sed et hoc notandum, quod quisque eorum in loco, quem ipse construxit, requiescit. Gebehardus namque coenobium quod Admunt dicitur construxit, in hoc ipse sepultus requiescit; monasterium Lambach ab Adalberone aedificatur in hoc et ipse nunc tumulatur; coenobialis vero ecclesia in monte gotewich ab altmanno construitur; in hac et ipse sepelitur.[9]

[At the time they were students, they sat one day at a river whose powerful stream was about to consume the bread, but it was not saturated; and so one after the other they con-

---

[7] Morris, *The Papal Monarchy*, p. 79.
[8] A. Krause, 'Das Dreigestirn', in S. K. Landersdorfer (ed.), *Der heilige Altmann Bischof von Passau: sein Leben und sein Werk* (Göttweig, 1965), pp. 39–47, at p. 39.
[9] W. Wattenbach, 'Vita Altmani Episcopi Pataviensis', in G. Pertz (ed.), *MGH SS* XII (Hanover, 1856), pp. 226–43, at p. 231.

cluded, and predicted that they would themselves be bishops. Gebhard said, he would be future bishop in the church of Salzburg; Adalbero said that he would attain the seat of the church of Würzburg; Altmann in truth said that he would possess the Passau cathedral: in this way the whole thing proved to be so. For Gebhard was vested bishop in the Salzburg church, and Adalbero was elevated bishop of the seat of Würzburg; truly, Altmann was installed bishop in the Passau cathedral. But this ought to be noted, that each of them rested in the very place he had built; for Gebhard built the monastery that is called Admont, [and] in that very place he lies buried; the Lambach monastery was built by Adalbero and in that very place he is now entombed; indeed the church of the abbey on the mountain of Göttweig was constructed by Altmann; in that very place he is buried.][10]

Their support of the pope bonded these and other local monasteries together, and their relationships were in other respects very close. Berthold, one of the first monks at Göttweig, went on to become Abbot of Garsten. One of the monks who was a novice during his abbotcy, Alram, later became Abbot of Kremsmünster.[11] Another monk, Sigibold, was simultaneously Abbot of Lambach and Melk in 1116 – hard to imagine, but apparently true, as recorded in the twelfth-century Lambach chronicle.[12] A monk trained at Lambach went on to become Abbot of Göttweig, the abbey that trained St Lambrecht's first abbot. These are just a few examples of the connections forged by the bonds between the abbeys of the Passau diocese, originally based on the friendship of the Austrian 'Dreigestirn' (trio of stars).

The three founders remained closely associated even after their prophetic visions were realized. It was Altmann who dedicated the Lambach abbey church and its altars to the Assumption of Mary and to St Kilian, the patron of Würzburg, in 1089. The original Romanesque abbey church was replaced in the fourteenth century by a Gothic church, which was itself replaced by the extant Baroque structure. The Romanesque building was double-choired, with altars at both the east and west ends (see Fig. 1). The high altar was located in the west end of the church. Of the original Romanesque church, only this western choir remains intact, forming the foundation of the modern belltower. In the 1080s, frescoes were painted in the western choir depicting scenes from the life of Christ on the walls and the Epiphany story on the ceiling cupolas.

Adalbero died on 6 October, 1090 and was entombed beneath the nave of the Lambach abbey church. His life and posthumous miracles are recorded in a

---

[10] It should be noted that the Latin here appears to be somewhat corrupt, and some liberties have had to be taken in the translation.

[11] W. Neumüller, 'Zur Benediktinerreform des heiligen Altman', in Landersdorfer (ed.), *Der heilige Altmann Bischof von Passau*, p. 20.

[12] 'Sigiboldus abbas . . . qui plures rexisse abbatias fertur, inter quas et Medeliccam tenuit.' W. Wattenbach, 'Vita Adalberonis Episcopi Wirziburgensis', in G. Pertz (ed.), *MGH SS* XII (Hanover, 1856), pp. 127–38, at p. 136.

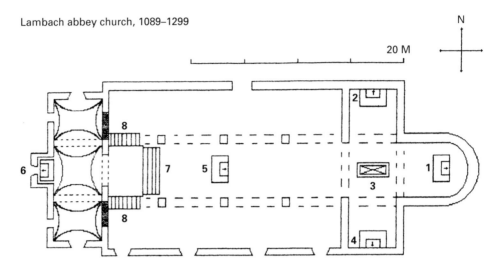

Lambach abbey church, 1089–1299

N

20 M

1 Altar dedicated to John the Baptist   [1089]
2 Altar dedicated to Martin and Nicholas   [date unknown]
3 Adalbero's tomb   [after 1090]
4 Altar dedicated to Leonard   [date unknown]
5 Altar dedicated to the Cross   [date unknown]
6 High Altar, dedicated to Mary and Kilian *et al.* [1089]
7 Stairs up to West Choir
8 Stairs down to crypt

major arch   window

minor arch, one level high   door

[see ÖKT, fig. 56 and Nachtrag, p. 502]

1. The Lambach Abbey Church (1089–1299)

Lambach manuscript of the twelfth century, Codex membranaceus lambacensis (Cml) LIV. Although he has been venerated locally as a saint since his death, Adalbero was not officially canonized until 1883.[13]

3. MONASTIC REFORM AT LAMBACH

In twelfth-century Lambach, as elsewhere, all aspects of monastic life – from the liturgy the monks recited to the books they produced – were heavily influenced by eleventh- and twelfth-century monastic reform movements. Along with the papacy's

[13] A. Wendehorst, 'Adalbero, Bischof von Würzburg und Gründer Lambachs', in *900 Jahre Klosterkirche Lambach. Oberösterreichische Landesausstellung 1989* (Linz, 1989), pp. 17–24, at p. 24.

programme of ecclesiastical and clerical reform came a renewal and dissemination of monastic reform. There was a feeling that monasticism had strayed from its ascetic and contemplative roots, tending more towards politics and a concern for wealth. With the support of the papacy, monastic leaders such as William of Dijon helped to disseminate this reformative fervour, which had its roots at centres such as Cluny and Gorze. Different centres re-created monasticism in their own ways, composing customaries to cement the new policies and traditions, and lending their names to movements such as the Cluniac reform (of which most other movements were a refinement), the St Blasien reform, the Hirsau reform, and so on. It was through Lambach's first abbot, Ekkebert, that the Junggorze monastic reform movement moved into southern Germany and Austria.[14] From Lambach, the reform spread to the nearby Austrian abbeys at Kremsmünster, Admont and Melk.

Although the abbey of the Virgin and St Kilian at Lambach was founded as part of the Junggorze reform movement, this fervour was not inherited by the next generation of monks; the Junggorze abbot Bero, who had been transferred to Lambach when the monks at Schlüchtern rejected his abbacy, was equally opposed by many of the Lambach monks.[15] In 1116, when Bishop Erlang of Würzburg appointed Bero as abbot against the will of the monks, many were so distraught that they left Lambach for Göttweig. In 1120, Bero was removed from office by the bishops of Passau and Würzburg.[16] The monastery in Göttweig had recently adopted the Fruttuarian reform movement from St Blasien, and it was via Göttweig that the Fruttuarian (also known as the St Blasien) reform came to Lambach with the return of the monks from that abbey in 1124. A new abbot, Helmbert, was elected to oversee the institution of Fruttuarian reforms.[17]

The Fruttuarian reform movement originated around the year 1030, when William of Dijon (himself formerly a monk at both Cluny and Hirsau) came to Fruttuaria as abbot and instituted intense reforms of the Cluniac traditions there.[18] William's goal was to give the Cluniac reform new spirit and ideals; his movement can be seen as a more intense version of the Cluniac reform. While the Cluniac abbot had his own sleeping quarters, the Fruttuarian abbot slept in the common room with the rest of the monks; the Cluniac hand-kiss became the Fruttuarian foot- and knee-kiss; the abbot's washing the feet of three and of twelve peasants was expanded, in Fruttuaria, to a hundred peasants.[19] The reform was brought to St

---

[14] *Ibid.*, p. 22.
[15] K. Hallinger, *Gorze-Kluny: Studien zu den monastischen Lebensformen und Gegensätzen im Hochmittelalter* (Rome, 1950), p. 228.
[16] A. Eilenstein, *Die Benediktinerabtei Lambach in Österreich ob der Enns und ihre Mönche* (Linz, 1936), p. 22.   [17] Hallinger, *Gorze-Kluny*, p. 229.
[18] Fruttuaria, now San Benigno Canavese, is located slightly north of Turin.
[19] L. Spätling, *Consuetudines Fructuarienses–Sanblasianae*, 2 vols., Corpus Consuetudinum Monasticum, 12 (Siegburg, 1985/1987), vol. I, p. LII.

Blasien by Henry IV and his mother Agnes, who stopped in Fruttuaria on their way through Italy to Rome and were much impressed by the reforms which had been instituted by Abbot William. From St Blasien, the Fruttuarian reform spread throughout the Germanic lands, and its houses traditionally supported the pope against the king.[20] In Austria, the reform spread from Göttweig to Lambach, Garsten, Seitenstetten and St Lambrecht, among others. The shared reform movement strengthened pre-existent ties and forged new ones, as monks of the St Blasien movement copied each other's liturgy and texts, commemorated each other in necrologies, and influenced each other artistically.[21]

The Fruttuarian *Consuetudines* (the customary) survives in several manuscripts.[22] One of these, Göttweig, Stiftsbibliothek, cod. 53b, originated in Göttweig or St Blasien, spent several centuries in Lambach (as Cml CVI), and has been in Göttweig since 1929.[23] This early twelfth-century manuscript is incomplete, containing only book 2 (detailed liturgical directions for the yearly cycle) and book 3 (the responsibilities of each monk's office). Book 1, directions for the daily liturgical ritual, is missing from this copy.

Several passages in the Gottschalk Antiphonary appear to quote from the *Consuetudines*, implying that the reform movement truly affected the Lambach liturgy. In addition to the Antiphonary's dependence on the Customary, the influence of the Fruttuarian reform movement on the Lambach liturgy is demonstrated by the manuscript's similarity to liturgical books produced in other centres of the reform movement. This issue is explored further in Chapter 4.

[20] *Ibid.*, p. XVI.
[21] I am currently working on an extended study of the impact of the reform movement on various aspects of book production in the region.
[22] Göttweig, Stiftsbibliothek, cod. 53b (formerly Lambach Cml CVI); Königswart, Schloßbibliothek, codd. 78 and 52; Linz, Studienbibliothek, cod. 313 (121); Munich, Bayerische Staatsbibliothek, Clm 14765; St-Paul-im-Lavanttal, Stiftsarchiv, cod. Sanblas. chart. 268 (32.2.28) and cod. Hosp. chart. 198 (29.1.1).   [23] Spätling, *Consuetudines Fructuarienses – Sanblasianae*, vol. I, p. XXXII.

2

The Lambach scriptorium in the late twelfth century

I. THE LAMBACH LIBRARY

A study of the Gottschalk Antiphonary must perforce begin with a survey of the palaeographical and art historical context within which the manuscript was created, that is, an overview of the Lambach scriptorium in the late twelfth century. The scriptorium existed in the shadows of the prolific scriptoria at Admont and Melk, which were themselves working under the influence of Salzburg, as were most of the scriptoria of this region.[1] The white-vine penwork initials in red and purple and the Byzantine features of the human figures all reveal the influence of the Salzburg style that is best manifested, perhaps, in the great St Peter Antiphonary.[2] The manuscript decoration to come out of Lambach during this period is not elaborate, consisting almost entirely of red and purple penwork initials and miniatures, occasionally filled with green or blue wash; there is no painting or gold leaf. Early studies of the Lambach scriptorium were critical of this paucity of illumination, claiming that it revealed the inferiority of the scriptorium in comparison to Salzburg.[3] However, as Robert Babcock points out in his study of the Beinecke Lambach fragments, 'the simplicity of the decoration does not result from a poverty of resources or ability, but rather from a conscious desire to avoid excessive luxury'.[4] The Lambach customary makes only one direct reference to manuscript illumination, declaring that it is not the custom of the abbey that the Gospel book carried before the priest at High Mass on Maundy Thursday be decorated with gold or silver, but 'that it be pure and lenten, as is suited to carrying throughout Lent'.[5] It is certainly possible that this reference,

---

[1] See G. Swarzenski, *Die Salzburger Malerei* (Leipzig, 1913), pp. 153–8.
[2] O. Demus and F. Unterkircher (eds.), *Das Antiphonar von St Peter: Codex Vindobonensis S. N. 2700* (Graz, 1969–73).   [3] Swarzenski, *Die Salzburger Malerei*, pp. 154–6.
[4] R. G. Babcock, *Reconstructing a Medieval Library: Fragments from Lambach* (New Haven, 1993), p. 53.
[5] 'Non est usus noster textum euangelii, qui ad maiorem missam in Cena Domini ante sacerdotem ad altare portatur, auro uel argento esse adornatum, sed ab his purum et quadragesimalem, qui per totam Quadragesimam portati solet.' L. Spätling, *Consuetudines Fructuarienses: Sanblasianae*, Corpus Consuetudinum Monasticum, 12 (Siegburg, 1985 and 1987), vol. II, p. 61.

disparaging as it is towards the use of gold and silver, might have led the monks at Lambach to avoid manuscript illumination in general.[6]

The script used at Lambach during this period is rather conservative:

The manuscripts copied in twelfth-century Lambach are impressive for the clarity of their script and for the solid durability of their construction rather than for any ornamental or decorative features. Many of the scribes at Lambach continued to use a clear and legible Caroline minuscule script as late as the year 1200, well after the introduction of proto-Gothic and Gothic scripts in many European scriptoria. Although this conservatism may seem provincial, it certainly resulted in the Lambach library having comparatively readable manuscripts, and it is not impossible that the retention of the older style of writing was intentional.'[7]

This 'transitional' script, lying somewhere between Caroline and Gothic, has never been satisfactorily named – it has been called 'proto-Gothic' (above), and both 'rounded primitive Gothic' and 'slanted-oval' (a description of the [o] grapheme), by Bernard Bischoff.[8] The term 'Romanesque' will be used here, as it designates the time-period in question and seems in this case to best describe the interim between Caroline and Gothic. The minims have feet, in a Gothic fashion, but the base-line is uneven, and the top line of writing is above the top line of ruling. There is also none of the 'biting', or joining of bows, that would characterize the script as a true Gothic.

The style of illustration and script practised at Lambach can be found through-out the Upper Austrian region, in other scriptoria such as Mondsee,[9] Kremsmünster, Seitenstetten and Göttweig. Of the latter it is thought 'that the influence of the Salzburg style of book-decoration came via Lambach'.[10]

Though its production was less prolific and luxurious than great Austrian centres such as Melk or Admont, the Lambach abbey has still achieved some measure of renown as a centre of book production; the monks produced illustrated manu-scripts of many literary genres, keeping up with the latest intellectual trends and newest works (early copies of works by Bernard of Clairvaux were written there, for example), as well as crafting beautifully blind-stamped and incised Romanesque and Gothic bindings.[11]

The contents of the abbey library have been laid out in detail by Robert Babcock,

---

[6] Babcock, *Reconstructing a Medieval Library*, p. 53.   [7] *Ibid.*, p. 53.
[8] B. Bischoff, 'La Nomenclature des écritures livresques du IXᵉ au XIIIᵉ siècle', in *Nomenclatures des écritures livresques du IXᵉ au XVIᵉ siècle* (Paris, 1954), pp. 7–14, figs. 1, 2, 7 and 8, and, for 'slanted-oval'; Bischoff, *Latin Paleography*, trans. D. Ó. Cróinín and D. Ganz (Cambridge, 1990), p. 120.
[9] C. Pfaff, *Scriptorium und Bibliothek des Klosters Mondsee im hohen Mittelalter*, Veröffentlichungen der Kommission für Geschichte Österreichs, 2 (Vienna, 1967).
[10] M. Pippal, 'Mittelalterliche Buchmalerei in Göttweig bis zum internationalen Stil', in *900 Jahre Stift Göttweig* (Göttweig, 1983), pp. 542–70, at p. 549.
[11] K. Holter, 'Romanische Bucheinbände des 12.Jahrhunderts aus Kloster Lambach, Oberösterreich', *Gutenberg Jahrbuch* (1965), pp. 343–7, and Holter, 'Zum gotischen Bucheinband in Österreich: Die Buchbinderwerkstatt des Stiftes Lambach O.-Ö.', *Gutenberg Jahrbuch* (1954), pp. 280–9.

and are here merely outlined.[12] According to the twelfth-century booklist preserved in Cml XCIII,[13] classical Latin authors represented at the Lambach school library included Terence, Persius, Vergil and Ovid. There were copies of several Ovidian texts, among them the *Metamorphoses*, *Heroides*, *Fasti*, *De remedia amoris*, *Ibis* and *Amores*. According to Babcock, 'The popularity of Ovid at Lambach in the twelfth century is a good indication of how up-to-date the curriculum was, for Ovid was widely read at that time in the leading schools in France and Germany'.[14] Also represented are Latin poets of the Late Antique and early medieval periods, such as Theodolus, Maximianus, Prudentius, Aesop, and a Latin abridgement of Homer's *Iliad*. Twelfth-century poetic works are strongly represented as well: Abelard, Hildebert of Lavardin, Bernard of Marval, Vital and William of Blois, and others. 'It is remarkable that an abbey so distant from the French centers where these texts were written should have owned so many of them at such an early date.'[15] The French influence on Lambach will be revisited throughout this study.

In Cml XIX, another booklist from the same period preserves titles of liturgical, theological and patristic texts, many of which can be identified with extant manuscripts. This booklist has been analysed by Kurt Holter in some detail.[16] Authors listed include Augustine, Gregory the Great, Rupert of Deutz, Honorius of Autun, Haimo, Bede, Isidore, Bernhard, Hugh of St Victor, and Smaragdus. 'The large number of patristic, exegetical, and other theological texts in the twelfth-century Lambach library indicates that the abbey was becoming at that time a regional center for advanced theological studies.'[17] This booklist also records forty liturgical manuscripts. Seventeen of these can be found among the Beinecke fragments.[18] Only three of these liturgical manuscripts are known to have escaped the fifteenth-century binder's knife: the two rituales (Cml LXXIII and Cml LXXIIIa), and a newly identified missal that had left Lambach by that time (Melk, Stiftsbibliothek, MS 709).[19] The Gottschalk Antiphonary, however, may have been excluded from the list; the booklist records 'three poor antiphonaries'. Because all of the surviving Lambach antiphonaries, including Gottschalk's, would have been new and in fine condition when the list was compiled, it is difficult to imagine what is meant by this entry. The term 'vilia' is a slightly later insertion, so perhaps it was not meant to apply to the antiphonaries.

While most of the manuscripts remain in the abbey library, many have been

---

[12] Babcock, *Reconstructing a Medieval Library*, pp. 53–63.
[13] Folio 1r. See K. Holter, 'Zwei Lambacher Bibliotheksverzeichnisse des 13. Jahrhunderts', *Mitteilungen des Instituts für Österreichische Geschichtsforschung*, 64 (1956), pp. 262–76, at pp. 271–2.
[14] Babcock, *Reconstructing a Medieval Library*, p. 53.   [15] Ibid., p. 54.
[16] Folio 227v. See Holter, 'Zwei Lambacher Bibliotheksverzeichnisse', pp. 272–5.
[17] Babcock, *Reconstructing a Medieval Library*, p. 59.   [18] Ibid., pp. 59–63.
[19] The manuscript includes the liturgy for the feast of St Colomannus, the patron of Melk, only in late medieval marginalia, indicating that the manuscript was not made for the use of Melk, but had travelled there by the fifteenth century. The script and initials indicate an origin in Lambach.

scattered through the book trade. A concordance of the original Lambach shelf numbers and known current locations of the manuscripts comprises Appendix 1. The pre-sixteenth-century holdings of the library are divided into three sections: parchment manuscripts (indicated by the appellation 'codex membranaceus lambacensis', or Cml), paper manuscripts ('codex chartaceus lambacensis', or Ccl) and incunables (books printed before 1501). Cml shelf numbers are indicated by Roman numerals, Ccl shelf numbers by Arabic. Within these groupings, the books are arranged in descending order according to size. The modern shelf numbers were assigned to the manuscripts by P. Felix Resch (*d.* 1789) in his catalogue of the library's holdings, although the numbers were not adopted officially until 1827.[20] Pre-dating Resch's catalogue are the two booklists from the late twelfth century. The next detailed catalogue of the manuscript holdings was produced in 1924/5 by Hans Gerstinger.[21] When Kurt Holter wrote his catalogue of the art-historically significant Lambach manuscripts as part of the *Österreichische Kunsttopographie* series in 1959, many of the manuscripts Gerstinger had listed were gone.[22] Holter was forced to base his descriptions of the 'lost' manuscripts on Gerstinger's work.

The incunables are divided into two groups. Within these groups, whose shelf numbers begin with Roman numerals I or II, the books are arranged according to size. The earliest extant incunable catalogue is incomplete, a bound paper manuscript compiled by Ph. Goldschmidt for the Österreichische Inkunabel Kommission between 15 and 27 June 1916. An older numbering system is evident on the spines of some incunables and most of the manuscripts.

Several manuscripts and manuscript fragments which were at the abbey in the Middle Ages predate the monastery's foundation, and were probably brought to Lambach at its foundation to start the monastic library. These have been studied by Kurt Holter,[23] Bernhard Bischoff[24] and Hans Gerstinger.[25] Manuscript production at Lambach began soon after the abbey's foundation. The earliest manuscripts of probable Lambach origin date from the late eleventh or early twelfth century: Cml VI (Bede's *Expositio super apocalipsin* and Haimo of Halberstadt's work of the

---

[20] Holter, 'Zwei Lambacher Bibliotheksverzeichnisse', p. 263.

[21] *Ibid.* Gerstinger's manuscript catalogue was ÖNB MS autogr. 200, and is now MS ser. n. 9713: *Bericht über die verbotswidrigen Veräußerungen aus der Stiftsbibliothek Lambach* (Vienna, 1930). Although the catalogue was written in 1924/5, it was assembled and an introduction written in 1930.

[22] K. Holter, 'Die Handschriften und Inkunabeln', in E. Hainisch (ed.), *Die Kunstdenkmäler des Gerichtsbezirkes Lambach*, ÖKT 34/2 (Vienna, *c.* 1959), pp. 234–65.

[23] K. Holter, 'Zu einem Verzeichnis der frühmittelalterlichen Handschriften', in *Karolingische und Ottonische Kunst: Werden, Wesen, Wirkung (VI. Internationaler Kongress für Frühmittelalterforschung)* (Wiesbaden, 1957), pp. 434–42.

[24] B. Bischoff, *Die südostdeutschen Schreibschulen und Bibliotheken in der Karolingerzeit*, II (Wiesbaden, 1980), pp. 40–4.

[25] H. Gerstinger, 'Zwei Fragmente einer altlateinschen Übersetzung des Buches der Richter in einem Codex der Bibliothek des Benediktinerklosters Lambach in Oberösterreich', *Mitteilungen des Vereines klassischer Philologen in Wien*, 6 (1929), p. 95.

same name), and Cml CXXXI (a martyrology, the Benedictine rule, and the Lambach necrology in one volume).[26] By the middle of the twelfth century, the scriptorium was flourishing. Under Abbots Bernhard (*c.* 1148–67) and Pabo (1167–94), manuscript production reached its literary and artistic high point, and the library was greatly expanded.

2. THE LAMBACH SCRIPTORIUM AND GOTTSCHALK

During the latter half of the twelfth century, many scribes and artists were working in the Lambach scriptorium. One artist's work is predominant throughout this period. Some of the finest examples of his work, intricate Romanesque initials and penwork miniatures, can be found in Berlin, Staatsbibliothek, MS Theol. lat. qu. 140 (formerly Cml XCIII, also known as the 'Williram manuscript' for its contents, among other texts Williram von Ebersberg's commentary on the *Song of Songs*). Opposite a donor's portrait is found the inscription 'Hic liber est Gotscalci de Lambach', written by the rubricating hand. Because the rubricator, scribe and artist appear to have been one man, this artist is known as Gottschalk, or the Gottschalk-master.[27] The booklist at the beginning of the Berlin manuscript is written in Gottschalk's hand, suggesting that he may have had some connection to the school; it has been suggested that he was the librarian.[28] Librarians often doubled as cantors during this period;[29] Gottschalk's musical interests are attested by the creative musical elements in the Gottschalk Antiphonary and the verses he composed which are found at the end of the Berlin manuscript.

Although few details are known of Gottschalk's life, his name is well known to modern scholarship.[30] He was active throughout the second half of the twelfth

---

[26] *ÖKT*, p. 214 and figs. 223, 224, 226 and 227. The necrology is edited in M. Fastlinger, 'Notae necrologicae et fragmentum necrologii monasterii lambacenses', *MGH Necr.* IV (Berlin, 1920), pp. 404–6.

[27] Holter, 'Zwei Lambacher Bibliotheksverzeichnisse', p. 266. It is important to distinguish Gottschalk of Lambach from the 'Cotescalco' active in St Gall in the mid-twelfth century.

[28] Holter, 'Zwei Lambacher Bibliotheksverzeichnisse', p. 270.

[29] M. Fassler, 'The Office of the Cantor in Early Western Monastic Rules and Customaries: A Preliminary Investigation', *Early Music History*, 5 (1985), p. 29.

[30] See references in: Babcock, *Reconstructing a Medieval Library*; R. G. Babcock and L. F. Davis, 'Two Romanesque Manuscripts from Lambach', *Codices Manuscripti*, 8 (1990), pp. 137–47; R. G. Babcock, L. F. Davis and P. Rusche, *Catalogue of Medieval and Renaissance Manuscripts in the Beinecke Rare Book and Manuscript Library, Yale University*, vol. IV; *MSS 481–485*, Medieval and Renaissance Texts and Studies, 176 (Forthcoming, Tempe, 1999); L. F. Davis, 'Epiphany at Lambach: The Evidence of the Gottschalk Antiphonary', unpublished Ph.D. diss., Yale University (1993); *eadem*, 'Tonary-letters in Twelfth-Century Lambach', *Plainsong and Medieval Music*, 5 (1996), pp. 131–52; *eadem*, 'Two Leaves of the Gottschalk Antiphonary', *Harvard Library Bulletin*, New Series 5/3 (1994), pp. 38–44; G. Heilingsetzer and W. Stelzer (eds.), *Kurt Holter: Buchkunst – Handschriften – Bibliotheken: Beiträge zur mitteleuropäischen buchkultur vom Frühmittelalter bis zur Renaissance*, 2 vols. (Linz, 1996); K. Holter, 'Beiträge zur Geschichte der Stiftbibliothek Lambach', *Jahrbuch des Musealvereines Wels*, 15 (1969), pp. 96–123;

century. Holter dates the Berlin manuscript to *c.* 1180, and gives Gottschalk a productivity span of about thirty years.[31] Evidence within several of the manuscripts themselves pinpoints his period of scribal productivity to between 1197 and 1204 (see below). As an artist, however, he was so prolific that his career must have begun much earlier, perhaps as early as the middle of the twelfth century; initials in his style can be found in the early Lambach rituale (Cml LXXIIIa), a manuscript known to have been produced during the abbacy of Bernhard (*c.* 1148–67). It is quite possible, however, that Gottschalk's work on this manuscript was added several decades later. The initials in the first five folios of the manuscript, which are not by Gottschalk, are thought by Holter to be later additions. It is unlikely that Gottschalk, if working at the time the manuscript was produced, would have left blank the initial spaces in the first five folios. It is more likely that he, too, added the initials later. Gottschalk's scribal hand is found at the very end of this manuscript, where he records a psalm and notated litany (folios 76^v–78^v). This work also seems to have been added at a later date; a second rituale, Cml LXXIII, which is a copy of Cml LXXIIIa made around the year 1200, does not include the psalm and litany recorded by Gottschalk in the earlier manuscript, implying that the psalm and litany were in all likelihood added to the early rituale after the turn of the century. Two other Lambach manuscripts retain evidence of Gottschalk's period of scribal activity: Cml LIV (the Life and Miracles of Adalbero) and CVP 373 (a Lambach chronicle).

Cml LIV

Gottschalk is thought to be the author, as well as the scribe and artist, of the first part of this manuscript, which records the life and posthumous miracles of

---

Footnote 30 (*cont.*)

idem, 'Die Handschriften und Inkunabeln'; *idem,* 'Initialen aus einer Lambacher Handschrift des 12.Jahrhunderts', *Wiener Jahrbuch für Kunstgeschichte*, 46/7 (1993/94), pp. 255–65 and 433–6; *idem,* 'Das mittelalterliche Buchwesen des Benediktinerstiftes Lambach', *900 Jahre Klosterkirche Lambach: Oberösterreichische Landesausstellung 1989* (Linz, 1989), pp. 53–64; *idem,* 'Neue Beiträge zur Geschichte der Stiftsbibliothek von Lambach im hohen Mittelalter', in G. Heilingsetzer (ed.), *Kunstgeschichtsforschung und Denkmalpflege (Festschrift für Norbert Wibiral zum 65. Geburtstag)* (Linz, 1986), pp. 85–98; *idem,* 'Die romanische Buchmalerei in Oberösterreich', *Jahrbuch des Ober-Österreichisches Musealvereins*, 101 (1956), pp. 221–50; *idem,* 'Zwei Lambacher Bibliotheksverzeichnisse'; W. Luger, *Der älteste Bibliothekskatalog des Klosters Lambach*, Oberösterreichische-Kulturberichte, 16 (Linz, 1953); O. Mazal, *Buchkunst der Romanik* (Graz, 1978); J. Neuwirth, 'Studien zur Geschichte der Miniaturmalerei in Oesterreich', *Sitzungsberichte der kaiserlichen Akademie der Wissenschaften, Philosophisch-Historische Klasse*, 130 (1886), pp. 129–39; O. Pächt and J. J. G. Alexander, *Illuminated Manuscripts in the Bodleian Library, Oxford*, I (Oxford, 1966), p. 6 (no. 80), pl. VII; H. Paulhart, *Mittelalterliche Bibliothekskataloge Österreichs*, V (Vienna, *c.* 1915), pp. 49–58, at p. 55; C. Pfaff, *Scriptorium und Bibliothek des Klosters Mondsee im hohen Mittelalter*, Veroffentlichungen der Kommission für Geschichte Österreichs, 2 (Vienna, 1967), G. Swarzenski, *Die Salzburger Malerei* (Leipzig, 1913), pp. 153–6, figs. 413–20; H. Swarzenski, 'Two Romanesque Illuminated Manuscripts in the Princeton University Library', *The Princeton University Library Chronicle*, 9 (1947/48), pp. 64–7.

[31] Holter, 'Zwei Lambacher Bibliotheksverzeichnisse', p. 268.

Adalbero and brief biographical sketches of the early Lambach abbots. Gottschalk's work extends to the initials, the *Vita*, part of the *series abbatum*, and the first few miracles. When copying an abbey charter which was written in a notarial hand, Gottschalk imitates the notary style by extending his ascenders and making their wavy nature even more pronounced.[32] His work as scribe and author ends on folio 27[v].[33]

On folio 11[r], Gottschalk records brief biographical sketches of the Lambach abbots from the first abbot, Ekkebert, through to the election of Waesigrimmus in 1197. Gottschalk describes the abbacy of Waesigrimmus, but a new hand records his death in 1209. Gottschalk had stopped working by then, but was still working five years earlier; the last miracle in his hand is dated 1204. In his study of Cml LIV, Trinks claims that the miracles in Gottschalk's hand (which he refers to as the 'Haupthand') were written between 1201 and 1204, and that the *Vita* and the beginning of the *series abbatum* were written during the early part of the abbacy of Waesigrimmus, between 1197 and 1200.[34] The first part of his argument is based on the internal evidence of dates in the miracles themselves. The second part is based on the assumption that Gottschalk recorded all of the abbatial biographies through to the death of Waesigrimmus in 1209, implying that the entire *series* up to that point was written at the same time. But a closer examination of folio 11[r] shows a change in ink (to a slightly lighter tint) and a change in the line of writing (which begins to slant) between the descriptions of the abbacy and the death of Swarzmannus. This implies that the first break in writing came during the abbacy of Swarzmannus, not between the ascension and death of his successor, Waesigrimmus. This places the composition of the *Vita* and *series abbatum* in the years 1196 or 1197.

Gottschalk's work on this manuscript stretched over a period of seven or eight years, from 1196 or 1197 to 1204. This same period of activity is seen in Gottschalk's work on the Lambach Annals, CVP 373.

---

[32] About this copy of a forged document, see K. Rumpler, 'Die Gründung Lambachs unter besonderer Berücksichtigung der Gründungsurkunden', in *900 Jahre Klosterkirche Lambach*, pp. 25–32; E. Trinks, 'Die Gründungsurkunden und Anfänge des Benediktinerklosters Lambach', *Jahrbuch des Oberösterreichischen Musealvereins*, 83 (1930), pp. 76–152; H. Koller, 'Die königliche Klosterpolitik im Südosten des Reiches. Ein Beitrag zum Niedergang der Reichsgewalt', *Archiv für Diplomatik: Schriftgeschichte Siegel- und Wappenkunde*, 20 (1974), pp. 1–38; E. Boshof, 'Gefälschte "Stiftsbriefe" des 11./12. Jahrhunderts aus bayerisch-österreichischen Klöstern', in *Fälschungen im Mittelalter: internationaler Kongress der Monumenta Germaniae Historica, München, 16.-19. September 1986, MGH Schriften* 33:1 (Hanover, 1988), pp. 519–50.

[33] This manuscript has been edited: see W. Wattenbach, 'Vita Adalberonis Episcopi Wirziburgensis', in G. Pertz (ed.), *MGH SS* XII (Hanover, 1856), pp. 127–38, and I. Schmale-Ott, *Vita Sancti Adalberonis* (Würzburg, 1954).

[34] E. Trinks, 'Die Gründungsurkunden und Anfänge des Benediktinerklosters Lambach', pp. 122–3.

2. Vienna, Österreichische Nationalbibliothek, CVP 373, folio 3ᵛ (detail)

CVP 373

Codex vindobonensis palatinus 373 is a compilation of several manuscript fragments, bound together before acquisition by the Österreichische Nationalbibliothek.[35] The first eight pages comprise the Lambach Annals.[36] From the years 1177 to 1197, this chronicle is a slightly condensed copy of the Kremsmünster Annals and is written by several different hands.[37] New, original material begins in the middle of the entry for 1197, with Gottschalk's hand (see Fig. 2 – Gottschalk's work begins on line 4, with 'Inter quos episcopus'). Once again, Gottschalk writes from 1197 to 1204, but no later (see Fig. 3); this is a reliable range of dates for his period of original composition. There are no new entries in the annals until 1207, when a new hand takes over. The year 1204 seems to be a reliable *terminus ante quem* for Gottschalk's career.

Contemporary abbey records add to the knowledge of Gottschalk's life. He has been identified as the 'Gotscalcus Presbyter et m[onacus] n[ostri] c[oenobii]' ('Gottschalk, priest and monk of our monastery') whose death is noted in the Lambach necrology on 2 January.[38] He is also mentioned in a newly discovered thirteenth-century Lambach mortuary list as 'Gotscalcus scolaris et monacus'.[39] The title 'scholaris' suggests that he was the schoolmaster, which would explain his recording of the list of school-texts in the Berlin manuscript.

Further evidence of Gottschalk's identity is found in the dedication panel of the Berlin manuscript (see Fig. 4); a monk (probably Gottschalk) is shown presenting his work to the Virgin and child, surrounded by a border of twelve saints. Depicted directly across from St Nicholas, patron of the Passau diocese, is St Gall. He reaches

---

[35] F. Unterkircher, *Die datierten Handschriften der Österreichischen Nationalbibliothek bis zum Jahre 1400*, I (Vienna, 1969), pp. 21–2 and pl. 40.
[36] W. Wattenbach, 'Annales Austriae', in G. Pertz (ed.), *MGH SS* IX (repr. Stuttgart, 1983), pp. 479–61, at pp. 555–61. See also the study in E. Klebel, 'Die Fassungen und Handschriften der österreichischen Annalistik', *Jahrbuch für Landeskunde und Heimatschutz von Niederösterreich und Wien*, 20 (1926–7), pp. 47 and 137. [37] The Kremsmünster Annals are also edited in *MGH SS* IX.
[38] A. Eilenstein, *Die Benediktinerabtei Lambach in Österreich ob der Enns und ihre Mönche* (Linz, 1936), p. 23. See also Fastlinger, 'Notae necrologicae et fragmentum necrologii monasterii lambacensis', p. 406. [39] Stiftsbibliothek Lambach, Frag., no number.

3. Vienna, Österreichische Nationalbibliothek, CVP 373, folio 4ʳ (detail)

out of his frame to present Gottschalk to the Virgin, perhaps suggesting that Gottschalk had some personal devotion to St Gall. This contention is supported by two other portraits in the border, depictions of saints closely connected to St Gall. In the lower-right corner of the dedication panel, St John, Bishop of Constance (*d.* 639) is identified as 'Sanctus Iohannes episcopus, discipulus sancti galli'. St Othmar, depicted in the lower-left corner, was abbot at St Gall from 720 to 759. Gottschalk's knowledge of music suggests that he may have had a direct connection with the abbey at St Gall, perhaps as a student at the choir school there.

The identification of Gottschalk's work is somewhat problematic. The scribe of the Gottschalk inscription seems to have written the rubrics of the rest of the Berlin manuscript, and the letter forms of the rubrics are those used for capital letters in the text. This suggests that Gottschalk was the scribe of at least the first portion of the manuscript. Other hands, similar to Gottschalk's, work later in the manuscript. The identification of Gottschalk as the artist rests on the nature of the rubrics in the dedication panel and in the other full-page miniature in the Berlin manuscript: an illustration of four parts of the life of St Nicholas. The rubrics are an integral part of the design of the miniatures, not afterthoughts or later additions. The initials elsewhere in the manuscript were produced by the same artist (see Fig. 5). The work of this scribe/artist, referred to hereafter as Gottschalk, can be identified in a number of other Lambach manuscripts.

Gottschalk's script is found in seven complete and two fragmentary manuscripts, in the Lambach Annals (CVP 373), and on a fragmentary chronicle/calendar. The extant manuscripts are: Cml CXL (sermons of Hugh of St Victor);[40] Cml L (Augustine, *Tractatus in evangelium Johannis*, I–XLV); Cml CXLIII (miracles of the

---

[40] *ÖKT*, p. 249 and fig. 233.

4. Berlin, Staatsbibliothek, MS Theo. lat. qu. 140, folio 2ʳ

5. *Berlin, Staatsbibliothek, MS Theo. lat. qu. 140, folio 107ʳ (detail)*

Virgin Mary, the dispute of Charlemagne and Alcuin on Dialectics, and Marian sermons, now Princeton University Library, MS 51); Cml XCIII (the Berlin manuscript);[41] Cml LIV (Life and Miracles of Adalbero); Kremsmünster, Stiftsbibliothek, CC 35 (Bernard of Clairvaux, *Sermones super Cantica Canticorum*);[42] and Cml LXXIIIa.

Codex Cremifarensis 35, Bernard of Clairvaux's *Sermones super Cantica Canticorum*, has not previously been identified as a Lambach product. In his catalogue of Kremsmünster manuscripts, H. Fill does not recognize this script, and attributes the manuscript to Kremsmünster based on its modern location in that monastery's library.[43] The script, however, is definitely Gottschalk's. In addition, faint marginal animals very similar to those in Cml L and Beinecke Rare Book and Manuscript Library (BRBL) MS 481.93 appear throughout this manuscript. This manuscript may in fact be the 'sermones Bernhardi' mentioned in the Cml XIX booklist.[44]

The copy of Augustine's Tracts on John was written in two volumes: the booklist in Cml XIX records 'Opera Augustini . . . Super Johannem duo volumina'.[45] The first volume is Cml L, Tracts I–XLV. The second volume, ostensibly containing

---

[41] *ÖKT*, pp. 245–6, figs. 292–300.
[42] H. Fill, *Katalog der Handschriften des Benediktinerstiftes Kremsmünster* (Vienna, 1984), pp. 99–100 and pl. 25.   [43] *Ibid.*, p. 99.
[44] Holter, 'Zwei Lambacher Bibliotheksverzeichnisse', p. 274. Although Holter offers possible identifications for many of the texts listed in the Cml XIX booklist, he makes no suggestion for the identity of the 'sermones Bernhardi'.
[45] Holter, 'Zwei Lambacher Bibliotheksverzeichnisse', p. 268.

Tracts XLVI–CXXIV, is not extant, and is not included in Resch's list (i.e., it was no longer part of the library by the late eighteenth century). One folio of the manuscript, written by Gottschalk, was used as a wrap-around binding and has survived as BRBL MS 481.93. The fragment includes part of Tract CXXIV, and was probably the penultimate folio of the manuscript.[46] Gottschalk also produced the initials in Cml L, and the marginal bird on folio 40ᵛ. A faint marginal sketch of a cat, also by Gottschalk, is visible on the recto of BRBL 481.93.[47] The Gottschalk Antiphonary is the other fragmentary manuscript written in Gottschalk's hand. In the margins of the calendrical fragment (Lambach, Stiftsbibliothek, Frag. 2), Gottschalk records the elections and deaths of eleventh- and twelfth-century abbots, up to the election of Waesigrimmus in 1197. These notations may have been added at the same time as the *series abbatum* in Cml LIV was composed. Of these manuscripts, only two combine Gottschalk's script with his initials: Cml XCIII (the Berlin manuscript) and the Gottschalk Antiphonary. The Gottschalk Antiphonary is one of his finest works, with sixteen characteristic initials in the recovered portion of the manuscript.

Although the total number of artists working in Lambach during this period is unclear since several artists used a very similar style, Gottschalk's initials remain somewhat distinctive:

The stems of the letters are typically interrupted by small bands, usually in purple ink, which wrap around the body of the letters. The bands are divided into three parts: narrow strips at the top and bottom of the band define a wider central panel, which is filled with rows of tiny circles. A primitive form of modeling of the bands attempts to make them look three-dimensional (i.e. circular). This is accomplished by extending the bands beyond the body of the letter, by rounding the ends of the narrow strips (as well as the sides of the central panel), and by extending a line a short distance up or down along the stem of the letter. . . . The effect is that the bands appear to squeeze the stem of the letter and to bulge from the pressure. . . . Another common decorative device on initials of the Gotscalcus group is a ring attached to a stem (sometimes two or three rings are together). These rings may represent berries or buds. . . . A further characteristic feature of the initials in this group is a single, detached leaf (rounded on one end and pointed on the other) split down the middle by a wavy line. The stem of the letter pierces the leaf through the wavy line.[48]

In the Gottschalk Antiphonary, examples of the band and detached leaf are evident in the initial [Q] on folio 52ʳ. The berries can be seen in the historiated initial [V] on folio 131ʳ. The artist has a particular predilection for birds and rabbits; these are found in the initial [E] on folio 121ᵛ.

Gottschalk's human figures are equally distinctive:

Typical features are the halo outlined by a ring of circles, the sinuous curve along the top of a two-pointed crown, the heavy eyebrows, the representation of the chin by a circle at

---

[46] Babcock, *Reconstructing a Medieval Library*, pp. 102–4 and fig. 15.   [47] *Ibid.*, fig. 15.
[48] Babcock and Davis, 'Two Romanesque Manuscripts from Lambach', p. 138.

the bottom of the face and of the nose by a three-leaf clover pointing downward, the single red dots on each cheek, and the heavy outline of the forehead and hair.[49]

These features are evident in all of the figural initials in the Gottschalk Antiphonary.

Gottschalk's work as an artist is well documented. His initials, or initials in his style, are found in at least twenty-five other manuscripts: Leutkirch, Fürstlich Waldburgschen Gesamtarchiv, MS 5 (formerly Cml XVII); Cml XVIII; Cml XXI; Cml XXII; Cml XXVIII; Cml XXIX; Cml XXXIII; Oxford, Bodleian Library, MS Lyell 56 (formerly Cml XLIII); Cml XLVIII; a fragmentary missal (fragments of which survive in the bindings of Ccl 308[50] and Göttweig, Stiftsbibliothek, MS 1117); BRBL MS 699 (formerly Cml LXIV); Cml LXV; Cml LXXIIIa (only a few initials in this manuscript are by Gottschalk); Vienna, Österreichische Nationalbibliothek (ÖNB), ser. n. 3600 (formerly Cml LXXIV); Cml LXXVI; ÖNB ser. n. 39,678 (formerly Cml LXXIX[51]); ÖNB ser. n. 3606 (formerly Cml CV); Cml CXIX; Linz, Studienbibliothek, MSS 290 and 466; Kremsmünster Stiftsbibliothek, CC 344 and 371; Melk, Stiftsbibliothek, MS 709 (a missal apparently written for the use of Lambach); and Baltimore, Walters Art Gallery, MS 29 (formerly Cml XCIV) and MS 30. Many of these manuscripts are listed in the booklist in Cml XIX.

Five of these manuscripts were apparently produced not for Lambach, but for nearby centres: Kremsmünster, Stiftsbibliothek, CC 344 and CC 371, Linz, Studienbibliothek, MS 290 and MS 466, and Baltimore, Walters Art Gallery, MS 30. CC 371 is the second of a four-volume set of Augustine's *In Psalmos* (CC 370, CC 371, CC 39, CC 372). Holter argues that because the initials in this manuscript were produced by Gottschalk, the manuscript can be attributed to Lambach 'with certainty'.[52] It is more likely, however, that the manuscript was produced in Kremsmünster; the script is not found in other Lambach manuscripts. Since many scribes only appear once in the extant Lambach manuscripts, however, this alone is insufficient evidence that CC 371 was not produced in Lambach. More convincing is that the ruling pattern in CC 371 – three ruling lines along the upper and lower margins and two along the outer and inner margins – is a pattern never used in Lambach during this period.[53] The majority

---

[49] *Ibid.*, p. 139.   [50] *ÖKT*, p. 218, fig. 232.

[51] This manuscript was sold at Sotheby's on 16 June 1997 (lot 6), and was acquired by the Österreichische Nationalbibliothek. See Sotheby & Co., *The Beck Collection of Illuminated Manuscripts* (London, 16 June 1997).

[52] Holter, 'Buchmalerei und Federzeichnungsinitialen im hochmittelalterlichen Skriptorium von Kremsmünster', in O. Mazal (ed.), *Handschriftenbeschreibung in Österreich* (Vienna, 1975), p. 47.

[53] In Fill, *Katalog der Handschriften des Benediktinerstiftes Kremsmünster*, this is ruling pattern no. 13. The next volume of the series, CC 39, is written in a style very similar to CC 371, but with no initials. Although it also uses the triple-ruling scheme, CC 39 has also been tentatively attributed to Lambach because of its visual similarity to CC 371. See Fill, *ibid.*, p. 475.

of Lambach manuscripts produced during the latter half of the twelfth century uses instead double ruling lines along each margin. The script of CC 344 (Origenes, varia) is not a Lambach style, but could have been produced there; the initials are definitely Gottschalk's work, and the ruling scheme has double margins on all sides.

Linz, Studienbibliothek, MS 290 (a breviary/psalter) appears to have been created for Kremsmünster (detailed liturgy is given for St Agapitus, the patron of Kremsmünster), but was decorated by Gottschalk.[54] The script and the unusual ruling pattern used in about half of this manuscript (a single upper margin, triple lower margin, and double inner and outer margins) may testify to an origin outside Lambach; perhaps Gottschalk travelled to Kremsmünster to decorate the manuscript. Linz 466 (a missal), which has the greatest number of initials of any Gottschalk manuscript, was probably created for the use of Garsten.[55] Almost every Office in the manuscript, no matter how abbreviated, is given an ornate initial. The most important Offices, those with expanded liturgy, have historiated initials. For the Office of St Kilian, on folio 42^r, Gottschalk was required by the liturgical needs of Garsten to abbreviate the Office of his patron. Even so, he did manage to squeeze a small portrait of the saint into the space he was allotted. Baltimore, Walters Art Gallery, MS 30, a missal created for the use of Melk, includes illustrations by a number of artists. Gottschalk's work is limited to the intricate white-vine monogram initials at the beginning of the manuscript – the miniatures are by another artist.

Kremsmünster, Garsten, and Melk: although it is unclear whether Gottschalk lived part of his life at these neighbouring abbeys, visited them as a travelling artist for specific commissions, or performed work for them at Lambach, the existence of the manuscripts indicates that Gottschalk's talent was recognized beyond the abbey's walls.

Gottschalk appears to have served the Lambach abbey in a number of capacities, perhaps including librarian, cantor, schoolmaster, scribe and artist. If the Gottschalk listed in the necrology is indeed our Gottschalk, he was also a priest. He had a hand in the original texts composed at the abbey during the 1190s: the *Vita* and *Miracula Adalberonis*, the *series abbatum*, and the poetry in the Berlin manuscript. His artistic talent was clearly admired by other houses, to which the manuscripts created for Kremsmünster, Garsten and Melk testify. He was also an accomplished poet and musician, composing rhymed verse and revising liturgical melodies.

---

[54] M. Czernin, 'Das Breviarium Monasticum Cod.290 (183) der Bundesstaatlichen Studienbibliothek in Linz', unpublished dissertation, University of Vienna (1992).

[55] K. Holter, 'Das mittelalterliche Buchwesen im Kloster Garsten', *Kirche in Oberösterreich, Katalog der Landesausstellung in Garsten* (Linz, 1985), pp. 91–102 and pp. 370–85, at p. 371.

3. OTHER SCRIBES AND ARTISTS

Many Lambach scribes used a script which was very similar to Gottschalk's. This style is characterized in part by the wavy nature of minims, ascenders and abbreviation strokes. In the bottom line of a page, the descenders are often extended, producing an effect that has been called notary-inspired.[56] Gottschalk's hand is distinguishable from the others by the distinctive rounding at the base of minims, which curve into their feet instead of turning abruptly, and by the slight slant to the right. He uses suprascript letters as abbreviations quite frequently. His [ct] ligature is also distinctive; the top of the [t]-ascender curls left into an almost complete circle.[57]

In this survey, I have focused on the scribes who were Gottschalk's contemporaries, that is, those who worked in manuscripts with his script or his initials, in an attempt to analyse the context within which Gottschalk was working. I have further restricted this study to scribes whose work appears more than once (with the exception of Scribe A6).[58] Each of the scribes is assigned a number or letter designation.

Many of the manuscripts surveyed are listed in the booklist in Cml XIX, and can be dated in relation to it, that is, before the turn of the century.[59] Because the list in Cml XIX is incomplete, no conclusions can be based on the apparent exclusion of particular manuscripts. It is possible that unlisted manuscripts post-date the catalogue, especially manuscripts of authors listed in the early, and presumably complete, part of the list. The booklist at the front of Cml XCIII was written by Gottschalk. The books listed there can be dated with relative security to the period before or during Gottschalk's career. Paulhart, following Holter, dates this booklist to *c.* 1210,[60] but since the year 1204 has been shown to be a reliable *terminus ante quem* for Gottschalk's career, the list should be assigned a slightly earlier range of dates, *c.* 1200–1204. Most of these manuscripts I examined in person, but some I

---

[56] Fill, *Katalog der Handschriften des Benediktinerstiftes Kremsmünster*, p. 99; 'Unterlängen in den letzten Zeilen manchmal verlängert: Einfluß der Urkundenschrift' ('The descenders in the bottom lines (of each page) are quite elongated: influence of notarial script'). Fill is here discussing the hand of CC 35 (Bernard of Clairvaux, *Sermones super Cantica canticorum*) which appears to be Gottschalk's, although Fill does not identify it as such.

[57] The script is also described by Holter in 'Zwei Lambacher Bibliotheksverzeichnisse', p. 266.

[58] Many scribes have been excluded: those whose work is found in only one manuscript, and/or those whose manuscripts do not include any work by Gottschalk.

[59] Holter claims that this booklist was written by Gottschalk (Holter, 'Zwei Lambacher Bibliotheksverzeichnisse', p. 268), but a close examination of the script proves that this is not so. The general character of the script is more pointed than Gottschalk's, and the [ct] ligature in particular is clearly different from Gottschalk's practice: in the booklist, the two letters are connected by a stroke from the top of the [t] back to the [c]. In addition, the lower bowl of the [g] is oversized in comparison to the upper bowl, as opposed to the bowls of Gottschalk's [g] which are closer to one another in size.   [60] Paulhart, *Mittelalterliche Bibliothekskataloge Österreichs*, V, p. 55.

have studied only on microfilm. A very few I know only from published photographs (for example, the manuscripts sold by Sotheby's in 1929 which are now untraced); in these cases, the data are of course incomplete.

3.1. Scribes

'A' Style

This style is distinctive of Lambach scribes, and was used in the late twelfth century by many of the monks, including Gottschalk. The characteristics of this style are the broken, wavy minims, the [ct] ligature with either the curled [t] ascender or a hair-stroke connecting the two letters, and the elongated round-[s]. The scribes who used this style are distinguishable from one another by various means.

A1

I have designated Gottschalk, whose script is the clearest and most consistent example of the A style, as scribe A1. His script is described in detail in Chapter 3; Gottschalk's hand can be differentiated from the other A-style scribes by the distinctive rounding at the base of the minims, which curve into their feet instead of turning abruptly, and by the slight rightward slant of the script. In addition to the booklist in Cml XCIII, Gottschalk wrote all or part of many other manuscripts, including the Gottschalk Antiphonary (see p. 21 above).

A2

This script is very similar to Gottschalk's. The primary difference is the ampersand; the cross-stroke is forked instead of slightly thickened (see Fig. 6). The head-line of the script is more ordered than Gottschalk's, and the spatulate ascenders add a sharper caste to the script. This hand can be found in four manuscripts: Cml XLIV, Cml XLV, Cml XLVI and Göttweig, Stiftsbibliothek, MS 1112 (formerly Cml XCV). Of these, only the Göttweig manuscript is illustrated by Gottschalk. Cml XLIV, XLV and XLVI are the first three volumes of a six-volume copy of Gregory's *Moralia in Job*. The last three volumes of the *Moralia* were completed by scribe B; the relationship between A2 and B is discussed below. With the exception of Göttweig 1112, all of the manuscripts written by scribe A2 are listed in the Cml XIX booklist.

A3

The hand of scribe A3 is almost indistinguishable from Gottschalk's (see Fig. 7). The only clear difference is the [ct] ligature: while Gottschalk curls the top of the [t] into an almost complete circle, and completely crosses the stem with the cross-stroke, scribe A3 tops the [t] with a hairstroke back towards the [c], and does not completely cross the stem. This difference is clear in Cml L, which is written by

6. Göttweig, Stiftsbibliothek, Cod. 1112, folio 48ᵛ (detail): Scribe A2

7. Lambach, Stiftsbibliothek, Cml L, folio 58ʳ (detail): Scribes A3 and A1 (Gottschalk)

both Gottschalk and A3. Figure 7, folio 58ʳ of the manuscript, shows both scribes at work; A3 writes from the top of the page to the middle of line 8 (ending with 'hoc non sonet'). Gottschalk's work begins with the next sentence, and continues through to the end of the page. The two scripts alternate throughout the manuscript. The transitions usually occur at sentence breaks, but are not otherwise textually determined. A3 also wrote part of Leutkirch, Fürstlich Waldburgschen

8. Vienna, Österreichische Nationalbibliothek, MS ser. n. 3612, folio 56ʳ (detail): Scribe A4

9. Vienna, Österreichische Nationalbibliothek, MS ser. n. 3612, folio 56ʳ (detail): Scribe A5

Gesamtarchiv, MS 5 (the first of a five-volume copy of Augustine's *In Psalmos*, formerly Cml XVII)[61] and ÖNB 39768 (formerly Cml LXXIX).[62] A3 and Gottschalk were close collaborators, and not only as scribes; Gottschalk illustrated all of the manuscripts which include A3's hand. Only one of the manuscripts written by A3 is listed in the Cml XIX booklist: Cml L, the manuscript that Gottschalk also wrote.

A4 and A5

The work of scribe A4 is also very similar to Gottschalk's, though less carefully articulated and less consistent (see Fig. 8). Even so, this hand is not as poor as that of scribe A5 (see Fig. 9), whose script is the least successful imitation of Gottschalk's. A4 is found in two manuscripts; ÖNB ser. n. 3612 (formerly Cml CXXXIII)[63] and Princeton MS 51 (a collaboration with Gottschalk that was for-

---

[61] Holter, 'Initialen aus einer Lambacher Handschrift des 12. Jahrhunderts'. [62] See above, note 51.
[63] Holter identifies this script as Gottschalk's (see 'Zwei Lambacher Bibliotheksverzeichnisse', p. 267), but the style is clearly different.

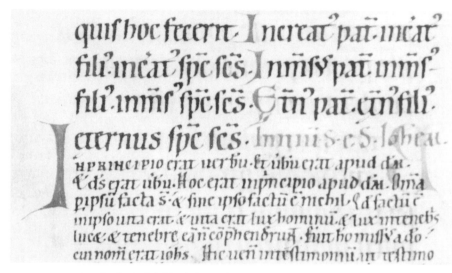

10. Lambach, Stiftsbibliothek, Cml LXXIIIa, folio 70ᵛ (detail): Scribe A6

merly Cml CXLIII). Both of these manuscripts are found in the Cml XCIII book-list, but not in Cml XIX. Most of the Princeton manuscript, which was illustrated by Gottschalk, was written by A5, alternating with samples of A4 which may have been produced as models for A5 to follow.

A6

A6 is the scribe of the early Lambach Rituale (Cml LXXIIIa), a manuscript which was produced during the abbacy of Bernhard (*c.* 1148–67) – the dedication panel shows the abbot presenting the book to the Virgin.[64] The hand of scribe A6 is similar to Gottschalk's, except for the [ct] ligature; the [t] is not completely crossed, and curves only slightly back towards the [c] at the top of the stem (see Fig. 10). Scribe A6 may have trained Gottschalk and taught him this script.

A7

Scribe A7, who also preceded Gottschalk, is primarily distinguishable from him by his [et] abbreviations; the back of the Tironian [et] is straight, not curved, and the final stroke of the ampersand curves upwards, mirroring the cross-stroke (see Fig. 11, line 12). He uses the elongated round-[s] inconsistently. Scribe A7 wrote the sections of the Lambach chronicle from 1191 to 1197, when Gottschalk's work begins (CVP 373, folios 2ʳ-4ᵛ). In addition, A7's hand is found in Cml XLII, a manuscript which is listed in the Cml XIX booklist.

[64] *ÖKT*, p. 217, fig. 230.

11. Lambach, Stiftsbibliothek, Cml XLII, folio 168ᵛ (detail): Scribe A7

B

Scribe B is by far the best-represented scribe of the Lambach scriptorium in this period, having written all or part of ten extant manuscripts: Cml XIV, Cml XVIII, Cml XXII, Cml XXIX, Cml XLVII, Cml XLVIII, Cml IL, Göttweig 1112 (formerly Cml XCV), ÖNB ser. n. 3605 (formerly Cml CII) and St Florian, Stiftsbibliothek, CFS XI/43.[65] Although his script and Gottschalk's do not ever appear in the same manuscript, they were definitely contemporaries; several of the manuscripts copied by B are illustrated with Gottschalk's work. Only four of the manuscripts by scribe B (Cml XIV, Cml XCV, Cml CII and St Florian XI/43) are not listed in Cml XIX.

The hand of scribe B is quite distinctive, with a pronounced pointed character (see Fig. 12). Ascenders end in sharp forks, and descenders are pointed at the bottom. The last minim of [m] and [n], as well as the down-stroke of [d], [i], [l], [t], [q] and [u], turns sharply to the right in an elongated final tick. The [g] and ampersand are particularly distinctive. The back of the [g] is clearly forked at the top, and makes a sharp right angle at the top of the lower bowl. The cross-stroke of the ampersand is also clearly forked.

Several manuscripts in B's hand warrant a more detailed discussion.

Cml XLVII, Cml XLVIII and Cml IL

These are the final three volumes of the six-volume copy of Gregory's *Moralia in Job* mentioned above. The first three volumes (Cml XLIV, Cml XLV and Cml

---

[65] V. Birke, ed., *Die Kunstsammlungen des Augustiner-Chorherrenstiftes St Florian* ÖKT 48 (Vienna, 1988), p. 63 and fig. 89. No Lambach shelf number is known for this manuscript, although the script and initials ensure a Lambach origin.

12. Lambach, Stiftsbibliothek, Cml XLVII, folio 2ʳ (detail): Scribe B

XLVI) were written by scribe A2. The preface in volume I of the set was written by a somewhat later scribe imitating the twelfth-century style, on a tipped-in bifolium. Marginal rubrication is found in the first three volumes and up to book 18 in the fourth volume (the first of B's work). The rubricator, who also added the table of contents to each of the first three volumes on a tipped-in first leaf, is neither A2 nor B. The last volume is completed by a tipped-in bifolium in yet another hand. The following scenario presents itself: A2 wrote the first three volumes, without rubrication. When B began work on the last three volumes, the rubrics were added. The scribe of the rubrics left the rubrics and the table of contents unwritten for the last three volumes.

3.2. Artists

There were many artists working at Lambach during the twelfth century. Although the general style of white-vine initials remained consistent throughout the century, there are stylistic variants and developments to be noted. In the early part of the century, the vines are quite thick, and appear almost tubular. Human figures are rather simple, not much more than line drawings. Vines end in rounded curls, without scallops.[66] This style persisted to the middle of the century, found in manuscripts such as Cml VI[67] and Cml XIX,[68] as well as the slightly later manuscripts Cml XLII,[69] Cml CIX, Cml CXXXI and Oxford, Bodleian Library, MS Lyell 56.[70] Also during this period, the vine pattern tends to be symmetrical, and the background of the initials may be coloured (e.g. Cml LXXIIIa). Occasionally, the wide stem-bands have a band at top and bottom filled with small circles in orderly patterns.[71] In one manuscript from the first half of the century

---

[66] *ÖKT*, pl. 223.   [67] *900 Jahre Klosterkirche Lambach*, p. 201, Katalog No. VIII.05.
[68] *ÖKT*, pl. 280.   [69] *Ibid.*, pl. 225.
[70] Pächt and Alexander, *Illuminated Manuscripts in the Bodleian Library, Oxford*, pl. VI, no. 73.
[71] *ÖKT*, pls. 280–1.

(Cml XLII), the stem-bands are flat, with darkened bands at top and bottom filled with a row of dots.

A few manuscripts from the middle of the century show elements of the early style as well as the beginnings of what would develop into the style used by Gottschalk. In Cml CLVI, for example, initials are still filled with very thick vines, but the vines terminate in scallops as well as curls.[72]

By the latter half of the century, the style had fully developed and reached its apex with Gottschalk's work. This later style is distinguished by thinner vines, not necessarily arranged symmetrically, and bands around the letter stems decorated with diamonds and small circles, or small circles filled with dots. The vines tend to terminate in full scallops, and the background is often coloured in.[73]

Besides Gottschalk, there is another artistic hand at Lambach distinctive enough to warrant individual attention – this is the so-called 'Rituale-Artist', named for his work on the Lambach Rituale, Cml LXXIII (*c.* 1200).[74] The style is thought by Holter to have been modelled on Gottschalk's work.[75] Though similar to Gottschalk's, the style is somewhat less elegant. The human figures are simpler and more round than Gottschalk's, with pronounced facial features such as nose and chin.[76] The features of the ornate initials are also more rounded than Gottschalk's, with vines terminating in large, full scallops. The vines within the body of a letter tend to be roughly symmetrical. This artist rarely uses bands around letter stems, although when he does the bands are narrow and rounded, appearing to truly circle the stem, not just lie on its surface. This feature in particular seems to have been inspired by Gottschalk's work. For simpler initials, without historiation or other elaboration, the style can be distinguished by the herringbone pattern which often crosses the stem of the letter.[77] Throughout, the white-vine initials are identifiable by the frequent use of red and green background wash. Gottschalk's work does not appear in any of the manuscripts illustrated in this style, which developed after Gottschalk began work and may have continued into the thirteenth century. This artist also worked on another late twelfth-century Lambach antiphonary: Beinecke Rare Book and Manuscript Library, MS 481.52.[78]

4. RULING PATTERNS

There were many different ruling patterns used in Lambach during the twelfth century (see Fig. 13). Of these, pattern 6 (double outer and inner margins) is by far

---

[72] *900 Jahre Klosterkirche Lambach*, p. 204, Katalog No. VIII.15.
[73] *ÖKT*, pl. 286.   [74] *Ibid.*, pls. 288–291.
[75] Holter, 'Neue Beiträge zur Geschichte der Stiftsbibliothek von Lambach', p. 97.
[76] *ÖKT*, pls. 240–3.   [77] Babcock, *Reconstructing a Medieval Library*, pp. 110–11 (fig. 60, cat. no. 30).
[78] *Ibid.*, p. 106 (fig. 57).

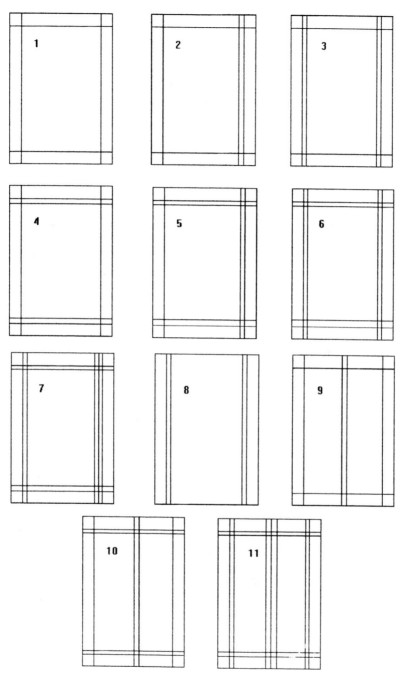

13. Ruling patterns used in the twelfth-century Lambach scriptorium

the most common, used in ten of the eighteen manuscripts examined in this chapter for which the ruling pattern is discernible. By contrast, patterns 3, 7, 9 and 10 are used in only two each of these manuscripts, and patterns 1 and 5 only once each. Pattern 6 is in fact the most common among all of the Lambach manuscripts of this period, used in seventeen of the twenty-eight twelfth-century manuscripts for which the ruling pattern is discernible. There is no clear correlation between scribe and ruling pattern. However, the preference of this ruling pattern in Lambach is of some use as additional evidence of a manuscript's Lambach origin when combined with other, more characteristic, types of evidence.

Most of Gottschalk's work as an author and annalist appears to date from after 1197, although his career as an artist almost certainly began much earlier. If it is true that Gottschalk served the abbey as librarian, 1197 may mark the beginning of his tenure. The Gottschalk Antiphonary contains no internal evidence that could help pinpoint its date of production. The evidence of Gottschalk's scribal activity detailed above, however, suggests that the manuscript was written sometime between the years 1197 and 1204.

5. THE LATER HISTORY OF THE LIBRARY

Lambach was sacked in 1233. A Lambach chronicle records the devastation:

Otto dux Bawarie terram nostram cum magno exercitu intravit, et magnam partem eiusdem rapinis et incendiis consumpsit. Et veniens ad civitatem Wels, Lambacensem locum et omnia adiacentia rapina et incendio totaliter vastavit, et sic ad terram suam rediit.[79]

[Otto, Duke of Bavaria, entered our land with a great army, and he destroyed a large part of it by plundering and burning. And coming to the city of Wels, he completely destroyed the Lambach area and all of the adjoining country by plundering and burning, and then he returned to his land.]

This destruction ended the period of manuscript production for over a century. Manuscript production had already begun to decline by this time, beginning, perhaps, with Gottschalk's death. Although the scriptorium was renewed in the fifteenth century, and many manuscripts with humanistic content were produced during the abbacy of Thomas Messerer (1436–74), the reputation of fifteenth-century Lambach book production rests with book bindings as much as with the books themselves.[80] When the monastery began acquiring printed books in the 1460s and 70s, the bindery expanded.[81] During this period, many of the older man-

---

[79] W. Wattenbach, 'Annales Austriae', p. 558.
[80] Holter, 'Zum gotischen Bucheinbände in Österreich'.
[81] Paulhart, *Mittelalterliche Bibliothekskataloge Österreichs*, V, p. 51.

uscripts were dismantled for use as book-binding material (as flyleaves, paste-downs, binding stays, or wrap-around bindings). It is clear that much of the dismantling occurred during an earlier period of book-binding, in the twelfth century; there is evidence of fragments having been used in twelfth-century bindings.[82] A small collection of former binding fragments survives in the abbey library. Many other former binding fragments are preserved among the fragment collections MS 481 and MS 482 at the Beinecke Rare Book and Manuscript Library at Yale University; their recent identification adds much to the knowledge of the history of the Lambach scriptorium and allows for the reconstruction of a significant portion of the library's medieval holdings.[83]

---

[82] Several Lambach fragments in the Beinecke collection show signs of having been used as flyleaves in two different books. For example, BRBL MS 481.48.3 and 4 were originally a bifolium, and show signs of having been used as an open bifolium pastedown in a large volume. Most recently, they were used as a folded bifolium (pastedown and flyleaf) in a Lambach manuscript bound in the fifteenth century. [83] Babcock, *Reconstructing a Medieval Library*.

3

The Gottschalk Antiphonary

I. THE HISTORY OF THE MANUSCRIPT

The Gottschalk Antiphonary was produced in the late twelfth or early thirteenth century at the Lambach abbey. Fifteenth-century marginal additions indicate that the manuscript was still being used three hundred years after it was written. In the late fifteenth century, however, the Antiphonary was dismembered and its pages used as flyleaves and pastedowns in books bound at the abbey. Most of the Antiphonary fragments were scattered as the abbey sold incunables and manuscripts throughout the modern era. Early in the twentieth century, Antiphonary fragments were removed from some of the bindings and sold separately, either by the monastery before the incunables were sold, or by a later owner. Fragments of the Gottschalk Antiphonary have been identified in six collections: the Stiftsbibliothek Lambach, the Beinecke Rare Book and Manuscript Library at Yale University, the Houghton Library at Harvard University, the Stiftsbibliothek St-Paul-im-Lavanttal, the St Louis Public Library, and a private Austrian collection.[1]

Four complete folios and fragments of six more remain in the Lambach abbey library. The four whole folios are flyleaves (two open bifolios) in an incunable with shelf number Ink. II.1.i (HC 13018*). The entry for this book in the handwritten Lambach incunable catalogue of 1916 records the presence of the manuscript flyleaves with the notation 'MS Perg. liturg. mit neumen', describing the Gottschalk Antiphonary as a liturgical manuscript on parchment with neumatic notation.[2]

---

[1] A preliminary list of Antiphonary fragments was published by Kurt Holter in 'Neue Beiträge zur Geschichte der Stiftsbibliothek von Lambach im hohen Mittelalter', in G. Heilingsetzer (ed.), *Kunstgeschichtsforschung und Denkmalpflege (Festschrift für Norbert Wibiral zum 65. Geburtstag)* (Linz, 1986), pp. 85–98, at p. 95. See also K. Holter, 'Das mittelalterliche Buchwesen des Benediktinerstiftes Lambach', in *900 Jahre Klosterkirche Lambach: Oberösterreichische Landesausstellung 1989* (Linz, 1989), pp. 53–64, at p. 58 and cat. # IX.13 (p. 213). He did not know of the Yale, Harvard or St Louis leaves.
[2] Lambach Incunable Catalogue, 1916 (Lambach, Stiftsbibliothek, no shelf number).

The left margin of one folio is a stub at the front of Lambach Stiftsbibliothek Ink. II.36 (Hain 11005). Because it is pasted down to the inner-front cover, only one side is legible. The original binding holes are preserved at the far left of the fragment, indicating that this is the inner margin of the recto side. In the back of the same incunable, the right margin of another folio is preserved. The binding holes are visible to the right, indicating that this is the inner margin of the verso side.

In Lambach Stiftsbibliothek Ink. I.95, strips from the top of two bifolios are preserved as remnants of flyleaves which have been cut out. The flyleaves (each bifolium is actually the full width of one folio and half the width of its conjugate) were originally bound into the incunable as open bifolios, with each bifolium folded approximately 14 mm from the top. The tab thus created protrudes after the first quire of the incunable (for the front bifolium) or before the last quire (for the back bifolium). When the flyleaves were cut out, the tabs remained in the incunable, preserving the upper few lines of four folios.

One of these cut-out leaves is now at the Beinecke Rare Book and Manuscript Library at Yale University, along with many other leaves of the Gottschalk Antiphonary; seventeen folios of the manuscript comprise Beinecke MS 481.51. This is the bulk of the extant portion of the manuscript. The three bifolios and eleven single leaves were acquired by the Swiss collector Rev. Franz Josef Zinniker, apparently in the 1950s.[3] Zinniker sold the fragments to the New York dealer Hans P. Kraus as part of an extensive fragment collection put together over many years. Many of the fragments in this collection have been identified since 1989 as having originated in Lambach.[4] Kraus split the collection into two parts. The larger portion was purchased for the Beinecke Library in 1965. This collection, BRBL MS 481, contained sixteen folios of the Gottschalk Antiphonary (as MS 481.51, A–N). When Kraus donated another large part of the Zinniker collection to the Beinecke Library later that same year, it was given the shelf number MS 482.[5] This collection contained one leaf of the Gottschalk Antiphonary, as

---

[3] In addition to Ink. II.1.i, listings for five other incunables in the handwritten incunable catalogue (all of which have left the abbey library and are untraced) include the notation 'MS Perg. liturg. mit neumen'. Some of these add the additional description 'mit initialen' ('with initials'). Four of these descriptions record the sale price of the incunable in the margin: Ink. I/10 (Hain 10367), Ink. I/150 (Hain 1182) and Ink. II/143 (HC 6717*) were sold for Swiss Francs. The Beinecke leaves came to the United States via Switzerland; some of them may have been removed from these incunables. Ink. I/23/4 (Hain 13015) was sold for German Marks. The entry for Ink. II/19 (HC 15192*), the fifth codex which is said to have had a binding fragment from the Gottschalk Antiphonary, bears no notation of sales price and is untraced.

[4] See R. G. Babcock, *Reconstructing a Medieval Library: Fragments from Lambach* (New Haven, 1993), pp. 13–34.

[5] See R. G. Babcock, L. F. Davis and P. Rusche, *Catalogue of Medieval and Renaissance Manuscripts in the Beinecke Rare Book and Manuscript Library, Yale University*, vol. IV: *MSS 481–485* (Medieval and Renaissance Texts and Studies, 176) (Forthcoming, Tempe, 1999).

MS 482.29. In 1990, the antiphonary leaf in MS 482 was reunited with its counterparts in MS 481; the fragments now bear the shelf numbers MS 481.51.1–17.

At Harvard University's Houghton Library, two folios of the Gottschalk Antiphonary bear the shelf numbers Pf Ms Typ 704 5 and Pf Ms Typ 704 6. Philip Hofer purchased the leaves from Bernard M. Rosenthal in 1956, and bequeathed them to the Houghton Library in 1984.[6] In 1988, during a tour of the Houghton exhibit 'The Bible in the Twelfth Century', Professor Barbara Shailor recognized the leaves as being related to the Yale fragments.

Two leaves of the Gottschalk Antiphonary were flyleaves in a Lambach incunable (a compilation of Hain 7053 and 13683 not listed in the 1916 Lambach incunable catalogue) which was acquired by the Stiftsbibliothek St-Paul-im-Lavanttal (fifteen miles north-east of Klagenfurt), where it bears the shelf mark Ink. 5.4.17. Recently, the flyleaves were removed from the incunable bindings and added to the St-Paul fragment collection as Frag. 54/8 1 and 54/8 2.[7]

At the St Louis Public Library, one leaf of the Gottschalk Antiphonary bears the shelf number Grolier #44. The leaf is part of a collection of about a hundred items originally assembled by bookdealer Frank Glenn and bibliophile Otto Ege as a travelling exhibition for the Grolier Society (not to be confused with New York's Grolier Club). The exhibit, titled 'The Magic Carpet on Wheels', toured the Midwest in an aluminium trailer for several years in the 1950s, introducing civic clubs, religious groups and students to the history of the book.[8] Glenn's source for the Antiphonary leaf is unknown. Although the collection was acquired by the library in 1956, Grolier #44 has only recently been identified as part of the Gottschalk Antiphonary.[9]

The final known leaf of the Gottschalk Antiphonary was acquired from the monastery by one Herr Pullirsch, a Lambach antiquarian. Pullirsch sold the leaf to a private collector in the 1960s; it remains in private hands, as part of a collection

---

[6] They are listed, albeit misidentified, on page 109 of the exhibition catalogue *The Bible in the Twelfth Century* (Cambridge, Mass., 1988). The description of the fragments (they are said to be from a 'Notated missal' from 'Milchstätt') is based on the notes of Hans Swarzenski found on the matte containing the fragments. It is worth noting that Swarzenski wrote an article in 1947 studying and correctly identifying Princeton University Library MS 51 as a Lambach manuscript written and illustrated by Gottschalk (H. Swarzenski, 'Two Romanesque Illuminated Manuscripts in the Princeton University Library', *The Princeton University Library Chronicle*, 9 (1947/48), pp. 64–7).

[7] Holter, 'Neue Beiträge', p. 95 and Holter, 'Das mittelalterliche Buchwesen des Benediktinerstiftes Lambach', p. 58. See also the description in W. Frodl, *Die Kunstdenkmäler des Benediktinerstiftes St Paul im Lavanttal und seiner Filialkirchen*, ÖKT 37 (Vienna, 1969), p. 440 and pl. 528.

[8] R. Baughman, *The Magic Carpet on Wheels* (*Catalogue of an Outstanding Collection of Authentic Books and Manuscripts Tracing the History of Writing and Printing for 4,500 years. Presented by the Grolier Society*) (New York, 1952), no. 44 and final page.

[9] I am grateful to Karen Gould of the St Louis Public Library and to Robert G. Babcock for bringing the existence of this leaf to my attention.

in the Alpine resort town of Badgastein, near Salzburg. Dr Kurt Holter identified the leaf as part of the Gottschalk Antiphonary.[10]

To date, thirty partial or complete folios of the Gottschalk Antiphonary have been identified: sixteen single folios, five bifolios, and four fragmentary folios being used as binding scrap in Lambach incunables. The original length of the manuscript can be approximated by comparison with coeval antiphonaries of a similar format. Of the antiphonaries surveyed for the present study, those from Rheinau and Einsiedeln are closest to the Gottschalk Antiphonary in format. The Rheinau Antiphonary (Zürich, Zentralbibliothek, Rh. 28) comprises 107 folios, with twenty-four lines per page. The Einsiedeln Antiphonary (Einsiedeln, Stiftsbibliothek, Hs 83) is eighty-seven folios long, with twenty-nine lines per page. The Gottschalk Antiphonary, with an average of twenty-seven lines per page, probably had an original length some-where between the Rheinau and Einsiedeln antiphonaries: approximately a hundred folios. The thirty extant folios represent about one-third of the original manuscript.

It is hoped that more folios of the Gottschalk Antiphonary will come to light in time. To facilitate their addition to the facsimile which follows, the extant folios have not been numbered consecutively. Instead, each folio has been assigned a number based on its position in its original quire. Portions of thirteen quires of the Gottschalk Antiphonary (*GA*) can be reconstructed, using two codicological rules:

(1) In his other manuscripts, Gottschalk consistently arranges his quires with the hair side of the outer bifolium facing out, and such that hair side always faces hair side.

(2) The folios are blind-ruled and arranged such that ridges face ridges, and troughs face troughs.

These quires are detailed in Figure 14. In this numbering system, what was origi-nally the third folio of the fifth (extant) quire, for example, is GA folio 53. If the place of the folio in its quire is uncertain, the folios are numbered consecutively beginning with [*]1, where [*] is the number assigned to the quire. For example, although the place of the first two extant folios of the manuscript in their original quire cannot be determined, they have been given the folio numbers 11 and 12 because they are consecutive (i.e. folios 1 and 2 of the first quire). It is important to note that while these numbers indicate in some fashion the general location of the folio in the original intact manuscript, they are in no way intended to indicate the exact original positions of the folios in the manuscript. This system leaves room for additional leaves, while at the same time indicating the placement of individ-ual folios relative to their neighbours. Each folio has also been assigned a siglum based on its current location and shelf mark.

---

[10] K. Holter, 'Beiträge zur Geschichte der Stiftsbibliothek Lambach', *Jahrbuch des Musealvereines Wels*, 15 (1969), pp. 96–123, at p. 103.

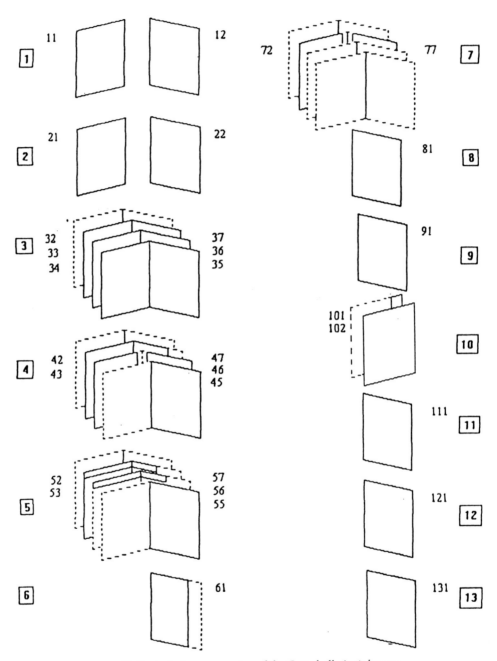

14. Codicological reconstruction of the Gottschalk Antiphonary

	Folio	Siglum	Location
Quire 1			
	11	B1	BRBL MS 481.51.1
	12	B2	BRBL MS 481.51.2
Quire 2			
	21	S1	St-Paul-im-Lavanttal, Stiftsbibliothek, Frag. 54/8, No. 1
	22	S2	St-Paul-im-Lavanttal, Stiftsbibliothek, Frag. 54/8, No. 2
Quire 3			
	32	B3	BRBL MS 481.51.3
	33	L1	Lambach, Stiftsbibliothek, flyleaf in Ink. II.1.i
	34	L2	Lambach, Stiftsbibliothek, flyleaf in Ink. II.1.i
	35	L3	Lambach, Stiftsbibliothek, flyleaf in Ink. II.1.i
	36	L4	Lambach, Stiftsbibliothek, flyleaf in Ink. II.1.i
	37	B4	BRBL MS 481.51.4
Quire 4			
	42	B5	BRBL MS 481.51.5
	43	B6	BRBL MS 481.51.6
	45	P	Private Collection
	46	H5	Cambridge Mass., Houghton Library, Pf MS Typ 704 5
	47	B7	BRBL MS 481.51.7
Quire 5			
	52	I.95.1 + B8	Lambach, Stiftsbibliothek, flyleaf-remnants in Ink. I.95; BRBL MS 481.51.8
	53	I.95.2	Lambach, Stiftsbibliothek, flyleaf-remnants in Ink. I.95
	55	B9	BRBL MS 481.51.9
	56	I.95.3	Lambach, Stiftsbibliothek, flyleaf-remnants in Ink. I.95
	57	I.95.4 + B10	Lambach, Stiftsbibliothek, flyleaf-remnants in Ink. I.95; BRBL MS 481.51.10
Quire 6			
	61	B11	BRBL MS 481.51.11
Quire 7			
	72	B12	BRBL MS 481.51.12
	77	B13	BRBL MS 481.51.13
Quire 8			
	81	B14	BRBL MS 481.51.14
Quire 9			
	91	St1	St Louis Public Library, Rare Books and Special Collections, Grolier #44
Quire 10			
	101	II.36.2	Lambach, Stiftsbibliothek, pastedown in Ink. II.36
	102	B15	BRBL MS 481.51.15

	Folio	*Siglum*	*Location*
Quire 11			
	111	B16	BRBL MS 481.51.16
Quire 12			
	121	B17	BRBL MS 481.51.17
Quire 13			
	131	H6	Cambridge Mass., Houghton Library Pf MS Typ 704 6
Uncertain			
	?	II.36.1	Lambach, Stiftsbibliothek, pastedown in Ink. II.36

2. DESCRIPTION

The Gottschalk Antiphonary (BRBL MS 481.51; Houghton Pf MS Typ 704 5 and 6; Lambach, Stiftsbibliothek, Ink. I.95, Ink. II.1.i, Ink. II.36 (flyleaves); Private Collection; St Louis Public Library, Rare Books and Special Collections, Grolier #44; St-Paul-im-Lavanttal, Stiftsbibliothek, MS 54/8). At least 334 × 244 (238 × 165) mm. Margins and writing lines of the manuscript are ruled with dry-point, the unruled side often reinforced with light lead. If the dry-point is particularly hard to distinguish, even the ruled side is reinforced, a practice which implies that several folios were ruled at once. Ruling side varies. The ruling pattern has double margins on all sides. True margin widths are not ascertainable, since all fragments have been trimmed, but an approximation can be given: upper, 32 mm; lower, 70 mm; inner, 31 mm; outer, 49 mm (see Appendix 2 for detailed measurements of each folio). Twenty-six lines per page, except for folios 91 and 102 (twenty-nine lines) and folios 111, 121 and 131 (twenty-eight lines); these leaves are written in a smaller module. Written in a Romanesque script by Gottschalk of Lambach. The neumes are of the St Gall style. Tonary-letters, indicating mode and final of each chant, are written in the outer margin on tiers of a column. In its original binding, five sewing holes were used. The distance between the sewing holes, from top to bottom, averages as follows: 42 mm, 84 mm, 88 mm, 42 mm (because upper and lower margins have been trimmed on every folio, the distance from the top of the folio to the first hole is not ascertainable, nor is the distance from the fifth hole to the bottom of the folio).

3. CONDITION

Many contemporary repairs are evident; parchment defects on folios 37, 43, 47, 55, 77, 81 and 102 were sewn before writing, although the thread is now gone. A hole on folio 121 was sewn after the folio was written, and some thread is extant. To repair a tear in the margin, an eleventh-century fragment of an unidentified text was pasted to the lower-left corner of folio 37^r. In the centre of the lower margin of that same folio is pasted a thirteenth-century fragment of an unidentified scholastic text.

When Lambach adopted the Melk reform in the fifteenth century, the liturgy of the twelfth-century Antiphonary became obsolete. The manuscript was dismantled, and all of the extant folios used as flyleaves in printed books (and possibly manuscripts) bound at the monastery in the latter half of the century. As flyleaves, the folios of the Gottschalk Antiphonary were cut, folded, pasted and defaced. Conjoint leaves appear to have been used as flyleaves in very large codices, as open bifolios. The single folios were used as flyleaves in quarto-size codices. The binding usage of individual fragments is described below:

- Folios 11 and 12 are consecutive, and may originally have been conjoint. They have been trimmed to practically the same size, indicating that they may have been used in the same binding.
- Folios 21 and 22 are known to have been used as flyleaves in a quarto incunable (a compilation of Hain 7953 and Hain 13683 that is now St-Paul-im-Lavanttal, Stiftsbibliothek, Ink. 5.4.17).
- When closed, no worm holes on the non-consecutive bifolium 32/37 align. This indicates that the bifolium was bound open, in a folio volume measuring approximately 477 × 323 mm.
- Folios 33–6 are still in the binding of Lambach, Stiftsbibliothek, Ink. II.1.i, two bifolios bound open; one bifolium in the front of the volume, and one in the back.
- The bifolium 42/47 seems to have been bound open in a codex with dimensions 412 × 270 mm.
- Fragment 52/57, a non-consecutive bifolium, has no aligning worm holes when closed, indicating that it, too, was bound open. Folio 57 has been cut in half along its vertical axis. The bifolium was used as a flyleaf in Lambach, Stiftsbibliothek, Ink. I/95; the upper three lines of the bifolium are still there, in the form of a stub left when the bifolium was cut out.
- The top margin and first few lines of bifolium 53/56 are still in the binding of Lambach, Stiftsbibliothek, Ink. I/95.
- Folios 72 and 77 were originally conjoint, and may have been removed from the same binding; they have been trimmed to practically the same size. Folio 77 was used as a flyleaf in Lambach, Stiftsbibliothek, Ink. II/34. The shelf number '98' is written on the leaf; Ink. II/34 (Cop. III n:5409), an incunable with the same dimensions as the fragment, was formerly #98.[11]

---

[11] This fragment is not noted in the Goldschmidt description of the incunable, and may have been removed before the catalogue was compiled in 1916.

- An offset of folio 121ʳ is visible inside the lower board of Lambach, Stiftsbibliothek, II/47/1 (H 8370).[12]
- Folios 43, 46, 61, 72, 77, 81, 91, 111, 121 and 131 were all used as flyleaves in volumes slightly smaller than the original size of the Antiphonary. Each has a fold approximately 14 mm from one vertical edge; the tab thus created would have protruded after the first or before the last quire of the bound codex.
- Folios 45 and 55 are severely damaged, and retain no evidence of binding usage.

In addition to being cut and folded while serving as flyleaves, the fragments were written on by Lambach monks. Thirteenth- to fifteenth-century marginal liturgical additions, mostly notations of hymns, indicate that the Gottschalk Antiphonary was used for over three centuries. These are found on folios 43, 46, 52 and 121ᵛ (see pp. 94–95 below). Several humanistic hands of the sixteenth century wrote classical, biblical, patristic and medieval theological quotations on folios 61, 72, 77 and 81. The classical authors cited are Aristotle, Ovid and Seneca. The patristic sources are Augustine, Gregory, Chrysostom and Ambrose. Of the later theologians, only Bernard of Clairvaux is cited. A. Eilenstein notes several sixteenth-century monks with humanistic interests; some of them may have been responsible for this marginalia.[13] Two unattributed quotes display a candid misogyny: 'Uxor autem est perpetuum tormentum' ('Indeed, Woman is perpetual torment') on folio 61ʳ, and 'Mulieris est oblivio rationis' ('women cause one to lose all sense of reason') on folio 61ᵛ. One of these humanistic hands can perhaps be identified from an ownership mark in a sixteenth-century book of Lambach provenance: the note '1564. Sum Adamii Schilheri' is found on the last page of a copy of Aurogallus' *Compendium hebreae chaldeaequae grammatices* (Wittenberg, 1525) (BRBL Fne20 523ac), and appears to have been written by the same hand which quotes Bernard on folio 72ʳ of the Gottschalk Antiphonary. This same hand, presumably that of one Adam Schilher, is found in several other Lambach books as a marginal notator.[14] One nineteenth-century notation concerns provenance: the very abraded hand-written ex-libris 'Stift Lambach' is found in the lower margin of folio 55ᵛ.

Most of the fragments bear twentieth-century notations of one form or another. After acquiring the Beinecke leaves, Zinniker added shelf numbers in pencil to each fragment.[15] An early owner, probably Zinniker, wrote German pencil notations on several leaves identifying some of their contents (see folio 121). Fragments 21 and

---

[12] See previous note.

[13] A. Eilenstein, *Die Benediktinerabtei Lambach in Österreich ob der Enns und ihre Mönche* (Linz, 1936), pp. 34–6.

[14] For example, in Lambach, Stiftsbibliothek, Ink. II/34, a quote from Ambrose is recorded in Schilher's hand on folio 1ʳ: 'Ambros. Pie clerite quid tibi cum. . .'.

[15] These are: 481.51.1 (145A); 481.51.2 (145B); 481.51.3/4 (147); 481.51.5/7 (146A); 481.51.6 (146B); 481.51.8/10 (153); 481.51.9 (152); 481.51.11 (150); 481.51.12 (144B); 481.51.13(144A); 481.51.14 (151); 481.51.15 (149); 481.51.16 (118); 481.51.17 (148).

22 bear the ex libris stamp of the Archiv des Benediktinerstiftes, St-Paul-im-Lavanttal. Folios 46 and 131 (the Houghton leaves) are marked 'II 8841' and 'II 8840' respectively; the import of these numbers is not known.

4. SCRIPT

The script of the Gottschalk Antiphonary is a Romanesque hand found in other late twelfth-century Lambach manuscripts: the hand of the monk Gottschalk. In the Antiphonary, Gottschalk writes in two modules; one with a 6 mm minim, the other with an 8 mm minim. The features of the script in each of these two modules are identical; only the size varies. The smaller module is used on folios 61 to 131.

Gottschalk uses two styles of rubrication; uncials with red highlighting, and capital letters. Directional rubrics, cross-referencing to another point in the manuscript, are black stroked with red, while titular rubrics, identifying the Offices and Hours, are red. In responsories, the first letter of the *repetendum* is highlighted with red in the text of the respond.

The distinguishing features of Gottschalk's script, all of which are used with varying degrees of consistency, are described below. Examples of each can be found on folio 33^r, on the line specified after the description of each feature. Several features of Gottschalk's script in this manuscript vary from his work in other manuscripts, changes which were necessitated by the fact that this is a musical manuscript, and abbreviation strokes or suprascript letters would have interfered with both the writing and the interpretation of musical notation.

4.1 Distinguishing features

(These descriptions are intended to convey the appearance of the letter forms, not their ductus.)

- [ct] ligature; The top of the [t]-ascender curls left into an almost complete circle (line 2). This series of letters is not a ligature in the most literal sense of the word, since the two letters are not in fact attached. However, because this mannerism appears to have developed from a pre-Caroline [ct] ligature such as that used at Fulda, where the join begins at the top of the [c] and curves to the top of the [t], it is a ligature in intention if not in fact.
- round [s]; at the end of a line, or in the bottom line of the page, the final stroke is extended far below the line of writing (line 24).
- Ascenders are slightly forked (line 1).

The script is difficult to distinguish from the hands of the many other Lambach scribes who used a similar style. The [ct] ligature, while somewhat distinctive, was imitated by other scribes, as was the elongated round [s]. Gottschalk's hand is distinguishable from the others by the rounding at the base of minims, which curve into their feet instead of turning abruptly. Also, the script tends to slant slightly to the right.

4.2 *Other distinctive letter forms*

- Both round and straight [d] are used (line 8).
- [e] at the end of a word: the cross-stroke is extended, ending with a downward tick (line 1).
- [g] before [e] and [o], and sometimes before [a] and [r], has a straight stroke connecting its back to the next letter (line 1). Otherwise, the back of the [g] is slightly forked (line 5).
- [m] at the end of a word is sometimes a capital uncial (line 8).
- [q]: the descender sometimes (more often in the smaller module) ends with a curl to the left, although a short horizontal tick is the rule (folio 81ʳ, line 24).
- [r]: at the end of a word, the shoulder is doubled (line 26).
- [x]: in the Antiphonary, unlike Gottschalk's other manuscripts, [x] does not descend below the line of writing (line 4).
- [z]: an [h] with a hook at the top and to the left of the ascender (line 16).

4.3 *Abbreviations*

Because this is a musical manuscript, abbreviations are generally avoided to facilitate a clear relationship between syllable and melody, and to avoid confusion of abbreviation strokes with neumes. Abbreviations of [et] and *nomina sacra*, however, are used frequently.

Tironian [et]:

- Although Gottschalk favours it elsewhere, the Tironian [et] is rarely used in this manuscript perhaps because it is more neume-like than the ampersand. It is only used in incipits or rubrics, when no music is supplied. The abbreviation is uncrossed (line 11).

Nomina sacra:

- Forms of [christus] ([xpc], [xpi], [xpo], [xpm]): the descender of the [p] is crossed with a horizontal stroke ending at the right with a downward tick (line 16). When used in a line with no music, a horizontal abbreviation stroke above the [p] is used instead of the lower cross-stroke (line 16).
- Forms of [deus] ([ds], [di], [dm] – [deo] is not abbreviated): the [d] is crossed with an upward curving stroke which is actually a continuation of the ascender

of the [d], curving to the right and back to cross itself (folio 34ᵛ, line 24). When used at the beginning of a phrase, i.e. with a capital [d], a horizontal abbreviation stroke is used instead (folio 34ᵛ, line 24).

- Forms of [dominus] ([dns], [dni], [dno], [dnm]): the [d] is crossed in the same manner as that in [deus] (line 3).
- Forms of [ihesus] ([ihu], [ihs], [ihm]): the ascender of the [h] is crossed in the same manner as the [d] of [deus] (folio 52ʳ, line 5).

Other abbreviations:

- -[m] is abbreviated with a horizontal abbreviation stroke – a horizontal line with a tick up at the left, down at the right. This stroke can also be used in abbreviations to indicate anything from one missing letter to most of a word (line 25).
- [con] is abbreviated by a backwards [c]. Other Lambach scribes using this style tend to use an abbreviation which more closely approximates the number [9] (line 23).
- -[er] is abbreviated by a suprascript comma (line 25). This abbreviation can also be used, in rubrics, in the same general manner as the horizontal abbreviation stroke (line 23).
- -[tur] is abbreviated with a suprascript [2] above [t] (line 17).

Gottschalk frequently uses suprascript letters as abbreviations (e.g. [qᵃ], [qᵉ], [gᵒ]) in his other manuscripts. In the Antiphonary, such abbreviations would have interfered with the neumes and are therefore avoided.

4.4 Ligatures

- [ct] (see above)
- [de] ligature: round [d] with the top of its ascender used as the back of the [e] (line 17).
- ampersand: the upper compartment of the ampersand is very narrow. The cross-stroke ends with a thick final stroke. The downward stroke descends slightly below the line of writing, and curves back up to meet it (line 2).
- -[nt]: at the end of a word, the final upright of [N] is used as the vertical stroke of the [T] (line 17).
- [st]: a long [s], with its upper bow joined to the back of the [t]. The [t] cross-stroke only barely crosses its back to the left (line 4). If the ligature occurs beneath a melismatic passage of music, the top curve of the [s] is extended across the passage as a wavy line, meeting the top of the [t] at the end of the melisma (folio 11ʳ, line 2).
- -[us]: at the end of a word, the right arm of an angled [v] is used as the lower bow of a round [s] (line 18).

- [ut]: the word [ut] is often abbreviated by an angled [v] with its right stroke used as the base of the [t] (line 23).

In other manuscripts, Gottschalk ligates [ae] with an e-cedilla. The cedilla is open at the right, and slightly disconnected from the [e]. In the Gottschalk Antiphonary, the cedilla is not used, probably to avoid confusion with the neumes below.

4.5 Punctuation

- A *punctus* in the shape of a flattened oval is used for all pauses except interrogative.
- *Interrogativus* is used rarely in the Gottschalk Antiphonary – one example can be found on folio 77ᵛ, line 10, after the word [Que].

5. TEXTUAL FORMAT

Gottschalk has formatted the text of his antiphonary in an extremely efficient manner, filling each line to the utmost to justify the right margin. Each responsory begins at the left margin and each set of antiphons at the beginning of a line (the only exceptions to these rules are pieces for which only the incipit is given; these may fall at any point in the line). In order to facilitate this efficient use of space, Gottschalk often completes chants by using the available space at the end of an immediately preceding or following line (e.g. folio 12ʳ, line 20). Such passages are separated from the rest of the text on their line by a decorative red bracket. This is a common formatting practice in liturgical manuscripts of the period.

When no space is available on the immediately preceding or following line, tie marks in the margin direct the reader to another point on the page where the chant is completed at the end of an earlier line which was not completely filled (e.g. folio 12ʳ, where line 16 cross-references to line 14). Again, these sections of text are distinguished from the main body of text by a red bracket. This particular system of omission marks is not found in any other Lambach manuscript of the period. The system commonly used to indicate textual omissions in late twelfth-century Lambach manuscripts, in fact the system used elsewhere by Gottschalk, employs neume forms as the reference marks. Using neumes as omission marks in a musical manuscript could lead to confusion. Instead, a system of arbitrary signs is used in the Gottschalk Antiphonary, similar to, although doubtless not directly influenced by, the system developed by Otfrid von Weissenburg in the ninth century.[16] The forms used by Gottschalk are not otherwise recognizable symbols, and are clearly distinct from the neumes.

---

[16] W. Kleiber, *Otfrid von Weissenburg* (Munich, 1971), pp. 391–2.

6. NOTATION

The Gottschalk Antiphonary is notated with St Gall neumes. This system of notation, adiastematic and unheighted, is a symbolic, as opposed to an iconic, method
of indicating monophonic melody.[17] The neumes bear little iconographic resem-
blance to the series of pitches they represent, functioning, rather, as abstract
symbols of particular melodic movements. Only relative pitch can be determined,
and that only in the most basic of relative movements, upward or downward. For
a modern-day singer untrained in monastic liturgy, the melodies would be impossible to interpret without reference to their heighted counterparts. Interpretation
by medieval monks was by convention and memorization; the neumes served to
remind the singer of a familiar tune.

The St Gall neumes in the Gottschalk Antiphonary include Germanic variants
typical of the period and area (see Fig. 15). Distinguishing features of the hand
include: the slight thickening at the upper left of virga and final stroke of franculus, torculus and porrectus (and other neumes using these forms); the flattened top
of the clivis (the left-hand stroke breaks at the top); the concavity of the top stroke
of the franculus and pressus; and the flattened-oval shape of the punctum.

Many neumes are combinations of those in Figure 15, and can be interpreted as
combinations of the relative pitch movements they represent. For example, on folio
34ᵛ, line 21, the word 'sedes' is notated by a ligature of scandicus, porrectus and
pressus, representing three notes in an upward progression, a movement downward, a movement upward, a repetition of that note, and a final movement downward. The specifics of interval and pitch are indeterminable. The use of ligation
follows the principles outlined by Cardine.[18]

It is likely that Gottschalk was also the neumator: space is left between syllables
in the text for melismatic passages (folio 11ʳ, line 4); the change in script module
corresponds to a similar change in neume size; and the neume forms used by
Gottschalk as omission marks in other manuscripts correspond to the neumes used
in the Gottschalk Antiphonary (see Fig. 16) – note particularly the broken clivis (at
the beginning of porrectus), and the tick at the upper left of the virga minim (seen
in Fig. 16, at the beginning of climacus).

7. DECORATION

The Gottschalk Antiphonary is decorated using a clear hierarchy of initials: plain,
white-vine, and historiated. Historiated and white-vine initials are never used con-

---

[17] L. Treitler, 'Paleography and Semiotics', in M. Huglo (ed.), *Musicologie Médiévale: Notations et Séquences* (Paris, 1987), pp. 17–28, at p. 24.

[18] E. Cardine, *Sémiologie Grégorienne*, Etudes Grégoriennes, II (1970), pp. 48–55.

Neume	Form
Punctum	.
Virga	∕
Podatus	♪
Clivis	⋀ ℗ ℘
Flexa	♪
Torculus	♫
Porrectus	ℕ
Scandicus	⸴∕
Salicus	⸴∕
Climacus	∕··
Qualisma	◢◢
Oriscus	⸡
Pressus	⸴⸴
Franculus	⸝
Trigon	·⁚
Tristropha	⸌⸌⸍
Bistropha	⸌⸍

15. Neume forms used in the Gottschalk Antiphonary

currently; Gottschalk chooses one or the other based on the importance of the feast in question.

7.1 *Plain initials*

Plain, red, single-line uncial capitals are used for pieces which commence at the beginning of a line.

7.2 *White-vine initials*

Two- to six-line white-vine initials begin the first responsory of Matins for feasts of lesser importance whose liturgy is given in full. These initials are characteristic of

16. Examples of neume omission marks used by Gottschalk in Berlin, Staatsbibliothek, MS Theo. lat. qu. 140: folio 107ʳ (detail): climacus; folio 38ᵛ (detail): porrectus; folio 40ʳ (detail): trigon

Gottschalk's work as described above: [D] (folio 35ʳ, the first responsory 'De psalmis', to be used between the Sunday after the Octave of Epiphany and Septuagesima); [Q] (folio 52ʳ, Quinquagesima Sunday); [T] (folio 55ᵛ, the second Sunday of Quadragesima); [O] (folio 61ʳ, Good Friday); [M] (folio 77ʳ, feria 2 of the week after Easter); [V] (folio 77ᵛ, feria 3 of the week after Easter); [D] (folio 81ᵛ, the first Sunday after the Octave of Easter); and [E] (folio 121ᵛ, the Common of Apostles).[19]

7.3 Historiated initials

Historiated initials are used for the first Matins responsory of particularly important feasts. The extant historiated initials are: Gideon blowing a trumpet in the letter [C] (folio 11ʳ, the fourth Sunday of Advent); a bust of Jeremiah holding a scroll, in the letter [C] (folio 11ᵛ, feria 2 of the fourth week of Advent); a bust of John the Evangelist in the letter [V] (folio 21ᵛ, his nativity); a bust of St Gregory in the letter [F] (folio 43ᵛ, his feastday); a bust of St Benedict (folio 45ʳ, his feastday); a full-length figure of the Angel Gabriel representing the letter [I] (folio 46ᵛ, the Annunciation); Pope Narcissus blessing St Afra in the letter [B] (folio 91ʳ, her feastday); and a virgin saint in the letter [V] (folio 131ʳ, the Common of Virgins). The portrait of Gabriel closely approximates the angel in the Berlin manuscript annunciation scene.[20]

All of the distinguishing characteristics of Gottschalk's style can be found in

---

[19] The highlighted uncials on line 5 of folio 57ᵛ indicate that originally an ornate initial [V] began the chant 'Videntes Joseph alonge', the first Matins responsory of the third Sunday of Quadragesima. The folio was severly trimmed, and the initial is not extant.   [20] *ÖKT*, p. 244, fig. 293.

these white-vine and historiated initials: the moulded bands, the berries, the detached leaf, the characteristic facial features. The main body of each initial is painted in red with purple highlights and facial features. Microscopic examination reveals that the purple highlights and flourishes were painted before the red body of the initial, implying that Gottschalk was tracing a detailed sketch. Evidence of this sketching is faintly visible beneath the initial [V] on folio 131^v.

8. CONTENTS OF THE GOTTSCHALK ANTIPHONARY: DETAIL

A detailed description of the contents of each quire of the Gottschalk Antiphonary is given below, followed by a summary inventory.

QUIRE 1

The extant liturgy begins with the first nocturn responsories of the fourth Sunday of Advent (folio 11^r). The dominical liturgy is given in full; ferias 2 to 6 are abbreviated (folios 11^v–12^v).

QUIRE 2

Folio 21 begins with the Little Hours for the feast of St Stephen (26 December). Commemorative antiphons in honour of the Nativity and in honour of the Virgin, the patroness of Lambach, follow Lauds and second Vespers. The feast of John the Apostle (27 December) is next, with the liturgy given in full, concluding at the bottom of folio 22^v. After Lauds and the Little Hours, commemorative antiphons in honour of the Nativity, the Virgin and St Stephen are supplied.

QUIRE 3

This quire preserves the Epiphany season. Folio 32 begins with the antiphons of the second nocturn of Epiphany Matins (6 January). On folio 32^v, at the end of Matins, is the sequence 'Quem non praevalent' (see pp. 113–119). The liturgy continues on folio 33 with the end of Lauds to the end of second Vespers. The liturgy for the days during the Octave of Epiphany follows.

The first indication of the combination of temporale and sanctorale in the manuscript is found on folio 34^r. The feast of a saint with very localized significance, St Valentine, Bishop of Passau (7 January), is acknowledged by a rubric referring the reader to the feast of St Odalricus.

Next is the liturgy for the Sunday during the Octave of Epiphany. A highly abbreviated liturgy for St Paul the First Hermit (10 January) follows, with most of the Offices referring back to the Epiphany liturgy. The liturgy for the Octave of Epiphany is next. Commemorative antiphons for St Hilary (13 January) are found at the beginning of Matins and after Lauds.

Next is the first Sunday after the Octave of Epiphany. The first portion of the liturgy (Vespers and the antiphons of the first nocturn of Matins) is specific to this day. The rest of the liturgy, which begins with the Matins responsories on folio 35ʳ, is differentiated by the rubric 'Responsoriae de psalmis ab octavo epiphaniae usque ad septuagesimam' ('Responsories from the Psalms [for use] from the Octave of Epiphany through Septuagesima'). 'Domine ne in ira' is the first of the thirteen Matins responsories for Sundays during this period (see below, p. 84). Ferias 2, 3 and 4 follow; folio 37 ends in the middle of the first nocturn of the fourth feria.

A brief biblical text is given after the third responsory of ferias 2 and 3 (Lamentations 2: 19 and Proverbs 3: 19–20, respectively). These readings, written in a larger script, are preceded by the rubric 'In aestate'. Depending on the date of Easter, the period between the Octave of Epiphany and Septuagesima can last from one to six weeks. If this period is less than six weeks long, the extra weeks are inserted after Trinity Sunday (in late May or June). The biblical texts labelled 'In aestate' are readings for these summer weeks.

QUIRE 4

Folio 42 is the next surviving leaf. This is the liturgy for the feast of St Agatha (5 February), beginning in the middle of the first Matins responsory. This feast is given in full, and ends on folio 43ʳ. A highly abbreviated liturgy for the feast of St Scholastica (10 February) follows, consisting only of a Vespers respond, the *Magnificat* antiphon and the invitatory. The rest of the liturgy is to be drawn from the Common of Virgins (found on folio 131); the invitatory is followed by the directional rubric 'Et cetera omnia ut de virginibus. Antiphona *Veni sponsa* [the first Matins responsory for the Common of Virgins] non canitur' ('All the rest as in the Common of Virgins. The antiphon "Veni Sponsa" is not sung'). The feast celebrating the dedication of St Peter's in Antioch (Cathedra St Petri – 22 February) is next, and is given almost completely in incipit form. The feast of Pope Gregory (12 March) begins on folio 43ᵛ, and is given in full. The folio concludes with the second responsory of Matins; folio 45 begins with the end of Lauds.

The feast honouring St Benedict (21 March) is given in full, beginning on folio 45ʳ and ending on folio 46ᵛ. The Annunciation (25 March) runs from folio 46ᵛ to 47ᵛ; first Vespers, Matins and two sets of Lauds antiphons are extant.

QUIRE 5

B8 (folio 52), a partial folio missing its first three lines, includes the end of Sexagesima Sunday, the *Magnificat* antiphons for the following week, and Quinquagesima Sunday. The next week is missing; two lines of one of the two missing folios survive in the fragment I.95.2 (folio 53). Folio 55 begins with the end of the first Sunday of Quadragesima, continuing with feria 2 to Saturday of the following week and the first nocturn of the second Sunday of Quadragesima. These weekdays are highly abbreviated, giving only Lauds antiphons and one or two antiphons for the Little Hours and Vespers. The second Sunday of Quadragesima is given in full. The rest of that Sunday and ferias 2 and 3 of the following week are extant only in the two-line fragment I.95.3 (folio 56). B10 (folio 57) contains ferias 4 to 6 of the second week of Quadragesima and the first nocturn of the third Sunday (the ferias are abbreviated, and the Sunday is given in full). Like its conjugate, B8, B10 has lost three lines at the top and is also missing its outer half. These three lines are preserved on the fragment bound in the front of Lambach, Stiftsbibliothek, Ink. I.95:

I.95.1ʳ [unknown] [*A* Cum turba plurima conveniret ad jesum et de civitatibus properarent ad eum dixit per similitudinem Exiit] qui seminat seminare semen suum *Ad 1a a* Exiit qui seminat semi

I.95.1ᵛ [holocaustum odoratus est domi]nus odorem [suavitatis et benedixit eis Crescite et multiplicamini et replete terram] E[cce ego] statuam pactum meum vobiscum vestra post [vos. Crescite]

I.95.4ʳ *a* E

I.95.4ᵛ patri et filio et spiritui sancto P[ ]em *in ev*

I.95.1ʳ begins with the Lauds antiphon 'Cum turba' for Sexagesima Sunday. The Prime antiphon, 'Exiit qui seminat', is completed at the first line of B8ʳ. Similarly, I.95.1ᵛ is consecutive with the last line of B8ʳ and the first line of B8ᵛ, preserving the responsory 'Aedificavit Noe altare' and its verse 'Ecce ego statuam'. The strip I.95.1–4 is the top of the bifolium B8/B10 which was bound into this incunable and cut out early in the twentieth century – together, they make up the complete bifolium 52/57.

In the back of the same Lambach incunable, another bifolium of the Gottschalk Antiphonary has been cut out. The top two lines of each folio are preserved, and have been given the sigla I.95.2 and 3:

I.95.2ʳ umen. *v* Et qui pr[ei]bant increpavit eum ut [taceret at ille ma] S[ecundum multitudinem] miserationem tuarum.*Ad laud*/gis clamabat. Rab

I.95.2ᵛ *a* Cum facis [elemosynam nesciat sinistra tua] quid faciat dextra tua *f. vi a* Nesciat sinistra tua quid faciat dextera tua. iii * *a* Tu autem cum [ora]veris intra

I.95.3ʳ [comedi ex omnibus priusquam tu veneris Benedixique ei et erit bene] dictus *v* Dominum tuum illum constitui et o *vel r* D²¹

---

²¹ The reference to an alternate responsory ('*v[e]l r* D . . .') may refer to the respond 'Dum iret Jacob' which is used as the fourth respond of the first nocturn of this feast in many of the surveyed manuscripts.

I.95.3ᵛ [R Minor sum cunctis . . . v Tu locutus es quod mihi bene faceres et dilatares sem]en meum sicut arenam maris Libera me *Sive*[22]

I.95.2ʳ preserves responsories and antiphons for Quinquagesima Sunday. The verso preserves antiphons for feria 6 of that week (the Friday after Ash Wednesday). Three marginal tonary-letters are visible on the verso: [a] for 'Cum facis', [ab] for 'Nesciat sinistra', and [a] for 'Tu autem cum' (this tonary-letter is preceded by a tie mark, indicated above by an asterisk [*]). The text on I.95.3 is from the second Sunday of Quadragesima. I.95.2 was the first of two folios which separated B8 and B9. I.95.3 immediately follows B9 (completing the respond 'Quis igitur ille' which begins at the last line of B9ᵛ), and was the folio between B9 and B10 (see Fig. 14).

QUIRE 6

The next surviving part of the Gottschalk Antiphonary (folio 61) is the end of Maundy Thursday, and Matins to Lauds of Good Friday (given in full). The outer half of this folio has been trimmed away.

QUIRE 7

Folio 72 begins with the end of Easter Lauds, continuing through to the Little Hours and Second Vespers. At the end of Lauds are commemorative antiphons in honour of the Cross, the Virgin, and St Kilian. A rubric directing the reader to a breviary refers to the suffrage which should follow Lauds: 'Suffragia sanctorum et de omnibus sanctis ut in breviario scriptum est' ('The suffrage of Saints and of All Saints as is written in the breviary'). On the verso is the stock repertory of twenty-five *Benedictus* antiphons for use during the Easter season. Incipits of antiphons for the week after Easter follow, beginning with the antiphons and versicles for feria 2 at the bottom of folio 72. Folio 77 begins with the antiphons and versicles for the Saturday of that week (the liturgy for ferias 3 to 6 is not extant). Next are the responsories and non-matinal antiphons for the week after Easter, beginning with the responsories of feria 2. The liturgy continues to feria 3.

QUIRE 8

Folio 81 includes the *Benedictus* antiphons for the third, fourth and fifth Sundays after Easter. The responsorial liturgy for the first Sunday after the Octave of Easter begins near the top of folio 81ᵛ. The folio ends in the middle of the second nocturn.

QUIRE 9

Folio 91 (St1) begins with the second antiphon of Matins for the feast of St Afra (7 August), and ends with the first antiphon of Lauds.

---

[22] The reference to an alternate verse, *sive*, was most likely followed by one of the five other verses that Hesbert associates with this respond (*CAO* 7156).

QUIRE 10

In the back of Lambach, Stiftsbibliothek, Ink. II.36, the inner margin of the verso of one folio of the Gottschalk Antiphonary is preserved as a stub (II.36.2). Only the last few letters of lines 8–26 are visible:

8   en
9   ia
10 ic
11
12 n
13
14
15 Cuius
16
17 n
18 e beata virgo maria exprogenie david ut
19 ipsa
20 Cuius
21
22
23 tella
24 c n
25 cta
26 s

At line 18, the text continues down the right-hand margin, providing more than enough text to ensure the positive identification of the Office: the Nativity of the Virgin (8 September). The phrase 'beata virgo maria exprogenie david . . .' is the end of the text 'Hodie nata est' used throughout this Office. The text runs down the right margin; this implies that Gottschalk felt obligated to complete the text without starting a new line. Because Gottschalk's formatting practice requires each respond to start at the beginning of a line, this text is probably the end of a verse. 'Hodie nata est' is the verse commonly used with the respond 'Beatissimae virginis Mariae'. The 'cuius' on line 15 (and on line 20) is formatted as a *repetendum* incipit (a single word with its initial highlighted in red). Two responds in this Office have a *repetendum* which begins with the word 'cuius': 'Hodie nata est' and 'Gloriosae virginis'. 'Hodie nata est' is usually used as the first respond of Matins. Folio II.36.2 must comprise the first nocturn of the Office, since the next folio, folio 102, begins with the verse of the first respond of the second nocturn. The verse's respond, 'Diem festum', must have been the last respond of II.36.2. Given these clues, and through the examination of this Office in other antiphonaries, it is possible to reconstruct at least part of this page, beginning with the first responsory of Matins at line 13.

After the three responsories of the first nocturn, which run from line 13 to line 23, only line 24 is left for the antiphons of the second nocturn. Because most of the antiphons for this Office are also used for the Assumption of the Virgin (15 August), they would not have been given here in full. As is Gottschalk's practice, antiphons which are found in full earlier in the manuscript would have been given in incipit form only. There is more than enough room on line 24 for these incipits. The end of line 25 must also be antiphon incipits (separated from the rest of the line by a bracket); the letter combination [cta] never occurs in the respond 'Diem festum'. The layout of the page, with spaces and hyphens indicating melismatic passages, would have been as follows (the letters in bold indicate the extant text):

13   *R* H-O-D-I-E N—A-T-A E-S-T beata virgo Maria exprogenie da-vid perquam
14   salus mun-di creden-tibus ap-paruit cuius vita glorio-sa lucem dedit seculo.
15   *v* Beatissime virginis Marie nativitatem devotissime celebre—mus **Cuius**
16   *R* Beatissime virginis Ma-rie nativitatem devotissi—me celebre—
17   mus ut ipsa pro no——bis intercedat ad dominum de ihesum x**pm**
18   *R* Gloriose virginis Marie ortu dignissimu recole—ntes cuius dominus/V
     Hodie beata virgo maria exprogenie david ut
19   humilitatem respici—ens angelo nunciate conce-pit salvato—rem mun—
     di/**ipsa**
20   *v* Beatissime virginis virginis Marie nativitate devotissime celebre—mus **Cuius**
21   *R* So—lem iustitie regem paritu—ra spremum stella maris hodie pro
22   ces——————————————————————————————
23   ——————-sit ad ortum. **v** Cernere divinum lumen gaude——te fideles. **Stella**
24   [antiphon incipits]
25   *R* Diem festum precelse genetri-cis dei vir-ginis Ma-rie/[antiphon incipits]**cta**
26   sollempniter celebre—-mus quo incoata es eius felix na——-tivitas

In sum,

1.1	*R* Hodie nata est	*V* Beatissime virginis Marie
1.2	*R* Beatissime virginis Marie	*V* Hodie nata est
1.3	*R* Gloriose virginis Marie	*V* Beatissime virginis Marie
1.4	*R* Solem justitie regem	*V* Cernere divinum lumen
2	[antiphon incipits]	
2.1	*R* Diem festum precelse	

This series of responsories is found in this sequence in only one of the surveyed manuscripts, Graz, Universitätsbibliothek, Nos. 29/30. The relationship of this manuscript and the Gottschalk Antiphonary is discussed in Chapter 4. Folio 102 follows II.36.2 (which can therefore be called folio 101), beginning with the verse of the respond 'Diem festum precelse' and continuing throughout the remainder of the feast. The Exaltation of the Cross (14 September) follows, an abbreviated

Office with rubrics referring the reader to the Invention of the Cross liturgy. Lauds is given in full, and the folio ends with the antiphons of second vespers.

Folio Sti precedes folios 101 and 102, and was located near these two leaves in the original manuscript. Because the original sewing holes on folio Sti are set at different distances from one another than those in folios 101 and 102, however, the three folios could not have been part of the same quire (see Appendix 2). Leaf Sti has therefore been labelled folio 91, having originally been part of the quire immediately preceding Quire 10.

QUIRE 11

Folio 111 consists entirely of the Office for St Andrew (30 November), from the middle of the first respond to the last antiphon of Lauds. Because it falls immediately before Advent, the Office of St Andrew is usually the last proper Office in an antiphonary. In the Gottschalk Antiphonary, however, this is not so. The Offices for St Lucy (13 December) and St Thomas (21 December) occur later in the manuscript, and immediately precede the Commons Offices.

QUIRE 12

Folio 121 begins with the end of Matins for St Lucy (13 December). The feast of St Thomas (21 December) follows the end of the Office, and is abbreviated with a directional rubric referring the reader to the Common of Apostles. The placement of these sanctorale Offices (Lucy and Thomas), which are often found in the Advent season near the beginning of a liturgical book, indicates that the Gottschalk Antiphonary follows a sanctorale system which runs from January to December, as opposed to beginning with Advent. Immediately before the Office for St Thomas is the rubric 'Hic incipiantur antiphona *O sapientia*', a reference to the series of elaborate *Magnificat* antiphons beginning with 'O' which are sung during the ferias before Christmas. Presumably, this series of antiphons would have been given in full in the Advent portion of the manuscript. The Common of Evangelists and the Common of Apostles are next, beginning the Commons Offices.

QUIRE 13

Folio 131, the final extant folio of the Gottschalk Antiphonary, consists entirely of the Common of Virgins, from the first nocturn to the responsories of the third nocturn. This folio may have been part of the same quire as folio 121, but as there is no direct evidence to justify affiliating the two folios, I have kept them distinct.

UNIDENTIFIED

The left margin of one folio of the Gottschalk Antiphonary (II.36.1) is preserved as a pastedown spine-liner in the front of Lambach, Sitftsbibliothek, Ink. II.36. Only lines 12–26 are legible:

12	*a*
13	n
14	x
15	
16	
17	*a* D
18	*a* C
19	f
20	*r* V
21	d
22	t
23	*v* Ci
24	r
25	n
26	*a* Q

The fragment preserves a series of antiphons, one respond (beginning with the letter [V]), its verse (beginning with the letters [Ci] or [Cu] – only one minim of the second letter is visible) and another antiphon (beginning with the letter [Q]). This is probably Vespers or Lauds, both of which consist of several antiphons, a respond/verse, and the antiphon 'in evangelio'. Gottschalk's tendency as evidenced elsewhere in the manuscript is to give only the respond/verse incipit at Lauds and the complete texts at Vespers. The three–line respond on this fragment is evidently given in full, making Vespers the most probable Office. As for the particular feast-day represented by this fragment, it must have at Vespers a respond beginning with [V] whose verse begins with [Ci] or [Cu], followed by a *Magnificat* antiphon beginning with [Q]. None of the responsories in *Corpus Antiphonalium Officii* or in any of the other surveyed manuscripts fulfils these requirements. While this fragment is clearly part of the Gottschalk Antiphonary, its exact location within the manuscript is unknown.

The contents are summarized below. For a more detailed analysis of the contents, see the CANTUS index of the Gottschalk Antiphonary.

9. CONTENTS OF THE GOTTSCHALK ANTIPHONARY: SUMMARY

Feast	Folio(s)
Dom. 4 Adventus	11r–11v
Fer. 2 Hebd. 4 Adv.	11v–12r
Fer. 3 Hebd. 4 Adv.	12r–12v
Fer. 4 Hebd. 4 Adv.	12v
Fer. 5 Hebd. 4 Adv.	12v
Fer. 6 Hebd. 4 Adv.	12v

Feast	Folio(s)
LACUNA	
de S. Stephani (26 December)	21r
de S. Joannis Evang. (27 December)	21r–22v
LACUNA	
Epiphania (6 January)	32r–33r
Epiphania, 8	33r–34r
Dom. 1 p. Epiph.	34r
de S. Pauli Heremitae (10 January)	34r
Octava Epiphaniae	34r–34v
Dom. 2 p. Epiph.	34v–35r
Dom. per annum	35r–36r
Feria 2 per annum	36r–37r
Feria 3 per annum	37r–37v
Feria 4 per annum	37v
LACUNA	
de S. Agathae (5 February)	42r–43r
de S. Scholasticae (10 February)	43r
Cathedra S. Petri (22 February)	43r–43v
de S. Gregorii (12 March)	43v–45r
de S. Benedicti (21 March)	45r–46v
Annuntiatio Mariae (25 March)	46v–47v
LACUNA	
Dom. Sexagesimae	52r
Hebd. Sexagesimae	52r
Dom. Quinquages.	52r–53r
LACUNA	
Fer. 6 post Cineres	53v
LACUNA	
Dom. 1 Quadragesimae	55r
Fer. 2 Hebd. 1 Quad.	55r
Fer. 3 Hebd. 1 Quad.	55r
Fer. 4 Hebd. 1 Quad.	55r
Fer. 5 Hebd. 1 Quad.	55r
Fer. 6 Hebd. 1 Quad.	55v
Sabb. Hebd. 1 Quad.	55v
Dom. 2 Quadragesimae	55v–56v
LACUNA	
Fer. 2 Hebd. 2 Quad.	57r
Fer. 3 Hebd. 2 Quad.	57r
Fer. 4 Hebd. 2 Quad.	57r
Fer. 5 Hebd. 2 Quad.	57r
Fer. 6 Hebd. 2 Quad.	57r
Sabb. Hebd. 2 Quad.	57r
Dom. 3 Quadragesimae	57r–57v
LACUNA	
Fer. 5 in Cena Dom.	61r

Feast	Folio(s)
Fer. 6 in Parasceve	61r–61v
LACUNA	
Dom. Resurrectionis	72r–72v
Fer. 2 p. Pascha	72v
LACUNA	
Fer. 6 p. Pascha	77r
Fer. 2 p. Pascha	77r–77v
Fer. 3 p. Pascha	77v
LACUNA	
Dom. 3 p. Pascha	81r
Dom. 4 p. Pascha	81r
Dom. 5 p. Pascha	81r
In Letaniis	81v
Dom. 2 p. Pascha	81v
LACUNA	
S. Afrae (7 August)	91r–91v
LACUNA	
Nativitas Mariae (8 September)	101r–102v
Exaltatio S. Crucis (14 September)	102v
LACUNA	
de S. Andreae (30 November)	111r–111v
LACUNA	
de S. Luciae (13 December)	121r
de S. Thomae Apost. (21 December)	121r
Comm. Evangelistorum	121r
Comm. Apostolorum	121r–121v
LACUNA	
Comm. Virginum	131r–131v

4

Liturgical analysis

An antiphonary is a musical Office book, containing only sung portions of the Divine Office. In general, only the liturgy of important feasts is given in full; the chants for other days would have come from the ferial Office or the preceding Sunday. In these cases, only new pieces are given in full, or incipits of those pieces which can be found elsewhere in the manuscript.

In the Gottschalk Antiphonary, a complete feast is structured as follows:

1 Vespers	(4A)RVvM
Matins	IP
nocturn 1	(6AP)v(4RV)
nocturn 2	(6AP)v(4RV)
nocturn 3	AvC(4RV)
Lauds	(5A)RVvB
Prime	Av
Terce	Av
Sext	Av
Nones	Av
2 Vespers	(4A)RVvM

A = antiphon; B = *Benedictus* antiphon; C = canticle; I = invitatory;
M = *Magnificat* antiphon; P = psalm; R = respond; V = verse; v = versicle.

Votive antiphons in honour of special saints or of saints whose Octave is being celebrated may be added to Matins, Lauds or Vespers. The four antiphons of the Little Hours are typically drawn from Matins (usually the antiphons of the first nocturn) or Lauds (antiphons 1, 2, 3 and 5). When liturgy for consecutive days is given, second Vespers of one feast is the first Vespers of the next; the liturgy of the more important feast takes precedence. Abbreviated versions of the Little Hours and Vespers suffice for most feasts, and incipits are used for pieces written out in full elsewhere. Rubrics may also direct the reader to the point in the liturgy where the appropriate pieces can be found (for example, on folio 34^r the rubric for the Little Hours of the Sunday during the Octave of Epiphany reads 'Ad horas ut in die sancto' ('At the Little Hours, as on the Holy Day'), referring the reader back to the Little Hours of Epiphany).

By comparing the text of the Gottschalk Antiphonary with coeval or related Office books, the direct influence of several different liturgical traditions on the manuscript can be clearly discerned. The manuscripts dating from the between the tenth and fifteenth centuries chosen for comparison were selected for one of several reasons:

(1) an origin in Austria or a neighbouring region;
(2) a connection with one of the reform movements with which Lambach was associated;
(3) the inclusion of the responsory trope 'Quem non praevalent' at Epiphany Matins.

Sixteen manuscripts were collated against the Gottschalk Antiphonary:

Aug60: Karlsruhe, Badische Landesbibliothek, Aug. LX, a twelfth-century antiphonary from Reichenau.

Berl40047: Berlin, Staatsbibliothek, Mus. ms. 40047, an eleventh-century antiphonary.[1]

Bodl287: Oxford, Bodleian Library, MS Canon. Liturg. 287, a late twelfth-century antiphonary from Würzburg (Münsterschwarzach).

Eng102: Engelberg, Stiftsbibliothek, MS 102, a mid-twelfth-century director-ium from Engelberg or St Blasien.[2]

Ein83: Einsiedeln, Stiftsbibliothek, MS 83, a mid-twelfth-century antipho-nary from Einsiedeln.

Gr29/30: Graz, Universitätsbibliothek, Nos. 29/30, a fourteenth-century antiphonary from St Lambrecht in two volumes.

Gr211: Graz, Universitätsbibliothek, No. 211, a late twelfth-century antiph-onary from Seckau.[3]

Gr258: Graz, Universitätsbibliothek, No. 258, a late twelfth-century antiph-onary from St Lambrecht (vol. I, Advent–Easter. Volume II is lost).

Lc601: Lucca, Biblioteca Capitolare, Cod. 601, the twelfth-century Lucca Antiphonary.[4]

---

[1] H. Möller, *Das Quedlinburger Antiphonar* (Tutzing, 1990).
[2] H. Houben, *St Blasianer Handschriften des 11. und 12. Jahrhunderts* (Munich, 1979), p. 63.
[3] Z. Falvy and L. Mezey, *Codex Albensis. Ein Antiphonar aus dem 12. Jahrhundert (Graz Universitats bib-liotek MS. Nr. 211)* (Graz, 1963).
[4] P. Puniet (ed.), *Antiphonaire monastique, XIIe siècle: Codex 601 de la Bibliothèque capitulaire de Lucques*, Paléographie Musicale, 9 (Tournai, 1906).

Lm:	Lambach 2 (Beinecke MS 481.52; binding fragments in Lambach, Stiftsbibliothek Cml V and Leutkirch, Fürstlich Waldburgschen Gesamtarchiv MS 5), a late twelfth-century antiphonary from Lambach.
Lz290:	Linz, Studienbibliothek, MS 290, a late twelfth-century breviary from Kremsmünster.[5]
Pas:	Passau Breviary, an amalgam of various manuscripts from the thirteenth to the fifteenth century.[6]
Pr:	Prague, Knihovna Metropolitní Kapitoly, Cap. P. VI, a fourteenth-century antiphonary from Prague.[7]
SG390:	St Gall, Stiftsbibliothek, MS 390–391, the Hartker Antiphonal (*c.* 996–1006).[8]
V2700:	Vienna, Österreichische Nationalbibliothek, ser. n. 2700 (a XII.7), a twelfth-century antiphonary from Salzburg.[9]
Zü28:	Zurich, Zentralbibliothek, Rh. 28, a twelfth-century antiphonary from Rheinau.

In addition, the monastic manuscripts of *Corpus Antiphonalium Officii* and the CANTUS on-line database of Gregorian chant were consulted in the analyses of unusual chants and Offices.

Every analysis of the liturgy in the Gottschalk Antiphonary shows an unquestionable relationship between Lambach and the Benedictine monastery in Engelberg, Switzerland. Matins responsories and unusual liturgical chants in the Gottschalk Antiphonary all show a remarkable similarity to the liturgy of the Engelberg Directorium, *Eng102*.[10] This correspondence can be easily explained: both manuscripts were products of the Fruttuarian reform movement, brought to Lambach and Engelberg from St Blasien in the second quarter of the twelfth century. Another house involved in the reform, St Lambrecht, shows this influence as well, in a twelfth-century (*Gr258*) as well as a fourteenth-century manuscript (*Gr29/30*). The evidence does not suggest a direct link between these three geographically and chronologically disparate codices. Rather, I would posit a common

---

[5] M. Czernin, 'Das Breviarium Monasticum Cod. 290 (183) der Bundesstaatlichen Studienbibliothek in Linz', unpublished Ph.D. dissertation, University of Vienna (1992).

[6] G.-H. Karnowka, *Breviarium Passaviense*, Münchener Theologische Studien, 44 (St Ottilien, 1983).

[7] See description in A. Podlaha, *Knihovna Kapitulni v Praze* (Prague, 1903).

[8] J. Froger, *Antiphonaire de Hartker: manuscrits Saint-Gall 390–391*, Paléographie musicale deuxième série, Monumentale, 1 (Berne, 1970).

[9] O. Demus and F. Unterkircher (eds.), *Das Antiphonar von St Peter: Codex Vindobonensis S. N. 2700* (Graz, 1969–73).

[10] The Engelberg Directorium may have originated in St Blasien after the adoption of the reform movement there, but was certainly in Engelberg by the thirteenth century (Houben, *St Blasianer Handschriften des 11. und 12. Jahrhunderts*, p. 63). Thirteenth-century additions to the manuscript can be positively attributed to Engelberg.

thread, perhaps an antiphonary from St Blasien that served as a source for these manuscripts. Each manuscript, while drawing from the liturgical traditions inherited through the reform movement, had its own local and traditional conventions to draw from as well. Gottschalk uses all of the traditions to which he had access – the reform movement (shown by similarities to *Eng102* and the St Lambrecht sources), the traditions of the mother house (shown by chants shared with *Bodl287*, from Münsterschwarzach) and local traditions (discernible through similarities to *V2700* and *Lz290*). A distant French influence is also evident at various points in the liturgy. All of these traditions will be discussed throughout the analyses which follow.

I. TONARY-LETTERS[11]

According to Andrew Hughes, the eight modes of Gregorian chant are 'theoretical abstractions by which medieval theorists attempted to classify the musical formulas which recur constantly in most plainsongs'. The determination of the mode of a chant requires the reader to be intimately familiar with the musical formulas employed throughout the corpus of Gregorian chant. Such familiarity is beyond the ken of even most musicologists – a set of 'rules of thumb', usually dependable though sometimes inaccurate, has therefore been worked out. Mode can be determined with some degree of surety based on (1) the pitch on which the melody ends, called the final, (2) the range of the chant with respect to that final, and (3) the pitch on which the recitation is sung, likely to be prominent as a repeated note.[12]

Medieval scribes often made modal assignment clear through the use of several different indicative systems. It is customary in many medieval liturgical manuscripts to indicate in particular the mode of each antiphon and the final cadence, or *differentia*, of the antiphonal psalm verse. The function of these *differentiae* is not completely understood. It has long been accepted that the variations in psalm-ending were designed to facilitate the melodic transition from the end of the psalm to the reprise of the antiphon, although this interpretation has been convincingly challenged.[13] In twelfth-century chant manuscripts, *differentiae* are customarily indicated in the outer margin by neumes written above the letters 'euouae', the vowels of the phrase 'seculorum amen' that ends the minor doxology sung at the conclusion of each antiphon's psalm. In the Gottschalk Antiphonary and several other Lambach fragments, mode and final are indicated using a system that originated in tenth-century St Gall, probably with the monk

[11] Portions of this section were originally published by L. F. Davis, 'Tonary-letters in Twelfth-Century Lambach', *Plainsong and Medieval Music*, 5 (1996), pp. 131–52.
[12] A. Hughes, *Medieval Manuscripts for Mass and Office* (Toronto, 1982), p. III.
[13] P. Merkley, *Italian Tonaries* (Ottawa, 1988), pp. 37–8.

and music theoretician Hartker. In this system, marginal tonary-letters indicate the mode and final.[14] These are indicated in the outer margins of the Gottschalk Antiphonary by letters written on tiers of a column drawn to resemble an architectural support. If two antiphons begin on the same line, a symbol in the style of the tie-marks is used to differentiate between them, marking the beginning of the antiphon in the text and its tonary-letter in the margin (folio 34ᵛ, line 19). Occasionally, the tonary-letter of the second antiphon is indicated in the inner margin (folio 12ᵛ, line 9, for 'Annunciate populis'). The margins of several folios have been severely trimmed, rendering the tonary-letters only partially legible or deleting them completely: folios 12ʳ, 21, 22, 45, 47, 57, 61, 72, 91, 111, 121 and 131. Even so, there are enough tonary-letters to make the following analyses statistically viable.

In the tonary-letter system, mode is indicated by one of eight vowels, one for each mode: the five vowels of the Latin alphabet (*a, e, i, o, u* = v) plus the Greek letters eta, upsilon and omega (in Gottschalk's hand *H, y* and *w*). The *differentiae* are indicated by one of eight consonants (*b, c, d, g, h, k, p* or *q*) paired with the vowel. The melodic interpretation of the tonary-letters might have been found in a section of the manuscript called the 'tonary'. This missing section of the Gottschalk Antiphonary would have listed not only the literal melodic interpretation of the *differentiae*, but also antiphon incipits grouped by mode and *differentia*.

Many Swiss and German antiphonaries use tonary-letters to indicate the mode and final of antiphons. In addition to the Lambach fragments, examples survive from St Gall, Einsiedeln, Rheinau, Engelberg, St Lambrecht and Bamberg.[15] Tonary-letters are used infrequently for pieces other than antiphons in Massbooks from some German and Swiss centres, and are used in a few antiphonaries to indicate explicitly the mode of select, important responsories.[16] Modal classification of responsories was not commonly indicated because formulaic melodies in the verse identify the mode of the responsory. In the Gottschalk Antiphonary, however, tonary-letters are used to indicate the mode and, if necessary, the *differentia* of every antiphon, every responsory, every invitatory, and the one extant responsory trope.[17]

This unique usage is demonstrated on folio 37ᵛ, in the liturgy for feria 4 of the weeks between the Octave of Epiphany and Septuagesima. At line 17, the invitatory 'In manu tua' is given the tonary-letter [H] in the left (outer) margin, while the tonary-letter [e] is assigned to the antiphon 'Da nobis domine' on the same line (the tonary-letters are distinguished from one another by the cross-reference

---

[14] See M. Huglo, *Les Tonaires: Inventaire, Analyse, Comparaison* (Paris, 1971), pp. 232–51.
[15] E. Omlin, *Die Sankt-Gallischen Tonarbuchstaben* (Engelberg, 1934), pp. 159–63.   [16] *Ibid.*, p. 175.
[17] In the Gottschalk Antiphonary, tonary-letters are given only the first time a particular piece is used. If the piece is used again later in the manuscript, only the incipit is given and no tonary-letter is provided.

symbol resembling the letter [y] with a dot above the fork). At line 21, the respond 'Exaudi deus deprecationem' and its verse 'Dum anxiaretur cor meum' are given the tonary-letters [yc].

1.1 Antiphons

In his study of tonary-letters, Omlin collates the tonary-letters for antiphons in eleven Office books that use Hartker's system: six manuscripts from St Gall, two from Engelberg (one printed in 1635), and one each from Einsiedeln, Rheinau and Bamberg. He did not know the Lambach or St Lambrecht sources. A comparison of the association of tonary-letters with antiphons in the Gottschalk Antiphonary, the St Lambrecht antiphonaries (*Gr29/30* and *Gr258*) and Omlin's eleven sources reveals much about liturgical influences on the abbey during the twelfth century. The conclusions of this collation are summarized in Table 4.1.[18]

While most of the antiphons in the Hartker Antiphonary (*SG390*) are also found in the Gottschalk Antiphonary (99 per cent – Line C), the two manuscripts are quite different in terms of tonary-letter usage (with only a 55 per cent correspondence – Line D). This difference can be explained. As demonstrated by Omlin in his study, the centres that use tonary-letters can be divided into familial groups according to graphemic usage: the St Gall group, the Rheinau group (which includes manuscripts produced in Engelberg, Rheinau, and Einsiedeln) and the Bamberg group. The results of the collation of tonary-letter usage in the Gottschalk Antiphonary against Omlin's data demonstrate that the Gottschalk Antiphonary belongs unequivocally to the Rheinau family: the Gottschalk Antiphonary agrees in usage with 92 per cent of corresponding antiphons in the Engelberg Directorium (*Eng102*) and with 82 per cent in the Rheinau Antiphonary (*Zü28*), and with 81 per cent in the Einsiedeln Antiphonary (*Ein83*). The two St Lambrecht sources belong to this group as well, with 87 per cent and 84 per cent correspondence. By contrast, Gottschalk's usage agrees with the seven St Gall antiphonaries in 55 per cent, 56 per cent, 59 per cent, 60 per cent, 81 per cent,[19] 36 per cent, and 61 per cent of corresponding antiphons respectively (Table 4.1, line D). The two families differ most in the seventh mode: where members of the St Gall family use one combination of letters to indicate mode and *differentia*, manuscripts of the Rheinau family consistently use another for the same chant. The characteristic usage of tonary-letters in mode 7 is summarized below:

---

[18] A collation of Omlin's data against tonary-letters in other Lambach sources comprises Appendix 3.
[19] This figure, for the Hartker Tonary, is reduced in significance by the small number of antiphons which the Gottschalk Antiphonary shares with this source (39 per cent – Table 4.1, line C). In addition, the tonary, which is a preface to the Hartker Antiphonary, is incomplete.

Table 4.1: Results of the collation of tonary-Letters in the Gottschalk Antiphonary with the surveyed sources

	GA	Eng102	Gr258	Gr29/30	Zü28	Ein83	SG390	SG388	SG389	SG413	SG390a	Clm14965b	SG414	Eng299
A: Total number of antiphons in each source with tonary-letters matching those in *GA*	319	232	155	209	203	196	148	146	141	122	87	85	76	70
B: Total number of antiphons in each source which are also found in *GA* and Omlin	271	253	179	248	247	242	267	261	241	205	107	235	124	113
C: B/271 (per cent of antiphons in each source which are also found in *GA* and Omlin)		93%	91%[a]	92%	91%	89%	99%	96%	89%	76%	39%	87%	46%	42%
D: A/B (per cent of antiphons in each source which use the same tonary-letter as *GA*)		92%	87%	84%	82%	81%	55%	56%	59%	60%	81%	36%	61%	62%

Notes:

[a] Because *Gr258* includes only Advent to Easter, this figure is actually Line B divided by 195, the number of antiphons found in that portion of both the Gottschalk Antiphonary and Omlin.

St Gall family	Rheinau family
y	yb
yb	yc
yc	yd
yd	yg

Gr258 and *Gr29/30* are exceptions to this rule – the St Lambrecht sources consistently use [y], according to the St Gall usage, instead of the Rheinau [yb].

It is possible, and, according to Omlin, likely, that the melodic interpretations of the tonary-letters [y] in St Gall and [yb] in Rheinau (and so on) were in fact identical. Omlin collates the letters each manuscript uses to indicate the various *differentia* melodies in a separate section of his work, but his musical interpretations are based primarily on later sources and are somewhat suspect. At any rate, it is the actual graphemic usage which is of interest for the present study, not the musical interpretation of the letters. Because no Lambach tonary is known to survive, the musical interpretation of the *differentiae* is not determinable with any real degree of certainty.

The Gottschalk Antiphonary agrees in almost every case with the Rheinau usage. If the calculations used in Table 4.1 are limited to mode 7 antiphons, the final percentages (Line D) make this quite clear. The percentages of antiphons with corresponding tonary-letters in the manuscripts affiliated with Rheinau (*Eng102, Zü28* and *Ein83*) remain relatively constant at 90 per cent, 86 per cent and 82 per cent, while the percentages in all of the St Gall sources are reduced to 0 (with the exception of *SG388*, at 5 per cent). The adherence of the Gottschalk Antiphonary to the Rheinau tradition of tonary-letter usage is easily explicable. A direct lineage from Rheinau to Lambach can be traced: Rheinau was the mother abbey of St Blasien, the centre which sent the Fruttuarian reform to Göttweig, Engelberg and Lambach. The St Lambrecht use of [y] where the other Rheinau sources use [yb] is as yet unexplained.

Six antiphons in the Gottschalk Antiphonary are assigned to a mode different from that used in the antiphonaries studied by Omlin. Two of these are 'Surrexit dominus de sepulchro' on folio 72ᵛ and 'Iterum autem videbo' on folio 81ʳ. Gottschalk records each of these antiphons twice, first assigned (as in Omlin) to mode 8, and then to mode 4. Each mode 4 melody is a legitimate melodic alternative found in other manuscripts. The mode 4 melody for 'Surrexit dominus de sepulchro' is also found, for example, in *Lz290, Gr211* and *V2700*. The mode 4 melody for 'Iterum autem videbo' is found in *Ein83*. The mode 8 melodies for both antiphons are more common. None of the manuscripts surveyed for the present study provides alternate melodies for any antiphons. That Gottschalk provided both melodies of these two pieces is one example of the way he combined the various sources and traditions that were available to him.

Table 4.2: Antiphons in the Gottschalk Antiphonary assigned to an unusual mode, compared with the surveyed sources

| | | Manuscript | | | | | | | | | | | | |
| | | St Gall group | | | | | | Rheinau group | | | | | | Bamberg |
GA	Antiphon	SG 390a	SG390	SG414	SG413	SG388	SG389	Ein83	Zü28	Eng102	Gr258	Gr29/30	Eng299	Cm14965b
a	Magi videntes stellam	—	wg	wg	wg	wg	wg	—	[a]	a	a	a	w	wb
i	Dominus legifer noster	.ı	i	.ı	.ı	.ı	.ı	.ı	aq	i	+	i	aq	ak
i	Laudate dominum omnes	—	oc	—	id	ic	oc	—	—	—	.ı	.ı	—	[eb]
i	Nonne sic oportuit	—	wd	—	wg	wd	[i]	+	w	w	Ø	i	+	[id]
ib	Cunctis diebus vitae	—	og	—	og	ib	og	id	+	ib	w	w	+	–
v	Alleluia × 2 (Ut non delinquam)	—	ok	—	ok	ok	ok	op	+	v	v	—	+	ok
v	Facti sumus sicut	—	ak	—	+	a	ak	op	v	?.	v	ap	—	ok
yb	Domine non habeo	—	yd	yd	wg	y	yd	yb	aq	yb	aq	aq	—	yc
w	Ego sum alpha et omega	—	yb	—	yb	yb	w	.ı	w	w	Ø	.ı	—	y
w	Et respicientes viderunt	.ı	w	—	.ı	.ı	.ı	w	w	w	Ø	w	w	id
w	Venite benedicti patris	—	yb	yb	yb	yb	yb	yc	w	yc	w	w	+	y
wg	Benediximus vobis in nomine	—	e	—	wg	wh	e	wg	e	wg	wg	wq	—	eb
wg	Domine in caelo	—	wh	—	wh	wh	wh	wg	e	wg	wg	wb	+	yg
wg	In tua justicia	—	wh	—	wg	wh	wh	wg	e	wg	wg	wb	+	eb
wg	Juste judicate filii	—	e	—	e	wh	e	wb	e	wg	wg	wg	+	eb
wg	Semen cecidit . . . aliud	—	yb	yb	yc	yb	yb	yc	w	w	wg	wg	yd	yd
wg	Semen cecidit . . . in patientia	—	yb	yb	+	yb	yb	yc	w	wb	wg	wg	yd	yd

The other four antiphons in the Gottschalk Antiphonary with a modal assignment not found among Omlin's sources have few correspondences with any of the antiphonaries surveyed in the present study. Two are in mode 6: 'Alleluia vi (In domino)' (folio 35ᵛ) and 'Omnes angeli eius' (folio 37ᵛ). Among Omlin's sources, 'In domino' is set either in mode 1 or mode 4. It is found in mode 6 only in *Aug60* and *Gr258*. 'Omnes angeli eius' is, in Omlin's sources, assigned to mode 5. In the Gottschalk Antiphonary, this antiphon has been moved from the authentic to the plagal, as it has in *Aug60* and the St Lambrecht sources. The antiphons 'Beatissime virginis Marie' and 'Cum venerit filius', which Omlin assigns to mode 8, are assigned to mode 7 in the Gottschalk Antiphonary.

The modal assignments of seventeen antiphons in the Gottschalk Antiphonary agree with only a few of Omlin's sources. These are listed in Table 4.2. A dash [-] indicates that the antiphon is not present in the surveyed manuscript. A plus sign [+] indicates that the antiphon is found in the source, but without a tonary-letter. An ought sign [Ø] indicates that the portion of the manuscript that should contain the antiphon is not extant. Square brackets indicate that the antiphon is found in the source with an alternate melody (i.e. different from the paradigm for this tone/difference). In the *Zü28* column, italics are used to indicate that the tonary-letter was taken from Zürich, Rh. 59 (*Zü59*) instead of Rh. 28.

This select group makes clear the adherence of the Gottschalk Antiphonary to the Rheinau usage of tonary-letters. Every one of these antiphons with an unusual modal assignment is set in the same mode as in at least one of the manuscripts in the Rheinau group. In addition, the Gottschalk Antiphonary always agrees with *Eng102* (the Engelberg Directorium) in the use of *differentiae*, with the exception of the last two antiphons on the list. These are assigned by Gottschalk to the fifth *differentia*, with the tonary-letters [wg], as opposed to [w] and [wb], the tonary-letters found in *Zü28* and *Eng102*. This represents not a change in the fundamental melody, but a change in classification. Gottschalk's modal classification matches that used in the St Lambrecht sources. The Gottschalk Antiphonary is closely related musically to the Engelberg and St Lambrecht sources. This relationship is due to the participation of all three centres in the St Blasien reform movement of the early twelfth century.

1.2 Responsories

In the Gottschalk Antiphonary, the usage of tonary-letters with responsories is particularly distinctive. Responsorial tonary-letters are somewhat redundant; melodies of the verse explicits are formulaic for each mode, and a glance at them reveals the mode of the responsory (see Fig. 17). Even so, Gottschalk indicates the mode of every responsory except those for which only the incipit is given (these were presumably found in full, with a tonary-letter, elsewhere in the manuscript). In several

Mode	Tonary Letter	Standard Verse Explicit
1	a	*(neume)*
	ab	*(neume)*
	ag	*(neume)*
2	e	*(neume)*
3	i	*(neume)*
	ik	inconclusive
4	o	*(neume)*
	oc	*(neume)*
	og	inconclusive
5	v	*(neume)*
	vb	*(neume)*
6	H	*(neume)*
7	y	*(neume)*
	yb	*(neume)*
	yc	*(neume)*
8	w	*(neume)*
	wd	*(neume)*

17. Formulaic verse endings for responsories in the Gottschalk Antiphonary

cases, the final verse melody does not follow the standard as detailed in Figure 17. For these few responsories, the indication of modal assignment is critical, as it cannot be determined by sight. This is particularly true for the St Benedict Office (the rhymed Office known as 'Praeclarum late'), which represents a newer, local tradition. Because none of the responsory verse melodies in the Benedict Office is formulaic, the modes must be identified using tonary-letters. The indication of responsorial mode elsewhere in the manuscript may have been intended to avoid any possible uncertainty, although this is a purely speculative interpretation.

Gottschalk often pairs responsory tonary-letters with a consonant, indicating a *differentia*, an optional change in, presumably, the melodic ending of the verse. The system of *differentiae* was developed for antiphonal psalmody, not for responsories. In practice, indicating a variable verse final may be a way of revising the transition from the end of the verse to the *repetendum*. As is possible in the use of *differentiae* with antiphons, however, these alternate verse endings may merely be a way of dividing the responsory repertory into groups of chants with similar melodies, to aid memorization. According to Apel, 'The classical system of the responsorial tones does not include any *differentiae*. There is only one termination for each tone. Attempts in the direction toward different endings can be traced in some of the earliest Antiphonaries . . . that this was not a general practice appears from other manuscripts of the same period (e.g. the *Codex Lucca* [*sic*]) in which these differences are absent.'[20] In the early twelfth-century antiphonary of St-Maur-des-Fossés (Paris, Bibliothèque Nationale, Lat. 12044), for example, the fourth responsorial mode has several options for verse melody explicit.[21] Gottschalk expands this usage to include alternate endings for the verses of responsories in modes 1, 3, 4, 5, 7 and 8.[22] The St-Maur antiphonary is the only other recorded source to regularly use responsorial *differentiae*. Here is yet another connection between Lambach and a French source, offering a tantalizing glimpse into Lambach's connections further afield about which, but for the Gottschalk Antiphonary, nothing would be known.

Not only are optional final verse melodies indicated in the Gottschalk Antiphonary by the use of consonants with modal letters, but in many cases the neumes are actually altered from the standard formula. These changes are detailed in Figure 17. For example, in the Gottschalk Antiphonary, as elsewhere, the standard verse melody for responsories of the first mode ends with a clivis.[23] Gottschalk's standard verse-explicit melody for the first mode, second *differentia*, indicated in Lambach by the letters [ab], consistently ends with a pressus, representing a change in the rhythm of the piece (see Fig. 18). By the same token, the standard verse-explicit for the fourth mode ends with a clivis. Gottschalk uses the clivis ending for responsories labelled [oc], and a scandicus for the one responsory labelled [o] (see Fig. 19). Although tonary-letters are also used to indicate *differentiae* for responsories in modes 3, 5, 7 and 8, the notation of the final verse melody of each indicated *differentia* does not vary from the standard notation for that mode (see Fig. 17). This indicates that responsories assigned to the same mode and *differentia* are grouped together not because they use the same final verse melody, but

---

[20] W. Apel, *Gregorian Chant* (Bloomington, 1966), p. 239.

[21] P. Wagner, *Gregorianische Formenlehre*, Einführung in die Gregorianischen Melodien, 3 (Leipzig, 1921), p. 210. Wagner gives only a few examples of fourth-mode *differentiae*. A thorough examination of fourth-mode responsories in the St-Maur-des-Fossés antiphonary reveals many more *differentiae* than he presents.

[22] These are the modes for which responsorial *differentiae* are extant. There may be additional modes with *differentiae* in the unrecovered portions of the antiphonary.

[23] See, for example, the Hartker Antiphonal (Froger, *Antiphonaire de Hartker*, p. 15).

& uertta   tis.

18. *New Haven, BRBL MS 481.51.13ᵛ (detail): formulaic verse explicit: first mode, second* differentia

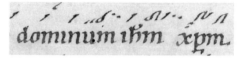

inmanu dei uuft

19(a). *New Haven, BRBL MS 481.51.2ʳ (detail): fourth mode, first* differentia

dominum ihm xpm

19(b). *New Haven, BRBL MS 481.51.5ʳ (detail): fourth mode, third* differentia

& uerutms· h.

20. *New Haven, BRBL MS 481.52.11ʳ (detail): formulaic verse-explicit, first mode, second* differentia

because of a commonality which has yet to be identified. The identification of such a commonality would presumably also explain the changes in notation which accompany changes in *differentiae* for responsory modes 1 and 4.

How and when the tradition of responsorial *differentiae* came to Lambach is unknown. Gottschalk seems not to have learned the method from an earlier Lambach source. He may have learned the practice from the French tradition which influenced the antiphonary of St-Maur-des-Fossés, in which case his use of responsorial *differentiae* would be another illustration of his use of French sources.

It is certainly possible that the responsorial *differentiae* were Gottschalk's own invention; among the Lambach sources which use tonary-letters, notational changes in the verse finals are found only in the Gottschalk Antiphonary. In a slightly later, and also fragmentary, Lambach antiphonary (*Lm*), the verse 'Non in fermento' ends with a clivis, as it does in all other surveyed manuscripts (see Fig. 20). On folio 77ᵛ of his antiphonary, however, Gottschalk labels this responsory [ab] and changes the end of the verse from clivis to pressus (see Fig. 18). This suggests that the revision of standard verse endings in the Gottschalk Antiphonary was Gottschalk's innovation.

1.3 Invitatories

Invitatory antiphons in the extant portion of the Gottschalk Antiphonary are found in modes 2, 3, 4, 6 and 7 only. In the vast majority of sources, there are no invitatory antiphons in modes 1 and 8, although there is more than one invitatory tone for invitatory antiphons of modes 3, 4 and 6. The Gottschalk Antiphonary indicates which of several tones should be used with invitatories of mode 4 in the same fashion used to indicate *differentiae* elsewhere in the manuscript, by the use of the letter [o] paired with a consonant. In the portion of the manuscript that has been recovered, only invitatory antiphons assigned to the tones [oc] and [og] survive. There may have been invitatories assigned to [o], [ob], [od], [oh] and [ok], but these are not extant. The same is true for modes 3 and 7: the use of invitatory tones [ik] and [yc] may indicate the existence of [i], [ib], [y], [yb] *et al.*, in the lost portions of the manuscript.

1.4 'Quem non praevalent'

There is one texted responsory trope in the extant portion of the Gottschalk Antiphonary. On folio 37ᵛ, the Epiphany responsory 'In columbae specie' and its verse 'Caeli aperti sunt' are followed by the trope 'Quem non praevalent'. The tonary-letter [e] which is written in the margin next to the trope's incipit indicates that modal classification of this work is the same as that of the responsory, mode 2 (see Chapter 5).

1.5 Summary of tonary-letter usage

The use of tonary-letters in the extant portion of the Gottschalk Antiphonary is summarized below. It should be noted that because the Gottschalk Antiphonary is fragmentary, this information may be incomplete.

Antiphons
   a ab ag ah ap aq
   e
   i ib id ik
   o oc od og oh
   v vb
   H
   yb yc yd yg
   w wb wd wg

Responsories
  a ab ag
  e
  i ik
  oc og
  v vb
  H
  yb yc
  w wd

Invitatories
  e
  ik
  oc og
  H
  yc

Because the Gottschalk Antiphonary has no tonary, nor is one extant in any other Lambach manuscript, it is impossible to determine with surety the melodic interpretation of the letters indicating *differentiae*. The Lambach tonary may have been descended from that used in Rheinau. The Engelberg Directorium, which is most similar to Lambach in its use of tonary-letters, inherited its tonary from Rheinau, via St Blasien.[24] Lambach also received its twelfth-century liturgical tradition from St Blasien, through its adoption of the Fruttuarian reform, and, in all probability, also used the Rheinau/Engelberg tonary. No reliable transcription of the Rheinau *differentiae* exists in modern notation; a detailed melodic study of the Lambach *differentiae* is therefore impossible, and would be extremely speculative even if one did have access to the literal interpretation of the Rheinau *differentiae*.[25] It is possible, however, to reconstruct a portion of the tonary: the list of incipits grouped by mode and difference. Appendix 4 comprises the CANTUS index of the Gottschalk Antiphonary, with chants sorted by genre, mode and *differentia*.

1.6 Other Lambach sources

Although Gottschalk's use of tonary-letters with responsories and invitatories appears to have been unique, he was not the first person at Lambach to use this system of modal identification with antiphons. Tonary-letters indicating the mode of antiphons can be found in three fragmentary liturgical manuscripts that were in

---

[24] Huglo, *Les Tonaires*, p. 242, and Omlin, *Die Sankt-Gallischen Tonarbuchstaben*, p. 143.
[25] Omlin transcribes the Rheinau *differentiae*, but his work is incomplete and, in several places, inaccurate.

Lambach in the Middle Ages: an eleventh-century notated breviary, a directorium from the middle of the twelfth century, and an antiphonary from the late twelfth century (*Lm*).

The eleventh-century breviary, the earliest of these manuscripts, may have introduced tonary-letters to Lambach. The script and the use of tonary-letters indicate a possible origin in St Gall.[26] Twenty-four folios are extant: twenty-two comprise Beinecke MS 481.25; two are an open bifolium being used as a flyleaf in Geneva, Bodmer Library, Cod. 161 (formerly Cml VII).

In the breviary, tonary-letters are used only for antiphons, and reflect the St Gall, as opposed to the Rheinau, usage. Where manuscripts of the Rheinau family use [yc], the breviary uses [yd], in the St Gall tradition. This indicates that the earliest tonary-letters at Lambach followed the St Gall practice. There are a few places where the surviving portion of the breviary overlaps with the Gottschalk Antiphonary and their texts can be compared. Textually, they are not particularly similar; the breviary gives unique readings in many places when compared with the other antiphonaries examined for this study. The breviary does not appear to have been used directly as a source for the Gottschalk Antiphonary.

The fragmentary directorium dates from the middle of the twelfth century. Only three folios and a few strips survive: Lambach, Stiftsbibliothek, Frag. 14 (two leaves); one folio pasted into the binding of Cml XXXII; and binding stays in Yale Law Library MssJ H358 no. 1, formerly Ccl 26.[27] Directoria provide incipits for Office and Mass liturgy, including chapter readings, hymns and other pieces not usually found in an antiphonary. The tonary-letters in the Lambach directorium are used only with antiphons, and correspond to the usage in the Gottschalk Antiphonary (see Appendix 3). As in Gottschalk's antiphonary, the use of tonary-letters in the directorium follows the Rheinau tradition, implying that at some point between the arrival of the breviary and the middle of the twelfth century a change in liturgical practice occurred at Lambach. This change almost certainly resulted from the adoption of the Fruttuarian reform movement in 1124, which evidently brought with it the musical practices of Rheinau.

There is some evidence, albeit slight, that the Lambach directorium was one of the sources of the Gottschalk Antiphonary. One of the binding stays in the Yale Law Library manuscript preserves part of the Office for St Benedict. The incipit for the chapter reading of that day is indicated – 'Dilectus d(e)o et h(omin)ibus' – followed by the responsory 'Alme pater'. Because they are music books, antiphonaries do not customarily include *capitula*. Even so, in the Gottschalk Antiphonary

---

[26] A Lambach provenance is certain; on MS 481.25.2ᵛ is found the nineteenth-century shelf number '261', the shelf number of the Lambach manuscript in which this bifolium was used as a flyleaf. In addition, there is evidence that two bifolios of this breviary were once flyleaves in Ccl 89.

[27] R. G. Babcock, *Reconstructing a Medieval Library: Fragments from Lambach* (New Haven, 1993), p. 118 (fig. 65).

Office for St Benedict, on folio 45^r, the following is found at Vespers; '*Cap.* Dilectus deo et hominibus *R* Alme pater'. This is the only *capitulum* found in the extant portion of the Gottschalk Antiphonary; that this particular chapter incipit is included may indicate that Gottschalk was referring to the directorium when he produced his antiphonary. In addition, Gottschalk uses the same abbreviations as the directorium. By habit, he never abbreviates the word 'deo', but does so at this point in the same manner as does the directorium. The abbreviation for 'hominibus' is also the same. Additional evidence for Gottschalk's use of a directorium in his work is found at the end of the Office for Maundy Thursday on folio 61^r, where incipits for both a prayer and a sermon ('Preces' and 'Oratio') are given. Neither of these pieces belongs in an antiphonary, although both could be found in this same format in a directorium.

There is also evidence that the directorium was not Gottschalk's only source. The directorium does not use the same Benedict Office as the Gottschalk Antiphonary; the respond 'Beatus Benedictus' and verse 'Recessit igitur', visible in the far-right column of the Yale Law Library fragment, are part of an older Benedict Office not used in the Gottschalk Antiphonary. Even so, there is plentiful evidence elsewhere in the antiphonary that Gottschalk drew on many different sources and traditions. It is certainly possible that the Benedict Office he uses did not come from a Lambach exemplar. Unfortunately, too little of the Lambach directorium survives to support a definite conclusion about Gottschalk's use of this manuscript in his work.

Nineteen leaves of another Lambach antiphonary also survive (*Lm*). The extant fragments are: Beinecke MS 481.52 (eleven folios);[28] binding fragments in Lambach, Stiftsbibliothek, Cml V (four folios); and four folios in the binding of Leutkirch, Fürstlich Waldburgschen Gesamtarchiv, MS 5 (formerly Cml XVII). The manuscript was written in part by a contemporary of Gottschalk who worked on Cml LXXIII and Cml CXIII. The two antiphonaries are nearly identical. Since each contains text not found in the other, however, their exact relationship to one another cannot be determined. In *Lm*, tonary-letters are used with antiphons only inconsistently, and very rarely with responsories, agreeing in all cases with the Gottschalk Antiphonary (see Appendix 3).

Gottschalk's use of tonary-letters for responsories and invitatories seems to be innovative. There is no evidence for the system's use in this manner at Lambach either before or after his day. Production of manuscripts at the monastery was cut short when the abbey was sacked in 1233. When new liturgical manuscripts were produced several centuries later, the tonary-letter system had fallen into disuse and was almost universally replaced by the 'euouae' system.

---

[28] Some of these fragments were removed from the bindings of Lambach manuscripts, now ÖNB ser. n. 3599, 3604, 3607 and 3608, before the manuscripts were purchased by the Österreichische Nationalbibliothek in 1953. See R. G. Babcock, *Reconstructing a Medieval Library*, p. 104 and fig. 57.

2. MATINS RESPONSORY CORRESPONDENCE

While creating a detailed collation in the manner of Hesbert's *Corpus Antiphonalium Officii*[29] would be the clearest way to analyse the enormous amount of data accumulated by the comparison of the Gottschalk Antiphonary with the sixteen coeval Office books listed above (pp. 65–66), such a format is not practical in this context. The general results are reflected in Table 4.3, showing the number of Matins responsories that each manuscript has in common with, and uses at exactly the same point in the liturgy as, the Gottschalk Antiphonary. Matins responsories were chosen for tabulation because they represent a relatively stable, and inheritable, segment of liturgy (as opposed to antiphons, whose usage varies widely from manuscript to manuscript). This methodology emulates Hesbert's.[30]

Several feasts in the Gottschalk Antiphonary do not provide Matins responsories, and are hence not included in this table. The bold-type figures for *Lm* indicate fragmentary Offices; all of the extant responsories in *Lm* correspond exactly to those in the Gottschalk Antiphonary. A blank space indicates that the Office is not extant in *Lm* or *Gr258*. An ought sign [Ø] indicates that the feast in question is not included in the surveyed manuscript, while a question mark [?] indicates that, because of manuscript inaccessibility, no comparison was possible.

Aside from *Lm* (which is nearly identical to the Gottschalk Antiphonary), it is the manuscripts from St Lambrecht and Engelberg which show the highest correspondence of Matins responsory usage, demonstrating the Gottschalk Antiphonary's dependence on the liturgical changes wrought by the Fruttuarian reform movement. The manuscripts that share over 50 per cent of their Matins responsories with the Gottschalk Antiphonary form a coherent group against those that share less than half. The manuscripts of the first group can all be connected with Lambach by proximity (Lambach, Salzburg and Kremsmünster), or by monastic lineage (Engelberg, St Lambrecht, Münsterschwarzach, Rheinau and Reichenau). The manuscripts that share less than 50 per cent of their Matins responsories with the Gottschalk Antiphonary – antiphonaries from Einsiedeln, St Gall, Quedlinburg, Seckau, late medieval Passau, Prague and Lucca – are those with no direct connection to twelfth-century Lambach.

Of the surveyed manuscripts, only *Lm* shares all of its Matins responsories with the Gottschalk Antiphonary. In fact, *Lm* and the Gottschalk Antiphonary are nearly identical; the slight differences between them make it impossible to ascertain whether they are copies of the same exemplar or directly related. *V2700* (the

---

[29] J. Hesbert, *Corpus Antiphonalium Officii*, Rerum Ecclesiasticarum. Documenta. Series maior. Fontes, 7–12, 6 vols. (Rome, 1963–79).   [30] See *CAO* V (Rome, 1975).

Table 4.3: Matins responsory correspondence

Office								Manuscript										
	GA	Lm	Gr258	Gr29	Eng102	V2700	Bodl287	Aug60	Lz290	Zü28	Ein83	SG390	Berr40047	Pa	Gr211	Pr	Lc601
Dom. 4 Adventus	12	8	12	12	12	11	12	11	11	11	7	4	9	8	7	3	6
Fer. 2 Hebd. 4 Adv.	12	1	12	11	10	3	3	11	3	10	10	9	10	1	3	3	3
S. Joannis Evang.	12		10	10	10	6	5	6	7	5	5	3	3	1	4	5	3
Epiphania	8		8	8	8	8	8	8	8	8	1	1	0	0	1	0	1
Dom. per annum	13		12	12	7	9	6	7	2	6	8	9	4	9	3	2	6
Feria 2 per annum	8		7	3	7	3	7	7	7	7	0	7	1	0	1	0	1
Feria 3 per annum	4		3	0	2	2	2	2	1	2	2	3	0	0	0	0	0
Feria 4 per annum	2		2	2	2	0	0	2	2	2	2	2	0	0	0	0	0
S. Agathae	12		12	12	9	7	8	7	8	7	8	8	5	4	7	4	4
Cathedra S. Petri	12		12	12	12	Ø	0	Ø	0	Ø	Ø	Ø	0	Ø	Ø	Ø	1
S. Gregorii	2		2	2	2	1	2	1	1	1	2	0	0	2	2	2	0
S. Benedicti	12	9	12	12	12	12	12	0	12	0	0	0	0	Ø	0	0	0
Annuntiatio Mariae	12	4	5	5	8	5	4	1	5	0	0	0	0	6	5	7	0
Dom. Quinquages.	12	4	12	11	12	11	12	12	10	12	8	9	11	8	8	8	1
Dom. 2 Quadrages.	4		4	4	4	3	3	3	3	3	3	3	3	3	3	3	1
Dom. 3 Quadrages.	5		5	3	3	5	5	5	5	5	5	5	5	5	5	4	2
Fer. 6 in Parasceve	9		9	9	9	9	9	7	9	9	9	7	9	8	7	0	1
Fer. 2 p. Pascha	3			3	3	3	3	3	3	3	3	3	3	3	3	3	0
Fer. 3 p. Pascha	3			3	3	3	3	3	3	3	3	3	3	3	3	3	0
Dom. 2 p. Pascha	7			0	6	6	3	4	5	3	3	6	6	3	3	3	3
S. Afrae	12			8	9	Ø	Ø	6	Ø	6	Ø	Ø	Ø	?	Ø	?	Ø
Nativitas Mariae	8			8	7	3	4	3	4	4	3	3	Ø	4	3	3	Ø
Exaltatio S. Crucis	4			0	0	4	2	1	0	0	Ø	3	3	Ø	0	0	0
S. Andreae	12			12	1	8	7	8	8	8	9	1	2	3	3	5	3
Comm. Apostolorum	4		4	4	4	4	4	4	4	4	4	3	3	3	3	0	3
Comm. Virginum	14		9	8	9	4	4	7	2	2	5	0	2	1	1	1	1
Total	218	26	152	176	171	130	128	129	123	126	100	89	82	75	75	59	40
% Correspondance	100	100	89	81	78	60	59	59	56	57	45	40	37	34	34	27	18

Note: for the incomplete sources *Lm* and *Gr258*, there were twenty-six and 173 responsories to compare, respectively.

Salzburg Antiphonary) and *Bodl287* (from Lambach's mother abbey) share with the Gottschalk Antiphonary 60 per cent and 59 per cent of their Matins responsories respectively. *Bodl287* is slightly later than the Gottschalk Antiphonary; their relationship is not a direct one. Of all of the manuscripts surveyed for this study, *V2700* is visually the most similar to the Gottschalk Antiphonary, both in script and decoration. It may be that Gottschalk modelled the appearance of his work in part on the great Salzburg antiphonary. *Lz290*, a breviary from the nearby monastery in Kremsmünster, also shares a majority of its Matins responsories with the Gottschalk Antiphonary. The two abbeys were in close contact during the twelfth century; some similarity between the Kremsmünster breviary and the Lambach antiphonaries is to be expected. Another manuscript which shares a majority of Matins responsories with the Gottschalk Antiphonary is *Zü28*, an antiphonary from Rheinau. Rheinau is also connected to Lambach by monastic reform; it was the mother house of St Blasien, the abbey which sent the Fruttuarian reform movement to Lambach and Engelberg.

An additional manifestation of the connection between the Gottschalk Antiphonary and Engelberg can be found in the responsories of the fourth Sunday of Advent. In the fifth volume of his *Corpus Antiphonalium Officii*, Hesbert uses the responsories of Advent Sundays to analyse the hundreds of manuscripts included in his study. The Gottschalk Antiphonary shares the responsories of the fourth Advent Sunday with Hesbert's Monastic Group VI, manuscripts with his responsories [41 42 43 44 45 46 47 48 49 59 81 91] (see folio 11). Twelve manuscripts are included in this group:[31]

Manuscript	*CAO*	Origin[32]	Date
Engelberg, Stiftsbibliothek, MS 42	672	Engelberg	s.XIV
Engelberg, Stiftsbibliothek, MS 100	673	Engelberg	s.XIV
Engelberg, Stiftsbibliothek, MS 105	675	Engelberg	s.XIII
Engelberg, Stiftsbibliothek, MS 106	676	Engelberg	s.XIV
Engelberg, Stiftsbibliothek, MS 114	677	Engelberg	s.XIII
Engelberg, Stiftsbibliothek, MS 133	678	Engelberg	s.XIII
Stuttgart, Landesbibliothek, H B I 55	855	Augsburg	s.XIV
Colmar Archives Départmentales, MS 36	647	Bavaria	s.XIII
Nuremberg, Mus. Germ. 672	751	Germany	s.XIII
Sarnen, Coll. 25	841	Germany	s.XV
Aarau	601	Muri	s.XIV
London, British Library, MS Add. 18306	699	Seckau	s.XV

[31] *Ibid.*, p. 413.
[32] These attributions are from K. Ottosen's revision of Hesbert's analyses, *L'antiphonaire latin au Moyen-Age* (Rome, 1986), pp. 178–9.

Once again, the connection between Lambach and Engelberg is made evident; half of the manuscripts in this group are from Engelberg. Absent from this list is manuscript *Eng102*, the Engelberg Directorium. Hesbert does not include this manuscript in his study. The responsories of the fourth Advent Sunday in *Eng102* are in fact the same as those in the Gottschalk Antiphonary. Of the other manuscripts surveyed for the present study, only the St Lambrecht sources and *Bodl287* (the twelfth-century breviary from Münsterschwarzach, Lambach's mother house) share this liturgy with the Gottschalk Antiphonary.

Another analysis of the use of Matins responsories involves the historia 'Domine ne in ira', the series of thirteen Matins responsories for use on Sundays between the Octave of Epiphany and Septuagesima, here found on folio 35 beneath the rubric 'Responsoriae de psalmis ab octavo epiphaniae usque ad septuagesimam' ('Responsories from the Psalms [for use] from the Octave of Epiphany to Septuagesima'). None of the 103 manuscripts surveyed by R. LeRoux in his study of the historia 'De Psalmis' uses this same series of responsories.[33] It is the third nocturn which is unique:

9.	*R.* Quam magna multitudo	*V.* Perfecisti eis qui
10.	*R.* Afflicti pro peccatis	*V.* Domine deus Israhel
11.	*R.* Peccata mea domine	*V.* Quoniam iniquitatem meam
12.	*R.* Fiat manus tua	*V.* Erravi sicut ovis
13.	*R.* Abscondi tamquam aurum	*V.* Quoniam iniquitatem meam

Among the manuscripts surveyed by LeRoux and for this study, none uses this exact series. That Gottschalk gives thirteen responsories instead of the standard twelve is unusual. Although the last may be a ferial responsory, it is possible that the thirteenth is meant to be an alternative to the twelfth – Gottschalk records the minor doxology, which is used in Matins only at the end of a nocturn, after responsory 12. If not an error, this would seem to indicate that the twelfth responsory was intended to finish the nocturn. If the respond 'Abscondi tamquam aurum' is in fact intended to be an alternative, the two options would be 9, 10, 11, 12, and 9, 10, 11, 13. Only *Gr29* and *Gr258* use the series 9, 10, 11, 12. Two of LeRoux's manuscripts, Monza Chapitre C.16/82 and Metz 83 (both early thirteenth-century manuscripts from Lombardy and Metz, respectively), record the second alternative – 9, 10, 11, 13.[34] *BN12044* also gives thirteen responsories, with Gottschalk's final responsory as the thirteenth, although it does not give the other responsories in this sequence.

---

[33] R. LeRoux, 'Les répons "de Psalmis" pour les Matines de l'Epiphanie à la Septuagésime', *Etudes grégoriennes*, 6 (1963), pp. 39–148 and table.

[34] R. LeRoux, 'Les répons "de Psalmis" pour les Matines de l'Epiphanie à la Septuagésime', table.

3. LAMBACH, ENGELBERG AND THE FRUTTUARIAN REFORM MOVEMENT

Eng102, the Engelberg Directorium, shares many other features with the Gottschalk Antiphonary, including the liturgy of the Epiphany season and the stock *Magnificat* antiphons for the weeks following Epiphany and Easter. These stock antiphon repertories vary widely from manuscript to manuscript. The lists in the Engelberg Directorium and in the St Lambrecht sources are practically identical to those in the Gottschalk Antiphonary. In addition, the anomalies elsewhere in the Gottschalk Antiphonary (Mass pieces which do not belong in an Office book) are found in the Engelberg Directorium. In all of the collations below, bold type indicates the liturgical classification of the piece, while italics are used to differentiate liturgical incipits from the surrounding rubrics.

Gottschalk Antiphonary	Engelberg Directorium
(S. Benedicti, folio 45ʳ)	(folio 48ᵛ)
Cap Dilectus deo et ho[minibus]	**Cap** Dilectus deo et hominibus
(Fer. 5 in Cena Dom., folio 61ʳ)	(folio 59ʳ)
V Custodi nos domine	**V** Custodi nos domine. Ut pupillam occuli
Pater noster	Pater noster
	Credo in deum
	Sine Kirie[leison]
V In pace in idipsum dormiam et r[equiescam]	
Preces Benedictus es domine deus p[atrum]	**Preces** Benedictus es domine deus patrum
Cum reliquis	**Cum reliquis**
P Miserere mei	**P** Miserere mei deus solus
Or Visit[a]	**Or** Visita quos domine

Many rubrics in the Gottschalk Antiphonary are found near verbatim in the Engelberg Directorium:

Gottschalk Antiphonary	Engelberg Directorium
Antiphona ad nocturno si quae sint de psalmis. Si autem nulla habetur de psalmis alternatim cantentur singulis noctibus duae ex istis (Epiphania, 8; folio 33ʳ)	Ad nocturnas antiphona si quae sint de psalmis. Si autem nulla habetur de psalmis alternatim cantentur singulis noctibus duae ex istis (folio 34ᵛ)
Singulis noctibus una **a** *Maria et flumina* non canitur (Epiphania, 8; folio 33ᵛ)	Singulis noctibus una a *Maria et flumina* non canitur (folio 34ᵛ)

Gottschalk Antiphonary	Engelberg Directorium
Semel cantate si necesse est repetantur (Octava Epiphaniae; folio 34ʳ)	Semel cantentur si vero necesse est repetantur (folio 35ʳ)
	In nativitate laudes
Post *benedicamus* non canitur de epiphania (Octava Epiphaniae; folio 34ʳ)	Post *benedicamus domino* non canitur de epiphania antiphona (folio 35ʳ)
Et cetera omnia ut de virginibus **A** *Veni sponsa* non canitur (S. Scholasticae; folio 43ʳ)	Et cetera omnia pleniter sicut de virginibus *Veni sponsa* non canitur (folio 45ʳ)
	In nativitate laudes
Post *Benedicamus domino* canitur *Nolite timere quinta* (S. Thomae Apost.; folio 121r)	post *benedicamus* canitur antiphona *Nolite timere quinta* (folio 120r)

The similarity between the Gottschalk Antiphonary and the Engelberg Directorium is due to their both being products of the Fruttuarian reform movement. The influence of the reform on the Lambach liturgy is also evident in the parallels between the Gottschalk Antiphonary and the Fruttuarian Customary. Several rubrics in the Gottschalk Antiphonary are identical to the instructions given in the customary (Göttweig, Stiftsbibliothek, MS 53b):

Gottschalk Antiphonary	Fruttuarian Customary
(1) (Exaltatio S. Crucis; folio 102ᵛ)	(Invention of the Cross, Spätling I: 209[35])
Ad canticum *Dulce lignum* **R** de inventionem **Cant**(icum) *Domine audivi* **C**(anticum) *Numquid in flum(inibus)* **C**(anticum) *Egressus es* **V** *Salva nos xpe*	**Ad canticum antiphona** *Alleluia, dulce lignum.* **Canticum** *Domine audivi* **tribus divisionibus** *Numquid in fluminibus* *Egressus es* **Versus** *Salva nos christi*
(2) (de S. Thomae Apost.; folio 121ʳ)	(St Thomas, Spätling I: 107) In natali sancti thomae finitus Matutinis Laudibus
Post *Benedicamus domino*	Post *Benedicamus domino* respondentibus omnibus *Deo gratias* eant duo fratres in medio ante altare et inchosent excelso voce
canitur **a** *Nolite timere quinta*	antiphonam *Nolite timere*

---

[35] Spätling, *Consuetudines Fructuarienses: Sanblasianae*, 2 vols., Corpus Consuetudinum Monasticum 12 (Siegburg, 1985 and 1987).

In the first example, for the Exaltation of the Cross, explicit instructions are given in the customary for a canticle in three parts. The Gottschalk Antiphonary follows suit, giving the three sections of the canticle in the same fashion. The second example is also found in the Engelberg Directorium.

There are several other places where the Gottschalk Antiphonary follows the instructions of the Fruttuarian Customary, but is not alone among the surveyed manuscripts in doing so:

Gottschalk Antiphonary	Fruttuarian Customary
(1) (Dom. Resurrectionis, folio 72ʳ)	(Spätling I: 194)
De sancta Cruce	Deinde antiphona de sancta Maria
A Crucem sanctam subiit qui infernum confregit accinctus est potentia surrexit die tercia alleluia	
De sancta Maria	ac de cruce
A Alleluia sancta dei genitrix maria intercede pro nobis alleluia alleluia	
De sancto Kyliano	et commemoratio sanctorum.
A Fulgebunt iusti sic[ut]	
Ad Vesperas	
A In tabernaculis iustorum	
Suffragia sanctorum et de omnibus sanctis ut in breviario scriptum est	Post haec eant ad processionem et canant matutinas de Omnibus Sanctis.
(2) (Fer. 2 p. Pascha, folio 72ᵛ)	(Spätling I: 201)
Feria secunda	Feria secunda ad
invitatorium	invitatorium revestiant se duo fratres in cappis.
Surrexit dominus	Antiphona *Surrexit dominus.*
(3) (Exaltatio S. Crucis, folio 102ᵛ)	(Spätling I: 209)
	In Inventione sanctae Crucis agatur in cappis. Ad Vesperam capitulum *Mihi autem,*
R Hoc signum crucis	responsorium *Hoc signum,*
	ymnus *Impleta sunt,*
V Adoramus te christe	versus *Adoramus te Christe*

In the first example, the customary instructs that antiphons are to be said after Easter Lauds in honour of the Virgin, the Cross, and in commemoration of the saints. The Gottschalk Antiphonary provides antiphons for the Cross, the Virgin, and the abbey's patron, St Kilian. This is followed, as the customary instructs, by a rubric directing the reader to the liturgy for All Saints found 'in breviario'.

Table 4.4: Liturgical alternatives in the Gottschalk Antiphonary

Feast	Folio	Liturgy	Lm	Gr258	Gr29/30	Eng102	Bodl287	Lz290	V2700	Zü28
Fer. 5 Hebd. 4 Adv.	12v	Lauds *Benedictus* antiphon	∅							
S. Stephani	21r	2nd Vespers *Magnificat* antiphon	∅							
S. Joannis Evang.	21r	Vespers processional responsory	∅							
		Vespers *Magnificat* antiphon	∅							
		Matins antiphons, 1st nocturn	∅							
	21v	Verse of Matins responsory 'In illo die'								
	22r	Matins antiphons, 2nd nocturn	∅							
	22v	2nd Vespers *Magnificat* antiphon	∅							
Octava Epiphaniae	34v	2nd Vespers responsory	∅							
Dom. per Annum	35r	Verse of Matins responsory 'A dextris est'	∅							
Annuntiatio Mariae	46v	Matins antiphons, 1st nocturn	∅							
	47v	Canticle antiphon	∅							
		Lauds antiphons	∅							
Dom. Quinquages.	52v	Verse of Matins responsory 'Deus domini mei'	∅							
Fer. 5 Hebd. 2 Quad.	57r	Matins antiphons	∅							
Dom. 2 p. Pascha	81v	Verse of Matins responsory 'Locutus est'	∅	∅						
Nativitas Mariae	102v	Prime antiphon	∅	∅						
Comm. Apostolorum	121r	Vespers responsory	∅							
	121v	Invitatory melody	∅							
		Matins antiphons, 1st nocturn	∅							
		Verse of Matins responsory 'Ecce ego mitto'	∅							
Comm. Virginum	131r	"Matins antiphons, 1st nocturn"	∅							
	131v	"Matins antiphons, 2nd nocturn"	∅							
		Canticle antiphon	∅							

= manuscripts using first alternative
= manuscripts using second alternative
= manuscripts using both alternatives
∅ = Office is not extant

Because none of the extant twelfth-century Lambach breviaries preserves the Easter season, this direction cannot be cross-referenced.

4. LITURGICAL ALTERNATIVES IN THE GOTTSCHALK ANTIPHONARY

Alternate forms of the liturgy are often provided in the Gottschalk Antiphonary, preceded by the rubric 'alia', 'alius', 'vel', 'sive' or 'aliter'. These alternatives are summarized in Table 4.4, where they have been compared with the liturgy in eight manuscripts closely related to the Gottschalk Antiphonary: *Lm*, *Gr258*, *Gr29/30*, *Eng102*, *Bodl287*, *Lz290*, *V2700* and *Zü28*. In order to be considered as shared liturgy in this analysis, the surveyed manuscript must use the chant in question at exactly the same point in the liturgy as does the Gottschalk Antiphonary. This analysis provides clear evidence of Gottschalk's use of multiple sources in compiling his antiphonary.

The results of this comparison are quite striking. In the majority of cases, the first alternative is found in the manuscripts of the Fruttuarian reform movement (*Lm*, *Gr258*, *Gr29/30* and *Eng102*), and the second comes from an older, Germanic tradition (*Bodl287*, *Lz290*, *V2700* and *Zü28*[36]). Gottschalk was quite clearly drawing on the two traditions inherited by the monks of his time – the original liturgical tradition dating from the abbey's foundation (represented by the Germanic manuscripts from Würzburg, Kremsmünster, Salzburg and Rheinau) and the newer tradition of the Fruttuarian reform movement.

On folio 43ᵛ, the first nocturn for Matins of the Annunciation has two options. *Bodl287* also offers both of these alternatives, suggesting that this particular set of choices was inherited from the mother house. Two different modes and melodies are provided for the invitatory for the Common of Evangelists, 'Regem apostolorum' (folio 121ᵛ). The first melody is found in *Bodl287* (as well as *Lc601*), the second in *Zü28*, *V2700* and the St Lambrecht sources. Both melodies are included in *Eng102*; the first is written in the body of the liturgy, while the second is written in the margin by a hand only slightly later than the primary hand.

Not every alternative can be found in one of these eight manuscripts, but most are included in at least one other source, even if one not obviously related to the Gottschalk Antiphonary. For example, the second *Magnificat* antiphon for second Vespers of the feast of St Stephen, not found in the eight sources of Table 4.4, does occur in *Aug60*. The primary Vespers processional responsory for the feast of John

---

[36] Even though Rheinau (represented by manuscript *Zü28*) was part of the Fruttuarian reform movement, there are only four cases where *Eng102* and *Zü28* use the same alternative; *Zü28*, written before the adoption of the reform in Rheinau, is firmly ensconced in the Germanic tradition, while *Eng102* was created in the context of the St Blasien reform movement.

the Evangelist occurs in the standard Passau breviary. The first set of Lauds antiphons for the Annunciation is found in the Hartker Antiphonary. The second
option for the verse of the Quinquagesima respond 'Deus domini mei' is found in
several manuscripts.

Two chants are found only in French and English, as opposed to Germanic,
sources, once again indicating a distant French influence on the liturgy of the
Gottschalk Antiphonary:

Feast	Folio	Incipit	Liturgy
S. Joannis Evang.	21r	*R.* Apparuit Caro	Vespers responsory, 2nd option
		V. Annuntiaverunt opera dei	
Dom. per Annum	35r	*V.* Dominus pars hereditatis	Verse of Matins responsory 'A dextris est', 2nd option

Both of these are found in Paris, Bibliothèque Nationale, Lat. 1535 (a ninth-
century manuscript from Fécamp), and the second is found in several other manuscripts as well.

All of the options can be accounted for in this manner, with one exception: the
first series of Lauds antiphons for feria 5 of the second week of Quadragesima.
These present an unusual case, and will be discussed below (p. 96).

In several cases, one of the two alternatives has been crossed out, presumably by
a later reader deleting the practices that were not in keeping with those he knew.
In second Vespers of the Octave of Epiphany, the second option for the respond
has been deleted (the first option is found only in *Gr258*). For the Annunciation,
two options are given for the antiphons of the first nocturn of Matins: 'Benedicta
tu in mulieribus' begins the first series, and has been deleted. The second set of
antiphons for feria 5 of the second week of Quadragesima has been crossed out
(folio 57ʳ), leaving the first set (which is unattested) unscathed.

This unusual tendency of Gottschalk to provide liturgical alternatives provides strong evidence that, as the scribe and neumator, he was also the compiler
of the manuscript. The codex was not copied from one source; throughout the
compilation process, the compiler drew on multiple sources, and, rather than
select one of these various options for inclusion in the manuscript, offered them
all to his readers, letting the singer make the decision as to which option to use.
It is certainly possible that Gottschalk was taking dictation, as it were, from a
higher monastic authority, but given his status at the abbey it seems more likely
that he was himself the authority making these liturgical decisions. The decision
he made in these cases was to draw upon two traditions inherited by the monks
– that of the Germanic origins of the abbey and that of the newer liturgy of the

St Blasien reform movement. Rather than conflate the two sources or choose one over the other, Gottschalk used both. It is rare that one finds such clear finger-prints of the patterns of liturgical transmission as are found in the Gottschalk Antiphonary.

5. NUMERICAL SETS OF ANTIPHONS

Several sets of antiphons are numerical, meaning that the modal assignments of the antiphons increase incrementally throughout the series – 1, 2, 3, 4, 5, 6, or 2, 3, 4, 5, for example. These are detailed below. The tonary-letters from *Gr29/30* have been used to identify the mode and *differentia* of those antiphons whose tonary-letters are not extant. These are indicated by italic type.

Folio	Feast	Position	Incipit	Mode	Tonary-letter
21ʳ	de S. Joannis Evang.	Matins 1.1	Joannes apostolus et evangelista	*1*	*a*
		Matins 1.2	Supra pectus domini Jesu	2	e
		Matins 1.3	Quasi unum de paradisi	3	i
		Matins 1.4	In ferventis olei dolium	4	oc
		Matins 1.5	Propter insuperabilem	5	v
		Matins 1.6	Occurrit beato Joanni	6	H
43ᵛ	de S. Gregorii	Matins 1.1	Gregorius ortus Romae	1	ag
		Matins 1.2	Lineam sui generis factis	2	e
		Matins 1.3	Adhaerebat moralibus	3	i
		Matins 1.4	Gregorius ut creditur	4	oc
		Matins 1.5	Studiis liberalibus nulli	5	v
		Matins 1.6	Hic ab adolescentia divina	6	H
		2 Vespers 1	Gregorius vigiliis	2	e
		2 Vespers 2	Lentis quidem	*3*	*i*
		2 Vespers 3	Caelesti cinctus	4	*o*
		2 Vespers 4	Bissenos nummos	5	v
45ʳ	de S. Benedicti	Matins 1.1	Benedictus tam nomine	*1*	a
		Matins 1.2	Hic ergo romae traditus	2	e
		Matins 1.3	Mundum suis cum floribus	3	ik
		Matins 1.4	Sanctum Romanus habitum	4	og
		Matins 1.5	In specu sub quo latitat	5	v
		Matins 1.6	Athleta dei gravibus	6	H
46ʳ		Lauds 1	Armis precinctus vere	2	e
		Lauds 2	Huic jubiliate quo	3	ik
		Lauds 3	Quem quam non lesit	4	oc
		Lauds 4	Laus puerilis hunc	5	v
		Lauds 5	Tympana laeta chori	6	H

Folio	Feast	Position	Incipit	Mode	Tonary-letter
46ᵛ		2 Vespers 1	Praeclarum late tibi vir	1	a
		2 Vespers 2	Membra specu claudis	2	e
		2 Vespers 3	Instar tu Christi patiens	3	ik
		2 Vespers 4	Hic probris actus tumidisque	4	oc
	Annunc. Mariae	Matins 1.1	Missus est angelus	1	ab
		Matins 1.2	Ingressus angelus ad Mariam	2	e
		Matins 1.3	Maria turbatur in sermone	3	ik
		Matins 1.4	Respondens angelus dixit	4	oc
		Matins 1.5	Ecce concipies et paries	5	vb
		Matins 1.6	Dabit illi deus	6	H
47ᵛ		Lauds 1	Quando venit ergo	2	e
		Lauds 2	Verbum supernum a patre	3	ik
		Lauds 3	Beatus auctor saeculi	4	oc
		Lauds 4	Clausa parentis viscera	5	v
91ʳ	S. Afrae	Matins 1.2[37]	In qua civitate cum puellis	2	e
		Matins 1.3	Cujus prostibulum cum	3	ik
		Matins 1.4	Cum psalmis deo et hymnis	4	og
		Matins 1.5	Audiens vero beatum	5	vb
		Matins 1.6	Quam vir sanctus verbis	6	H

Three of these antiphon series are presented as liturgical alternatives – the first nocturns of John the Evangelist and the Annunciation, and Lauds of the Annunciation. The second option given in these cases is not numerical. One might hope that some interesting conclusions about the tradition of numerical antiphons could be drawn by determining which other manuscripts use each alternative – those from the Fruttuarian reform, or those from the older, Germanic tradition. A reference to Table 4.4, however, confirms that such conclusions are not forthcoming. Each of the three cases collates differently against the eight manuscripts. In the case of John the Evangelist, the Fruttuarian manuscripts all use the numerical series, and form a clear group against the Germanic codices which use the second, non-numerical series. This might suggest that the numerical series represents a newer tradition transmitted in part by the Fruttuarian reform movement. In Matins of the Annunciation, the single surveyed manuscript which includes only the non-numerical alternative is the tenth-century Hartker Antiphonal. *Bodl287*, from Münsterschwarzach, gives both. Other manuscripts from both the Fruttuarian and Germanic traditions use the numerical alternative, suggesting that these numerical antiphons represent a liturgical tradition which predates the St Blasien reform

[37] The first antiphon of Matins is not extant.

movement, and was not solely dependent on the reform for transmission to this region.

Unlike the Offices for St John, the Annunciation and St Afra, the Offices for St Gregory and St Benedict are truly numerical throughout, with numerical modal series preserved among the responsories as well as the antiphons. As pointed out by Andrew Hughes in his studies of numerical Offices, the numerical sequence is preserved among antiphons and responsories distinctly, that is, continuing from the last antiphon of one nocturn to the first of the next, and from the last responsory of one nocturn to the first of the next, skipping the intervening responsories or antiphons respectively.[38] Most of the Gregory Office is missing, but enough survives to show that the Office is in fact numerical:

Numerical sequence of modes in the Gregory Office

Antiphons	1.1 1.2 1.3 1.4 1.5 1.6		[lacuna] B V1 V2 V3 V4 M
Mode	1 2 3 4 5 6		7 2 3 4 5 6
Responsories		1.1 1.2 [lacuna]	
Mode		1 2	

The same is true for the Benedict Office, but on a larger scale since the Office is intact (with the modes of the cut-away tonary-letters taken from *Gr29/30*):

Numerical sequence of modes in the Benedict Office

Antiphons	1.1 1.2 1.3 1.4 1.5 1.6	2.1 2.2 2.3 2.4 2.5 2.6	3	L1 L2 L3 L4 L5 B V1 V2 V3 V4 M
Mode	1 2 3 4 5 6	7 8 1 4 5 6	1	2 3 4 5 6 7 1 2 3 4 1
Responsories	1.1 1.2 1.3 1.4	2.1 2.2 2.3 2.4	3.1 3.2 3.3 3.4	
Mode	1 2 3 4	5 6 7 8	1 2 3 1	

This near-perfect numerical system breaks down at only a few places, notably after the third antiphon of the second nocturn, where we find the expected sequence 7, 8, 1 followed not by 2, 3, 4 but by 4, 5, 6, itself a numerical sub-series. A similar break-down occurs with the responsories of the third nocturn, which read 1, 2, 3, 1 instead of 1, 2, 3, 4. According to Hughes, these anomalies (and he is referring to a copy of this exact Office) are the result of the composer's wish to avoid ending each of these groups with a chant set in mode 4, which Hughes considers to be 'unstable' and 'not favored in the rhymed Office repertory'.[39]

[38] A. Hughes, 'Modal Order and Disorder in the Rhymed Office', *Musica Disciplina*, 37 (1983), pp. 29–52.   [39] *Ibid.*, pp. 37–8.

6. MARGINAL LITURGY FROM THE LATER MIDDLE AGES

The notation of hymns, antiphons and responsories in the margins of the Gottschalk Antiphonary by several thirteenth- to fifteenth-century hands indicates that the manuscript was used and adapted for several hundred years, probably until the time of Lambach's adoption of the Melk reform in the mid-fifteenth century. At least three hands are discernible.

In the lower margin of folio 43^r, a thirteenth-century reader has added alternate liturgy for St Scholastica (10 February), the sister of St Benedict. Because the lower margin has been severely trimmed, only the first line of text is visible. According to this marginal note, the Vespers respond 'Benedictus' and its verse 'Uterque' are to be followed by the minor doxology. The incipit of the respond is included in Gottschalk's version of the Office, although the verse and doxology are not. The respond and the verse are found in full in the Benedict Office on folio 45^v. The text is pertinent to both Offices:

> R. Benedictus quam devotas
> deo solvebat gratias
> ire videns ut columbam
> celo sororis animam.
>
> V. Uterque duxit gaudia
> soror celo hic in cella.

[R. Benedict, seeing, like a dove, the soul of his sister ascend to heaven, sent out such devoted thanks to God. V. Each one led forth their joys, [his] sister in heaven, he in his cell.]

Among the surveyed manuscripts, only *Eng102, Bodl287* and *Lz290* give any respond at all at this point in the Office for St Scholastica. All three use responsories from the Common of Virgins: *Eng102* uses 'Adiuvabit eam', while *Bodl287* and *Lz290* use 'Concupivit rex'. *Eng102* and *Bodl287* use the same Benedict Office as Gottschalk, and could have given 'Benedictus quam devotas' for St Scholastica; they did not.[40] Gottschalk's borrowing of 'Benedictus quam devotas' from the Benedict Office is most unusual – among the surveyed manuscripts, only a fourteenth-century French antiphonary (Arras, Bibliothèque Municipale, 465 (893)) uses the respond in this context. The later annotator of the Gottschalk Antiphonary, seeking to expand the liturgy given in the body of the manuscript itself, sought and found the appropriate chants in the Benedict Office.

A fifteenth-century annotator has written interlinear hymn incipits at appropriate points in several Offices:

---

[40] The version of the Benedict Office in *Lz290* is a fourteenth-century replacement.

Office	Hymn	Folio
S. Gregorii	Confessor dei (*Analecta Hymnica [AH]*[41] 52: 286?)	43ᵛ
S. Benedicti	Christus sanctorum (*AH* 14: 63)	46ʳ
	Rex benedicte (*AH* 4: 103)	46ᵛ
Dom. Quinquages.	Dies absoluti (*AH* 52: 3)	52ʳ

On folio 121ᵛ, an early fifteenth-century hand has written a third series of antiphons for the first nocturn of the Common of Apostles, complete with psalm verses and tonary-letters. Among the surveyed manuscripts, this series of antiphons and psalms corresponds only with *BN17296*, the twelfth-century antiphonary from St-Denis:

Antiphon	Psalm verse	Tonary-letter
In omnem terram	Celi enarrant	e
Hec est generatio	Domini est terra	ik
Letamini in domino	Beati quorum	v
Clamaverunt	Benedicam	og

It is worth noting that in two of these cases, direct correspondences have been found only in French manuscripts. This is somewhat indicative of the French influence on the liturgical traditions at Lambach that cannot be explained by the transmission of monastic reform.

7. UNUSUAL CHANTS

There are several chants and Offices that appear to be unusual, or even unique, when compared with the surveyed manuscripts. These consist of unattested or unusual antiphons, uncommon respond/verse combinations, and three unusual Offices.

7.1 Antiphons
Unique antiphons

Three antiphons do not occur in *CAO*, Omlin, CANTUS or any of the other manuscripts surveyed for this study:

---

[41] G. Dreves and C. Blume (eds.), *Analecta Hymnica medii aevi* (Leipzig, 1886–1922).

95

Incipit	Folio	Feast	Position
Si veritatem dico	55ᵛ	Fer. 6 Hebd. 1 Quad.	Matins
[Non quaero] voluntatem [?]	57ʳ	Fer. 5 Hebd. 2 Quad.	Matins
[Ego veni in nomi]ne [?]	57ʳ	Fer. 5 Hebd. 2 Quad.	Matins

Gottschalk's source for these antiphons is unknown. He may have composed them himself, or drawn from a source which is now lost.

Si veritatem dico. This Matins antiphon for feria 6 of the first week of Quadragesima, on folio 55ᵛ, appears to be unique: 'Si veritatem dico quare non creditis mihi qui est ex deo verba dei audit'. The text is John 8: 46–7.

Non quaero voluntatem and **Ego veni in nomine.** Two sets of antiphons are given for feria 5 of the second week of Quadragesima (folio 57ʳ). The second set (which has been crossed out) is given in incipit form only. This is the common series beginning with 'Pater abraham' and 'Fili recordare' (the third incipit has been trimmed away, but was almost certainly 'Dives ille guttam', which usually follows these antiphons). The first set begins with 'Non possum ego', a fairly common antiphon for this feast, but is followed by text (probably comprising two antiphons) which does not fit any of the other known antiphons used for this day. The outer edge of the folio has been trimmed, so the incipits of the two antiphons are not extant. They appear to be unique, and to have been drawn from the gospel for this day:[42]

[Non quaero] voluntatem meam sed voluntatem eius qui [misit me] (John 5: 30b)

[Ego veni in nomi]ne patris mei et non accepistis me si alius [venerit in nomine suo illum] accipietis (John 5: 43)[43]

Uncommon antiphons

While not unique, two other antiphons are quite rare:

O gloriosa femina. This antiphon is found among the surveyed sources only in *Bodl287* and in the margins of *Lz290*, written there by a thirteenth-century annotator updating the liturgy. In the Gottschalk Antiphonary, this is the canticle antiphon for Matins of the Annunciation, on folio 47ᵛ (in *Lz290*, it is used for Terce):

O gloriosa femina, non solum benedicta inter mulieres, sed inter mulieres benedictas maiori, benedictione specialiter in signis.

Alleluia viii (Praebe fili). This chant, eight alleluias sung to the melody of 'Praebe fili', is found among the surveyed manuscripts only in *Gr29/30*, the

---

[42] I am grateful to Charles Downey for determining the probable texts of these antiphons.
[43] A variant of this antiphon, using a slightly different text and melody, is found in the Florentine antiphonary, Florence, Arcivescovado, S.C., folio 84ʳ.

fourteenth-century antiphonary from St Lambrecht. The base antiphon 'Praebe fili' (*CAO* 4351) is used in several manuscripts for the Summer Sunday drawn from the book of Wisdom. That section of the Gottschalk Antiphonary is not extant, although since the antiphon in question is given in incipit form, and the alleluias are to be sung 'as is Praebe fili', it must be assumed that the antiphon was given in full elsewhere in the manuscript.

'Christus resurgens ex mortuis' and 'Dicant nunc Judei'

The chants 'Christus resurgens ex mortuis' and 'Dicant nunc Judei' for Easter Vespers on folio 72^r present another set of difficulties. In the transcription below, rubrics are in italics, and line breaks have been preserved.

> *A.* Christus resurgens ex mortuis iam non moritur mors illi ultra non domina-
> bitur quod enim vivit vivit deo alleluia *ITEM.*
> *A.* Dicant nunc iudei Quomodo milites custodientes sepulchrum perdiderunt
> regem ad lapidis positionem Quare non servabant patram iusticie aut se-
> pultum reddant aut resurgentem adorent nobis cum
> dicentes. Quod enim vivit vivit deo alleluia alleluia.

Gottschalk calls both of these texts 'antiphons', and instructs that they are 'ad processionem' for Easter Vespers. In other words, these are two Easter processional antiphons. 'Christus resurgens' is recorded first, followed by the rubric 'item' and the chant 'Dicant nunc Judei'. The use of the rubric 'item', which means 'in the same manner', implies that Gottschalk considers these to be two antiphons to be used for the same function, as opposed to alternative antiphons of which one should be chosen. This is the only place in the manuscript where the term 'item' is used.

Other manuscripts handle these chants differently. When it appears alone, 'Christus resurgens' is universally considered a processional antiphon. In three manuscripts (Cambrai, Bibliothèque Municipale MSS 38 and XVI, and Graz, Universitätsbibliothek, 30), these chants are presented in the opposite order, and labelled as a verse and an antiphon. In one manuscript, Paris, Bibliothèque Nationale, Lat. 15181, 'Christus resurgens' is called a respond, and 'Dicant nunc Judei' its verse. This is the assignation used in the modern liturgy.[44] Another solution is adopted in Paris, Bibliothèque Nationale, Lat. 17296 (from St-Denis) and Worcester, Cathedral Library, folio 160. In these manuscripts, 'Christus resurgens' is considered an antiphon, with 'Dicant nunc' as an accompanying verse, which is the assignation given to the chants by Hesbert.[45] These chants were clearly considered somewhat problematic. Gottschalk's solution of calling each chant a processional antiphon appears to be unique.

Several features could warrant considering the chants a respond and a verse. The

---

[44] L. Pothier, 'Répons de la Procession pascale', *Revue du Chant Grégorien*, 3 (1894), pp. 35–40.
[45] *CAO* III, p. 96.

final phrase of 'Dicant nunc Judei' is the same as the conclusion of 'Christus resurgens', and that phrase, 'Quod enim . . . alleluia', has the same melody each time it is recorded. None of the other manuscripts concludes 'Dicant nunc Judei' in this fashion – usually, the text ends with 'dicentes . . . alleluia' instead of 'dicentes . . . quod enim . . . alleluia'. By concluding both texts the same way, Gottschalk has fashioned a *repetendum* of sorts, giving the impression that 'Dicant nunc Judei' is indeed a verse of 'Christus resurgens'. However, the two formatting features that accompany responds and their verses throughout the manuscript (highlighting the beginning of the *repetendum* text in the body of the respond, and not habitually beginning a verse on a new line if there is room after the end of the respond) are not present here. Gottschalk does *not* highlight the beginning of the repeated phrase within the text of 'Christus resurgens', and he *does* begin 'Dicant nunc Judei' on a new line, which would seem to negate the idea that 'Dicant nunc Judei' is intended to function as a verse of 'Christus resurgens'. In addition, both texts are given tonary-letters (these have unfortunately been trimmed away, although the tier on which the letter was written is still visible for each chant). For each respond/verse series elsewhere in the manuscript, only the respond is assigned a tonary-letter. In addition to his calling both texts 'antiphons', these additional features indicate that Gottschalk does not consider the texts to be related as are a respond and its verse. Gottschalk has instead chosen a compromise, relating the two texts through the use of the rubric 'item', but calling them antiphons, perhaps because he was not convinced of the more hierarchical relationship (antiphon/verse or respond/verse) used in other manuscripts. In his brief discussion of the chants, Jacques Handschin notes that he believes 'processional antiphon' to have been the original function of both pieces.[46] Whether Gottschalk, by calling both chants 'antiphons', was transmitting an ancient tradition, or reverting to one, is unknown.

7.2 Responsories

Two responsories use a verse that is not one of those paired with the respond in *CAO*, CANTUS or in any of the manuscripts surveyed for this study:

Feast	Respond	Verse	Folio
S. Joannis Evang.	Apparuit caro suo	Annuntiaverunt opera dei	21^r
Comm. Apostolorum	Ecce ego mitto vos	Ut filii lucis sitis	121^v

---

[46] J. Handschin, 'Sur quelques tropaires Grecs traduits en Latin', *Annales Musicologiques*, 2 (1954), pp. 47–8.

There are four responsories whose verse is found among the surveyed sources only in *Eng102* and/or the St Lambrecht sources, revealing yet again the impact on the Lambach liturgy of the adoption of the St Blasien reform:

Feast	Respond	Verse	Folio
Dom. 4 Adventus	Radix Jesse qui	Deus a libano	11ᵛ
S. Joannis Evang.	Iste est Joannes cui	Mulier ecce filius tuus	22r
Epiphania	Omnes de Saba venient	Et laudem domino	33ʳ
S. Agathae	Agathes laetissima et	Beata agathes ingressa	42ᵛ

7.3 Unusual Offices

Several complete Offices in the Gottschalk Antiphonary are seen to be unusual when compared with the surveyed manuscripts. These are: the dedication of St Peter's in Antioch (Cathedra S. Petri); the Exaltation of the Cross; and the Office of St Benedict.

Cathedra S. Petri

The celebration of the dedication of St Peter's in Antioch is given in a highly abbreviated fashion in most manuscripts, with incipits of only a few pieces. On folio 43, Gottschalk also provides only incipits for Cathedra S. Petri, but he gives the incipit of every chant. The liturgy is identical to that in the Engelberg Directorium (*Eng102*) and *Gr258*, the only other surveyed manuscripts to provide such detail, implying that the Office is connected to the transmission of the St Blasien reform.

The Exaltation of the Cross

The liturgy commemorating the Exaltation of the Cross, on folio 102ᵛ, has no exact correlation among any of the surveyed manuscripts. The tripartite canticle and the Vespers respond are found in the Fruttuarian Customary, and the commemorative antiphon 'Isti sunt sancti' is found in *Eng102*. Both of these items are also found in *Lc601*, suggesting that they may come from an Italian tradition. The responsories and Lauds antiphons, however, are found only in the Germanic manuscripts *Zü28*, *Bodl287* and *V2700*. The Little Hours correspond with none of the surveyed sources. The Office is a pastiche of influences, a microcosm of the entire manuscript.

St Benedict

Particularly noteworthy is the Office for St Benedict (folios 45ʳ–46ᵛ). The Office in the Gottschalk Antiphonary is one of the earliest examples of the rhymed Benedict Office 'Praeclarum late', a version of the Office which became very popular in the later Middle Ages. Of the surveyed manuscripts, *Eng102*, *Gr258*, *V2700*, *Bodl287*, *Lm* and *Zü28* include contemporary versions of the Office.[47] The rhymed Office was appendixed to *Aug60* in the thirteenth century, and, in the fourteenth century, was used to replace the original liturgy in *Lz290*.[48] The Office is also used in the fourteenth-century manuscript *Gr29/30*.

The published text in *Analecta Hymnica* (25: 145–9) claims to know sixty-two manuscripts using this Office (including none of the early sources described above). In the study preceding his edition of the music, Willibrord Heckenbach cites the thirteenth-century 'Nachtrag' in *Aug60* as the oldest notated source.[49] Presumably, he means 'notated' as in 'on a staff': the neumed offices in the Gottschalk Antiphonary and *V2700* predate the version in *Aug60* by perhaps as much as fifty years. *V2700* and *Eng102* (which is not fully notated) are slightly older than the Gottschalk Antiphonary, and may represent the earliest known copies of the Office.[50] In order to understand more fully the place of this copy in the history of the transmission of the Office, the Benedict historia has been collated below against nine early versions, from manuscripts which have been compared elsewhere in this study with the Gottschalk Antiphonary: *Aug60*, *Bodl287*, *Eng102*, *Gr29/30*, *Gr258*, *Lm*, *Lz290*, *V2700* and *Zü28*.

Office of St Benedict, folios 45r–46v

Vespers

A.	Sanctissime confessor domini monachorum pater et dux Benedicte intercede pro nostra omnium salute.[51]
Cap.	Dilectus d[e]o et ho[minibus][52]
R.	Alme pater[53]
v.	Os iusti[54]

---

[47] Again, the relationship between *Lm* and the Gottschalk Antiphonary is indeterminable based on the variants in this Office. The Gottschalk Antiphonary agrees at some points with *Lm* against *V2700*, in others with *V2700* against *Lm*, and often with both manuscripts against *AH*.

[48] See Czernin, 'Das Breviarium Monasticum Cod. 290 (183) der Bundesstaatlichen Studienbibliothek in Linz', pp. 140–9.

[49] W. Heckenbach, 'Das mittelalterliche Reimoffizium "Praeclarum late" zu den Festen des Heiligen Benedikt', in *Itinera Domini: gesammelte Aufsätze aus Liturgie und Mönchtum: Emmanuel v. Severus OSB zur Vollendung des 80. Lebensjahres am 24. August 1988 dargeboten* (Aschendorff, 1988), pp. 189–210, at pp. 190–1.

[50] The St Peter Antiphonary has been dated on art historical grounds to around 1160 (Demus and Unterkircher (eds.), *Das Antiphonar von St Peter*, Kommentarband, p. 17).

[51] Lacking in all manuscripts.   [52] Lacking in all manuscripts except *Bodl287* and *Eng102*.

[53] *Bodl287*, *Gr29/30*, *Zü28*: O laudanda sancti; lacking in all others except *Eng102* and *Gr29/30*. *Eng102*, *Gr29/30*: followed by the hymn 'Christi sanctorum'.

[54] *Bodl287*, *Gr29/30*, *Zü28*: Inter choros confessorum; lacking in all others except *Gr29/30*.

In ev.

> Magna semper et preclara
> deum decent preconia
> cuius igne spernens mundum
> fulges in turba celitum
> o confessor Benedicte
> vota servorum suscipe.[55]

Matins

Invit.

> Ut christo celebri iubilemus laude venite.
> Qui dedit eterne Benedicto gaudia vite.

First nocturn

A I.1.   Benedictus tam nomine
quam gratiarum munere
e nursia progenitus
claris fulsit parentibus.

A I.2.   Hic ergo rome traditus
disciplinis scolaribus
nil scire duxit commodum
nisi crucis mysterium.

A. I.3   Mundum suis[56] cum floribus
scienter sprevit[57] nescius
iesuque ferens stigmata
spelunce petit abdita.

A. I.4   Sanctum romanus habitum
dans[58] illi fert subsidium
sed magister invidie
sevit in illum lapide.

A. I.5   In specu sub quo latitat[59]
dei miles se cruciat.
Sed rex mundi cui militat
hunc sacerdote visitat.

A. I.6   Athleta[60] dei gravibus
penis ardens exterius[61]
hostis in mente iacula
igne restrinxit ignea.

---

[55] *Gr29/30*: followed by processional respond 'O laudanda sancti' and verse 'Inter choros confessorum'.
[56] *Lz290*: suum.   [57] *Aug60*: sprevit scienter.   [58] *Aug60*: dum.   [59] *Bodl287*: habitat.
[60] *Aug60, Lz290*: Adleta; *Gr29/30*: Adthleta.   [61] *Bodl287*: interius.

R. I.1   Florem mundi periturum[62]
Despexit tamquam aridum
ut floreat in eternum
Benedictus ante deum.

V.   Pennas sumens [ut] columbe
recessit gaudens requie.

r.   Ut floreat . . .

R. I.2   Puer fletum subsecute
consolatus nutricule
vas ubi prece solidat
fugit ne laude pereat.

V.   Elongatus a nutrice
mansit in solitudine.

r.   Ne laude pereat.[63]

R. I.3   Agnosce dei famule
surrexit christus hac die
assunt quas misit epule
cu[ius] amore percipe.

V.   Hec dies quam fecit deus
in qua iubet exultemus.

r.   [Cuius amore percipe.][64]

R. I.4   Electo grex mortiferum
patri ferebat poculum.
Sed vir dei si[gno] vite
vas rupit tamquam lapide.

V.   Intenderunt arcum suum
ut perderent innoxium.

r.   Sed vir . . . (minor doxology)

Second nocturn

A. II.1   Iam latius innotuit
quasi lampas emicuit
fit benedictus celebris
frequentatur a populis.

---

[62] *Bodl287*: 'periturum' added in margin.
[63] *Aug60, Eng 102, Gr29/30, Lz290, V2700*: Fugit ne laude pereat.
[64] Although the *repetendum* incipit has been trimmed away, it is determinable from the red-stroked text in the main body of the respond. *Aug60, Bodl287, Eng 102, Gr29/30, Lz290, V2700*: Assunt quas misit.

A. II.2   Eius ergo sub tramite
             multi dum certant vivere
             locis florent duodenis
             fulget ipse miraculis.

A. II.3   Hic non impar helyseo
             ciet[65] ferrum de profundo
             sensus et corda perspicit
             presens absentes arguit.

A. II.4   Maurus verbo currens patris
             petri fertur vestigiis
             super liquens elementum
             mersumque trahit placidum.

A. II.5   Favent cuncta benedicto
             vas sponte manat oleo
             fugit vita spernit terra[66]
             eius privatum gratia.

A. II.6   O quanta plenus gratia
             qui respectu rumpit[67] vincla
             sedens curvat imperia
             Benedictus per secula.[68]

R. II.1   Servus dei Benedictus
             stetit misertus illius
             qui clamitabat o meum
             o redde redde filium.

V.   Orans iacentem suscitat
             reddit patri qui clamitat.

r.   O meum . . .

R. II.2   Benedictus quam[69] devotas
             deo[70] solvebat gratias
             ire videns ut columbam
             celo sororis animam.

V.   Uterque duxit gaudia
             soror celo hic in cella.

r.   Ire . . .

R. II.3   O israhelita verus
             cor in deum dilatatus

[65] *Gr29/30, V2700*: sciet; *Lz290*: ciget.   [66] *Lz290*: vaga.   [67] *Aug60*: vicit; *Gr29/30*: rupit.
[68] *Eng102, Gr29/30, Lm*: followed by versicle 'Amavit eum dominus'.
[69] There is a hole through the first letter of this word, but what remains appears to read '[q]uam', as in all but one of the surveyed mansucripts. *Lm*: tam.   [70] *Lz290*: celo.

qui infra se angustatam
vidit omnem creaturam.

V.   Celo quoque ferri sanctam
Germani cernens animam.

r.   Qui infra . . .

R. II.4   Alme pater qui prescius
tui sacrati transitus
hunc prenotasti fratribus
tuere nostros exitus.

V.   Per te ducem clarissimum
ut transeamus ad deum.

r.   Tuere . . . (minor doxology)

Third nocturn

A.   Benedictum propheticis
condecoremus canticis
qui tam fulsit prophetia
quam et doctrine gratia.[71]

R. III.1   Grandi pater fiducia
Morte stetit preciosa
qui elevatis manibus
celos scandit in precibus.

V.   Fecit[72] christe quod iussisti
te secutus spe premii.

r.   Qui elevatis . . .

R. III.2   Fratribus illuxit
Benedictum que[73] via duxit
usque polum surgens
et multa lampade[74] fulgens.

V.   Virque super candens
micuit que sit via pandens.

r.   Usque polum . . .

R. III.3   Ecce iam cari noscite
quam claro scandit[75] tramite
Benedictus ad sydera
Qui hic reliquit omnia.

---

[71] *Eng102, Gr29/30, Lm*: followed by versicle 'Justus ut palma'.   [72] *Aug60*: feci.
[73] *Lz290*: quem.   [74] *Lz290*: laude.   [75] *Lm*: csandit [*sic*].

V.	Accepit ergo centuplum et vitam in perpetuum.
r.	Qui hic . . .
R. III.4	Gloria christe tuo tibi personat in benedicto quem faciens te eum sanctis regnantibus equum. Iam quibus equasti gaudentibus associasti.
V.	Nos eius norma rege serva terge reforma.
r.	Iam quibus . . . (minor doxology)

Lauds

A.	Armis precinctus vere fidei Benedictus ydola dum stravit sedem tibi christe paravit.
A.	Huic iubilate quo[76] pater iste par fit[77] helye[78] par quoque moysi dum lapis illi flumina fundit[79] corvus obaudit.
A.	Quem quam non lesit post te dominator adhesit. Utque david doluit hostis ut occubuit.[80]
A.	Laus puerilis hunc benedicit[81] qui puerorum per Benedictum corpora vite trinus et unus trina reformat.
A.	Tympana leta chori mens consona concitet ori ac dominum laudet quo servus in ethere gaudet.
R.	Amavit eum[82]

---

[76] *Gr29/30*: quod.   [77] *Gr29/30*: sit.   [78] *Lz290*: elyseo.   [79] *Aug60*: fudit.
[80] *Aug60*: obcubuit; *Gr29/30*: ocubuit.   [81] *Aug60, Bodl287*: benedicat; *Gr29/30*: benedixit.
[82] Responsory and verse lacking in all manuscripts except *Eng102* and *Gr29/30*. *Eng102, Gr29/30*: hymn 'Huius o christe' follows the responsory. A fourteenth-century interlinear note indicates that the hymn 'Christus sanctorum' is to be sung at this point.

v.   Os iusti

In ev.

A.   Benedictus es domine
            qui benedicti anime
            dum et celi con[fe]rs gaudia
            glorificas terris membra
            dum et specu quo latuit
            per te virtus emicuit.

Horae[83]

Prime

A.   Benedictus tam no[mine][84]

Terce

A.   Hic non impar[85]

Sext

A.   Favent cuncta[86]

Nones

A.   O quanta pl[enus][87]

2nd Vespers[88]

A.1   [89]Preclarum late tibi[90]
            vir sine fine beate.
            Nomen non ficte fidei
            manet o Benedicte.

A.2   [91]Membra specu claudis
            quo factus es hostia laudis
            carnem districte
            dum frenas o Benedicte.

A.3   [92]Instar tu christi
            patiens ad cuncta fuisti
            pacis et indicte[93]
            cultor pius o Benedicte.

---

[83] The Little Hours are lacking in all manuscripts except *Eng102* and *Gr29/30*.
[84] *Eng102*: Preclarum late.   [85] *Eng102*: Membra specu.   [86] *Eng102*: Instar [tu Christi].
[87] *Eng102*: Hic probis.   [88] All surveyed manuscripts use these antiphons for first Vespers instead.
[89] *Eng102*: Erat vere vir.
[90] *Gr29/30*, *Lm*: the antiphons of second Vespers end at this point – the next chant is the antiphon 'in evangelio'.   [91] *Eng102*: Coram omni plete.   [92] *Eng102*: Dum clamaret.   [93] *Lz290*: invicte.

A.4 [94]Hic probis actus
tumidisque peripsima factus
iam[95] noys[96] invicte
palmam geris o Benedicte.

R. Iustus ut palma[97]

v. Os iusti meditab[itur] s[apientiam]

in ev.

A. O celestis norma vite
doctor et dux Benedicte
cuius cum christo spiritus
exultat in celestibus
gregem pastor alme serva
sancta prece corrobora[98]
via celos clarescente
fac te duce penetrare.

The assignment of antiphons to Vespers and the Little Hours deserves further clarification:

First Vespers

Gottschalk Antiphonary	Surveyed manuscripts
Sanctissime confessor domini	Preclarum late tibi
	Membra specu claudis
	Instar tu christi
	Hic probis actus

Little Hours

	Gottschalk Antiphonary[99]	Eng102
Prime	Benedictus tam nomine	Preclarum late tibi
Terce	Hic non impar	Membra specu claudis
Sext	Favent cuncta	Instar tu christi
Nones	O quanta plenus	Hic probis actus

[94] *Eng102*: Ad te deus rex.   [95] *Lz290*: nam.   [96] *Aug60*: novis.
[97] Responsory and verse are lacking in all manuscripts except *Eng102*. Another fourteenth-century interlinear note indicates that the hymn 'Rex benedicte' is to be sung at this point.
[98] *V2700*: serva sancta prece corrobora (the melody has been revised to accommodate the additional syllables).   [99] *Gr29/30* also uses these antiphons for the Little Hours.

Second Vespers

Gottschalk Antiphonary	Eng102
Preclarum late tibi	Erat vere vir
Membra specu claudis	Coram omni plete
Instar tu christi	Dum clamaret
Hic probis actus	Ad te deus rex

None of the early sources uses the Vespers antiphon 'Sanctissime confessor domini' in this context. Among manuscripts that use a different Benedict Office, the antiphon is used at first Vespers only in the antiphonary of St-Maur-des-Fossés, Paris, Bibliothèque Nationale, Lat. 12044 – this is not only a French source, but it is the only recorded source to regularly use responsorial tonary-letters. *Aug60*, which in the original portion of the manuscript gives the unrhymed Benedict Office, assigns this antiphon to second Vespers, while *Gr29/30* uses it for the Translation of Benedict. At this point in the Office, Gottschalk has conflated two distinct liturgical traditions, combining a feature from the older Office (which apparently was inherited from a French source) with the newer, rhymed historia. This suggests a certain creativity in Gottschalk's liturgical work.

The compiler of *Eng102* has drawn the antiphons of the Little Hours from first Vespers. Throughout the Gottschalk Antiphonary, antiphons for the Little Hours are drawn from Matins or Lauds. In this case, Gottschalk has drawn from Matins, as has the scribe of *Gr29/30*, using antiphons I.1, II.3, II.5 and II.6. This is an unusual method of assigning the antiphons for the Little Hours – usually, if drawn from Matins, the four antiphons chosen for the Little Hours are those of the first nocturn.

Of the surveyed manuscripts, only Gottschalk and *Eng102* give antiphons for second Vespers. The series used by Gottschalk is used by the other manuscripts for first Vespers. A new series is given in *Eng102* at this point. It is impossible to determine if this final series in *Eng102* is also rhymed, because (1) only incipits are given, (2) the series is not included in *Analecta Hymnica* or in Heckenbach's edition of the historia, and (3) the antiphons are not found in *CAO*, Omlin or CANTUS.

For several responsories, Gottschalk uses *repetenda* which vary from many of the early sources. The responds of this historia are for the most part composed of two rhyming couplets. Each corresponding verse is a single couplet. The *repetendum* adds a fourth couplet by repeating lines 3 and 4 of the respond. In the Gottschalk Antiphonary, however, the *repetenda* of responsories I.2 and I.3 begin respectively in the middle of, and at the beginning of, the fourth line of the respond. This disruption of rhythm is not unheard of elsewhere in the Office. In all of the early sources, the *repetenda* of responsories II.1, II.3 and II.4 also begin at, or during, the fourth line.

8. RESPONSORIAL TROPING IN THE GOTTSCHALK ANTIPHONARY

A common method of musical elaboration in medieval liturgical sources is the addition of interpolative chants known as 'tropes' to the base chant. This can be accomplished in a number of ways: adding a purely musical trope to the chant by interpolating a newly composed melisma; writing text to the melody of a pre-existent melisma; or composing both text and melody to be added to a liturgical chant. Examples of all three can be found in the Gottschalk Antiphonary. While tropes of the Mass have been the subject of numerous studies, Office tropes such as the responsory tropes of the Gottschalk Antiphonary have received less attention. Thomas F. Kelly analysed responsory tropes, primarily in English and French sources, in his doctoral dissertation, 'Responsory Tropes'.[100] Helma Hofmann-Brandt covered several hundred sources in her two-volume study, 'Die Tropen zu den Responsorien des Officiums'.[101] Because most of Hofmann-Brandt's sources are from Germanic lands, her work is more useful than Kelly's for studying the tropes of the Gottschalk Antiphonary.

The performance of a responsory without a trope can be represented as [AB-V1–B] (where [A] is the first half of the respond, [B] is the *repetendum*, and [V1] is the verse). In the Gottschalk Antiphonary, the verse is immediately followed by the incipit of the *repetendum*, cuing the reader back to the middle of the respond. The incipit of the *repetendum* in the original respond is highlighted in red. When the doxology is performed, the liturgy is expanded to [AB-V1–B-V2–B(′)]. In this case, [V2] is the doxology and [B′] represents an alternate *repetendum* beginning at a different point in the respond, a *repetendum* which may or may not be present. An example of this is found on folio 35ʳ, where the respond 'Notas mihi' has two *repetenda*, one for the first verse and one for the minor doxology, beginning at 'Delectationes' and 'Usque' respectively. Gottschalk makes this order of performance explicit on folio 35ᵛ, line 13, where the respond 'Fiat manus' is followed by the verse 'Erravi sicut ovis', the *repetendum* cue ('concupivi'), the minor doxology, and the second *repetendum* cue (in this case, the first *repetendum*, 'concupivi', is repeated). When a trope is added to the responsory, the order of performance becomes [AB-V1–B*] or [AB-V1–B-V2–B(′)*] (where [B(′)*] represents the troped *repetendum*).[102] The trope is sung after the final performance of the *repetendum*, or is interpolated into it.

The extant portion of the Gottschalk Antiphonary preserves a number of examples of melismas that have been interpolated into responsories. Several pre-existent melismas found in the Gottschalk Antiphonary were later texted elsewhere (for example, the melismas in the responsory 'Stirps Jesse virgam' on folio 102ʳ). Two

---

interpolative melismas are extant, and one sequence (which is discussed in Chapter 5). Each responsory trope is formatted differently.

On folio 22^r, line 20, the respond 'Apparuit caro suo' (the last responsory of the second nocturn of Matins for the Nativity of John the Evangelist) is troped by a melisma above the syllabic notation of the penultimate word, 'fratribus'. The melisma is relatively short, a minor musical trope. Gottschalk's general practice in transcribing melismatic passages is to leave space between syllables for the melisma. That he has in this case written the passage *above* the primary text seems to indicate that the melisma is indeed a trope, an addition to the responsory as it was originally conceived, and was intended for performance during the *repetendum*, not during the primary performance of the respond. The melisma is short enough that it could be inserted above the word it tropes without disrupting the format of the page.

The second example of melismatic troping provides clear evidence as to the performance of these tropes within the context of the individual responsories. On folio 22^v, line 10, the responsory 'In medio ecclesiae' (the last responsory of Matins for the Nativity of John the Evangelist) is troped by an extraordinarily long melisma. The format of the trope on the page is as follows: respond, verse ('Misit dominus manum'), *repetendum* cue ('Et imple . . .'), and the words 'Et intellectus', with the melisma inserted between the two words. 'Et intellectus' is the final phrase of the respond. In the original respond, only a brief melisma separates the first two syllables of 'intellectus'. The elongated melisma was intended to be performed during the *repetendum*, when these words are sung for the second time. According to Kelly, this is in fact the 'normal' format for responsory tropes:

the respond is normally written only once, to conserve space. . . . If [the responsory] includes new material the second time, at least that section which is to differ from the original must be written out.[103]

The order of performance is clearly demonstrated by the format of 'In medio ecclesiae': respond, verse, *repetendum* with trope. The trope itself is so long that it could not have been written above the original notation of 'et intellectus' without disrupting the format of the page. Interpolating the melisma into the primary text of the respond would have left the singer with no way of recognizing that this chant was intended to be performed only during the *repetendum*, not during the original performance of the respond.

The melisma of 'In medio ecclesiae' is divided into seven sections, with red lines delineating the individual segments of the passage. This creates a trope of seven melodic sections, or stanzas. The melody of the trope is the 'alternate melisma' of

---

[103] T. F. Kelly, 'New Music from Old: The Structuring of Responsory Prosas', *Journal of the American Musicological Society*, 30 (1977), pp. 366–90, at p. 366.

the third neuma of the *neuma triplex*, the great triple melisma which was originally attached to this responsory.[104] At a later date, the seven-stanza poem 'Indutum pro nobis' was written to this melody and added to the responsory as a prosula. According to Hofmann-Brandt, who did not know the Gottschalk Antiphonary, this particular melody is found as a trope to this responsory in only one other manuscript, a fourteenth-century antiphonary (Prague, Knihovna Kapitoly, Cap. P. VI, vol. I, folios 174–175ᵛ). This later manuscript includes the entire prosula, not just the melisma.[105] This is also the only other recorded manuscript to include the chant 'Quem non praevalent', a sequence whose function in the Gottschalk Antiphonary is the subject of Chapter 5.

CONCLUSIONS

These comparisons of the Gottschalk Antiphonary with other coeval antiphonaries have clearly demonstrated both Gottschalk's use of other sources and his independence from them. The impact of the St Blasien reform movement on the Lambach liturgy is demonstrated in two ways: directly, by the similarity of rubrics and liturgy in the Antiphonary to directions in the Customary; and indirectly, by the connections between Lambach and the other houses (Engelberg, St Lambrecht, Rheinau) that were connected to the reform centre, as demonstrated by the use of tonary-letters, the correspondence of Matins responsories and the use of liturgical alternatives. The liturgical alternatives also reveal the influence of local traditions from such nearby centres as Kremsmünster and Salzburg. Similarities to the breviary from Münsterschwarzach reveal the enduring legacy of a liturgical tradition dating back to the foundation of the abbey.

Finally, a distant, but palpable, French influence is manifested in several ways. Several of these are incidental, due perhaps to the vagaries of manuscript survival: in the Office for St Benedict, only the antiphonary of St-Maur-des-Fossés (Paris, Bibliothèque Nationale, Lat. 12044) uses the same Vespers antiphon as does Gottschalk, even though the St-Maur antiphonary otherwise uses a different Office; one combination of respond and verse ('Apparuit Caro' with 'Annuntiaverunt opera dei') is unknown except for its use in Paris, Bibliothèque Nationale, Lat. 1535, while one verse ('Dominus pars hereditatis') is found only in that manuscript and a few English sources; finally, the use of the Benedict respond 'Benedictus quam devotas' for the Office of St Scholastica occurs outside the Gottschalk Antiphonary only in a fourteenth-century French antiphonary (Arras, Bibliothèque Municipale, 465 (893)). Regarding Gottschalk's use of tonary-letters with responsories, however, the

---

[104] Hofmann-Brandt, 'Die Tropen zu den Responsorien des Officiums', vol. I, p. 70.
[105] *Ibid.*, vol. I, p. 70, and vol. II, p. 63.

evidence is much more convincing. The only other known manuscript to regularly use tonary-letters with responsories is the French antiphonary of St-Maur-des-Fossés.

This French influence is not easily explained. It must be remembered, however, that the Lambach library was strong in holdings of twelfth-century French authors such as Abelard, Hildebert of Lavardin, Bernard of Marval, Vital and William of Blois, Bernard of Clairvaux, and others. The existence of so many early copies of these French texts may indicate a direct point of contact between Lambach and a French centre – someone bringing exemplars of these texts to Lambach, or perhaps a Lambach monk travelling far afield to copy or borrow them, along the way viewing, copying or acquiring the French liturgical texts whose influence is felt in the Gottschalk Antiphonary.

Gottschalk was not merely copying or randomly bringing together these disparate sources. He was making choices about which chants to use, or leaving the choice up to the singer in the cases where he presents liturgical alternatives. He tinkered with the standard verse-final melodies to create responsorial *differentiae*. He came up with an original way of presenting the problematic chants 'Christus resurgens ex mortuis' and 'Dicant nunc Judei'. And as we shall see in the next chapter, he found a way to use the manuscript as a tool for encoding and transmitting the abbey's historical and political traditions.

5

'Quem non praevalent' and the importance of Epiphany at Lambach[1]

1. 'QUEM NON PRAEVALENT'

The only responsory trope given a text in the extant portion of the Gottschalk Antiphonary is found at the end of Epiphany Matins, on folio 32ᵛ. The responsory 'In columbae specie' (line 5) is followed by a lengthy melisma on the last word. The melisma is divided into seven sections. This is followed by the verse ('Caeli aperti sunt'), the *repetendum* cue and the incipit of the minor doxology. Following this respond/verse, the rhymed, metrical sequence 'Quem non praevalent' is written out in full, line by line. Each line is labelled 'v', for 'versus'. The tonary-letter column in the outer (left) margin is interrupted at this point by a secondary column that runs alongside the trope as a kind of bracket around the text. The primary column fades into a dotted line and then vanishes altogether after the first couplet, reappearing again as a dotted line next to the final verse and then returning to its original solidity to the left of the piece immediately following 'Quem non praevalent', the first antiphon of Lauds. The mode of 'Quem non praevalent' is indicated next to its first line with the tonary-letter 'e', indicating mode 2. 'Quem non praevalent' is written in the same mode as the responsory.

In this context, 'Quem non praevalent' tropes the respond 'In columbae specie'. The melisma at the end of the respond is divided into seven sections; 'Quem non praevalent' is made up of six couplets and one final verse. Each line, syllabically neumed, is followed by its melismatic counterpart. These pairs of melismas match the sections of the responsory melisma.

The order of performance of this respond, verse and trope is [AB-V1–B-V2–B*], where [A] is the first half of the respond ('In columbae...audita est'), [B] is the second half of the respond (also the *repetendum*), [V1] is the verse ('Caeli aperti

[1] Portions of this chapter were first presented in a paper entitled 'Epiphany at Lambach: The Ritualization of Monastic Memory' at the annual meeting of the Medieval Academy of America, Boston, Massachusetts, 1995.

sunt'), [V2] is the minor doxology and [B*] is the troped *repetenda* (see p. 109 above). Sections [A], [V1] and [V2] were sung by the soloist. Section [B] was sung by the choir.[2] The format of the trope indicates its probable manner of performance: each verse was sung by the cantor, with the matching melisma sung by the choir after each verse. This is the standard manner of performance of this genre of trope: 'the prosa is sung in sections by soloists, each section being repeated melismatically by the choir'.[3] Because the syllabic and neumatic melodies are slightly different, verse and melisma could not have been sung simultaneously. According to Kelly, 'such pieces are probably designed for performance in the texted version by a soloist, this being followed by a choral neuma'.[4] Such is the case here. The number of notes in the neumatic version consistently exceeds the number of notes in the syllabic version, though differing by no more than three. For example, the syllabic notation above the first line of 'Quem non praevalent' totals fourteen notes: four puncta, eight virgae and a franculus. The melismatic version of the same melody, shown to the right of the text, has seventeen notes, and while the two melodies may be almost the same, they could not have been performed simultaneously. It is also possible that the neumatic version functioned as a mnemonic device for the singers.

The Gottschalk Antiphonary is the earliest-known source to use 'Quem non praevalent' in this context, where the text of the sequence has been adapted for use as a responsory trope. The text has been recorded as a responsory trope in only one other manuscript, the fourteenth-century antiphonary from Prague (Prague, Knihovna Metropolitní Kapitoly, Cap. P. VI).[5] Although the liturgy of the Prague antiphonary is otherwise unrelated to that of the Gottschalk Antiphonary, the fact that the two manuscripts share two unusual features (the tropes 'Indutum pro nobis' and 'Quem non praevalent') suggests that they may be connected.

Although the Gottschalk Antiphonary is the earliest-known manuscript to use 'Quem non praevalent' as a responsory trope, it is not the earliest copy of the chant itself. 'Quem non praevalent' is found free-standing in two earlier contexts: collections of sequences, and Magi plays. One of these must have been the source for the version in the Gottschalk Antiphonary. The edition of 'Quem non praevalent' in *Analecta Hymnica*[6] cites four early manuscripts: London, British Library, Add. 19768 (*BL19768*; a proser with sections from Tegernsee, saec. XI); Munich, Bayerische Staatsbibliothek, Clm 18955 (a passionale from Tegernsee, saec. XI);

---

[2] A. Hughes, *Medieval Manuscripts for Mass and Office* (Toronto, 1982), p. 27.
[3] T. F. Kelly, 'Melisma and Prosula: The Performance of Responsory Tropes', in *Liturgische Tropen: Referate zweier Colloquien des Corpus Troporum in München (1983) und Canterbury (1984)* (Munich, 1985), p. 173.
[4] T. F. Kelly, 'Responsory Tropes' unpublished Ph.D. dissertation, Harvard University (1973), p. 252.
[5] H. Hofmann-Brandt, 'Die Tropen zu den Responsorien des Officiums', Inaugural-Dissertation, Erlangen-Nürnberg (1971), vol. II, p. 108.   [6] *AH* 54: 9.

Munich, Bayerische Staatsbibliotheek, Clm 14845 (a troper from Regensburg, 1106–25); and Leiden, Bibliotheek der Rijksuniversiteit, Gronov. 70 (a miscellany from Germany, saec. XI).[7] In addition to its use as a sequence, 'Quem non praevalent' is also found in a dramatic context: the piece is sung by the three kings as they process from Jerusalem to the scene of the Nativity in some Magi plays. According to Norbert King six Magi plays include this particular feature:[8] a play from southern Germany (now lost);[9] Madrid, Biblioteca Nacional, MS 288; Brussels, Bibliothèque des Bollandistes, MS 229;[10] Orléans, Bibliothèque de la Ville, MS 201; Montpellier, Bibliothèque de la Faculté de Médecine, MS H.304;[11] and Madrid, Biblioteca Nacional, MS 289.[12] The hymns that King calls 'Quem non praevalent' in the first three of these manuscripts are only loosely based on the whole text of 'Quem non praevalent', and will not be considered here.[13]

There are, then, nine reported copies of 'Quem non praevalent' in various contexts: two antiphonaries, four troper-prosers and three Magi plays. All of the plays, and *only* the plays, include a variant fourth stanza and delete stanzas 9 to 13. There are two melodies for the piece as well, one for sequences, another for plays. Gottschalk's version uses the sequence melody, as in *BL19768*. The version in the Gottschalk Antiphonary, then, must have come from a proser, a source which included all thirteen stanzas set to the sequence melody. A collation of the text in the Gottschalk Antiphonary against the prosers and the Prague antiphonary follows. The base text is from *BL19768*, the eleventh-century proser from Tegernsee that is one of the earliest exemplars of the text.

(1) Quem non praevalent
propria
magnitudine

(2) Caeli terrae atque
maria
amfisaepire

(3) De virgineo
natus utero
ponitur in praesaepio

(4) Ut propheticus
sermo nuntiat
stant simul bos et asinus.

(5) Sed oritur stella lucida
praebitura
domino obsequia

(6) Quam balaam ex iudaica
orituram
dixerat prosapia.

---

[7] The *AH* edition also cites Orléans, Bibliothèque de la Ville, MS 201 (*olim* 178) via the edition in C. de Coussemaker's *Drames liturgiques du moyen âge* (Rennes, 1860), pp. 153–4. Because 'Quem non praevalent' occurs in a completely different context in Orléans 201, I have not included it in this list. It is discussed below.   [8] N. King, *Mittelalterliche Dreikönigsspiele* (Freiburg, 1979).
[9] K. Young, *The Drama of the Medieval Church* (Oxford, 1933), II, pp. 448–9.   [10] *Ibid.*, II, p. 75.
[11] *Ibid.*, II, pp. 68–74.   [12] *Ibid.*, II, pp. 59–62.
[13] King's edition of 'Quem non praevalent', *Mitelalterliche Dreikönigsspiele*, p. 200, is somewhat misleading: he gives the entire text in his study, without noting that 'Quem non praevalent' is always truncated in a dramatic context. He cites many manuscripts, but lists only the variants of Orléans MS 201.

(7) Haec magorum oculos
fulguranti lumine
praestrinxit providos.

(8) Atque ipsos praevia
Christi ad cunabula
perduxit vilia.

(9) Illi at exiguis
adorant obsitum pannulis

(10) Offerentes regia
aurum tus et myrrham munera.

(11) Ipsa sed tamen mysticis
non carent munera figuris

(12) Aurum ut regi tus deo
et magno offerunt sacerdoti

(13) Atque myrrham
in sepulturam.

[The one born from the virginal womb whom even the heavens, lands and seas cannot contain for all their own magnitude is placed in a manger [where] the ox and the ass stand together, as the prophetic word declared. But the shining star rises, [it is] going to offer homage to the Lord which Balaam had said is going to rise from the Jewish people. By its dazzling light it struck the eyes of the farseeing Magi, and the precursor led them to the humble cradle of Christ. Even thus they worship the one covered in poor rags, offering royal gifts of gold, frankincense and myrrh. But nevertheless these gifts do not lack mystical qualities; they offer the high priest gold, as of a king, frankincense to God, and myrrh in burial.]

'Quem non praevalent' as a sequence (my sigla – *AH* sigla in square brackets):

Clm18955 [B]: Munich, Bayerische Staatsbibliothek, Clm 18955
Tegernsee, saec. XI
Clm14845 [C]: Munich, Bayerische Staatsbibliothek, Clm 14845
Regensburg, 1106–25
Lei70 [D]: Leiden, Bibliotheck der Rijksuniversiteit, Gronov. 70
Germany, saec. XI

'Quem non praevalent' as a responsory trope (my sigla)

GA: Gottschalk Antiphonary, saec. XII
Pr: Prague, Knihovna Metropolitní Kapitoly, Cap. P. VI, saec. XIV

Variants:

2,1 celi terrae] celi terra *Clm14845*
2,2 maria] mare *Clm14845*
2,3 amfisaepire] amphisepere *Clm18955*, *Lei70*, *GA*
4,3 stant] stat *GA*; stans *Pr*
6,1 balaam] balaan *Pr*
7,3 praestrinxit providos] perstrinxit providos *Clm18955*, *Clm14845*, *GA*; prestrinxit providos *Lei70*; perstrinxit pavidos *Pr*
9,1 illi at exiguis] illi exiguis *Clm18955*, *Lei70*, *GA*; illum exiguis *Pr*
11,1 sed tamen] sed tantum *Clm14845*
12,1 Aurum ut regi thus deo] Aurum regi tus ut deo *Clm18955*

The Gottschalk Antiphonary shares most of its variants with *Clm18955*, a Tegernsee troper/proser from the eleventh century (Gottschalk's reading of 'stat' for 'stant' in verse 4 is grammatically incorrect and is probably a scribal error). None of Gottschalk's variants is found in the Prague antiphonary, and the manuscripts are otherwise dissimilar – although this is the only other manuscript known to include 'Quem non praevalent' as a responsory trope, its connection to the Gottschalk Antiphonary, if any, must be indirect.

Gottschalk's source for the text was apparently a Germanic troper-proser. But which one? 'Quem non praevalent' appears in no known Austrian troper-prosers. However, a troper-proser from Lambach does survive in fragments, with one leaf preserving tropes for Epiphany and a Magi play (Lambach, Stiftsbibliothek, Frag. 1; see below, pp. 119–121). Several other leaves of this manuscript, from the proser section, are Beinecke MS 481.39 and flyleaves in Ccl 314. 'Quem non praevalent' is not among the surviving texts. The question is – could it have been? Can the original contents of the troper-proser be reconstructed by determining the sources of the extant chants? Collation of the surviving texts against the contents of the troper-prosers studied by W. von den Steinen in his seminal work on Notker the Stammerer helps to resolve this issue: there is no known manuscript which could clearly have served as a model for the Lambach troper-proser.[14] The series of sequences preserved in the Lambach troper-proser corresponds almost exactly with the twelfth-century St Gall, Stiftsbibliothek, MS 375, while major textual variants ally the manuscript instead with von den Steinen's 'German' group, which includes manuscripts from Einsiedeln, Rheinau and Reichenau.

The tropes which surround the Lambach Magi play also cannot help determine the source of this Lambach troper-proser. On folio 1ᵛ of the Magi play fragment, part of the Epiphany Mass is extant (primarily consisting of tropes of the introit antiphon 'Ecce advenit'), running from lines 5 to 23. The missing text (supplied in brackets) is taken from Drumbl's edition.[15] Rubrics are indicated in italics.

5. [   ] *Cantores:* Deo gracias
6. [   ] *Populus:* Kyrieleison
7. *[Chorus redit] cum processione, iam preparatus ad missam,*
8. *[perlecta sanc]ti oratione:* Omnis terra adoret te deus.
9. *[Oratione fi]nita vadunt in chorum cantantes*
10. *[et portantes] magna veneratione imaginem*
11. *[et stat]im imponunt antiphonam:* A.Ecce advenit
12. [Ecclesie sponsus illuminator] gentium *Tropi*
13. [Baptismatis sacrator orbis redempt]or *A.* Ecce advenit.Iesus quem reges
14. [gentium cum muneribus mysticis hi]erosolymam requirunt dicentes: ubi est

[14] W. von den Steinen, *Notker der Dichter und seine geistige Welt* (Berne, 1948).
[15] J. Drumbl, *Quem Quaeritis: Teatro Sacro dell'Alto Medioevo* (Rome, 1981), pp. 301–2.

15. [qui natus est Dominator Dominus. Vi]dimus stellam eius in oriente et agno
16. [vimus regem regum natum esse.] Et regnum eius. Cui soli debetur honor
17. [gloria laus et iubilatio Et pote]stas. Deus iudicium. Ipsi soli omnipotenti
18. [Deus pater Deo eternus regi eter]no. Gloria patri. Qui credentes in se
19. [coronas et lapsis donas veniam] miserando *A.* Ecce advenit
20. [Forma speciosissimus manuque po]tentissimus *Item tropi*
21. [Ex davidis origine natus maria] virgine. *A.* Ecce advenit. Olim promissus
22. [ac cupitus, patribus venerandis D]ominator dominus. Laxare vincula strictum
23. [quibus humanum detinebtur g]enus. Et regnum.

The introit tropes begin at line 12. Altogether, nine tropes are listed (for two performances of the introit antiphon 'Ecce advenit' – one complete, one fragmentary – and the minor doxology):

Trope	Phrase	Corpus Troporum[16]	
Ecclesiae sponsus	Ecce advenit	I: 85	(Epiph. Intr. 15)
Iesus quem reges	dominator dominus	I: 117	(Epiph. Intr. 17)
Vidimus stellam	et regnum eius	I: 213	(Epiph. Intr. 18)
Cui soli debetur	et potestas.	I: 72	(Epiph. Intr. 19)
Ipsi soli omnipotenti	Gloria Patri	(not in *CT*)	
Qui credentes in	Ecce advenit	I: 177	(Epiph. Intr. 33)
Forma speciosissimus	Ecce advenit	I: 96	(Epiph. Intr. 40)
Olim promissus ac	dominator dominus	I: 148	(Epiph. Intr. 23)
Laxare vincula strictum	et regnum	I: 133	(Epiph. Intr. 24)

None of the sixty-three troper-prosers surveyed in *Corpus Troporum* (*CT*) includes these tropes in this particular order. The first series – 15, 17, 18, 19 – is fairly common, used in close to half of the *CT* manuscripts.[17] The final series – 40, 23, 24 – is much less common, used in only three troper-prosers: Oxford, Bodleian Library, Selden Supra 27 (Heidenheim, saec. XI[in]), Munich, Bayerische Staatsbibliothek, Clm 14083 (Regensburg, 1024/1040) and Verona, Biblioteca Capitolare, XC (Monza, saec. X[med]). All three of these manuscripts use the first set of tropes as well. In addition, Munich 14083 gives the psalm incipit 'Deus iudicium' found on line 17 of the Magi play fragment. None of these manuscripts, however, includes 'Qui credentes' (*CT* Epiph. Intr. 33). That trope is found in only three manuscripts: St Gall, Stiftsbibliothek, MSS 484 and 381 (both c. 965) and Berlin, Staatsbibliothek, MS Theo. lat. qu. 11 (Minden, 1024/27). These manuscripts include all of the other tropes found in the Magi play fragment, but not in the same order. The St Gall manuscripts use 'Qui credentes' with the phrase 'In iudicio'. The

---

16 R. Jonsson, *Corpus Troporum I: Tropes du propre de la messe*, vol.1: *Cycle de Noël* (Stockholm, 1975).
17 *Ibid.*, I:1: 244–5.

Heidenheim and St Gall manuscripts are also included in von den Steinen's survey, but have no significant correlation to the sequences preserved in the Lambach troper-proser.

None of the aforementioned manuscripts includes 'Quem non praevalent'. In fact, the only manuscript in von den Steinen's work to include 'Quem non prae-valent' is *BL19768*, a manuscript which contains *none* of the sequences preserved in the Lambach troper-proser.[18] It therefore seems unlikely that Gottschalk inherited 'Quem non praevalent' from the Lambach troper-proser, a source which was close at hand. While looking for an Epiphany sequence to append to 'Caeli aperti sunt', Gottschalk could have used the text that is preserved in the Lambach troper-proser, 'Festa Christi omnis'. But he went further afield instead, somehow finding and then incorporating 'Quem non praevalent'. His exact source, while likely Germanic, must for the time remain a mystery.

The use of this particular responsory trope has important implications for understanding the significance and celebration of Epiphany at Lambach in the Middle Ages. Epiphany was, of course, an extremely important feast everywhere, but at Lambach it attained an uncommon resonance. The use of 'Quem non prae-valent' allows one to place the other elements of Epiphany at Lambach into a rel-evant liturgical context, and to posit an answer to the question of why Epiphany was so important there.

2. THE LAMBACH MAGI PLAY

The first element of Epiphany at Lambach is the mid-eleventh-century Lambach Magi play, which is now only a fragment in the Lambach library.[19] The fragment bears the shelf mark Stiftsbibliothek Fragment 1. Only a few other pages of this manuscript, which was almost certainly a troper-proser, survive, among which are several leaves at the Beinecke library (MS 481.39). Originally, the play was part of a liturgical manuscript whose origins are undetermined – at one point, Bernhard Bischoff judged the script to be from the early eleventh century, which would imply that the manuscript pre-dated the abbey's foundation. Because of Bischoff's opinion, the Lambach Magi play has traditionally been attributed to Lambach's mother abbey, Münsterschwarzach, and is thought to have been brought to Lambach with the first group of monks, as part of the original monastic library. On another occasion, however, Bischoff dated leaves from the same manuscript,

---

[18] Von den Steinen, *Notker der Dichter und seine geistige Welt*, table 1. *BL19768* is von den Steinen's [Mz].

[19] For an edition, see Drumbl, *Quem Quaeritis: Teatro Sacro dell'Alto Medioevo*, pp. 299–301. See also the plates in N. Wibiral, 'Beiträge zur Ikonographie der frühromanischen Fresken im ehemaligen Westchor der Stiftskirche von Lambach (Oberösterreich)', *Würzburger Diözesangeschichtsblätter*, 25 (1963), pp. 63–91, Abb. 1–2.

written by the same hand, to the *late* eleventh century, which would make a Lambach origin possible. Where the manuscript was actually written, however, is not important for this argument – what matters is that the manuscript was *in* Lambach by the late eleventh century. It was presumably one of the three troper-prosers listed in a twelfth-century Lambach booklist.[20]

Of the various liturgical dramas which developed during the Middle Ages, those of the Christmas season are the most diverse and complex in origin and scope. One genre, the Magi play, developed specifically for performance on Epiphany. Magi plays first appeared in the eleventh century, probably in France, although both the date and place of origin of the earliest examples are still disputed. In its simplest form, the Magi play presents the Adoration of the Magi at the scene of the Nativity, with the altar usually serving as the manger. This scene was evidently inspired by Easter *Visitatio* plays (re-enactments of the Visit of the three Marys to the Holy Sepulchre), which were themselves brief scenes performed before the high altar. The textual kernel of the Magi play is drawn in part from the Matins antiphon 'Ab oriente' ('From the East'), itself based loosely on Matthew 2: 11 with an added explanation of the significance of the gifts brought by the Magi:

Ab oriente venerunt magi in bethleem adorare dominum, et apertis thesauris suis preciosa munera obtulerunt, aurum sicut regi magno. Thus sicut deo vero. Myrram sepulturae eius, alleluia. (*CAO* 1205 and *GA* folio 33ʳ)

[From the East came the Magi to adore the Lord in Bethlehem, and opening their treasures they offered precious gifts, gold as to a great king, frankincense as to the true God, myrrh for his burial, hallelujah.]

The plot outline is also drawn from the apocryphal Gospel of James.[21]

Soon after the earliest plays appeared, the genre branched out to extend both forward and backward in the narrative. The twenty-five known Magi plays are quite complex in their development and structure, with as few as eight or as many as thirty-nine plot components. The Lambach Magi play is unique in its combination of narrative elements.[22]

The Lambach play presents the following story: the Magi enter the scene, singing about their intent to follow the star which heralds the birth of the Messiah. Herod intercepts them in Jerusalem, and interrogates them about their intentions. They respond that they are bringing gifts to the newborn child. Herod instructs his scribes to see if there is anything written in their books concerning the infant. They search their books, and find the prophecy of Isaiah that the Messiah was to have been born in Bethlehem from the line of David. The antiphon praising Bethlehem is sung

[20] R. G. Babcock, *Reconstructing a Medieval Library: Fragments from Lambach* (New Haven, 1993), pp. 43–5.
[21] S. J. Strycker, *La forme la plus ancienne du Protévangile de Jacques* (Brussels, 1961), pp. 457–8.
[22] King, *Mittelalterliche Dreikönigspiele*, p. 16.

('Bethlehem non est minima'). Herod orders the Magi to continue on their way, and
to report back to him. The Magi resume their journey, singing again about the star
and declaring the nature of the gifts they bring: gold, frankincense and myrrh.

When they reach Bethlehem, the Magi encounter the midwives who ask them
to identify themselves and their intentions. They respond that they are kings from
Tharsis, Arabia and Saba, come to bring gifts to the infant Messiah. The midwives
lead them to the child, and the Magi sing the antiphon 'Ab oriente'. This is followed by the incomplete rubric 'Et duos versus de y[mno . . .]', presumably a reference to the hymn 'Hostis Herodes' that is usually sung at this point.

The Magi genuflect before the infant and present their gifts, explaining their
mystical significance: gold because he is King, frankincense because he is divine
and myrrh because he is mortal. Later, while they are sleeping, an angel speaks to
the Magi, declaring that the prophecies have been fulfilled and telling the kings to
take an alternate route home in order to avoid Herod's wrath.

The Lambach Magi play is unique among the roughly two-dozen known Magi
plays. It includes more narrative elements than some plays, while excluding other
elements. For example, half of the known Magi plays include an extended scene
where Herod's guards intercept the Magi and bring them before their ruler. Several
plays begin instead with a visit to the manger by shepherds, before moving on to
the scene in Jerusalem. In the Lambach play, the Magi are intercepted by Herod
himself, and the shepherds are not included. On the other hand, many other plays
omit the scene in Jerusalem completely, and go directly from the Magi's entrance
to the scene at the manger. The Lambach play is more extensive than some, and
less so than others.

3. THE LAMBACH FRESCOES

The second piece of evidence for the celebration of Epiphany at Lambach is art historical. The original abbey church was Romanesque, built in the second half of the
eleventh century and dedicated in 1089. This was replaced in the fourteenth
century by a Gothic church, which was itself supplanted by the extant Baroque
structure. The Romanesque building was double-choired, with altars in both the
east and west ends. Only the west choir remains intact, serving as the foundation
of the modern belltower. Double-ended churches such as this are not particularly
unusual for the period. What is unusual is that documentary evidence indicates
that the high altar, dedicated to the Virgin and to St Kilian, was not in the east end
of the church, but in the west. A fifteenth-century manuscript titled 'Tractatus de
institutione et consecratione monasterii Lambacensis' ('Treatise on the foundation
and consecration of the Lambach monastery', Ccl 325) describes the Romanesque
church on folio 48ʳ:

De duplici choro monasterii Lambacensis. Fuit olim sicut modo est, duplex chorus ecclesiae Lambacensis, videlicet superior in posteriore [sic] parte ecclesiae et inferior in parte
anteriori. In choro superiori consecratum fuit olim per beatum Altmannum altare in
honore gloriosae Virginis Mariae, quae est principalis et primaria patrona monasterii
Lambacensis, et habetur in martyrologio, ubi dicitur: Dedicatio ecclesiae S. Mariae patro-
nae nostrae et in honore S. Kiliani Martyris et sociorum eius. Et illud fuit olim principale
et summum altare . . . et in illo choro olim fuerant cantatae horae canonicae usque ad
tempus . . . abbatis Joannis dicti Daxperger anno 1429. . . . In choro inferiori fuit olim a
principio fundationis per beatum Adalberonem consecratum altare in honore S. Joannis
apostoli, qui fuit alter principalis patronus ecclesiae huius.[23]

[Concerning the two choirs of the abbey of Lambach. The two choirs in the Lambach
church were made in this fashion in the past, that is, the upper in the rear part of the church
and the lower in the front part. In the upper choir the altar in honour of the glorious Virgin
Mary, who is the principal and primary patroness of the Lambach abbey, was consecrated
by the blessed Altmann [Bishop of Passau], and it is considered in the martyrology where
it is said: The dedication of the church of St Mary our patron and in honour of the martyr
St Kilian and his companions. And that was the principal and high altar…and in that choir
were sung the canonical hours until the time…of Abbot Johannes called Daxperger in the
year 1429. …In the lower choir there was from the time of the original foundation an altar
consecrated by blessed Adalbero in honour of St John the Apostle, who was the other principal patron of this church.]

The implications of this passage are manifold. The choir in the west part of the
church (*posterior*) is clearly referred to as the *superior* choir, with the double
meaning 'higher' or 'greater'. The *anterior*, or east, choir is *inferior*, 'lower' or
'lesser'. The altar dedicated to St Kilian and to the Virgin (the 'principal and
primary' patroness of the monastery) was in the west choir. This is also where the
canonical Hours were said prior to 1429.

The other altars were arranged as follows: in the *inferior* choir was the altar dedicated to John (here called the apostle, although elsewhere John the Baptist is said
to be the dedicatee – it is often the case in double-choired churches that the
'Nebenaltar', as opposed to the high altar, is dedicated to John the Baptist[24]). In
the small north chapel, an altar was dedicated to St Martin and St Nicholas (the
patron of the diocese), while the south chapel altar was dedicated to St Leonard.
An altar in the centre of the nave was dedicated to the Cross. The tomb of Adalbero
was (and still is) below the crossing (see Fig. 1).[25]

---

[23] H.-J. Genge, *Die liturgiegeschichtlichen Voraussetzungen des Lambacher Freskenzyklus*
(Münsterschwarzach, 1972), p. 4, n. 15.

[24] G. Bandmann, 'Früh- und hochmittelalterliche Altaranordnung als Darstellung', in V. Elbern (ed.),
Das erste Jahrtausend (Düsseldorf, 1963), vol. I, p. 394. As Bandmann notes (p. 410), this same arrange-
ment, with the Baptist altar in the east and the Marian altar in the west, is found in Hildesheim.

[25] See *ÖKT*, fig. 56 (p. 83) and Nachtrag, p. 502, as well as the diagram in *900 Jahre Klosterkirche
Lambach: Oberösterreichische Landesausstellung 1989* (Linz, 1989), p. 167 (cat.# IV.10).

A document at Lambach from 1431 begins with a description of the Romanesque church:

Neque etiam mulieres ad oratorium huius monasterii venientes ne ad cryptam ipsius intrent, seu etiam super basilicam retro ascendant, in qua ab olim usque modo a fratribus horae canonicae solebant decantari, quae nunc in choro anteriori noviter ad hoc aptato cantantur.[26]

[And let not the women coming into the place of prayer enter through the crypt of this abbey; rather indeed let them ascend to the rear above the basilica where formerly the canonical Hours used to be chanted by the brothers, which now are recently from this point appropriately chanted in the anterior choir.]

The phrase 'retro ascendant' again implies that the rear, or west, end of the church was somewhat higher than the east end. Architectural excavation beneath the modern church has confirmed this; the west choir was raised 187 cm above the nave,[27] and was accessible by a set of stairs leading from the nave to a platform extending from the centre of the choir. The choir itself was divided into three rooms, separated by arches. Each room was domed. The western wall of the choir had two small doors, one each in the south and in the north. Only the tops of these doors are visible today, since the modern floor cuts across them. Again, it appears from the above passage that, in the fifteenth century, saying the canonical Hours in the east end of the church was a new practice. Traditionally, the Hours had been said in the west end, before the high altar.

The west choir, raised above the nave and accessible by a short flight of steps, was decorated with frescoes. These frescoes depict scenes from the Bible, with the story of the Three Magi on the three ceiling cupolas.[28] Applied above the original location of the high altar, these ceiling frescoes are the architectural and artistic focus of the cycle. In the southern cupola (see Fig. 21), the Magi are intercepted by Herod, who interrogates them about the purpose of their journey. His scribes stand by to interpret the meaning of the Magi's words. A demon whispers in Herod's ear, presumably giving him bad advice. In the central cupola (see Fig. 22), the Magi travel to Bethlehem, pointing at the star which shines in the very centre of the dome. The Magi present their gifts to the enthroned Virgin and Child, who are flanked by the three midwives. As the Magi sleep, an angel warns them to return home via an alternate route to avoid being captured and interrogated by Herod. The north cupola is quite fragmentary (see Fig. 23), but appears to represent the Magi returning home (also in this cupola, the narrative moves on to the boyhood of Christ, with his presentation in the Temple).

---

[26] Genge, *Die liturgiegeschichtlichen Voraussetzungen des Lambacher Freskenzyklus*, pp. 4–5, n. 16.
[27] N. Wibiral, 'Die Wandmalereien des XI. Jahrhunderts im ehemaligen Westchor der Klosterkirche von Lambach', *Alte und moderne Kunst*, 13 (1968), pp. 2–13, at p. 5.
[28] See O. Demus, *Romanesque Mural Painting* (New York, 1970), pp. 137–8 and pls. 278–87.

21. Stift Lambach, west choir, south cupola: the Magi enter Jerusalem and meet with King Herod

22. Stift Lambach, west choir, central cupola: the Adoration

23. Stift Lambach, west choir, north cupola (fragmentary): in their sleep, the Magi are warned by an angel to flee Herod's wrath

The fresco cycle follows closely the plot of the Lambach Magi play, and was apparently inspired by it – no guards intercept the Magi, and no shepherds precede them. The frescoes serve as backdrops for the performance of the play, and the raised choir functions as a veritable proscenium stage. It is worth noting that the twelfth-century Lambach library contained copies of the plays of Terence and of other medieval comedies. The monks 'may have drawn on their own dramatic experience in explicating the plays or been influenced in their performances by their reading'.[29]

---

[29] Babcock, *Reconstructing a Medieval Library*, p. 54.

The connection between the play and the frescoes has been well studied, but never within a direct liturgical context. Karl Swoboda was the first to study the relationship of the frescoes to the Magi play.[30] His work of 1927 was expanded by Norbert Wibiral, who supervised the restoration of the frescoes in the 1960s. Wibiral adds to Swoboda's work a detailed description of the Magi play fragment, and examines the play in the context of the gospel readings for the Epiphany season indicated by a list of chapter readings in a ninth-century evangeliary that was in the medieval Lambach library (ÖNB ser. n. 3601).[31] While these chapter readings do provide a kind of liturgical context for the play, the connection is somewhat tenuous as the evangeliary pre-dates the frescoes by some two hundred years and provides only a small portion of the liturgy that may have surrounded the play. In the early 1970s, Hans-Joachim Genge returned primarily to the frescoes, describing them in detail and charting their relationship to the text of the play.[32] Genge also considers the frescoes in the context of the chapter readings, concluding that the subject matter of the frescoes was additionally inspired by the gospel readings for the Epiphany season. Genge and Wibiral both attempt to study the liturgical context of the play and frescoes, but because the sources known to them were so limited, their studies can present only partial and fragmented conclusions. In his study of the frescoes and the play, Wibiral laments the paucity of extant liturgy from medieval Lambach, noting in particular that he knew of no extant antiphonary.[33] In addition, none of these publications considers the evidence for performance of the play in the context of the decorated abbey church, because until now no such evidence has been known to exist. The Gottschalk Antiphonary provides that evidence.

4. EPIPHANY AT LAMBACH

When considered in tandem with the play and the frescoes, the Gottschalk Antiphonary helps to paint a vivid picture of the celebration of Epiphany at Lambach, as it allows at last for the placement of the dramatic and artistic elements of the feast in their appropriate context of prayer and performance. The bulk of the extant Epiphany liturgy is not particularly unusual. In fact, the liturgy for the

---

[30] K. Swoboda, 'Der romanische Epiphaniezyklus in Lambach und das lateinische Magierspiel', in *Festschrift für Julius Schlosser zum 60. Geburtstage* (Leipzig, 1927), pp. 82–7.

[31] 'Beiträge zur Ikonographie der frühromanischen Fresken im ehemaligen Westchor der Stiftskirche von Lambach'. See B. Bischoff, *Die südostdeutschen Schreibschulen und Bibliotheken in der Karolingerzeit*, 2 vols. (Wiesbaden, 1940 and 1980), vol. II, pp. 43–4, for a description of the evangeliary.   [32] Genge, *Die liturgiegeschichtlichen Voraussetzungen des Lambacher Freskenzyklus*.

[33] Wibiral, 'Beiträge zur Ikonographie der frühromanischen Fresken im ehemaligen Westchor der Stiftskirche von Lambach', p. 70.

Epiphany season in the Gottschalk Antiphonary is in most respects identical to that in the Engelberg Directorium. The most important difference is the use of the responsory trope 'Quem non praevalent' in the Gottschalk Antiphonary. It is the combination of elements at Lambach – the frescoes, the play, the liturgy and the trope – that makes the celebration of Epiphany there so unusual, even unique.

'Quem non praevalent' summarizes the journey of the Magi and explains the mystical interpretation of their gifts. No other sequence relates so closely to the tradition of liturgical drama performed on Epiphany. As was discussed above, the piece is actually included as part of several Magi plays, although that could not have been the context from which Gottschalk inherited it. Most Epiphany sequences mention the Magi (those which do not are concerned solely with the Baptism), but only a few include the mystical interpretation of the gifts which figures so prominently in the Lambach Magi play. Of the twenty-two Epiphany sequences listed in *Analecta Hymnica*, ten include the mystical interpretation of the Magi's gifts. Of these, three are late medieval compositions, two are part of the French/English liturgical tradition ('Epiphaniam domino', from St Martial, and 'Gaudete vos fideles', an English or French composition), and four include some reference to the Baptism. Of the pre-thirteenth-century Germanic sequences, only 'Quem non praevalent' follows the journey of the Magi and describes their gifts without any reference to the Baptism of Christ. It is the perfect complement to the performance of the Lambach Magi play.

The dramatic, artistic and liturgical evidence is clear – Epiphany was a day of unusual import at Lambach. Not only the feast itself, but the very *images* of the Epiphany story resonated at Lambach throughout the liturgical year. Every time the high altar was used, every time Mass was said, the image of the Magi bowing before the infant Christ stared down at the monks and layfolk. No one has ever asked why this particular emphasis should have existed at Lambach. The traditional explanations for such red-letter days elsewhere can be dismissed – the relics of the Magi were in Cologne, nowhere near Lambach. The church was neither dedicated on Epiphany nor was it dedicated to the Magi. A possible explanation is suggested when one remembers that Epiphany commemorates the baptism of Jesus by John. The altar in the east end of the church *was* dedicated to St John – in some early sources John the Evangelist, but in others John the Baptist. Could this veneration of John be related to the choice of Epiphany as a particularly critical time in the Lambach liturgical year? Perhaps, but probably not. The iconography of the church decor and the liturgy of the Gottschalk Antiphonary actually *de*-emphasize the baptism. The frescoes include only a minor scene of the baptism, while the central focus of the ceiling frescoes is the visitation of the Magi. The most interesting part of the Epiphany liturgy in the Gottschalk Antiphonary, the sequence 'Quem non praevalent', is one of only a handful of Epiphany sequences that neglect the baptism completely. Of the events commemorated on the feast of

24. Stift Lambach, western choir, south-west corner, upper register: the death of Herod Agrippa

Epiphany, the adoration of the Magi was particularly stressed at Lambach, musically, liturgically and visually. The emphasis on Epiphany was in place by 1089 at the latest, when the frescoes were presumably completed and the high altar dedicated beneath them. It is during the early years of the monastery's existence, then, that an explanation may be sought.

To this end, one of the wall frescoes in the southern room of the west choir deserves special attention (see Fig. 24). On the left, a crowned figure is enthroned in robes of state, holding an orb and sceptre. A figure kneels at his right hand, perhaps an advisor of some sort. Above, an angel gestures threateningly. A figure is stricken below, being assisted by two other men, while a crowd of onlookers shield their eyes from the scene. The other frescoes in this part of the choir deal primarily with the life of Herod. Originally, this fresco was interpreted in that context, as Herod (the fallen figure) collapsing at the sight of Christ in his majesty.[34] This interpretation, however, fails to account for most of the details of the fresco.

---

[34] Demus, *Romanesque Mural Painting*, p. 624, pl. 279.

129

Wibiral has offered an alternative interpretation which takes into account additional aspects of the scene. The fresco shows the death of Herod Agrippa, in two scenes: Herod enthroned, addressing his subjects and threatened by an angel; and then after having been struck down by the angel. Wibiral has argued that the scene illustrates a conflation of two sources.[35] The primary source is the book of Acts (12: 21–3);

Herod, wearing his robes of state and enthroned on a dais, made a speech to them. The people acclaimed him with, 'It is a god speaking, not a man!', and at that moment the angel of the Lord struck him down, because he had not given the glory to God. He was eaten away with worms and died.[36]

Several details in the fresco are not found in the biblical account: the star above the angel, and the three white rays which run from the crowned man to the cowering crowd. These details are found in the secondary source, Josephus' *Antiquitates Judaicae* (Book 19, chapter 8, lines 343–50). This is a lengthy and more detailed account of Herod's speech and subsequent death. Josephus writes that:

clad in a garment woven completely of silver so that its texture was indeed wondrous, [Herod] entered the theatre at daybreak. There the silver, illumined by the touch of the first rays of the sun, was wondrously radiant and by its glitter inspired fear and awe in those who gazed intently upon it. Straightaway his flatterers raised their voices from various directions…addressing him as a god. …The king did not rebuke them nor did he reject their flattery as impious.[37]

The star above the scene represents the sun, and the white rays the sun's reflection off Herod's robes. Wibiral notes that only Josephus describes a purely silver garment – all later exegetes clothe Herod in silver and gold. In addition, Herod's death as depicted in the fresco shows him prostrate on the ground, not being eaten away with worms. In the Josephus account, Herod dies after five days of illness, from a 'severe pain' in his belly.

In this interpretation, the fresco represents Adalbero's conflict with the emperor, who had ousted Adalbero from his bishopric in 1077, merely a decade before the frescoes were painted and the altar beneath them was dedicated. According to Wibiral, the scene functions as a diatribe against Emperor Henry IV by directly comparing him to the tyrannical Herod.[38] Herod holds the imperial regalia of orb and sceptre, and wears a crown that is similar in appearance to the 'Reichskron' worn by Henry.[39] His stature is that of a traditional 'majestic figure', quite similar,

---

[35] N. Wibiral, 'Apostelgeschichte und Jüdische Altertümer in Lambach', in *Festgabe für Kurt Holter* (Linz, 1991), pp. 73–96 and pls. 1–8.

[36] A. Jones (ed.), *The Jerusalem Bible* (New York, 1968), p. 172.

[37] L. Feldman (ed. and trans.), *Josephus,* Loeb Classical Library, Greek Authors, 9 (Cambridge, Mass., 1965), pp. 377–9.   [38] Wibiral, 'Apostelgeschichte und Jüdische Altertümer in Lambach'.

[39] R. Staats, *Theologie der Reichskrone*, Monographien zur Geschichte des Mittelalters, 13 (Stuttgart, 1976), pl. 5.

in fact, to contemporary illustrations of reigning emperors – the enthroned, crowned figure faces straight ahead, sitting formally upright, with the raised sceptre in his right hand, the orb in his left.[40]

Wibiral describes this scene as a political allegory. His interpretation, however, can be expanded to include the entire fresco cycle. The importance of Epiphany at Lambach may have been directly related to the turmoil surrounding Bishop Adalbero's support of Pope Gregory against the emperor. Lambach was founded in 1056 by Bishop Adalbero of Würzburg, who was a member of the local nobility. Adalbero was forcibly banished from Würzburg by Emperor Henry IV in 1077, and formally deposed from his bishop's throne four years later. He returned to Lambach, where, in 1089, the frescoes centred on the Epiphany story were presumably completed and the Lambach abbey church dedicated.

Those who supported Gregory believed Henry's quest for investiture rights, among other things, to be prideful and hubristic. Henry lacked humility in the face of divine authority – hence his excommunications, and the humiliation and penance at Canossa. And what is the central theme of Epiphany if not the image of secular rulers, the Magi, humbling themselves before the Divine, in contrast to the prideful, doubting Herod? What better way for Adalbero to express his continued support of Gregory and disapproval of Henry's actions than by devoting the decor of his monastery to the topic? Although the usual patristic interpretation of the Epiphany story construes the Magi as pagans bowing before the leader of the true faith, there is some justification for interpreting them as secular rulers deferring to divine authority. Medieval tradition holds that on Epiphany, Frankish kings would themselves re-enact the Adoration by offering gold, frankincense and myrrh at the church altar as a token of their veneration of the King of Kings.[41]

There also exists a strong contemporary *textual* precedent for the allegorical use of Herod to signify the improprieties of pride and vanity in the face of the Divine. Peter Damian, who was a supporter of Gregory, quotes Acts 12: 21–3 in his *Letters*, then writes the following (in letter 24, written between 1047 and 1054):

quia vanae gloriae deditus delatam sibimet in Deum transferre gloriam noluit, repetino superveniente iudicio consumptus a vermibus expiravit…erubescat ergo terrena superbia, confundatur et obstupescat arrogantia redempti hominis, ubi mox erumpentibus radiis exorti coruscat humilitas redempotoris.[42]

---

[40] See, for example, the frontispiece portrait of Henry IV dated 1112–13 in W. Landgraf, *Heinrich IV: Macht und Ohnmacht eines Kaisers: Biografie* (Berlin, *c.* 1991).

[41] H. Kehrer, *Die heiligen drei Könige in Literatur und Kunst* (Leipzig, 1908/9), p. 52, and G. Zappert, 'Epiphania', *Sitzungsberichte der philosophisch-historische Klasse der Kaiserliche Akademie der Wissenschaften*, 21 (1857), pp. 291–372, at p. 358.

[42] K. Reindel, *Die Briefe des Petrus Damiani, MGH*, Die Briefe der deutschen Kaiserzeit, 4 (Munich, 1983), vol. I, p. 231.

[Because [Herod] was overwhelmed by vainglory and would not give to God the honour offered to him, he became the victim of instant justice and died eaten away with worms. ... Worldly pride should therefore blush, and the arrogance of humanity that was granted redemption should be confounded and stand in wonder at the radiant humility of the newborn Redeemer whose light is about to break forth before men.][43]

Those who stand in awe before the infant Christ are contrasted with those who are full of hubristic pride. The exhortation to 'be confounded and stand in wonder at the radiant humility of the newborn Redeemer' conjures up images of the Magi bowing in awe before the Madonna and child, a vision which contrasts strongly with that of Herod being devoured by worms. Damian was a staunch supporter of Gregory. Although all of the early manuscripts of Damian's letters are Italian, Adalbero, as one of the pope's few firm friends, could certainly have been familiar with Damian's polemical works.

When one considers that Adalbero had already been banished from his bishopric when the Lambach abbey church was dedicated, the inclusion of a political allegory among the more traditional themes of the frescoes begins to make sense. The presentation of this political motif in the context of the Epiphany story takes the critique of Henry to a more complex allegorical level. The allegorical treatment of Emperor Henry IV, which depicts the chastisement of an earthly ruler for his rejection of the Divine authority, works in tandem with the ceiling frescoes to compare the emperor to Herod and contrast his behaviour with that of the Magi, in much the same way that Damian contrasts those who behave like Herod with those who behave like the three kings.

The Lambach Magi play pre-dates these political considerations, and was clearly not composed as a political diatribe. Even so, the play, in combination, perhaps, with Damian's words, seems to have inspired Adalbero's visual political invective. Though it is possible that, once in place, the original symbolism of Epiphany at Lambach was forgotten, freed from Adalbero's original purposes, it is much more likely that the Epiphany liturgy in the Gottschalk Antiphonary represents an early written expression of a very strong political attitude, even though the events surrounding the foundation of the abbey took place more than a hundred years before the Antiphonary was produced. This assertion is supported by the fact that Gottschalk was the author and scribe of the *Vita Adalberonis* (Cml LIV). The *Vita* records not just the life of the founder but the political mythology surrounding his deeds, here recorded for the monks of the twelfth century.

Adalbero's expulsion from Würzburg is described by Gottschalk as follows:

---

[43] O. J. Blum (trans.), *Peter Damian: Letters 1–30* (The Fathers of the Church, Mediaeval Continuation) (Washington, DC, *c.* 1989), p. 233.

episcopus Adelbero…collecto cum suis consilio, elegit abiectus esse in domo Domini, quam habitare in tabernaculis peccatorum.[44]

[Bishop Adalbero…together with his councillors, chose to be driven from the house of God, rather than to live in a tabernacle of sinners.] (Psalm 83: 11)

Gottschalk quotes Matthew 10: 23: if you are persecuted in one city, flee to another. Adalbero is 'by the grace of God prefect of the Würzburg church, by the hand of violence unjustly ejected'.[45] All of these references preserve inherent criticism of the emperor while at the same time showing Adalbero to be the innocent, martyred victim of Henry's quest for power. Although Gottschalk manages to preserve the sense of the actions surrounding Adalbero's expulsion, he does get his historical facts confused: he cites the conflict between 'Emperor Henry and his son', that is, Henry IV and Henry V, as the context for Adalbero's expulsion, a schism that took place after Adalbero's death.[46]

Gottschalk knew the effectiveness of these kinds of documents. Within the *Vita Adalberonis* is a copy of an earlier notarial document, the original of which is certainly a forgery. This document is one of a series of forged documents designed to ensure various fishing and forestry rights for the abbey. The 'original' is dated 1056, a slip-up that reveals the forgery since the author also mentions Pope Gregory VII and Bishop Altmann of Passau, neither of whom were in power at that date. Gottschalk apparently changed the date to 1089 in his version of the document, knowing it to be a more reasonable date.[47] In addition to securing fishing and forestry rights, Gottschalk's document shows Adalbero, Gregory and Altmann working together to establish the abbey, thus cementing the monastic tradition.[48]

When memorializing the events surrounding an abbey's foundation, many monastic writers tried to de-politicize their abbey's history, weaving mythological and miraculous tales around the events surrounding the foundation.[49] This is the case, for example, at Admont; the tale of the three future bishops, Adalbero, Altmann and Gebhard, and their joint vision of the monasteries they would later found, is preserved in the *Vita Altmanni* (see above, p. 8). It is not included in the *Vita Adalberonis*. Was Gottschalk not familiar with the legend? Or did he choose to exclude it in favour of a more political interpretation of events? There is no way

---

[44] I. Schmale-Ott, *Vita Sancti Adalberonis* (Würzburg, 1954), p. 26. [45] *Ibid.*, p. 30.
[46] *Ibid.*, p. 24 and n. 62.
[47] K. Rumpler, 'Die Gründung Lambachs unter besonderer Berücksichtigung der Gründungsurkunden', in *900 Jahre Klosterkirche Lambach: Oberösterreichische Landesausstellung 1989* (Linz, 1989), pp. 25–33, at p. 29.
[48] E. Boshof, 'Gefälschte "Stiftsbriefe" des 11./12. Jahrhunderts aus bayerisch-österreichischen Klöstern', in *Fälschungen im Mittelalter: internationaler Kongress der Monumenta Germaniae Historica, München, 16.–19. September 1986*, MGH *Schriften* 33:1 (Hanover, 1988), pp. 519–50, at p. 526.
[49] P. Geary, *Phantoms of Remembrance* (Princeton, 1994), p. 132.

to know for certain. It is often the case, however, that medieval records of the past were written with an eye on the present. The *Vita Adalberonis* and the Gottschalk Antiphonary may have been intentionally politicized, and not only as a way of commemorating Adalbero. The second half of the twelfth century was itself marked by continuing papal/imperial strife, and was a time of some upheaval for the Lambach abbey.

From the time of its foundation to the last quarter of the twelfth century, the Lambach abbey had been firmly in the control and under the influence of the Würzburg diocese and bishop. Adalbero's status as the Bishop of Würzburg had virtually assured this. During this period, it was the episcopal authority in Würzburg who had the greatest say in the selection of the Lambach abbot. By the middle of the twelfth century, however, the abbey began to seek some measure of independence from the distant episcopate, and was supported in this effort when Pope Alexander III granted monasteries the right to choose their own abbot in 1163. This new-found autonomy was compromised, however, when the territory of Steiermark (including Lambach) was given into the hands of the Babenbergers in 1186.[50] The hand-over of Lambach by Emperor Frederick Barbarossa from the Otakar counts (descendants of Adalbero's sister) to the Babenberger dukes left the abbey once again under the stewardship of a distant authority, forced to make donations to the administrative ministry.[51] This situation could not have left the monks with strong feelings of support for the emperor.

More generally, the reign of Emperor Frederick Barbarossa (1152–90) was marked by constant opposition to Pope Alexander III as the emperor tried to force a return to a papacy that was under imperial control. Barbarossa selected a pope to his own liking, Victor IV, leading to a schism that lasted seventeen years. Alexander waited out the schism in France. The schism ended with Frederick's surrender at Venice in 1177, after which Alexander took immediate steps to prevent such a situation from recurring. At the Third Lateran Council in 1179, he vested the exclusive power to elect the pope with a two-thirds majority of cardinals. Like his forebear, Henry IV, Frederick was excommunicated and suffered a crushing loss of support from the German princes and bishops. The next emperor, Henry VI (1190–97), had papal problems of his own. Adalbero's message of secular humility in the face of divine authority was still relevant a century later, in Gottschalk's time.

The situation in Lambach contrasts somewhat with that facing other monastic historians who were struggling to piece together an almost fictional monastic past based on oral and written fragments.[52] Gottschalk's recording of what had presumably been an oral tradition of the *Vita Adalberonis* shows an unbroken line of descent from Adalbero to Gottschalk. In Lambach, this understanding of Adalbero

[50] H. Dopsch, 'Das Kloster Lambach unter den Otakaren und Babenbergern', in *900 Jahre Klosterkirche Lambach*, pp. 73–80, at p. 78.   [51] *Ibid.*, p. 78.   [52] Geary, *Phantoms of Remembrance*, p. 115.

as a fast friend of the pope who was betrayed by the false emperor represented an interpretation of relatively recent history that was encoded within the frescoes, played out in the west choir, and perpetuated in the Gottschalk Antiphonary by the hymn 'Quem non praevalent', all three of which elements focus closely on the humility of secular authority in the face of the divine.

The Gottschalk Antiphonary, therefore, is in part a manifestation of the political propaganda inherited by successive generations of Lambach monks. The use of the sequence 'Quem non praevalent' as a responsory trope was directly inspired by the existence of the Magi play and the frescoes, and functions as yet another reminder of Adalbero's anti-imperial invective. There are other Epiphany sequences which could have been chosen; only 'Quem non praevalent' tells the story in the same way as the play and frescoes. In addition, the choice of a trope which focuses only on the Magi pushes the celebration of the Baptism to the background and centralizes the Magi's humility. The celebration of Epiphany was taken to an elaborate level, while the monks were reminded on a daily basis of the circumstances surrounding the abbey's origins. This combination of art, drama and music at Lambach represents a unique conflation of liturgical and extra-liturgical elements working together to commemorate a major event in the life of Christ, and to ritualize the communal monastic memory. The use of written *vitae* and notarial documents as political tools is common, and has been much studied.[53] Even documents for monastic use such as customaries, cartularies and necrologies can often be understood in this light.[54] To find such a device in a purely liturgical document is extraordinary.

There were two messages encoded in the celebration of Epiphany at Lambach. The first is political, the second personal. Adalbero was criticizing Henry's hubris, and at the same time pointing out his own unjust treatment at the hands of the emperor. Even today, there is a feeling at Lambach that Adalbero was betrayed by Henry. A modern publication in honour of the abbey recounts that, during Henry's minority, 'he had a true helper in his godfather, Adalbero'.[55] Then Henry grew up, grew ambitious, and forced Adalbero from his bishopric. The recollections reach across the centuries, painted on stone, written by hand, printed by press, as the political attitudes planted by Adalbero are perpetuated by each generation. He was a canny politician, and knew exactly how to preserve his tale of perceived injustices in perpetuity. Gottschalk was a willing participant in this chain of propaganda, not only through the composition of the *Vita Adalberonis*, but also through his use of the Antiphonary to pass along a message that, while somewhat obscure to us, would have been quite obvious to the Lambach monks of the twelfth century.

---

[53] See, for example, *Fälschungen im Mittelalter* and Geary, *Phantoms of Remembrance*.
[54] Geary, *Phantoms of Remembrance*, p. 105.
[55] P. W. Scheele, *Die Herrlichkeit des Herrn; Die Lambacher Fresken aus der Zeit des heiligen Adalbero* (Würzburg, 1990), p. 15.

5. GENERAL CONCLUSIONS

We have come full circle: from the political and historical context within which the Lambach abbey was built to a survey of its scriptorium; from the structure of one manuscript produced by the scriptorium, the Gottschalk Antiphonary, to a detailed examination of the manuscript's contents; from a study of its contents to one Office in particular, Epiphany; and from an examination of the celebration of Epiphany at Lambach back to the political and historical context surrounding the origins of the abbey. Each element sheds light on the others – to understand one, we must examine them all.

I began studying the Gottschalk Antiphonary as a graduate student at Yale University in 1989. As part of my responsibilities as Assistant to the Curator of Pre-1600 Books and Manuscripts at the Beinecke Rare Book and Manuscript Library, I was assigned the task of organizing and cataloguing the library's monumental collection of over four hundred manuscript fragments: removing the fragments from the brittle mattes in which they were stored; performing conservation work when necessary (to remove tape residue, for example); housing the fragments in individual mylar sleeves; storing each group of leaves that came from the same manuscript together in a non-acidic folder; organizing the folders in archival boxes; and, finally, cataloguing the individual leaves. Fragments that had come from the same manuscript needed to be put in the correct order before they could be catalogued. It was during this phase of the project that what would come to be known as the Gottschalk Antiphonary caught my eye.

When I began studying the seventeen Beinecke leaves of the Gottschalk Antiphonary, I thought of them only as a codicological exercise, an interesting intellectual puzzle. The Lambach origin of the Antiphonary and the other Beinecke fragments was not known to me or anyone else. The discovery that these and many other Beinecke leaves had come from Lambach is a story that has been told elsewhere.[56] But once the Beinecke leaves of the Gottschalk Antiphonary were discovered to have come from Lambach, leaves at other collections were easily identified. With such a large body of liturgy, it then became possible to pursue any number of angles of investigation into the manuscript: the physical object, its decoration and script, its music, its contents, and the politicization of the celebration of Epiphany.

In 1989, however, I had no idea where these enquiries would lead or that I would discover new aspects of the manuscript with each revision of my work: the unique aspects of Gottschalk's use of tonary-letters, the influence of monastic reform on the liturgy, the implications of the elaboration of the Epiphany Office, and so on. If so much can be teased out of three-dozen randomly preserved leaves from one

---

[56] Babcock, *Reconstructing a Medieval Library.*

manuscript, how much is yet to be found in the tens of thousands of unstudied manuscript fragments? The case of the Gottschalk Antiphonary demonstrates the need for close study of manuscript fragments. Working with individual leaves presents unique challenges, but has been made more feasible with the advent of on-line textual and liturgical databases. As demonstrated by the Gottschalk Antiphonary, such manuscripts are full of surprises. Even complete liturgical manuscripts need to be examined not just from a liturgiological or musicological point of view, or as of purely palaeographical or art historical relevance. The makers of the manuscripts did not think of them that way. They are rich, multi-dimensional documents, containing evidence of the daily monastic ritual and of the functions of the scriptoria in which they were produced, of course, but also preserving hints of the larger context within which the monks lived and worked.

Appendix 1 Extant twelfth-century Lambach codices

Cml	Modern (if no longer at Lambach)
II	
III	
VI	
XII	
XIV	
XVII	Leutkirch, Fürstlich Waldburgschen Gesamtarchiv, MS 5
XVIII	Sotheby's 1929 no. 389
XIX	
XXI	Göttweig, Stiftsbibliothek, cod. 1116
XXII	
XXIV	Oxford, Bodleian Library, Lyell 55
XXVII	
XXVIII	Göttweig, Stiftsbibliothek, cod. 1115
XXIX	Stuttgart, Württembergische Landesbibliothek, MS. Th. et phil. 2.351
XXX	
XLII	
XLIII	Oxford, Bodleian Library, Lyell 56
XLIV	
XLV	
XLVI	
XLVII	
XLVIII	
IL	
L	
LII	
LIV	
LX	
LXI	
LXII	Private Collection (Dr Jörn Günther – Antiquariat, Hamburg) (formerly J. Paul Getty Museum, MS Ludwig I 3)
LXIII	Sotheby's, 1929 no. 388
LXIV	New Haven, Beinecke Rare Book and Manuscript Library, MS 699
LXV	Frankfurt, Stadt- und Universitätsbibliothek, Lat. qu. 64
LXVII	Vienna, Österreichische Nationalbibliothek, ser. n. 3599

LXIX	Sotheby's, 1929 no. 387
LXX	
LXXIII	
LXXIIIa	
LXXIV	Vienna, Österreichische Nationalbibliothek, ser. n. 3600
LXXVII	
LXXIX	Vienna, Österreichische Nationalbibliothek, ser. n. 39678 (Sotheby's, 16 June 1997, lot 6)
LXXXVI	Vienna, Österreichische Nationalbibliothek, ser. n. 3602
XCIII	Berlin, Staatsbibliothek, Theo. lat. qu. 140
XCIV	Baltimore, Walters Art Gallery, MS 29
XCV	Göttweig, Stiftsbibliothek, cod. 1112
XCVI	Vienna, Österreichische Nationalbibliothek, ser. n. 3604
C	Berlin, Staatsbibliothek, Theo. lat. qu. 915
CII	Vienna, Österreichische Nationalbibliothek, ser. n. 3605
CIII	
CIV	
CV	Vienna, Österreichische Nationalbibliothek, ser. n. 3606
CVI	Göttweig, Stiftsbibliothek, cod. 53b
CVII	Stuttgart, Württtembergische Landesbibliothek, Brev. 166
CVIII	Vienna, Österreichische Nationalbibliothek, ser. n. 3607
CIX	Vienna, Österreichische Nationalbibliothek, ser. n. 3608
CXIII	Vienna, Österreichische Nationalbibliothek, ser. n. 3610
CXIV	Sotheby's, 1929 no. 386
CXV	Oxford, Bodleian Library, R 820
CXIX	Vienna, Österreichische Nationalbibliothek, ser. n. 4837
CXXII	
CXXV	
CXXVII	
CXXXI	
CXXXIII	Vienna, Österreichische Nationalbibliothek, ser. n. 3612
CXXXVIII	
CXXXIX	
CXL	
CXLIII	Princeton University Library, MS 51
CLII	Vienna, Österreichische Nationalbibliothek, ser. n. 14000
CLVI	

Appendix 2 Dimensions of the Gottschalk Antiphonary

Folio	Dimensions	Writing space	Margins			
			upper	lower	inner	outer
11	319 × 210	240 × 170	27	44		41
12	317 × 214	237 × 165	**32**	42		40
21	305 × 217	236 × 165				
22	304 × 217	239 × 165				
32	**323** × 236	240 × 167	15	**70**	30	45
33	326 × 244	235 × 163				
34	334 × 242	240 × 162				
35	334 × 238	240 × 162				
36	326 × 237	235 × 163				
37	322 × 241	239 × 170	14	70	**31**	47
42	270 × **244**	237 × 163	13	13	30	47
43	289 × 225	232 × 163	31	26	24	39
45	294 × 205	235 × 165	20	39	9	31
46	288 × 215	235 × 153	26	27	22	40
47	271 × 168	238 × 138	15	29	30	
52	256 × 242	209 × 173		46	30	**49**
55	314 × 208	241 × 173	29			39
57	255 × 127	205 × 99		46	30	
61	313 × 157	237 × 124	27	52	30	
72	306 × 227	237 × 170	26	42	28	36
77	306 × 234	236 × 165	29	43	27	42
81	316 × 230	235 × 167	25	51	22	43
91	260 × 210	242 × 170	10	8	20	20
102	312 × 229	244 × 162	27	39	22	47
111	277 × 227	240 × 161	28	16	18	49
121	290 × 206	239 × 164	21	28	23	22
131	278 × 221	239 × 171	20	19	12	38

bold = largest dimensions

Original sewing holes

Folio	Sewing holes*					Distance between sewing holes			
	1	2	3	4	5	1/2	2/3	3/4	4/5
21	35	78	150	224	300	43	72	74	76
22	34	76	149	223	300	42	73	74	77
32/37	25	67	150	237	279	42	83	87	42
33/36	45	87	171	259	301	42	84	88	42
34/35	33	75	159	246	289	42	84	87	43
42/47	27	70	154	242		43	84	88	
52/57	30	113	201	242			83	88	41
61	36			270	292				22
72				255					
77	40		166	254				88	
91	23	60	133	204		37	73	71	
101	41	85	170	255		44	85	85	
II.36.1	41	85	169	256	300	44	84	87	44

*distance from the top of the folio to the sewing hole

Appendix 3 Collation of tonary-letters in other Lambach manuscripts against Omlin's data and the Gottschalk Antiphonary

Because these manuscripts are fragmentary, these data are difficult to interpret. For the Gottschalk Antiphonary, an ought symbol [Ø] indicates that the portion of the antiphonary which should include the antiphon is not extant.

[−] indicates that the antiphon in question is not found in the source.
[+] indicates that the antiphon is found in the source, but with no tonary-letter.
[?] indicates that the reading of the tonary-letter is uncertain.

| | | Omlin's manuscripts and data | | | | | | | | | |
| | | St Gall group | | | | | | Rheinau group | | |
Antiphon	GA	SG390a	SG390	SG414	SG413	SG388	SG389	Ein83	Zü28	Eng102
St Gall Breviary (BRBL MS 481.25 etc.)										
Mode 1										
Tonary-letter [a]										
Ad hanc vocem	Ø	a	a	a	a	a	a	a	a	a
Beatus calistus	Ø	a	a	a	a	a	a	a	a	—
Christi virgo nec	Ø	a	a	a	a	a	a	a	a	a
Tonary-letter [ab]										
Mel et lac ex	+	aq	aq	aq	aq	aq	aq	aq	aq	aq
Tonary-letter [ac]										
Beatus es et bene	Ø	wh	wh	wh	wh	wh	wh	wg	wg	wg
Mode 3										
Tonary-letter [id]										
Secus decursus	Ø	—	od	od	od	od	od	od	od	oc
Mode 4										
Tonary-letter [o]										
Iste est discipulus	+	not in Omlin								

Antiphon	GA	St Gall group						Rheinau group		
		SG390a	*SG390*	*SG414*	*SG413*	*SG388*	*SG389*	*Ein83*	*Zü28*	*Eng102*
Mode 6										
Tonary-letter [H]										
Predicantes preceptum	Ø	–	ag	ag	ag	ag	ag	i	i	i
Mode 7										
Tonary -letter [yb]										
Quomodo fiet istud	yc	–	yb	yb	yb	yg	yb	yc	yc	yc
Tonary-letter [yc]										
Christo quotidie	Ø	–	y	yh	yb	y	yb	yb	yc	yc
Dexteram meam et	+	–	yc	yc	yc	yc	yc	yd	yd	yd
Induit me dominus	+	–	yc	yc	yc	yc	yc	yd	yd	yd
Mode 8										
Tonary-letter [w]										
Discede a me pabulam	Ø	–	w	w	w	w	w	w	w	w
Istorum est enim	Ø	–	w	w	w	w	w	w	w	w
Nolite timere non	Ø	–	w	w	w	w	w	w	w	w
Nos famuli domini	Ø	–	w	w	w	w	w	w	w	w
Ut vidit beatus Seb[astianus]	Ø	–	w	w	+	w	w	w	w	w
Zoe uxor Nicostrati	Ø	–	w	w	w	w	w	w	w	w

**Lambach Directorium
(Lambach frag. 14, binding stays in
Cml XXII and Yale Law Library
MssJ H358 no. 1)**

Antiphon	GA	*SG390a*	*SG390*	*SG414*	*SG413*	*SG388*	*SG389*	*Ein83*	*Zü28*	*Eng102*
Mode 1										
Tonary-letter [a]										
Beatus Januarius	Ø	not in Omlin								
Benedictus es in templo	Ø	–	a	–	+	a	a	a	–	a
Cum beatus martyris	Ø	not in Omlin								
Dedit illi dominus	Ø	a	a	a	a	a	a	a	a	a
Ecce puer meus	+	a	a	a	a	a	a	a	a	a
Hec est domus	Ø	–	a	a	+	a	a	a	a	a
Hec est vera	Ø	not in Omlin								
In medio ecclesiae	+	ab	a	ab	a	ab	a	a	a	a
Lapides preciosi	Ø	ac	ac	a	+	ac	ac	a	a	a
Sanctificavit	Ø	ac	ac	ac	+	ac	ac	a	+	ag
Templum domini	Ø	–	a	a	+	a	a	a	a	a
Tonary-letter [ab]										
Domus mea domus	ab	ab	ab	ab	+	ab	ab	ab	ab	ab
Ecce ego mitto	+	ab	ab	ab	ab	–	ab	ab	ab	ab

Antiphon	GA	Omlin's manuscripts and data								
		St Gall group						Rheinau group		
		SG390a	SG390	SG414	SG413	SG388	SG389	Ein83	Zü28	Eng102
Tonary-letter [ag]										
Astiterunt justi ante	Ø	ag	ag	—	ag	ag	ag	ag	ag	ag
Iste sanctus	Ø	ag	ag	—	ag	ag	ag	ag	ag	ag
Tonary-letter [ap]										
Nisi tu domine	Ø	ap	aq	—	a	e	—	ap	—	ap
Mode 2										
Tonary-letter [e]										
Defuncto itaque papa	Ø	not in Omlin								
Spiritu sapientiae	+	e	e	e	e	e	e	e	e	e
Mode 3										
Tonary-letter [i]										
Corpus autem	Ø	i	i	—	+	i	i	i	i	i
Presta domine utque	Ø	not in Omlin								
Quem apicem atentis	Ø	not in Omlin								
Tollite portas	Ø	i	i	i	+	i	i	i	i	i
Vota mea d[omino]	Ø	i	i	—	—	i	—	id	i	—
Mode 4										
Tonary-letter [o]										
Erit mihi	Ø	o	o	o	+	o	o	o	o	o
Tonary-letter [oc]										
Isti sunt viri sancti	+	—	wd	—	—	wd	wd	—	—	wd
Letamus coeli et	Ø	not in Omlin								
Mane surgens Ja[cob]	Ø	—	oc	oc	oc	oc	oc	oc	oc	oc
Tandem electus domini	Ø	not in Omlin								
Tonary-letter [oh]										
In domum domini	Ø	—	a	—	—	w	—	op	—	oh
Mode 5										
Tonary-letter [vb]										
Rex omnis terrae	Ø	wh	wh	wh	wh	wh	wh	wb	wb	wb
Mode 6										
Tonary-letter [H]										
Aedificavit Moys[es]	Ø	H	H	H	+	H	H	H	H	H
Habuit vir dei	Ø	H	H	—	+	H	H	H	H	H

Collation of tonary-letters

Antiphon	GA	Omlin's manuscripts and data								
		St Gall group						Rheinau group		
		SG390a	*SG390*	*SG414*	*SG413*	*SG388*	*SG389*	*Ein83*	*Zü28*	*Eng102*
Notum fecit dominus	Ø	–	H	H	H	H	H	H	H	H
Sanctimonialis autem	H	–	H	H	H	H	H	H	–	H

Mode 7

Tonary-letter [yc]

Antiphon	GA	*SG390a*	*SG390*	*SG414*	*SG413*	*SG388*	*SG389*	*Ein83*	*Zü28*	*Eng102*
Benedicta gloria	Ø	–	y	yb	+	yb	y	yb	yc	yc
Cognoscentes [duo ex]	Ø	not in Omlin								
Cum evigilasset	Ø	not in Omlin								
Cum judex	Ø	not in Omlin								
Domum tuam	Ø	o	yb	o	+	yg	yb	yc	yc	yc
Huius ipse calve	Ø	–	yb	–	+	yb	yb	yc	yc	yc
In templo domini	Ø	not in Omlin								
Juravit dominus et	Ø	–	yb	yb	+	yb	yg	yc	yc	yc
Sanctus Januarius	Ø	not in Omlin								
Vidit Jacob	Ø	–	yb	yg	+	yb	yg	yc	yc	yc

Tonary-letter [yd]

Antiphon	GA	*SG390a*	*SG390*	*SG414*	*SG413*	*SG388*	*SG389*	*Ein83*	*Zü28*	*Eng102*
Cibavit illum dominus	+	–	yc	yc	yc	yg	yc	yd	yd	yd
Homo natus est	Ø	–	yc	yc	yb	yc	yd	yh	yh	yd
Justorum autem	Ø	–	yc	yd	yc	yg	–	yd	yd	yd
Non est hic	Ø	–	yc	yc	yc	yc	yc	yd	yd	yd

Tonary-letter [yg]

Antiphon	GA	*SG390a*	*SG390*	*SG414*	*SG413*	*SG388*	*SG389*	*Ein83*	*Zü28*	*Eng102*
Misit dominus manum [...et replevit]	Ø	–	yd	yd	yd	yd	yd	yg	yg	yg

Mode 8

Tonary-letter [w]

Antiphon	GA	*SG390a*	*SG390*	*SG414*	*SG413*	*SG388*	*SG389*	*Ein83*	*Zü28*	*Eng102*
In principio et ante	Ø	–	w	w	w	w	w	w	w	w
Non vos me elegi[stis]	Ø	w	w	w	w	w	–	w	w	w
Potens in terra	Ø	w	w	–	+	w	–	–	w	w
Qui habitat in		–	w	w	w	w	w	w	w	w
Zacheae festinans	Ø	w	wg	+	+	wg	wg	w	w	+

Tonary-letter [wb]

Antiphon	GA	*SG390a*	*SG390*	*SG414*	*SG413*	*SG388*	*SG389*	*Ein83*	*Zü28*	*Eng102*
Bene fundata est	Ø	–	wh	wh	+	wh	wh	wb	wd	wb
Collocet	Ø	–	wh	wh	+	wh	–	wg	wb	wb
Dominus in te[mplo]	Ø	–	wb	–	+	wb	wh	wb	wb	wb
Veritas de terra	Ø	wh	wh	wh	wh	wh	wh	wd	wb	wb

Tonary-letter [wd]

Antiphon	GA	*SG390a*	*SG390*	*SG414*	*SG413*	*SG388*	*SG389*	*Ein83*	*Zü28*	*Eng102*
Quoniam confortavit	Ø	–	+	–	–	+	–	wd	wd	–

		St Gall group						Rheinau group		
Antiphon	GA	SG390a	SG390	SG414	SG413	SG388	SG389	Ein83	Zü28	Eng102
Tonary-letter [wg]										
Erat autem	Ø	not in Omlin								
Euntes ibant	Ø	−	+	−	−	+	−	wg	−	−
Invitatories										
Mode 6										
Tonary-letter [H]										
Fidei sancte veni	Ø	not in Omlin								
Lambach 2 (*Lm*: BRBL MS 481.52, etc.)										
Mode 1										
Tonary-letter [a]										
Angelus domini nuntiavit	Ø	a	a	a	+	a	a	a	a	a
Antequem conveniret	Ø	a	a	a	a	a	a	a	a	a
Dominus veniet ocurrite	a	a	a	a	a	a	a	a	a	a
In tuo adventu	Ø	ad	ad	ac	ad	ad	ad	−	a	a
Tonary-letter [ag]										
Erunt prava indirecta	ag	ag	ag	ag	ag	ag	ag	ag	ag	ag
Mode 2										
Tonary-letter [e]										
De Syon exhibit	+	e	e	e	e	e	e	e	e	e
Omnipotens sermo tuus	e	eb	eb	eb	e	eb	eb	e	e	eb
Mode 4										
Tonary-letter [o]										
Ecce veniet propheta	Ø	o	o	o	o	o	o	o	o	o
Tuam domine excita	Ø	o	o	o	o	o	o	o	o	o
Tonary-letter [oc]										
Quaerite dominum dum	Ø	ob	ob	oc	ob	ob	ob	ob	oc	oc
Qui venturus est	Ø	−	oc	oc	−	oc	oc	oc	oc	oc
Mode 5										
Tonary-letter [v]										
Ecce dominus veniet	Ø	−	v	v	v	v	v	v	v	v
Mode 7										
Tonary-letter [y]*										
Si culmen veri	yd	−	yc	yc	+	yc	yc	yd	yd	yd
Si vere fratres	yd	−	yc	yc	yc	−	yc	yd	yd	yd

Collation of tonary-letters

| | | Omlin's manuscripts and data | | | | | | | | |
| | | St Gall group | | | | | | Rheinau group | | |
Antiphon	GA	SG390a	SG390	SG414	SG413	SG388	SG389	Ein83	Zü28	Eng102
Tonary-letter [yc]										
Hierusalem respice ad	Ø	y	y	y	?	yg	y	y	yc	yc
Tonary-letter [yd]										
Omnes sicientes venite	Ø	–	yc	yc	yg	yc	yc	yd	yd	yd
Mode 8										
Tonary-letter [w]*										
Multi enim sunt	Ø	–	wd	wd	+	wg	w	wd	wd	wd
Sic erunt novissimi	Ø	–	w	wd	+	w	w	w	w	w
Tonary-letter [w]										
Ne timeas Maria	Ø	–	w	w	w	w	wg	w	w	w
Spiritus sanctus in	+	–	w	w	w	w	–	w	w	w
Veni et libera	Ø	–	wg	wd	?	wg	wd	wd	wd	wd
Tonary-letter [wd]										
Missus est Gabriel	+	–	wg	wg	wd	wg	wg	wd	wd	wd
Tu es qui veturus [...an]	Ø	–	wg	wg	wd	wg	wg	wd	wd	wd
Tonary-letter [wg]										
Veniet fortior me	Ø	wh	wh	wg	wh	wh	wh	wg	wg	wg
Responsories		not in Omlin								
Mode 1										
Tonary-letter [a]										
Ostende nobis	+									
Mode 2										
Tonary-letter [e]										
Clama in fortitudine	H									
Mode 4										
Tonary-letter [oc]										
Tu exsurgens domine	+									

Appendix 4 Chants in the Gottschalk Antiphonary, sorted according to mode and differentia

In the lists which follow, each section begins with a group of texts whose tonary-letter was trimmed away or is otherwise illegible, and which have been given a modal assignment based on that used in *Eng102*, the Engelberg Directorium (or *Gr29/30*, if the chant is not included in Engelberg). Chants given in incipit form have been assigned the mode given when, and if, the chant appears in full elsewhere in the manuscript. Where possible, the mode of responsories has been deduced from the formulaic verse endings.

Mode	Differentia	Incipit	Feast	Office	Pos.	Folio
Invitatories						
2	e	Surgite vigilemus quia veniet	Hebd. 4 Adventus	M		11v
2	e	Tu es pastor ovium princeps	Cathedra S. Petri	M		43r
3	ik	Regem apostolorum dominum	Comm. Apostolorum	M		121v
4	*	Adoremus regem apostolorum	S. Joannis Evang.	M		21r
4	*	Regem apostolorum dominum	Comm. Apostolorum	M		121v
4	*	Regem virginum*	S. Scholasticae	M		43r
4	*	Ut Christo celebri jubilemus	S. Benedicti	M		45r
4	oc	Adoremus deum quia ipse fecit	Dom. Quinquagesimae	M		52r
4	oc	Venite exsultemus domino	Feria 2 per annum	M		36r
4	og	Ad dominum vigiles cuncti	S. Gregorii	M		43v
4	o-	Regem virginum*	Comm. Virginum	M		131r
6	*	Christus apparuit*	Dom. 1 p. Epiph.	M		34r
6	*	Surrexit dominus vere*	Fer. 3 p. Pascha	M		77v
6	H	Christus apparuit*	Epiphania,8	M		33r
6	H	In manu tua domine omnes	Feria 4 per annum	M		37v
6	H	Jubilemus deo salutari nostro	Feria 3 per annum	M		37r
6	H	Non sit vobis vanum surgere	Fer. 2 Hebd. 1 Quad.	M		55r
6	H	Prope est jam dominus venite	Hebd. 4 Adventus	M		12r
6	H	Surrexit dominus vere	Fer. 2 p. Pascha	M		72v
7	*	Alleluia ii	Dom. 2 p. Pascha	M		81v
7	*	Deus magnus dominus et rex	Dom. 3 Quadragesimae	M		57v
7	yc	Ave Maria gratia plena	Annuntiatio Mariae	M		46v
7	yc	Praeoccupemus faciem domini	Dom. per annum	M		34v
7	yc	Quoniam deus magnus dominus	Dom. 2 Quadragesimae	M		55v

Mode	*Differentia*	Incipit	Feast	Office	Pos.	Folio
Antiphons						
I	*	Ab insurgentibus in me libera	Fer. 6 in Parasceve	M	3.1	61v
I	*	Afra priscam Rahab	S. Afrae	M	2.3	91r
I	*	Ait latro ad latronem nos	Fer. 6 in Parasceve	L	3	61v
I	*	Ave Maria gratia*	Annuntiatio Mariae	L	2	47v
I	*	Beata Agatha*	S. Agathae	S		43r
I	*	Benedictus tam nomine quam	S. Benedicti	M	1.1	45r
I	*	Benedictus tam nomine*	S. Benedicti	P		46r
I	*	Canite tuba*	Dom. 4 Adventus	P		11v
I	*	Columna es immobilis Lucia	S. Luciae	L	B	121r
I	*	Continet in*	S. Joannis Evang.	L	R	22v
I	*	Cum autem esset*	S. Stephani	P		21r
I	*	Cum reverteretur Joannes ab	S. Joannis Evang.	M	2.6	22r
I	*	Dabit illi dominus*	Annuntiatio Mariae	M	3	47v
I	*	Dedit illi dominus claritatem	S. Joannis Evang.	M	1.6	21v
I	*	Dixit autem Maria ad angelum	Annuntiatio Mariae	M	2.3	47r
I	*	Dixit dominus matri suae	S. Joannis Evang.	M	2.4	22r
I	*	Dixit dominus matri suae*	S. Joannis Evang.	M	2.3	22r
I	*	Dulce lignum*	Exaltatio S. Crucis	M	3	102v
I	*	Dulce lignum*	Exaltatio S. Crucis	N		102v
I	*	Dum conturbata fuerit anima	Fer. 6 in Parasceve	L	4	61v
I	*	Ecce ego Joannes vidi ostium	Comm. Evangelistarum	V	M	121r
I	*	Ecce ego mitto vos sicut oves	Comm. Apostolorum	V	2M	121v
I	*	Ecce in nubibus caeli filius	Dom. 4 Adventus	M	3	11v
I	*	Ecce puer meus electus quem	S. Joannis Evang.	L	1	22v
I	*	Ecce veniet*	Dom. 4 Adventus	T		11v
I	*	Erunt prava*	Dom. 4 Adventus	S		11v
I	*	Exiit sermo inter fratres	S. Joannis Evang.	M	2.5	22r
I	*	Exiit sermo inter fratres*	S. Joannis Evang.	M	2.4	22r
I	*	Exiit sermo inter fratres*	S. Joannis Evang.	V2	1M	22v
I	*	Gregorius ortus*	S. Gregorii	P		45r
I	*	Hic non impar Eliseo ciet	S. Benedicti	M	2.3	45v
I	*	Hic non impar*	S. Benedicti	T		46r
I	*	In medio ecclesiae aperuit	S. Joannis Evang.	L	B	22v
I	*	In tabernaculis justorum*	Dom. Resurrectionis	V2	R	72r
I	*	In tua patientia possedisti	S. Luciae	V2	M	121r
I	*	Inclinavit dominus aurem suam	Feria 2 per annum	V2	2	37r
I	*	Inclinavit se Maria prospexit	In tempore Paschae	E	II	72v
I	*	Invicta Christi testis Afra	S. Afrae	L	1	91v
I	*	Ipsi soli*	Comm. Virginum	M	2.6	131v
I	*	Iste est Joannes cui Christus	S. Joannis Evang.	M	2.6	22r
I	*	Iste est Joannes cui*	S. Joannis Evang.	M	2.5	22r
I	*	Iste est Joannes qui supra	S. Joannis Evang.	M	3	22r
I	*	Jesus haec dicens*	Dom. Sexagesimae	T		52r
I	*	Jesus haec dicens*	Hebd. Sexagesimae	E	2	52r
I	*	Joannes apostolus et	S. Joannis Evang.	M	1.1	21r
I	*	Joannes apostolus*	S. Joannis Evang.	P		22v
I	*	Joannes autem apostolus virgo	S. Joannis Evang.	L	5	22v

Mode	*Differentia*	Incipit	Feast	Office	Pos.	Folio
I	*	Jucundus homo qui miseretur	S. Stephani	V2	I	21r
I	*	Lapidabant*	S. Stephani	T		21r
I	*	Magna semper et praeclara	S. Benedicti	V	M	45r
I	*	Medicinam carnalem*	S. Agathae	V2	2	43r
I	*	Mel et lac ex*	Comm. Virginum	M	2.4	131v
I	*	Posuerunt super*	Fer. 6 in Parasceve	L	B	61v
I	*	Qui me misit mecum est et non	Fer. 2 Hebd. 2 Quad.	V2	M	57r
I	*	Qui vicerit faciam illum	S. Joannis Evang.	M	1.1	21v
I	*	Quid retribuam domino pro	S. Stephani	V2	2	21r
I	*	Sunt de hic stantibus qui non	S. Joannis Evang.	L	4	22v
I	*	Tecum principium*	Epiphania	V2	I	33r
I	*	Thomas qui dicitur*	S. Thomae Apost.	L	B	121r
I	*	Tradetur enim gentibus ad	Fer. 4 Hebd. 2 Quad.	P		57r
I	*	Tu es discipulus meus in te	S. Joannis Evang.	M	2.1	22r
I	*	Tu es pastor ovium*	Cathedra S. Petri	T		43r
I	*	Unguentum effusum nomen tuum	Comm. Virginum	M	1.2	131r
I	*	Vado ad patrem meum et dicam	Sabb. Hebd. 2 Quad.	L	B	57r
I	?	Pulchra es et decora filia	Comm. Virginum	M	2.2	131v
I	a	Ave Maria gratia plena	Fer. 4 Hebd. 4 Adv.	T		12v
I	a	Biduo vivens pendebat in	S. Andreae	M	2.3	111r
I	a	Canite tuba in Sion quia	Dom. 4 Adventus	L	I	11v
I	a	Dabit illi dominus sedem	Fer. 4 Hebd. 4 Adv.	S		12v
I	a	Deficiente vino jussit Jesus	Dom. 2 p. Epiph.	V2	2M	36r
I	a	Descendentibus illis de monte	Sabb. Hebd. 1 Quad.	S		55v
I	a	Deus a Libano veniet et*	Fer. 6 Hebd. 4 Adv.	L	4	12v
I	a	Dixerunt pharisaei ad Joannem	Dom. 4 Adventus	L	B	11v
I	a	Dominus veniet occurrite illi	Dom. 4 Adventus	L	4	11v
I	a	Ecce veniet desideratus	Dom. 4 Adventus	L	2	11v
I	a	Euge serve*	S. Hilarii	L	R	34v
I	a	Gloriosa sanctissimi	S. Gregorii	V	M	43v
I	a	Ille me clarificabit quia de	Dom. 4 p. Pascha	E	7	81r
I	a	Joannes quidem clamabat	Epiphania,8	E	3	33v
I	a	Lex per Moysen data est gra-	Fer. 3 Hebd. 4 Adv.	L	5	12v
I	a	Magi videntes stellam obtule-	Epiphania	L	5	32v
I	a	Medicinam carnalem corpori	S. Agathae	L	2	42v
I	a	Mulier cum parit tristitiam	Dom. 3 p. Pascha	E	4	81r
I	a	Nemini dixeritis visionem	Dom. 2 Quadragesimae	V	M	55v
I	a	O caelestis norma vitae	S. Benedicti	V2	M	46v
I	a	Omnis qui petit accipit et	In Letaniis	E	2	81v
I	a	Per arma justitiae virtutis	Fer. 2 Hebd. 1 Quad.	N		55r
I	a	Post passionem domini factus	In tempore Paschae	E	I	72v
I	a	Praeclarum late tibi vir sine	S. Benedicti	V2	I	46r
I	a	Prophetae praedicaverunt	Fer. 4 Hebd. 4 Adv.	L	I	12v
I	a	Qui me sanum fecit ille mihi	Fer. 6 Hebd. 1 Quad.	T		55v
I	a	Qui verbum dei retinent corde	Hebd. Sexagesimae	E	8	52r
I	a	Quod uni ex minimis meis	Fer. 2 Hebd. 1 Quad.	V2	M	55r
I	a	Sacerdos et pontifex*	S. Hilarii	V	R	34r
I	a	Tribus miraculis ornatum diem	Epiphania	V2	M	33r

Chants in the Gottschalk Antiphonary, sorted according to mode and *differentia*

Mode	*Differentia*	Incipit	Feast	Office	Pos.	Folio
1	a	Tu es pastor ovium princeps	Cathedra S. Petri	V	M	43r
1	a	Vado ad eum qui misit me sed	Dom. 4 p. Pascha	E	1	81r
1	a	Visionem quam vidistis nemini	Sabb. Hebd. 1 Quad.	N		55v
1	a-	Egredietur virga de radice	Fer. 2 Hebd. 4 Adv.	L	B	12r
1	ab	Beata Agatha ingressa	S. Agathae	M	2.4	42r
1	ab	Dixit quidam ad Jesum ecce	Fer. 4 Hebd. 1 Quad.	V2	M	55r
1	ab	Domus mea domus orationis	Fer. 3 Hebd. 1 Quad.	L	B	55r
1	ab	Missus est angelus Gabriel a	Annuntiatio Mariae	M	1.1	46v
1	ab	Non in solo pane vivit homo	Dom. 1 Quadragesimae	V2	M	55r
1	ab	Nonne cor nostrum ardens erat	In tempore Paschae	E	9	72v
1	ab	Quia fecit mihi dominus magna	Feria 3 per annum	V2	M	37v
1	ab	Si quis fecerit voluntatem	Fer. 4 Hebd. 1 Quad.	T		55r
1	ab	Similabo eum*	S. Pauli Heremitae	V	M	34r
1	ab	Super omnia ligna cedrorum tu	Exaltatio S. Crucis	L	B	102v
1	ag	Erunt prava in directa et	Dom. 4 Adventus	L	3	11v
1	ag	Et incipiens a Moyse et	Fer. 2 p. Pascha	S		77r
1	ag	Gregorius ortus Romae ex	S. Gregorii	M	1.1	43v
1	ag	Qui diligitis dominum	Cathedra S. Petri	M	2.3	43r
1	ag	Tu solus peregrinus es et non	Fer. 2 p. Pascha	P		77r
1	ag	Venit lumen tuum Jerusalem et	Epiphania	L	2	32v
1	ah	Ecce quam bonum et quam	Feria 3 per annum	V2	4	37v
1	ah	Salutis nostrae auctorem magi	Epiphania	N		33r
1	ap	Apertis thesauris suis	Epiphania	L	3	32v
1	ap	De Sion veniet dominus	Fer. 5 Hebd. 4 Adv.	L	1	12v
1	ap	De Sion veniet qui regnaturus	Fer. 5 Hebd. 4 Adv.	L	2	12v
1	ap	Domine quinque talenta*	S. Pauli Heremitae	T		34r
1	ap	Secundum magnam misericordiam	Feria 3 per annum	L	1	37v
1	aq	Benedictum propheticis	S. Benedicti	M	3	46r
1	aq	Domine bonum est nos hic esse	Sabb. Hebd. 1 Quad.	P		55v
1	aq	Domine deus meus in te	Feria 3 per annum	P		37v
1	aq	Dominus defensor vitae meae	Dom. per annum	M	2.1	35r
1	aq	O crux admirabilis evacuatio	Exaltatio S. Crucis	L	3	102v
2	*	Ante luciferum*	Epiphania,8	L	1	33v
2	*	Christus resurgens ex mortuis	Dom. Resurrectionis	X	P	72r
2	*	Crucem sanctam subiit qui	Dom. Resurrectionis	L	R	72r
2	*	Crucem sanctam subiit*	In tempore Paschae	E	23	72v
2	*	Crucem sanctam subiit*	Dom. Resurrectionis	V2	R	72r
2	*	Cujus pulchritudinem*	Comm. Virginum	M	2.5	131v
2	*	Dum steteritis ante reges et	Comm. Apostolorum	V	3M	121v
2	*	Fulgebunt justi sicut*	Dom. Resurrectionis	L	R	72r
2	*	Gregorius vigiliis*	S. Gregorii	V2	1	45r
2	*	Hic ergo Romae traditus	S. Benedicti	M	1.2	45r
2	*	In omnem terram exivit sonus	Comm. Apostolorum	M	1.1	121v
2	*	In omnem terram*	Cathedra S. Petri	M	1.1	43r
2	*	In omnem terram*	Comm. Apostolorum	M	1.1	121v
2	*	In qua civitate cum puellis	S. Afrae	M	1.2	91r
2	*	Ista est speciosa*	S. Luciae	V2	3	121r
2	*	Isti sunt sancti qui pro*	Exaltatio S. Crucis	V	R	102v

151

Mode	*Differentia*	Incipit	Feast	Office	Pos.	Folio
2	*	Lineam sui generis*	S. Gregorii	T		45r
2	*	O*	Dom. 4 Adventus	V2	M	11v
2	*	O sapientia*	Antiphonae Majores	V	M	121r
2	*	O Thoma Didyme per Christum	S. Thomae Apost.	V	M	121r
2	*	Omnipotens sermo*	Dom. 4 Adventus	N		11v
2	*	Post abscessum angeli Maria	Annuntiatio Mariae	M	2.4	47r
2	*	Quando venit ergo sacri	Annuntiatio Mariae	L	1	47v
2	*	Spiritu sapientiae salutaris	S. Joannis Evang.	M	1.5	21v
2	*	Supra pectus domini Jesu	S. Joannis Evang.	M	1.2	21r
2	*	Supra pectus*	S. Joannis Evang.	T		22v
2	*	Unus est enim magister vester	Fer. 3 Hebd. 2 Quad.	L	B	57r
2	e	Alleluia iv (De Sion exibit)	Dom. per annum	M	3	35v
2	e	Alleluia vi (Ortus conclusus)	Dom. per annum	P		35v
2	e	Ante luciferum genitus et	Epiphania	L	1	32v
2	e	Armis praecinctus verae fidei	S. Benedicti	L	1	46r
2	e	Assumpsit Jesus discipulos	Sabb. Hebd. 1 Quad.	L	B	55v
2	e	Constantes estote videbitis	Fer. 6 Hebd. 4 Adv.	L	1	12v
2	e	Da nobis domine auxilium de	Feria 4 per annum	M	1.1	37v
2	e	Et coegerunt illum dicentes	Fer. 2 p. Pascha	N		77r
2	e	In columbae specie spiritus	Octava Epiphaniae	M	3	34v
2	e	Ingressus angelus ad Mariam	Annuntiatio Mariae	M	1.2	46v
2	e	Lineam sui generis factis et	S. Gregorii	M	1.2	43v
2	e	Membra specu claudis quo	S. Benedicti	V2	2	46r
2	e	Omnipotens sermo tuus domine	Dom. 4 Adventus	L	5	11v
2	e	Petite et dabitur vobis	In Letaniis	E	1	81v
2	e	Sana domine animam meam quia	Feria 2 per annum	M	2.3	36v
2	e	Spiritus domini super me	Fer. 4 Hebd. 4 Adv.	L	2	12v
2	e	Usque modo non petistis	Dom. 5 p. Pascha	E	1	81r
2	e-	Dicant nunc Judaei quomodo	Dom. Resurrectionis	X	01	72r
3	*	Adhaerebat moralibus*	S. Gregorii	S		45r
3	*	Cujus prostibulum cum Felice	S. Afrae	M	1.3	91r
3	*	Cum esset rex in accubitu suo	Comm. Virginum	M	2.1	131v
3	*	Fili tu semper mecum es et	Dom. 3 Quadragesimae	V	M	57v
3	*	Haec est generatio	Comm. Apostolorum	M	1.2	121v
3	*	Haec est quae*	Annuntiatio Mariae	M	2.1	47r
3	*	Hic est discipulus ille qui	S. Joannis Evang.	M	1.2	21r
3	*	Hic est discipulus meus sic	S. Joannis Evang.	L	2	22v
3	*	Lentis quidem*	S. Gregorii	V2	2	45r
3	*	Lignum vitae*	Exaltatio S. Crucis	T		102v
3	*	Mundum suis cum floribus	S. Benedicti	M	1.3	45r
3	*	Quaerentes eum tenere	Fer. 6 Hebd. 2 Quad.	V2	M	57r
3	*	Quasi unum de paradisi	S. Joannis Evang.	M	1.3	21r
3	*	Quasi unum*	S. Joannis Evang.	S		22v
3	*	Salva nos Christe*	Exaltatio S. Crucis	V2	2	102v
3	*	Sic eum volo manere donec	S. Joannis Evang.	M	1.3	21r
3	*	Spiritu sancto repleta	Annuntiatio Mariae	M	2.5	47r
3	*	Tollite jugum*	Cathedra S. Petri	M	2.2	43r
3	*	Veni electa*	S. Luciae	V2	2	121r

Mode	Differentia	Incipit	Feast	Office	Pos.	Folio
3	*	Verbum supernum a patre ante	Annuntiatio Mariae	L	2	47v
3	*	Vidi speciosam*	S. Luciae	V2	1	121r
3	?	Nigra sum sed formosa filia	Comm. Virginum	M	2.5	131v
3	i	Alleluia v (Inter natos mu-)	Dom. per annum	S		36r
3	i	Dominus legifer noster	Fer. 5 Hebd. 4 Adv.	L	5	12v
3	i	Justus cor suum*	S. Pauli Heremitae	L	B	34r
3	i	Laudate dominum omnes gentes	Feria 2 per annum	V2	3	37r
3	i	Nonne sic oportuit pati	Fer. 2 p. Pascha	T		77r
3	i	Quid est hoc quod dicit nobis	Dom. 3 p. Pascha	E	2	81r
3	i	Salva nos Christe salvator	Exaltatio S. Crucis	L	2	102v
3	i	Tu Bethleem terra Juda non	Fer. 3 Hebd. 4 Adv.	L	B	12v
3	ib	Cunctis diebus vitae nostrae	Feria 3 per annum	L	4	37v
3	id	Vivo ego dicit dominus nolo	Fer. 2 Hebd. 1 Quad.	P		55r
3	ik	Adhaerebat moralibus seniorum	S. Gregorii	M	1.3	43v
3	ik	Huic jubilate quo pater iste	S. Benedicti	L	2	46r
3	ik	Instar tu Christi patiens ad	S. Benedicti	V2	3	46v
3	ik	Maria turbatur in sermone	Annuntiatio Mariae	M	1.3	46v
3	ik	Quando nata est virgo	Nativitas Mariae	V2	M	102v
3	ik	Si veritatem dico quare non	Fer. 5 Hebd. 1 Quad.	V2	M	55v
4	*	Adest namque*	Nativitas Mariae	T		102v
4	*	Alieni insurrexerunt in me et	Fer. 6 in Parasceve	M	2.3	61r
4	*	Annuntiate populis et dicite	Fer. 4 Hebd. 4 Adv.	L	3	12v
4	*	Ante torum hujus virginis	Comm. Virginum	M	1.1	131r
4	*	Anxiatus est in me spiritus	Fer. 6 in Parasceve	L	2	61v
4	*	Beata quae credidit quoniam	Annuntiatio Mariae	M	2.6	47r
4	*	Beatus auctor saeculi servile	Annuntiatio Mariae	L	3	47v
4	*	Benedicta tu in mulieribus*	Annuntiatio Mariae	M	1.1	46v
4	*	Bethleem non*	Dom. 4 Adventus	M	2	11r
4	*	Caelesti cinctus*	S. Gregorii	V2	3	45r
4	*	Confundantur et revereantur	Fer. 6 in Parasceve	M	2.2	61r
4	*	Cum psalmis deo et hymnis	S. Afrae	M	1.4	91r
4	*	Custodiebant*	Cathedra S. Petri	M	2.5	43r
4	*	Domine suscipe me ut cum	S. Joannis Evang.	M	2.3	21v
4	*	Domine suscipe me*	S. Joannis Evang.	V	1M	21r
4	*	Domine suscipe*	S. Joannis Evang.	V2	2M	22v
4	*	Ecce rex veniet dominus	Fer. 6 Hebd. 4 Adv.	L	2	12v
4	*	Exiit qui seminat seminare	Dom. Sexagesimae	P		52r
4	*	Exiit qui seminat*	Hebd. Sexagesimae	E	1	52r
4	*	Gregorius ut creditur*	S. Gregorii	N		45r
4	*	Imbuta verae fidei rudimentis	S. Afrae	M	2.4	91r
4	*	In ferventis olei dolium	S. Joannis Evang.	M	1.4	21r
4	*	In ferventis olei*	S. Joannis Evang.	N		22v
4	*	Intuens in caelum*	S. Stephani	V2	1M	21r
4	*	Isti sunt viri sancti quos	Comm. Apostolorum	V	1M	121r
4	*	Laeva ejus sub capite meo et	Comm. Virginum	M	1.6	131r
4	*	Maria et flumina*	Epiphania,8	L	4	33v
4	*	Maurus verbo currens patris	S. Benedicti	M	2.4	45v
4	*	Mentem sanctam*	S. Agathae	N		43r

Mode	*Differentia*	Incipit	Feast	Office	Pos.	Folio
4	*	O Gregori dulcissime sancti	S. Gregorii	V2	M	45r
4	*	O regem caeli*	S. Joannis Evang.	V2	R	22v
4	*	Omnes gentes*	Epiphania,8	M	2.1	33r
4	*	Omnis terra*	Epiphania,8	M	1.5	33r
4	*	Ornatam*	S. Luciae	V2	4	121r
4	*	Petre amas me*	Cathedra S. Petri	L	1	43r
4	*	Petre amas*	Cathedra S. Petri	P		43r
4	*	Rectos decet*	Fer. 2 Hebd. 1 Quad.	M	1.1	55r
4	*	Sanctum Romanus habitum dans	S. Benedicti	M	1.4	45r
4	*	Simile est regnum caelorum	Comm. Virginum	V	M	131r
4	*	Simon Bar Jona*	Cathedra S. Petri	V2	M	43v
4	*	Tria sunt munera*	Epiphania	T		33r
4	*	Vidimus stellam*	Epiphania,8	L	R	34r
4	o	Commendemus nosmetipsos in	Fer. 2 Hebd. 1 Quad.	S		55r
4	o	Da mercedem domine	Fer. 3 Hebd. 4 Adv.	L	4	12v
4	o	Ecce veniet dominus ut sedeat	Fer. 4 Hebd. 4 Adv.	L	4	12v
4	o	Faciamus hic tria tabernacula	Sabb. Hebd. 1 Quad.	T		55v
4	o	Intuemini quantus sit	Fer. 5 Hebd. 4 Adv.	L	1B	12v
4	o	Propter Sion non tacebo donec	Fer. 4 Hebd. 4 Adv.	L	5	12v
4	o	Sicut fuit Jonas in ventre	Fer. 4 Hebd. 1 Quad.	P		55r
4	o	Veni domine et noli tardare	Fer. 6 Hebd. 4 Adv.	L	3	12v
4	o-	Ecce veniet dominus princeps	Fer. 2 Hebd. 4 Adv.	L	1	12r
4	o-	Egredietur dominus de loco	Fer. 2 Hebd. 4 Adv.	L	5	12r
4	o-	Magnus dominus et laudabilis	Feria 3 per annum	M	1.3	37r
4	o-	Surrexit enim sicut dixit	Dom. Resurrectionis	V2	M	72r
4	oc	Alleluia viii (Praebe fili)	Dom. per annum	T		36r
4	oc	Alleluia viii (Surrexit)	Fer. 2 p. Pascha	V2	p	77v
4	oc	Angelus domini descendebat de	Fer. 6 Hebd. 1 Quad.	L	B	55v
4	oc	Clamavi et exaudivit me	Feria 3 per annum	T		37v
4	oc	Dominus regit me et nihil	Dom. per annum	M	1.3	34v
4	oc	Emitte agnum domine	Fer. 3 Hebd. 4 Adv.	L	2	12v
4	oc	Et omnis mansuetudinis ejus	Feria 3 per annum	V2	3	37v
4	oc	Exivi a patre et veni in	Dom. 5 p. Pascha	E	3	81r
4	oc	Gregorius ut creditur	S. Gregorii	M	1.4	43v
4	oc	Hic probris actus tumidisque	S. Benedicti	V2	4	46v
4	oc	Ingressus angelus ad Mariam	Annuntiatio Mariae	V	p	46v
4	oc	Ite nuntiate fratribus meis	In tempore Paschae	E	13	72v
4	oc	Iterum autem videbo vos et	Dom. 3 p. Pascha	E	8	81r
4	oc	Laudabo deum meum in vita mea	Dom. per annum	V	2	34v
4	oc	Maria et flumina benedicite	Epiphania	L	4	32v
4	oc	Mentem sanctam spontaneam	S. Agathae	M	3	42v
4	oc	Oculi mei semper ad dominum	Dom. per annum	M	1.5	34v
4	oc	Parce tuis ovibus quos raptor	Cathedra S. Petri	V2	01	43v
4	oc	Quemquam non laesit post te	S. Benedicti	L	3	46r
4	oc	Respondens angelus dixit ad	Annuntiatio Mariae	M	1.4	46v
4	oc	Rorate caeli desuper et nubes	Fer. 3 Hebd. 4 Adv.	L	1	12v
4	oc	Sanctifica nos domine	Exaltatio S. Crucis	V	M	102v
4	oc	Simon Bar Jona tu vocaberis	Cathedra S. Petri	V2	M	43v

Mode	Differentia	Incipit	Feast	Office	Pos.	Folio
4	oc	Speret Israel in domino	Feria 3 per annum	V2	2	37v
4	oc	Stella nobis visa est rex	Epiphania,8	M	1.1	33r
4	oc	Stella nobis visa*	Dom. 1 p. Epiph.	M	1.1	34r
4	oc	Surrexit dominus de sepulcro	In tempore Paschae	E	19	72v
4	oc	Tria sunt munera quae	Epiphania	M	3	32r
4	oc	Ut cognoscamus domine in	Fer. 3 Hebd. 4 Adv.	L	3	12v
4	oc	Vide humilitatem meam domine	Feria 2 per annum	N		37r
4	oc	Vidimus stellam ejus in	Epiphania	S		33r
4	oc	Vigilate animo in proximo est	Fer. 5 Hebd. 4 Adv.	L	2B	12v
4	oc	Vox de caelis sonuit et vox	Epiphania,8	E	1	33v
4	od	Alleluia vii (Dico vobis)	Dom. per annum	L	p	35v
4	od	Alleluia vii (Innuebant pa-)	Dom. per annum	N		36r
4	og	Cum factus esset Jesus	Dom. 1 p. Epiph.	L	B	34r
4	og	Hodie nata est beata virgo	Nativitas Mariae	P		102v
4	og	Quod autem cecidit in terram	Dom. Quinquagesimae	V	M	52r
4	oh	Adjutor in tribulationibus	Feria 3 per annum	M	1.1	37r
4	oh	Custodit dominus omnes	Dom. per annum	V	1	34v
4	oh	Expugna impugnantes me	Feria 2 per annum	M	1.3	36r
4	oh	Fidelia omnia mandata ejus	Dom. per annum	V2	2	36r
4	oh	In mandatis ejus volet nimis	Dom. per annum	V2	3	36r
4	oh	Nisi diligenter perfeceris	S. Agathae	M	2.1	42r
4	oh	Rectos decet collaudatio	Feria 2 per annum	M	1.1	36r
4	oh	Vade jam et noli peccare ne	Fer. 6 Hebd. 1 Quad.	V2	M	55v
4	-c	Surrexit Christus et illuxit	In tempore Paschae	E	21	72v
5	*	Alleluia quem quaeris*	In tempore Paschae	E	16	72v
5	*	Alleluia sancta dei genetrix	Dom. Resurrectionis	L	R	72r
5	*	Audiens vero beatum virum	S. Afrae	M	1.5	91r
5	*	Bissenos nummos*	S. Gregorii	V2	4	45r
5	*	Clausa parentis viscera*	Annuntiatio Mariae	L	4	47v
5	*	Favent cuncta Benedicto vas	S. Benedicti	M	2.5	45v
5	*	Favent cuncta*	S. Benedicti	S		46r
5	*	In specu sub quo latitat dei	S. Benedicti	M	1.5	45r
5	*	Propter insuperabilem	S. Joannis Evang.	M	1.5	21r
5	*	Quae beatum virum noctu ad se	S. Afrae	M	2.5	91r
5	v	Alleluia ii (Ut non delin-)	Feria 2 per annum	M	2.1	36v
5	v	Alleluia noli flere Maria	In tempore Paschae	E	17	72v
5	v	Alleluia resurrexit dominus	In tempore Paschae	E	15	72v
5	v	Caeli aperti sunt super eum	Epiphania,8	E	2	33v
5	v	Facti sumus sicut consolati	Feria 3 per annum	N		37v
5	v	Laus puerilis hunc benedicit	S. Benedicti	L	4	46r
5	v	Studiis liberalibus nulli	S. Gregorii	M	1.5	43v
5	v	Ut non delinquam in lingua	Feria 2 per annum	M	2.1	36v
5	v-	Ecce jam veniet plenitudo	Fer. 2 Hebd. 4 Adv.	L	3	12r
5	v-	Haurietis aquas in gaudio de	Fer. 2 Hebd. 4 Adv.	L	4	12r
5	vb	Adhuc multa habeo vobis	Dom. 4 p. Pascha	E	4	81r
5	vb	Ecce concipies et paries	Annuntiatio Mariae	M	1.5	46v
5	vb	Paganorum multitudo fugiens	S. Agathae	L	B	43r
6	*	Adorate dominum alleluia in	Epiphania	M	2.3	32r

Mode	*Differentia*	Incipit	Feast	Office	Pos.	Folio
6	*	Athleta dei gravibus poenis	S. Benedicti	M	1.6	45r
6	*	Exaltabuntur cornua*	Cathedra S. Petri	M	2.1	43r
6	*	Miserere mei deus*	Fer. 2 Hebd. 1 Quad.	L	1	55r
6	*	Modicum et non videbitis me	Dom. 3 p. Pascha	E	1	81r
6	*	Nesciens mater*	S. Stephani	V2	R	21r
6	*	O quanta plenus*	S. Benedicti	N		46r
6	*	O quanta plenus gratia qui	S. Benedicti	M	2.6	45v
6	*	Occurrit beato Joanni ab	S. Joannis Evang.	M	1.6	21r
6	*	Quam vir sanctus verbis	S. Afrae	M	1.6	91r
6	*	Regali ex progenie*	Nativitas Mariae	S		102v
6	*	Sancta et immaculata*	S. Stephani	L	R	21r
6	*	Virginum tria milia Romae	S. Gregorii	L	5	45r
6	H	Adorate dominum alleluia om-	Epiphania	M	2.4	32r
6	H	Alleluia vi (Crucifixus)	Dom. Resurrectionis	V2	p	72r
6	H	Alleluia vi (In domino)	Dom. per annum	L	5	35v
6	H	Benedicite gentes deo nostro	Feria 4 per annum	M	1.3	37v
6	H	Benedictus deus Israel	Feria 2 per annum	L	B	36v
6	H	Benedixit filiis tuis in te	Dom. per annum	V	4	34v
6	H	Cognoverunt discipuli dominum	In tempore Paschae	E	10	72v
6	H	Crucifixus resurrexit	In tempore Paschae	E	25	72v
6	H	Crucifixus surrexit a mortuis	In tempore Paschae	E	22	72v
6	H	Dabit illi deus sedem David	Annuntiatio Mariae	M	1.6	46v
6	H	Eructavit cor meum verbum	Feria 2 per annum	M	2.5	36v
6	H	Exivi a patre meo et veni in	Dom. 5 p. Pascha	E	4	81r
6	H	Hic ab adolescentia divina	S. Gregorii	M	1.6	43v
6	H	In excelsis laudate deum	Feria 2 per annum	L	5	36v
6	H	Intende in me et exaudi me	Feria 3 per annum	M	2.4	37r
6	H	Miserere mei deus	Feria 2 per annum	L	1	36v
6	H	Ne in ira tua arguas me	Feria 2 per annum	M	1.6	36r
6	H	Notum fecit dominus alleluia	Epiphania	M	2.5	32r
6	H	Omnes angeli ejus laudate	Feria 3 per annum	L	5	37v
6	H	Puer Jesus proficiebat aetate	Epiphania,8	E	3	34r
6	H	Puer Jesus proficiebat*	Dom. 2 p. Epiph.	V	M	34v
6	H	Regali ex progenie Maria	Nativitas Mariae	L	3	102r
6	H	Revela domino viam tuam	Feria 2 per annum	M	1.4	36r
6	H	Salutare vultus mei deus meus	Feria 3 per annum	L	2	37v
6	H	Sanctimonialis autem femina	S. Scholasticae	V	M	43r
6	H	Tristitia vestra alleluia	Dom. 3 p. Pascha	E	6	81r
6	H	Tympana laeta chori mens	S. Benedicti	L	5	46r
6	H	Vobis datum est nosse	Dom. Sexagesimae	V2	M	52r
7	*	Adjuvabit eam*	Comm. Virginum	M	1.5	131r
7	*	Afferte domino*	Dom. 1 p. Epiph.	M	2.1	34r
7	*	Agatha laetissima*	S. Agathae	T		43r
7	*	Agatha sancta dixit*	S. Agathae	P		43r
7	*	Apparuit caro suo Joanni	S. Joannis Evang.	M	2.1	21v
7	*	Auditis praesul sanctus	S. Afrae	M	2.6	91r
7	*	Beatissimae virginis*	Nativitas Mariae	N		102v
7	*	Christi fidelis famulus	S. Gregorii	L	B	45r

Mode	Differentia	Incipit	Feast	Office	Pos.	Folio
7	*	Christus circumdedit me*	Comm. Virginum	M	2.2	131v
7	*	Cibavit eum dominus pane	S. Joannis Evang.	M	1.4	21v
7	*	Clamaverunt justi et dominus	Comm. Apostolorum	M	1.2	121v
7	*	Clamaverunt justi*	Comm. Apostolorum	M	1.4	121v
7	*	Confortatus*	Cathedra S. Petri	V2	4	43v
7	*	Constitues eos principes	Comm. Apostolorum	M	1.3	121v
7	*	Constitues eos principes*	Comm. Apostolorum	M	1.5	121v
7	*	Dextram meam*	Comm. Virginum	M	1.1	131r
7	*	Dixit autem Maria ad angelum	Annuntiatio Mariae	M	2.1	47r
7	*	Dixit dominus*	Dom. 1 Quadragesimae	V2	1	55r
7	*	Domine libera animam meam a	S. Stephani	V2	3	21r
7	*	Ecce ascendimus Jerusalem et	Fer. 4 Hebd. 2 Quad.	L	B	57r
7	*	Fili tu semper mecum fuisti	Sabb. Hebd. 2 Quad.	T		57r
7	*	Gratias tibi ago*	S. Agathae	V2	3	43r
7	*	Hosanna filio David	Fer. 3 Hebd. 1 Quad.	P		55r
7	*	Induit me*	Comm. Virginum	M	1.3	131r
7	*	Ipsi sum desponsata*	Comm. Virginum	M	2.1	131v
7	*	Jam latius innotuit quasi	S. Benedicti	M	2.1	45v
7	*	Jugum enim*	Cathedra S. Petri	M	2.4	43r
7	*	Juravit dominus et*	S. Joannis Evang.	V2	1	22v
7	*	Juravit dominus*	Cathedra S. Petri	V2	1	43v
7	*	Lucia virgo quid a me petis	S. Luciae	L	2	121r
7	*	Lucia virgo*	S. Luciae	T		121r
7	*	Misit dominus manum suam et	S. Joannis Evang.	L	3	22v
7	*	Nativitas est hodie*	Nativitas Mariae	V2	1	102v
7	*	Nos autem gloriari*	Exaltatio S. Crucis	P		102v
7	*	O magnum pietatis*	Exaltatio S. Crucis	V2	1	102v
7	*	O quam pulchra es*	Comm. Virginum	M	1.6	131r
7	*	Orante sancta Lucia apparuit	S. Luciae	L	1	121r
7	*	Orante sancta Lucia*	S. Luciae	P		121r
7	*	Pastores loquebantur*	S. Joannis Evang.	L	R	22v
7	*	Posuit signum*	Comm. Virginum	M	1.2	131r
7	*	Proprio filio suo non	Fer. 6 in Parasceve	L	1	61v
7	*	Qui me dignatus*	S. Agathae	V2	4	43r
7	*	Quis es tu qui venisti*	S. Agathae	V2	1	43r
7	*	Salvator mundi salva*	Exaltatio S. Crucis	S		102v
7	*	Sancto pontifice in divinis	S. Afrae	M	2.1	91r
7	*	Scio quod Jesum quaeritis*	Fer. 2 p. Pascha	M	2	77r
7	*	Sedere autem mecum non est	Fer. 4 Hebd. 2 Quad.	V2	M	57r
7	*	Si culmen*	Hebd. Sexagesimae	E	6	52r
7	*	Si vere fratres*	Hebd. Sexagesimae	E	5	52r
7	*	Specie tua*	Comm. Virginum	M	1.4	131r
7	*	Tanto pondere eam fixit	S. Luciae	L	5	121r
7	*	Tanto pondere*	S. Luciae	N		121r
7	*	Tu es Petrus et*	Cathedra S. Petri	S		43r
7	*	Veterem hominem*	Octava Epiphaniae	P		34v
7	*	Videntes stellam*	Epiphania,8	V2	R	34r
7	?	Surge aquilo et veni auster	Comm. Virginum	M	2.4	131v

Mode	*Differentia*	Incipit	Feast	Office	Pos.	Folio
7	y-	Specie tua et pulchritudine	Comm. Virginum	M	1.4	131r
7	y-	O quam pulchra est casta	Comm. Virginum	M	1.3	131r
7	y-	Adjuvabit eam deus vultu suo	Comm. Virginum	M	1.5	131r
7	yb	Aqua comburit peccatum hodie	Epiphania,8	E	4	33v
7	yb	Baptista contremuit et non	Octava Epiphaniae	L	3	34v
7	yb	Caput draconis salvator	Octava Epiphaniae	L	4	34v
7	yb	Domine non habeo hominem ut	Fer. 6 Hebd. 1 Quad.	P		55v
7	yb	Magnum mysterium declaratur	Octava Epiphaniae	L	5	34v
7	yb	Pater de caelis filium	Epiphania,8	E	5	33v
7	yb	Praecursor Joannes exsultat	Octava Epiphaniae	L	B	34v
7	yb	Scio quod Jesum quaeritis	In tempore Paschae	E	4	72v
7	yb	Te qui in spiritu et igne	Octava Epiphaniae	L	2	34v
7	yb	Veterem hominem renovans	Octava Epiphaniae	L	1	34v
7	yc	Baptizatur Christus et	Epiphania,8	E	6	33v
7	yc	Beata Agatha ingressa	S. Agathae	V2	M	43r
7	yc	Beatissimae virginis Mariae	Nativitas Mariae	M	3	102r
7	yc	Benedictus es domine qui	S. Benedicti	L	B	46r
7	yc	Cito euntes dicite discipulis	In tempore Paschae	E	6	72v
7	yc	Concede nobis hominem justum	S. Andreae	M	3	111v
7	yc	Cum autem venerit ille	Dom. 4 p. Pascha	E	5	81r
7	yc	Cum venerit filius hominis in	Fer. 2 Hebd. 1 Quad.	L	B	55r
7	yc	Ego veritatem dico vobis	Dom. 4 p. Pascha	E	2	81r
7	yc	Erexit dominus nobis cornu	Feria 3 per annum	L	B	37v
7	yc	In Galilaea Jesum videbitis	In tempore Paschae	E	14	72v
7	yc	Qui persequebatur justum	S. Andreae	L	4	111v
7	yc	Quid mihi et tibi est mulier	Dom. 2 p. Epiph.	V2	1M	36r
7	yc	Quomodo fiet istud angele dei	Fer. 4 Hebd. 4 Adv.	L	B	12v
7	yc	Servite domino in timore et	Feria 2 per annum	P		36v
7	yc	Videntes stellam magi gavisi	Epiphania,8	M	1.4	33r
7	yd	Cum jucunditate nativitatem	Nativitas Mariae	L	5	102v
7	yd	Dignum sibi dominus	S. Andreae	M	2.5	111r
7	yd	Ego Christum confiteor labiis	S. Agathae	M	2.3	42r
7	yd	Et ecce terraemotus*	Fer. 3 p. Pascha	L		77v
7	yd	Gratias tibi ago domine quia	S. Agathae	L	3	42r
7	yd	Justum deduxit*	S. Pauli Heremitae	P		34r
7	yd	Mens mea solidata est et a	S. Agathae	M	2.2	42r
7	yd	Nativitas est hodie sanctae	Nativitas Mariae	L	2	102r
7	yd	Nos autem gloriari oportet in	Exaltatio S. Crucis	L	4	102v
7	yd	O magnum pietatis opus mors	Exaltatio S. Crucis	L	1	102v
7	yd	Propter fidem castitatis	S. Agathae	M	2.6	42r
7	yd	Quis es tu qui venisti ad me	S. Agathae	L	1	42v
7	yd	Salve crux pretiosa suscipe	S. Andreae	L	1	111v
7	yd	Si culmen veri honoris	Dom. Sexagesimae	N		52r
7	yd	Si gloriam dignitatum	Hebd. Sexagesimae	E	7	52r
7	yd	Si vere fratres divites esse	Dom. Sexagesimae	S		52r
7	yd	Sit nomen domini benedictum	Dom. per annum	V2	4	36r
7	yd	Solve jubente*	Cathedra S. Petri	N		43v
7	yd	Vidisti domine agonem meum	S. Agathae	M	2.5	42r

Mode	*Differentia*	Incipit	Feast	Office	Pos.	Folio
7	yg	Dixit dominus domino meo sede	Dom. per annum	V2	I	36r
7	yg	Stella ista sicut flamma	Epiphania,8	M	1.3	33r
7	yh	Qui me dignatus est ab omni	S. Agathae	L	5	42v
8	*	Advenerunt nobis*	Dom. 2 Quadragesimae	M	I	55v
8	*	Annuntiaverunt opera dei et	Comm. Apostolorum	M	1.6	121v
8	*	Astiterunt reges terrae et	Fer. 6 in Parasceve	M	1.1	61r
8	*	Beatus venter*	S. Joannis Evang.	V2	R	22v
8	*	Benedico te pater domini mei	S. Luciae	L	4	121r
8	*	Captabant in animam justi et	Fer. 6 in Parasceve	M	3.3	61v
8	*	Collocet eum*	Cathedra S. Petri	V2	3	43v
8	*	Cumque dulcem sanae doctrinae	S. Afrae	M	2.2	91r
8	*	Dedisti hereditatem	Comm. Apostolorum	M	1.5	121v
8	*	Diviserunt sibi vestimenta	Fer. 6 in Parasceve	M	1.2	61r
8	*	Dixit autem pater ad servos	Sabb. Hebd. 2 Quad.	P		57r
8	*	Domine in virtute*	Dom. Quinquagesimae	M	1.1	52r
8	*	Ecce advenit*	S. Stephani	L	R	21r
8	*	Ecce ancilla domini fiat*	Annuntiatio Mariae	L	5	47v
8	*	Ejus ergo sub tramite multi	S. Benedicti	M	2.2	45v
8	*	Expandens manus suas ad deum	S. Joannis Evang.	M	2.2	21v
8	*	Exsultate justi in domino	Comm. Apostolorum	M	1.3	121v
8	*	Fili recordare*	Fer. 5 Hebd. 2 Quad.	E	5	57r
8	*	Gratias tibi domine Jesu	S. Afrae	M	3	91v
8	*	Ideoque et quod nascetur ex	Annuntiatio Mariae	M	2.2	47r
8	*	Insurrexerunt in me testes	Fer. 6 in Parasceve	M	1.3	61r
8	*	Jesum qui crucifixus est	In tempore Paschae	E	5	72v
8	*	Longe fecisti notos meos a me	Fer. 6 in Parasceve	M	3.2	61v
8	*	Malos male perdet et vineam	Fer. 6 Hebd. 2 Quad.	P		57r
8	*	Malos male perdet et vineam	Fer. 6 Hebd. 2 Quad.	L	B	57r
8	*	Manete*	Cathedra S. Petri	M	2.6	43r
8	*	Memento mei domine deus dum	Fer. 6 in Parasceve	L	5	61v
8	*	Missus est Gabriel*	Fer. 4 Hebd. 4 Adv.	P		12v
8	*	Missus est Gabriel*	Annuntiatio Mariae	L	I	47v
8	*	Nativitas gloriosae*	Nativitas Mariae	P		102v
8	*	Ne timeas Maria invenisti*	Annuntiatio Mariae	L	4	47v
8	*	Nolite expavescere*	In tempore Paschae	E	3	72v
8	*	Nolite expavescere*	Fer. 2 p. Pascha	M	I	72v
8	*	Nolite timere quinta*	S. Thomae Apost.	L	R	121r
8	*	Patefactae sunt januae caeli	S. Stephani	L	B	21r
8	*	Pater Abraham*	Fer. 5 Hebd. 2 Quad.	E	4	57r
8	*	Per te Lucia virgo civitas	S. Luciae	L	3	121r
8	*	Per te Lucia virgo*	S. Luciae	S		121r
8	*	Ponam te signaculum dicit	S. Joannis Evang.	M	2.2	22r
8	*	Potens in terra*	Cathedra S. Petri	V2	2	43v
8	*	Principes populorum	Comm. Apostolorum	M	1.4	121v
8	*	Principes populorum*	Comm. Apostolorum	M	1.6	121v
8	*	Qui major est vestrum erit	Fer. 3 Hebd. 2 Quad.	V2	M	57r
8	*	Quia vidisti me*	S. Thomae Apost.	V2	M	121r
8	*	Sepelierunt*	S. Stephani	N		21r

Mode	*Differentia*	Incipit	Feast	Office	Pos.	Folio
8	*	Spiritus sanctus*	Annuntiatio Mariae	L	3	47v
8	*	Stephanus autem*	S. Stephani	V2	2M	21r
8	*	Stephanus vidit*	S. Joannis Evang.	L	R	22v
8	*	Stephanus vidit*	S. Stephani	S		21r
8	*	Surgens Jesus*	In tempore Paschae	E	2	72v
8	*	Sustinuit anima mea in verbo	S. Stephani	V2	4	21r
8	*	Valde honorandus est beatus	S. Joannis Evang.	V	2M	21r
8	*	Veni sponsa*	S. Scholasticae	M	3	43r
8	*	Verbum caro*	S. Stephani	V2	R	21r
8	*	Vim faciebant qui quaerebant	Fer. 6 in Parasceve	M	2.1	61r
8	?	Jam hiems transiit imber	Comm. Virginum	M	2.3	131v
8	w	Ab oriente venerunt magi in	Dom. 1 p. Epiph.	V	M	34r
8	w	Adjuva me et salvus ero	Feria 2 per annum	T		37r
8	w	Advenerunt nobis dies	Fer. 2 Hebd. 1 Quad.	T		55r
8	w	Amen amen dico vobis quia	Dom. 3 p. Pascha	E	3	81r
8	w	Andreas Christi famulus	S. Andreae	M	2.4	111r
8	w	Angelus autem domini*	Fer. 2 p. Pascha	L		77r
8	w	Avertit dominus captivitatem	Feria 3 per annum	M	2.2	37r
8	w	Baptizat miles regem servus	Epiphania,8	E	8	33v
8	w	Beatus Andreas orabat dicens	S. Andreae	L	3	111v
8	w	Benedico te pater domini mei	S. Agathae	L	4	42v
8	w	Christo datus est principatus	Octava Epiphaniae	V2	M	34v
8	w	Conversus est furor tuus	Feria 2 per annum	L	4	36v
8	w	Convertere domine aliquantu-	Fer. 5 Hebd. 4 Adv.	L	3	12v
8	w	Corde et animo Christo	Nativitas Mariae	L	4	102r
8	w	Crux benedicta nitet dominus	Exaltatio S. Crucis	L	5	102v
8	w	Dilexit Andream dominus in	S. Andreae	M	2.6	111r
8	w	Dum venerit paraclitus spiri-	Dom. 4 p. Pascha	E	3	81r
8	w	Ecce deus meus et honorabo	Fer. 5 Hebd. 4 Adv.	L	4	12v
8	w	Ego sum alpha et o. primus et	In tempore Paschae	E	18	72v
8	w	Et recordatae sunt verborum	In tempore Paschae	E	7	72v
8	w	Fontes aquarum sanctificati	Octava Epiphaniae	V	M	34r
8	w	Generatio haec prava et	Fer. 4 Hebd. 1 Quad.	L	B	55r
8	w	Hymnum dicamus alleluia	Dom. per annum	L	4	35v
8	w	Inventa bona margarita dedit	Comm. Virginum	M	3	131v
8	w	Jesum quem quaeritis non est	In tempore Paschae	E	24	72v
8	w	Jesum qui crucifixus est*	Fer. 3 p. Pascha	M	1	77v
8	w	Jesus junxit se discipulis	Fer. 2 p. Pascha	L	B	77r
8	w	Magnificat anima mea dominum	Feria 2 per annum	V2	M	37r
8	w	Maria autem conservabat omnia	Epiphania,8	E	2	34r
8	w	Maximilla Christo amabilis*	S. Andreae	L	5	111v
8	w	Miserere mei fili David quid	Dom. Quinquagesimae	M	3	52v
8	w	Nativitas gloriosae virginis	Nativitas Mariae	L	1	102r
8	w	Nativitatem hodiernam	Nativitas Mariae	L	B	102v
8	w	Non enim loquetur a semetipso	Dom. 4 p. Pascha	E	6	81r
8	w	Non me permittas domine	S. Andreae	L	2	111v
8	w	Petite et accipietis ut	Dom. 5 p. Pascha	E	2	81r
8	w	Qui habitas in caelis	Feria 3 per annum	S		37v

Mode	Differentia	Incipit	Feast	Office	Pos.	Folio
8	w	Quid est quod me quaerebatis	Epiphania,8	E	1	34r
8	w	Quodcumque ligaveris super	Cathedra S. Petri	L	B	43r
8	w	Recipe me ab hominibus et	S. Andreae	M	2.2	IIIIr
8	w	Si ergo vos cum sitis mali	In Letaniis	E	3	8Ir
8	w	Si manseritis in sermone meo	Fer. 5 Hebd. 1 Quad.	L	B	55r
8	w	Stetit Jesus in medio	Fer. 3 p. Pascha	L	B	77v
8	w	Super ripam Jordanis stabat	Epiphania,8	E	7	33v
8	w	Surrexit dominus de sepulcro	In tempore Paschae	E	20	72v
8	w	Tristitia implebit cor	Dom. 3 p. Pascha	E	5	8Ir
8	w	Veni sponsa Christi accipe	Comm. Virginum	M	3	131v
8	w	Venient ad te qui detrahebant	Epiphania,8	M	1.2	33r
8	w	Venite benedicti patris mei	Fer. 2 Hebd. 1 Quad.	P		55r
8	w	Venite et videte*	Fer. 3 p. Pascha	M	2	77v
8	w-	Dum venerit filius hominis	Fer. 2 Hebd. 4 Adv.	L	2	12r
8	w-	Et respicientes viderunt	Dom. Resurrectionis	S		72r
8	w-	Nolite expavescere Jesum	Dom. Resurrectionis	N		72r
8	w-	Surgens Jesus mane prima	Dom. Resurrectionis	P		72r
8	wb	Aspice in me et miserere mei	Feria 2 per annum	S		37r
8	wb	De profundis clamavi ad te	Feria 3 per annum	V2	1	37v
8	wb	Deo nostro jucunda sit	Dom. per annum	V	3	34v
8	wb	Deus deorum dominus locutus	Feria 3 per annum	M	1.5	37r
8	wb	Domus Jacob de populo barbaro	Feria 2 per annum	V2	1	37r
8	wb	Ecce advenit dominator*	Epiphania	M	2.6	32r
8	wb	Intellege clamorem meum	Feria 2 per annum	L	2	36v
8	wb	Lux de luce apparuisti	Epiphania	P		33r
8	wb	Salve crux quae in corpore	S. Andreae	M	2.1	IIIIr
8	wd	Adorate dominum in aula	Dom. per annum	M	2.3	35r
8	wd	Ardens est cor meum desidero	In tempore Paschae	E	12	72v
8	wd	Ave spes nostra dei genetrix	Annuntiatio Mariae	V	M	46v
8	wd	Domine in virtute tua	Dom. per annum	M	1.1	34v
8	wd	Ecce ancilla domini fiat mihi	Fer. 4 Hebd. 4 Adv.	N		12v
8	wd	Ecce nunc palam loqueris et	Dom. 5 p. Pascha	E	5	8Ir
8	wd	Et dicebant ad invicem quis	Dom. Resurrectionis	T		72r
8	wd	Fili quid fecisti nobis sic	Dom. 1 p. Epiph.	V2	M	34r
8	wd	Hodie caelesti sponso juncta	Epiphania	L	B	33r
8	wd	In ecclesiis benedicite	Feria 4 per annum	M	1.5	37v
8	wd	Iterum autem videbo vos et	Dom. 3 p. Pascha	E	7	8Ir
8	wd	Nuptiae factae sunt in Cana	Dom. 2 p. Epiph.	L	B	35v
8	wd	Oportebat pati Christum et	In tempore Paschae	E	8	72v
8	wd	Qui sunt hi sermones quos	Fer. 2 p. Pascha	V2	M	77v
8	wd	Quoniam in te confidit anima	Feria 3 per annum	L	3	37v
8	wd	Scriptum est enim quia domus	Fer. 3 Hebd. 1 Quad.	V2	M	55r
8	wg	Alleluia iii (Juste judicate)	Feria 3 per annum	M	2.1	37r
8	wg	Benediximus vobis in nomine	Feria 2 per annum	V2	4	37r
8	wg	Domine in caelo misericordia	Feria 2 per annum	L	3	36v
8	wg	In tua justitia libera me	Dom. per annum	M	2.5	35r
8	wg	Juste judicate filii hominum	Feria 3 per annum	M	2.6	37v
8	wg	Semen cecidit in terram bonam	Hebd. Sexagesimae	E	4	52r

Mode	*Differentia*	Incipit	Feast	Office	Pos.	Folio
8	wg	Semen cecidit in terram bonam	Hebd. Sexagesimae	E	3	52r
8	-G	Aquae multae non potuerunt	Comm. Virginum	M	2.6	131v

Responsories

1	*	Audivi voces in caelo*	Dom. 2 p. Pascha	V		81v
1	*	Beatus pontifex Narcissus cum	S. Afrae	M	1.1	91r
1	*	Dixit angelus ad Mariam ne	Annuntiatio Mariae	M	2.1	47r
1	*	Dixit autem Maria ad angelum	Annuntiatio Mariae	M	3.3	47v
1	*	Egredietur virga*	Hebd. 4 Adventus	M	II	12r
1	*	Florem mundi periturum	S. Benedicti	M	1.1	45r
1	*	In medio ecclesiae aperuit os	S. Joannis Evang.	M	3.4	22v
1	*	In omnem terram exivit sonus	Comm. Apostolorum	M	1.4	121v
1	*	In omnem terram*	Comm. Apostolorum	V		121r
1	*	Iste est Joannes qui supra	S. Joannis Evang.	M	3.1	22v
1	*	Multis hinc inde sermonum	S. Afrae	M	3.3	91v
1	*	Posuit Moyses bissenas virgas	Annuntiatio Mariae	M	1.4	47r
1	*	Qui sunt hi qui ut nubes	Comm. Evangelistarum	V		121r
1	*	Quomodo fiet istud respondens	Annuntiatio Mariae	M	3.1	47v
1	*	Salve nobilis virga Jesse	Annuntiatio Mariae	M	2.4	47r
1	a	Audivi voces in caelo angelo-	Dom. 2 p. Pascha	M	2.2	81v
1	a	Beata Agatha ingressa	S. Agathae	M	3.3	42v
1	a	Canite tuba in Sion vocate	Dom. 4 Adventus	M	1.1	11r
1	a	Domine ne in ira tua arguas	Dom. per annum	M	1.1	35r
1	a	Dum staret Abraham ad radicem	Dom. Quinquagesimae	M	2.2	52v
1	a	Egredietur virga de radice	Dom. 4 Adventus	M	3.3	11v
1	a	Fulgebat in venerando duplex	S. Gregorii	M	1.1	43v
1	a	Gaudeamus omnes in domino	S. Agathae	M	3.4	42v
1	a	Germinaverunt campi eremi	Hebd. 4 Adventus	M	9	12r
1	a	Nativitas gloriosae virginis	Nativitas Mariae	M	3.2	102r
1	a	Nativitas tua dei genetrix	Nativitas Mariae	M	3.1	102r
1	a	Peccata mea domine sicut	Dom. per annum	M	3.3	35v
1	a	Ponam arcum meum in nubibus	Dom. Quinquagesimae	M	1.2	52r
1	a	Quam magna multitudo	Dom. per annum	M	3.1	35v
1	a	Quis igitur ille est qui	Dom. 2 Quadragesimae	M	1.4	55v
1	a	Regali ex progenie Maria	Nativitas Mariae	M	2.3	102r
1	a	Surge illuminare Jerusalem	Epiphania	L		33r
1	a	Tria sunt munera pretiosa	Epiphania	M	3.1	32r
1	a	Veni hodie ad fontem aquae et	Dom. Quinquagesimae	M	3.3	52v
1	ab	Expurgate vetus fermentum ut	Fer. 3 p. Pascha	M	1.3	77v
1	ab	Felix namque es*	Nativitas Mariae	M	3.3	102r
1	ab	Grandi pater fiducia morte	S. Benedicti	M	3.1	46r
1	ab	Ingressus angelus ad Mariam	Annuntiatio Mariae	M	1.1	46v
1	ag	Cum vidisset beatus Andreas	S. Andreae	M	2.1	111r
1	ag	Sedes tua deus in saeculum	Feria 2 per annum	M	1.3	36v
1	ag	Statuit dominus supra petram	Feria 2 per annum	M	1.1	36v
2	*	Angelus domini*	Dom. Quinquagesimae	V		52r
2	*	Barabbas latro dimittitur et	Fer. 6 in Parasceve	M	2.3	61v
2	*	Christi virgo dilectissima	Annuntiatio Mariae	M	3.4	47v

Mode	*Differentia*	Incipit	Feast	Office	Pos.	Folio
2	*	Christi virgo dilectissima*	Annuntiatio Mariae	V		46v
2	*	Puer fletum subsecutae	S. Benedicti	M	1.2	45v
2	*	Qui vicerit faciam illum	S. Joannis Evang.	M	1.4	21v
2	*	Sancto praesule precibus	S. Afrae	M	1.2	91r
2	*	Valde honorandus est beatus	S. Joannis Evang.	M	1.1	21v
2	*	Velum templi scissum est et	Fer. 6 in Parasceve	M	1.2	61r
2	e	Ad te domine levavi animam	Dom. per annum	M	2.3	35r
2	e	Angelus domini vocavit	Dom. Quinquagesimae	M	2.4	52v
2	e	Auribus percipe domine	Feria 2 per annum	M	1.4	36v
2	e	Bonum mihi domine quod	Dom. 1 Quadragesimae	V2		55r
2	e	Emitte agnum domine	Hebd. 4 Adventus	M	7	12r
2	e	Fratribus illuxit Benedictum	S. Benedicti	M	3.2	46r
2	e	Gloria Christe tuo tibi	S. Benedicti	M	3.4	46r
2	e	Homo dei ducebatur ut	S. Andreae	M	1.4	IIIIr
2	e	In columbae specie spiritus	Epiphania	M	3.4	32v
2	e	Ista est speciosa inter	Comm. Virginum	M	3.2	131v
2	e	Locutus est ad me unus ex	Dom. 2 p. Pascha	M	2.1	81v
2	e	Locutus est dominus ad Abra-	Dom. Quinquagesimae	M	2.1	52v
2	e	Non auferetur sceptrum de	Dom. 4 Adventus	M	1.3	IIIr
2	e	Rorate caeli desuper et nubes	Hebd. 4 Adventus	M	8	12r
2	e	Stirps Jesse virgam produxit	Nativitas Mariae	M	2.4	102r
2	e	Temptavit deus Abraham et	Dom. Quinquagesimae	M	2.3	52v
2	e	Videns Romae vir beatus	S. Gregorii	M	1.2	43v
2	e?	Veni electa mea et ponam in*	Comm. Virginum	M	3.3	131v
3	*	Agnosce dei famule surrexit	S. Benedicti	M	1.3	45v
3	*	Diligebat autem eum Jesus	S. Joannis Evang.	M	3.2	22v
3	*	Doctor bonus et amicus dei	S. Andreae	M	2.4	IIIIv
3	*	Dum steteritis ante reges et	Comm. Apostolorum	M	1.3	121v
3	*	Hostis antiquus caelesti	S. Afrae	M	1.3	91r
3	*	Intuemini quantus sit iste	Dom. 4 Adventus	M	3.1	IIv
3	*	Martyr sancta dei quae	S. Afrae	M	3.4	91v
3	*	Omnes amici mei dereliquerunt	Fer. 6 in Parasceve	M	1.1	61r
3	*	Veni sponsa Christi accipe	Comm. Virginum	M	1.1	131r
3	?	Ad nutum domini nostrum	Nativitas Mariae	M	3.4	102r
3	i	Congratulamini mihi omnes qui	Fer. 2 p. Pascha	M	1.3	77r
3	i	Deus in te speravi domine ut	Feria 4 per annum	M	1.2	37v
3	i	Ego sicut vitis fructificavi	Dom. 2 p. Pascha	M	1.2	81v
3	i	Egredietur dominus et proeli-	Hebd. 4 Adventus	M	4	12r
3	i	Me oportet minui illum autem	Dom. 4 Adventus	M	1.4	IIIr
3	i	Vir iste in populo suo	S. Andreae	M	3.3	IIIIv
3	i	Virtute magna reddebant	Fer. 3 p. Pascha	M	1.1	77v
3	ik	Mox ut vocem domini	S. Andreae	M	1.3	IIIIr
3	ik	Videbis o Jerusalem et	Epiphania,8	M	3	33v
4	*	Adjuva nos tuis*	Nativitas Mariae	V2		102v
4	*	Dabit illi dominus deus sedem	Annuntiatio Mariae	M	2.3	47r
4	*	Deus qui sedes*	Dom. per annum	V		34v
4	*	Dilexisti justitiam et odisti	Comm. Virginum	M	1.4	131r
4	*	Dum deambularet dominus juxta	S. Andreae	M	1.1	IIIIr

Mode	Differentia	Incipit	Feast	Office	Pos.	Folio
4	*	Electo grex mortiferum patri	S. Benedicti	M	1.4	45v
4	*	Propulso post longum	S. Afrae	M	2.1	91v
4	?	Diffusa est gratia in labiis	Comm. Virginum	M	2.1	131v
4	o-	Videbunt gentes justum tuum	Hebd. 4 Adventus	M	6	12r
4	oc	Benedicta tu in mulieribus et	Annuntiatio Mariae	M	1.2	46v
4	oc	Deus qui sedes super thronum	Dom. per annum	M	1.2	35r
4	oc	Dilexit Andream dominus in	S. Andreae	M	3.4	111v
4	oc	Diligam te domine virtus mea	Dom. per annum	M	2.1	35r
4	oc	Ecce jam cari noscite quam	S. Benedicti	M	3.3	46r
4	oc	Ego autem adjuta a domino	S. Agathae	M	2.4	42v
4	oc	Ego dixi domine miserere mei	Feria 2 per annum	M	1.2	36v
4	oc	Expandi manus meas tota die	S. Andreae	M	3.2	111v
4	oc	Fiat manus tua ut salvum me	Dom. per annum	M	3.4	35v
4	oc	Interrogabat magos Herodes	Epiphania	M	2.2	32r
4	oc	Pastores prae claritate	Epiphania,8	M	4	33v
4	oc	Videntes stellam magi gavisi	Epiphania	M	2.4	32r
4	oc	Vox domini super aquas deus	Octava Epiphaniae	V2		34v
4	og	Adjuva nos tuis precibus	Nativitas Mariae	L		102v
5	*	Caligaverunt oculi mei a	Fer. 6 in Parasceve	M	3.3	61v
5	*	Cum fontem vitae sitientes et	S. Afrae	M	2.2	91v
5	*	Grata facta est a domino in	S. Luciae	M	3.4	121r
5	*	Joseph dum intraret in terram	Dom. 3 Quadragesimae	M	1.4	57v
5	*	Servus dei Benedictus stetit	S. Benedicti	M	2.1	45v
5	?	Pulchra facie sed pulchrior	Comm. Virginum	M	2.3	131v
5	v	Paratum cor meum deus paratum	Feria 3 per annum	M	1.2	37r
5	v	Vidisti domine et exspectasti	S. Agathae	M	1.2	42r
5	v-	Delectare in domino et dabit	Feria 2 per annum	M	1.2	36r
5	vb	Benedicam domino in omni	Feria 2 per annum	M	1.1	36r
5	vb	Ecce jam veniet plenitudo	Dom. 4 Adventus	M	2.1	11r
5	vb	Quadraginta dies et noctes	Dom. Quinquagesimae	M	1.1	52r
5	-B	Concupivit rex speciem tuam	Comm. Virginum	M	2.2	131v
6	*	Benedictus quam devotas deo	S. Benedicti	M	2.2	45v
6	*	Benedictus quam devotas*	S. Scholasticae	V		43r
6	*	Benedictus*	S. Scholasticae	M		43r
6	*	Hoc signum crucis*	Exaltatio S. Crucis	V		102v
6	*	Hoc signum crucis*	Exaltatio S. Crucis	M	3.2	102v
6	*	Induit me dominus*	S. Agathae	M	3.1	42v
6	*	Mox omnibus in fide Christi	S. Afrae	M	2.3	91v
6	*	Omnes de Saba*	Dom. 1 p. Epiph.	V		34r
6	*	Omnes de Saba*	Epiphania,8	V2		34r
6	*	Omnes de Saba*	Octava Epiphaniae	V2		34v
6	*	Reges Tharsis*	Octava Epiphaniae	L		34v
6	*	Surrexit dominus vere*	Fer. 2 p. Pascha	L		77r
6	*	Tradiderunt me in manus	Fer. 6 in Parasceve	M	3.1	61v
6	*	Videns Jacob vestimenta	Dom. 3 Quadragesimae	M	1.3	57v
6	*	Vox tonitrui tui deus in rota	S. Joannis Evang.	V		21r
6	H	Abscondi tamquam aurum	Dom. per annum	M	13	35v
6	H	Adjutorium nostrum in nomine	Feria 2 per annum	V2		37r

Mode	*Differentia*	Incipit	Feast	Office	Pos.	Folio
6	H	Benedicam domino in omni	Feria 2 per annum	M	1.4	36v
6	H	Clama in fortitudine qui	Hebd. 4 Adventus	M	1	11v
6	H	Decantabat populus in Israel	Dom. 2 p. Pascha	M	2.3	81v
6	H	Deus in nomine tuo salvum me	Feria 3 per annum	M	1.4	37r
6	H	Domine in caelo misericordia	Feria 2 per annum	L		36v
6	H	Exaltent eum in ecclesia	Cathedra S. Petri	L		43r
6	H	Hoc signum crucis erit in	Exaltatio S. Crucis	L		102v
6	H	Induit me dominus vestimento	Comm. Virginum	M	3.1	131v
6	H	Miserere mei deus miserere	Feria 3 per annum	L		37v
6	H	Modo veniet dominator dominus	Hebd. 4 Adventus	M	3	12r
6	H	Ne perdideris me domine cum	Feria 3 per annum	M	1.1	37r
6	H	Omnes de Saba venient aurum	Epiphania	V2		33r
6	H	Per memetipsum juravi dicit	Dom. Quinquagesimae	M	1.3	52r
6	H	Quam magnificata sunt opera	Dom. per annum	V2		36r
6	H	Reges Tharsis et insulae	Epiphania,8	L		33v
6	H	Resurrexit dominus alleluia	Dom. 2 p. Pascha	M	1.4	81v
6	H	Surrexit dominus de sepulcro	Fer. 2 p. Pascha	V2		77v
6	H	Surrexit dominus de sepulcro	Dom. Resurrectionis	V2		72r
6	H	Surrexit dominus vere	Fer. 3 p. Pascha	L		77v
7	*	Cibavit eum dominus pane	S. Joannis Evang.	M	3.3	22v
7	*	Conversus Ezechiel ad	Annuntiatio Mariae	M	3.2	47v
7	*	Dixit Judas fratribus suis	Dom. 3 Quadragesimae	M	1.2	57v
7	*	Dum ingrederetur beata Agatha	S. Agathae	M	1.1	42r
7	*	Ecce ego mitto vos sicut oves	Comm. Apostolorum	M	1.1	121v
7	*	Ecce puer meus quem elegi	S. Joannis Evang.	M	2.1	22r
7	*	Haec est virgo sapiens quam	Comm. Virginum	M	1.2	131r
7	*	Hic est discipulus qui	S. Joannis Evang.	M	2.2	22r
7	*	Maria ut audivit turbata est	Annuntiatio Mariae	M	1.3	47r
7	*	Memento mei dum bene tibi	Dom. 3 Quadragesimae	M	2.1	57v
7	*	O Israelita verus cor in deum	S. Benedicti	M	2.3	45v
7	*	Pater peccavi in caelum et	Sabb. Hebd. 2 Quad.	X		57r
7	*	Postquam novellam conversa	S. Afrae	M	3.1	91v
7	*	Specie tua et pulchritudine	Comm. Virginum	M	1.3	131r
7	*	Tenebrae factae sunt dum	Fer. 6 in Parasceve	M	2.2	61r
7	*	Tollite jugum meum super vos	Comm. Apostolorum	M	1.2	121v
7	*	Tollite jugum*	Comm. Apostolorum	V		121r
7	y-	Praecursor pro nobis	Hebd. 4 Adventus	M	5	12r
7	yb	Nascetur nobis parvulus et	Dom. 4 Adventus	M	3.4	11v
7	yc	Adjutor meus tibi psallam	Feria 3 per annum	M	1.3	37r
7	yc	Agatha laetissima et	S. Agathae	M	2.2	42v
7	yc	Audiam domine vocem laudis	Dom. per annum	M	2.4	35r
7	yc	Audivi vocem de caelo tamquam	Dom. 2 p. Pascha	M	1.3	81v
7	yc	Cum ceciderit justus non	Feria 2 per annum	M	1.3	36r
7	yc	Det tibi deus de rore caeli	Dom. 2 Quadragesimae	M	1.3	55v
7	yc	Dignus es domine accipere	Dom. 2 p. Pascha	M	1.1	81v
7	yc	Ecce odor filii mei sicut	Dom. 2 Quadragesimae	M	1.2	55v
7	yc	Exaudi deus deprecationem	Feria 4 per annum	M	1.1	37v
7	yc	Hic est dies praeclarus in	Epiphania	M	3.3	32v

Mode	_Differentia_	Incipit	Feast	Office	Pos.	Folio
7	yc	Maria Magdalena et altera	Fer. 2 p. Pascha	M	1.1	77r
7	yc	Qui me dignatus est ab omni	S. Agathae	M	3.2	42v
7	yc	Salve crux quae in corpore	S. Andreae	M	2.2	IIIr
7	yc	Surgens Jesus dominus noster	Fer. 2 p. Pascha	M	1.2	77r
7	yc	Tolle arma tua pharetram et	Dom. 2 Quadragesimae	M	1.1	55v
7	yc	Vicesima quarta die decimi	Dom. 4 Adventus	M	1.2	IIr
8	*	Alme pater qui praescius tui	S. Benedicti	M	2.4	45v
8	*	Ecce concipies et paries	Annuntiatio Mariae	M	2.2	47r
8	*	Fervente interim immani	S. Afrae	M	3.2	91v
8	*	Hic est beatissimus	S. Joannis Evang.	M	1.2	21v
8	*	In illo die suscipiam te	S. Joannis Evang.	M	1.3	21v
8	*	Iste est Joannes cui Christus	S. Joannis Evang.	M	2.3	22r
8	*	Jesum tradidit impius summis	Fer. 6 in Parasceve	M	3.2	61v
8	*	Propter veritatem et	Comm. Virginum	M	1.5	131r
8	*	Propter veritatem*	S. Agathae	M	2.3	42v
8	*	Radix Jesse*	Hebd. 4 Adventus	M	10	12r
8	*	Tamquam ad latronem existis	Fer. 6 in Parasceve	M	2.1	61r
8	*	Videntes Joseph a longe	Dom. 3 Quadragesimae	M	1.1	57v
8	*	Vinea mea electa ego te	Fer. 6 in Parasceve	M	1.3	61r
8	w	A dextris est mihi dominus ne	Dom. per annum	M	1.3	35r
8	w	Afflicti pro peccatis nostris	Dom. per annum	M	3.2	35v
8	w	Caecus sedebat secus viam	Dom. Quinquagesimae	M	3.4	52v
8	w	Corde et animo Christo	Nativitas Mariae	M	2.2	102r
8	w	Deus domini mei Abraham	Dom. Quinquagesimae	M	3.2	52v
8	w	Dies sanctificatus illuxit	Epiphania	M	3.2	32r
8	w	Domini est terra et plenitudo	Dom. per annum	M	2.2	35r
8	w	Juravi dicit dominus ut ultra	Dom. 4 Adventus	M	2.3	IIr
8	w	Magi veniunt ab oriente	Epiphania	M	2.1	32r
8	w	Non discedimus a te	Dom. 4 Adventus	M	2.4	IIr
8	w	Notas mihi fecisti domine	Dom. per annum	M	1.4	35r
8	w	O bona crux quae decorem et	S. Andreae	M	2.3	IIIr
8	w	Orietur stella ex Jacob et	Hebd. 4 Adventus	M	2	12r
8	w	Radix Jesse qui exsurget	Dom. 4 Adventus	M	3.2	IIv
8	w	Stella quam viderunt magi in	Epiphania	M	2.3	32r
8	w	Tulerunt dominum meum et	Fer. 3 p. Pascha	M	1.2	77v
8	w	Venit lumen tuum Jerusalem et	Epiphania,8	M	2	33r
8	w	Venite post me faciam vos	S. Andreae	M	1.2	IIIr
8	w	Virgo Israel revertere in	Dom. 4 Adventus	M	2.2	IIr
8	w	Vocavit angelus domini	Dom. Quinquagesimae	M	3.1	52v
8	wb	Quis es tu qui venisti ad me	S. Agathae	M	1.3	42r
8	wd	Ipse me coronavit qui per	S. Agathae	M	2.1	42r
8	wd	Medicinam carnalem corpori	S. Agathae	M	1.4	42r
8	wd	Oravit sanctus Andreas dum	S. Andreae	M	3.1	IIIv
8	-D	Ornatam in monilibus filiam*	Comm. Virginum	M	2.4	131v

Sequence

2		Quem non praevalent propria	Epiphania	M		32v

Bibliography

900 Jahre Klosterkirche Lambach: Oberösterreichische Landesausstellung 1989 (Linz, 1989).

Anschober, H., 'Die dramatische Dichtkunst im Stifte Lambach', *Oberösterreichische Heimatblätter*, 6 (1952), pp. 559–68.

Anz, H., *Die lateinischen Magierspiele* (Leipzig, 1905).

Apel, W., *Gregorian Chant* (Bloomington, 1966).

Babcock, R. G., *Reconstructing a Medieval Library: Fragments from Lambach* (New Haven, 1993).

Babcock, R. G., and L. F. Davis, 'Two Romanesque Manuscripts from Lambach', *Codices Manuscripti*, 8 (1990), pp. 137–47.

Babcock, R. G., L. F. Davis and P. Rusche, *Catalogue of Medieval and Renaissance Manuscripts in the Beinecke Rare Book and Manuscript Library, Yale University*, vol. IV: *MSS 481–485*, Medieval and Renaissance Texts and Studies, 176 (Tempe, 1998).

Bandmann, G., 'Früh- und hochmittelalterliche Altaranordnung als Darstellung', in V. Elbern (ed.), *Das erste Jahrtausend* (Düsseldorf, 1963), vol. I, pp. 371–411.

Baughman, R., *The Magic Carpet on Wheels* (*Catalogue of an Outstanding Collection of Authentic Books and Manuscripts Tracing the History of Writing and Printing for 4,500 years. Presented by the Grolier Society*) (New York, 1952).

Birke, V. (ed.), *Die Kunstsammlungen des Augustiner-Chorherrenstiftes St Florian*, Österreichische Kunsttopographie, 48 (Vienna, 1988).

Bischoff, B., 'La Nomenclature des écritures livresques du IXe au XIIIe siècle', in *Nomenclatures des écritures livresques du IXe au XVIe siècle* (Paris, 1954), pp. 7–14, figs. 1, 2, 7 and 8.

Die südostdeutschen Schreibschulen und Bibliotheken in der Karolingerzeit, 2 vols. (Wiesbaden, 1940 and 1980).

Bjork, D., 'On the Dissemination of "Quem Quaeritis" and the "Visitatio Sepulchri" and the Chronology of their Early Sources', in C. Davidson (ed.), *The Drama of the Middle Ages* (New York, 1982), pp. 1–24.

Blum, O. J. (trans.), *Peter Damian: Letters 1–30*, (The Fathers of the Church, Mediaeval Continuation) (Washington, DC, c. 1989).

Boshof, E., 'Gefälschte "Stiftsbriefe" des 11./12. Jahrhunderts aus bayerisch-österreichischen Klöstern', in *Fälschungen im Mittelalter: internationaler Kongress der Monumenta Germaniae Historica, München, 16.-19. September 1986*, MGH Schriften 33:1 (Hanover, 1988), pp. 519–50.

Cardine, E., *Sémiologie Grégorienne*, Études Grégoriennes, 11 (1970).

Coussemaker, C. de, *Drames liturgiques du moyen âge* (Rennes, 1860).

Czernin, M., 'Das Breviarium Monasticum Cod. 290 (183) der Bundesstaatlichen Studienbibliothek in Linz', unpublished Ph.D. dissertation, University of Vienna (1992).

Davis, L. F., 'Epiphany at Lambach: The Evidence of the Gottschalk Antiphonary', unpublished Ph.D. dissertation, Yale University (1993).

   'Tonary-letters in Twelfth-Century Lambach', *Plainsong and Medieval Music*, 5 (1996), pp. 131–152.

   'Two Leaves of the Gottschalk Antiphonary', *Harvard Library Bulletin*, New Series 5/3 (1994), pp. 38–44.

Demus, O., *Romanesque Mural Painting* (New York, 1970).

Demus, O., and F. Unterkircher, (eds.), *Das Antiphonar von St Peter: Codex Vindobonensis S. N. 2700* (Graz, 1969–73).

Dopsch, H., 'Das Kloster Lambach unter den Otakaren und Babenbergern', in *900 Jahre Klosterkirche Lambach*, pp. 73–80.

Dreves, G., and C. Blume (eds.), *Analecta Hymnica medii aevi* (Leipzig, 1886–1922).

Drumbl, J., *Quem Quaeritis: Teatro Sacro dell'Alto Medioevo* (Rome, 1981).

Eilenstein, A., *Die Benediktinerabtei Lambach in Österreich ob der Enns und ihre Mönche* (Linz, 1936).

   'Die Beziehungen des Stiftes Lambach zu Salzburg', in *Studien und Mitteilungen zur Geschichte des Benediktiner-Ordens*, N.F. 11 (Munich, 1924), pp. 196–232.

   'Zur Geschichte der Stiftsbibliothek in Lambach (Oberösterreich)', *Studien und Mitteilungen zur Geschichte des Benediktiner-Ordens und seiner Zweige*, 51 (Munich, 1933), pp. 205–17.

   'Zur Geschichte des Theaters im Stifte Lambach', *Linzer Volksblatt*, 6 (Linz, 1933).

Falvey, Z., and L. Mezey, *Codex Albensis. Ein Antiphonar aus dem 12. Jahrhundert (Graz Universitätsbibliothek MS. Nr. 211)* (Graz, 1963).

Fassler, M., 'The Office of the Cantor in Early Western Monastic Rules and Customaries: A Preliminary Investigation', *Early Music History*, 5 (1985), pp. 29–51.

Fastlinger, M., 'Notae necrologicae et fragmentum necrologii monasterii lambacenses', *MGH Necr.* IV (Berlin, 1920), pp. 404–6.

Feldman, L. (ed. and trans.), *Josephus*, Loeb Classical Library, Greek Authors, 9 (Cambridge, Mass., 1965).

Fichtenau, H., 'Neues zu den Lambacher Nekrologien', *MIÖG*, 59 (1951), pp. 416ff.

Fill, H., *Katalog der Handschriften des Benediktinerstiftes Kremsmünster* (Vienna, 1984).

Folliet, G., 'Deux nouveaux témoins du Sermonnaire carolingien récemment reconstitué', *Revue des Etudes Augustiniennes*, 23 (1977), pp. 155–98.

Frodl, W., *Die Kunstdenkmäler des Benediktinerstiftes St Paul im Lavanttal und seiner Filialkirchen*, ÖKT 37 (Vienna, 1969).

Froger, J., *Antiphonaire de Hartker: manuscrits Saint-Gall 390–391. Nouv. Ed.*, Paléographie musicale, deuxième série, Monumentale, 1 (Berne, 1970).

Geary, P., *Phantoms of Remembrance* (Princeton, 1994).

Genge, H.-J., *Die liturgiegeschichtlichen Voraussetzungen des Lambacher Freskenzyklus* (Münsterschwarzach, 1972).

Gerstinger, H., *Bericht über die verbotswidrigen Veräußerungen aus der Stiftsbibliothek Lambach* (Vienna, 1930) [Vienna, Österreichische Nationalbibliothek ser. n. 9713, früher MS autogr. 200l; enthält Vorarbeiten zu einem Katalog der Lambacher Hss, Vienna 1923–5].

'Zwei Fragmente einer altlateinischen Übersetzung des Buches der Richter in einem Codex der Bibliothek des Benediktinerklosters Lambach in Oberösterreich', *Mitteilungen des Vereines klassischer Philologen in Wien*, 6 (1929), pp. 94–107.

Grüll, G., 'Geschichte des Lambacher Klosterarchivs', *Mitteilungen des oberösterreichischen Landesarchivs*, 1 (1950), p. 156.

Hainisch, E. (ed.), *Die Kunstdenkmäler des Gerichtsbezirkes Lambach*, ÖKT 34/2 (Vienna, *c.* 1959).

Hallinger, K., *Gorze-Kluny: Studien zu den monastischen Lebensformen und Gegensätzen im Hochmittelalter* (Rome, 1950).

'Neunhundert Jahre Benediktinerabtei Lambach', *3. Jahrbuch des Musealvereines Wels* (1956–7) pp. 17–29.

Hammer, I., 'The Conservation in Situ of the Romanesque Wall Paintings of Lambach', in S. Cather, (ed.), *The Conservation of Wall Paintings* (London, 1987), pp. 43–56.

Handschin, J., 'Sur quelques tropaires Grecs traduits en Latin', *Annales Musicologiques*, 2 (1954), pp. 47–8.

Heckenbach, W., 'Das mittelalterliche Reimoffizium "Praeclarum late" zu den Festen des Heiligen Benedikt', in *Itinera Domini: gesammelte Aufsätze aus Liturgie und Mönchtum: Emmanuel v. Severus OSB zur Vollendung des 80. Lebensjahres am 24. August 1988 dargeboten* (Aschendorff, 1988), pp. 189–210.

Heilingsetzer, G. and W. Stelzer (eds.), *Kurt Holter: Buchkunst – Handschriften – Bibliotheken: Beiträge zur mitteleuropäischen buchkultur vom Frühmittelalter bis zur Renaissance*, 2 vols. (Linz, 1996).

Hesbert, J., *Corpus Antiphonalium Officii*, Rerum Ecclesiasticarum. Documenta. Series maior. Fontes, 7–12, 6 vols. (Rome, 1963–79).

'Les séries de répons des dimanches de l'Advent', *Les Questions liturgiques et paroissales*, 39 (1958), pp. 299–326.

Hoffmann, H., *Buchkunst und Königtum im ottonischen und frühsalischen Reich*, Schriften der MGH, 30 (Stuttgart, 1986).

Hofmann-Brandt, H., 'Die Tropen zu den Responsorien des Officiums', Inaugural-Dissertation, Erlangen-Nürnberg (1971).

Holter, K., 'Beiträge zur Geschichte der Stiftsbibliothek Lambach', *Jahrbuch des Musealvereines Wels*, 15 (1969), pp. 96–123.

'Buchmalerei und Federzeichnungsinitialen im hochmittelalterlichen Skriptorium von Kremsmünster', in Mazal (ed.), *Handschriftenbeschreibung in Österreich* (Vienna, 1975), pp. 41–50 and figs. 1–38.

'Graphische Kunst der Romanik aus alten Klöstern Oberösterreichs', *Oberösterreich*, 8 (Linz, 1958), pp. 36–42.

'Die Handschriften und Inkunabeln', in E. Hainisch (ed.), *Die Kunstdenkmäler des Gerichtsbezirkes Lambach*, ÖKT 34/2 (Vienna, *c.* 1959), pp. 213–68.

'Initialen aus einer Lambacher Handschrift des 12. Jahrhunderts', *Wiener Jahrbuch für Kunstgeschichte*, 46/7 (1993/94), pp. 255–65 and pp. 433–6.

'Das mittelalterliche Buchwesen des Benediktinerstiftes Lambach', in *900 Jahre Klosterkirche Lambach*, pp. 53–64.

'Das mittelalterliche Buchwesen im Kloster Garsten', in *Kirche in Oberösterreich, Katalog der Landesausstellung in Garsten* (Linz, 1985), pp. 91–102 and pp. 370–85.

'Neue Beiträge zur Geschichte der Stiftsbibliothek von Lambach im hohen Mittelalter', in

G. Heilingsetzer (ed.), *Kunstgeschichtsforschung und Denkmalpflege (Festschrift für Norbert Wibiral zum 65. Geburtstag)* (Linz, 1986), pp. 85–98.

'Romanische Bucheinbände des 12.Jahrhunderts aus Kloster Lambach, Oberösterreich', *Gutenberg Jahrbuch* (1965), pp. 343–7.

'Die romanische Buchmalerei in Oberösterreich', *Jahrbuch des Ober-Österreichischen Musealvereines*, 101 (1956), pp. 221–50.

'Zu einem Verzeichnis der frühmittelalterlichen Handschriften', in *Karolingische und Ottonische Kunst: Werden, Wesen, Wirkung (VI. Internationaler Kongress für Frühmittelalterforschung)* (Wiesbaden, 1957), pp. 434–42.

'Zum gotischen Bucheinband in Österreich: Die Buchbinderwerkstatt des Stiftes Lambach O.-Ö.', *Gutenberg Jahrbuch* (1954), pp. 280–9.

'Zwei Lambacher Bibliotheksverzeichnisse des 13. Jahrhunderts', *MIÖG*, 64 (1956), pp. 262–76.

Houben, H., *St Blasianer Handschriften des 11. und 12. Jahrhunderts* (Munich, 1979).

Hughes, A., *Medieval Manuscripts for Mass and Office* (Toronto, 1982).

'Modal Order and Disorder in the Rhymed Office', *Musica Disciplina*, 37 (1983), pp. 29–52.

Huglo, M., *Les Tonaires: Inventaire, Analyse, Comparaison* (Paris, 1971).

Jakobs, H., *Der Adel in der Klosterreform von St Blasien* (Graz, 1968).

Die Hirsauer (Cologne, 1961).

Jonsson, R., *Corpus Troporum I: Tropes du propre de la messe*, vol. I: *Cycle de Noël* (Stockholm, 1975).

Karnowka, G.-H., *Breviarium Passaviense*, Münchener Theologische Studien, 44 (St Ottilien, 1983).

Kehrer, H., *Die heiligen drei Könige in Literatur und Kunst* (Leipzig, 1908/9).

Kellner, A., *Musikgeschichte des Stiftes Kremsmünster, nach den Quellen dargestellt* (Kassel, 1956).

Kelly, T. F., 'Melisma and Prosula: The Performance of Responsory Tropes', in *Liturgische Tropen: Referate zweier Colloquien des Corpus Troporum in München (1983) und Canterbury (1984)* (Munich, 1985), pp. 163–80.

'New Music from Old: The Structuring of Responsory Prosas', *Journal of the American Musicological Society*, 30 (1977), pp. 366–90.

'Responsory Tropes', unpublished Ph.D. dissertation, Harvard University, 1973.

King, N., *Mittelalterliche Dreikönigsspiele* (Freiburg, 1979).

Klebel, E., 'Die Fassungen und Handschriften der österreichischen Annalistik', *Jahrbuch für Landeskunde und Heimatschutz von Niederösterreich und Wien*, 20 (1926–7), pp. 43–185.

Kleiber, W., *Otfrid von Weissenburg* (Munich, 1971).

Koller, H., 'Die königliche Klosterpolitik im Südosten des Reiches. Ein Beitrag zum Niedergang der Reichsgewalt', *Archiv für Diplomatik Schriftgeschichte Siegel- und Wappenkunde*, 20 (1974), pp. 1–38.

Korger, F., *Lambacher Fresken* ([Lambach], n.d.).

Krause, A., 'Das Dreigestirn', in S. K. Landersdorfer (ed.), *Der heilige Altmann Bischof von Passau: sein Leben und sein Werk* (Göttweig, 1965), pp. 39–47.

Lambach Incunable Catalogue, 1916 (unpublished manuscript, Lambach Stiftsbibliothek, no shelf number).

Landersdorfer, S. K. (ed.), *Der heilige Altmann Bischof von Passau: sein Leben und sein Werk* (Göttweig, 1965).

Landgraf, W., *Heinrich IV: Macht und Ohnmacht eines Kaisers: Biografie* (Berlin, *c.* 1991).

LeRoux, R., 'Les répons "de Psalmis" pour les Matines de l'Epiphanie à la Septuagésime', *Etudes grégoriennes*, 6 (1963), pp. 39–148 and table.

Leidinger, S., *900 Jahre Lambach* (Linz, 1956).

Lerner, K. F., 'Zur Lambacher Dreikönigspeil, einer liturgischen Dreikönigsfeier des 11.Jahrhunderts aus Schwarzach am Main', unpublished dissertation, Munich Hochschule für Musik (1957).

Light, L., *The Bible in the Twelfth Century* (Cambridge, Mass., 1988).

Lipphardt, W., *Lateinische Osterfeiern und Osterspiele* (Berlin, 1975).

Luger, W., 'Beiträge zur Musikgeschichte des Stiftes Lambach. I. Vom Mittelalter bis zum Barock', *Oberösterreichische Heimatsblätter*, 15 (1961), pp. 1–8.

Die Benediktiner-Abtei Lambach (n.p., 1952).

Der älteste Bibliothekskatalog des Klosters Lambach, Oberösterreichische-Kulturberichte, 16 (Linz, 1953).

Mazal, O., *Buchkunst der Romanik* (Graz, 1978).

Mazal, O. (ed.), *Katalog der abendländischen Handschriften der Österreichischen Nationalbibliothek*, Series nova, 3 (Vienna, 1967).

Merkley, P., *Italian Tonaries* (Ottowa, 1988).

Möbius, F., 'Die Chorpartie der westeuropäischen Klosterkirche zwischen dem 8. und 11. Jahrhundert. Kulturgeschichtliche Voraussetzungen, liturgischer Gebrauch, soziale Funktion', in F. Möbius, and E. Schubert (eds.), *Architektur des Mittelalters. Funktion und Gestalt* (Weimar, 1983), pp. 9–41.

Westwerkstudien (Jena, 1968).

Möller, H., *Das Quedlinburger Antiphonar* (Tutzing, 1990).

Neumüller, W., 'Zur Benediktinerreform des heiligen Altman', in S. K. Landersdorfer (ed.), *Der heilige Altmann Bischof von Passau: sein Leben und sein Werk* (Göttweig, 1965), pp. 16–22.

'Zur Geschichte der oberösterreichischen Benediktinerklöster im Mittelalter', *Christliche Kunstblätter*, 99 (1961), pp. 33–40.

Neuwirth, J., 'Studien zur Geschichte der Miniaturmalerei in Oesterreich', *Sitzungsberichte der kaiserlichen Akademie der Wissenschaften, Philosophisch-Historische Klasse*, 130 (1886), pp. 129–39.

Omlin, P., *Die Sankt-Gallischen Tonarbuchstaben* (Engelberg, 1934).

Ottosen, K., *L'Antiphonaire Latin au Moyen-Age* (Rome, 1986).

Pächt, O. and J. J. G. Alexander, *Illuminated Manuscripts in the Bodleian Library, Oxford*, I (Oxford, 1966).

Paulhart, H., *Mittelalterliche Bibliothekskataloge Österreichs*, V (Vienna, *c.* 1915), pp. 49–58.

Pfaff, C., *Scriptorium und Bibliothek des Klosters Mondsee im hohen Mittelalter*, Veroffentlichungen der Kommission für Geschichte Österreichs, 2 (Vienna, 1967).

Pippal, M., 'Mittelalterliche Buchmalerei in Göttweig bis zum internationalen Stil', in *900 Jahre Stift Göttweig* (Göttweig, 1983), pp. 542–70.

Podlaha, A., *Knihovna Kapitulni v Praze* (Prague, 1903).

Pothier, L., 'Répons de la Procession pascale', *Revue du Chant Grégorien*, 3 (1894), pp. 35–40.

Primisser, A., 'Reisenachrichten über Denkmale der Kunst und des Althertums in den österreichischen Abteien. Lambach, Benediktinerstift in Oberösterreich', *Archiv für Geographie, Historie, Staats- und Kriegskunst* (Hormayrs Archiv), XIII, No. 68 (Vienna, 1822), pp. 361–8.

Puniet, P. (ed.), *Antiphonaire monastique, XIIe siècle: Codex 601 de la Bibliothèque capitulaire de Lucques*, Paléographie Musicale, 9 (Tournai, 1906).

Puskás, R., *Die mittelalterlichen Messeresponsorien der Klosterkirche Rheinau: Studien zum Antiphonar in Hs Zentralbib. Zürich Rh. 28*, Collection d'études musicologiques-Sammlung musikwissenschaftlicher Abhandlungen, 68 (1984).

Quaritch, B., *Bookhands of the Middle Ages: Part V* (London, 1991), Catalogue 1147, Item 73, pp. 60–2, with plate.

Reindel, K., *Die Briefe des Petrus Damiani, MGH,* Die Briefe der deutschen Kaiserzeit, 4 (Munich, 1983).

Rumpler, K., 'Die Gründung Lambachs unter besonderer Berücksichtigung der Gründungsurkunden', in *900 Jahre Klosterkirche Lambach*, pp. 25–33.

Scheele, P.-W., *Die Herrlichkeit des Herrn: Die Lambacher Fresken aus der Zeit des heiligen Adalbero* (Würzburg, 1990).

Schiffmann, K., 'Drama und Theater in Österreich ob der Enns bis zum Jahre 1803', in *59.Jahresbericht des Museum Francisco-Carolinum* (Linz, 1905).

'Die lateinischen Magierspiele. Untersuchungen und Texte zur Vorgeschichte des deutschen Weihnachtsspiels. von A. Anz', *Anzeiger für deutsches Altertum und deutsche Literatur*, 31 (1908), pp. 12–17.

Schmale-Ott, I., *Vita Sancti Adalberonis* (Würzburg, 1954).

Schmeider, P., *Breve chronicon monasterii BMV Lambacensis OBS* (Linz, 1865).

Schubiger, A., *Die Sängerschule St Gallens vom achten bis zwölften Jahrhundert* (Einsiedeln, 1858).

Sotheby & Co., *The Beck Collection of Illuminated Manuscripts* (London, 16 June 1997).

Catalogue of Valuable Printed Books and Manuscripts (London, 16–19 July 1928).

Catalogue of Important Literary and Mediaeval Manuscripts, Autograph Letters, Valuable Printed Books, &c. (New York, 11 November 1929).

Catalogue of Western Manuscripts and Miniatures (New York, 9 December 1974).

Spätling, L., *Consuetudines Fructuarienses: Sanblasianae*, 2 vols. Corpus Consuetudinum Monasticum, 12 (Siegburg, 1985 and 1987).

Staats, R., *Theologie der Reichskrone*, Monographien zur Geshichte des Mittelalters, 13 (Stuttgart, 1976).

Steinen, W. von den, *Notker der Dichter und seine geistige Welt* (Berne, 1948).

Stemmler, T., *Liturgische Feiern und geistliche Spiele* (Tübingen, 1970).

Strunk, O., 'The Latin Antiphons for the Octave of the Epiphany', in *Mélanges G. Ostrogosky*, vol. II: *Receuil de travaux de l'Institut d'Etudes Byzantines*, 8/2 (Beograd, 1964), pp. 417–26.

Strycker, S. J., *La forme la plus ancienne du Protévangile de Jacques* (Brussels, 1961).

Sturm, A., *Theatergeschichte Oberösterreich im 16. und 17. Jahrhundert, Theatergeschichte Österreichs*, I: *Oberösterreich* (Vienna, 1964).

Swarzenski, G., *Die Salzburger Malerei* (Leipzig, 1913).

Swarzenski, H., 'Two Romanesque Illuminated Manuscripts in the Princeton University Library', *The Princeton University Library Chronicle*, 9 (1947/48), pp. 64–7.

Swoboda, K., 'Der romanische Epiphaniezyklus in Lambach und das lateinische Magierspiel', in *Festschrift für Julius Schlosser zum 60.Geburstage* (Leipzig, 1927), pp. 82–7.

Treitler, L., 'Paleography and Semiotics', in M. Huglo (ed.), *Musicologie Médiévale: Notations et Séquences* (Paris, 1987), pp. 17–28.

Trinks, E., 'Die Gründungsurkunden und Anfänge des Benediktinerklosters Lambach', *Jahrbuch des Oberösterreichischen Musealvereins*, 83 (1930), pp. 76–152.

Ulm, B., 'Die Westanlage der Stiftskirche von Lambach', *Christliche Kunstblätter*, 99 (1961), pp. 52–62.

Unterkircher, F., *Die datierten Handschriften der Österreichischen Nationalbibliothek bis zum Jahre 1400* (Vienna, 1969).

Wagner, P., *Gregorianische Formenlehre*, Einführung in die Gregorianischen Melodien, 3 (Leipzig, 1921).

Wattenbach, W., 'Annales Austriae', in G. Pertz (ed.), *MGH SS* IX (repr. Stuttgart, 1983), pp. 479–561.

'Vita Adalberonis Episcopi Wirziburgensis', in G. Pertz (ed.), *MGH SS* XII (Hanover, 1856), pp. 127–38.

'Vita Altmani Episcopi Pataviensis', in G. Pertz (ed.), *MGH SS* XII (Hanover, 1856), pp. 226–43.

Wendehorst, A., 'Adalbero, Bischof von Würzburg und Gründer Lambachs', in *900 Jahre Klosterkirche Lambach*, pp. 17–24.

Whiston, W. (trans.), *Josephus, Complete Works* (Michigan, 1978).

Wibiral, N., 'Apostelgeschichte und Jüdische Altertümer in Lambach' in *Festgabe für Kurt Holter* (Linz, 1991), pp. 73–96 and pl. 1–8.

'Die Arbeiten im alten Westchor von Lambach 1956–1966', *Kunstchronik. Monatsschrift für Kunstwissenschaft, Museumwesen und Denkmalpflege*, 19 (1966), pp. 113–22.

'Beiträge zur Erforschung der romanischen Westanlage der Stiftskirche in Lambach', *Österreichische Zeitschrift für Kunst und Denkmalpflege*, 13 (1959), pp. 17–27.

'Beiträge zur Ikonographie der frühromanischen Fresken im ehemaligen Westchor der Stiftskirche von Lambach (Oberösterreich)', *Würzburger Diözesangeschichtsblätter*, 25 (1963), pp. 63–91.

'Beobachtungen zur Krypta und zum Westchor der ersten Klosterkirche der Benediktiner in Lambach', *9. Jahrbuch des Musealvereines Wels* (1962/3), pp. 48–64.

'Le dégagement des peintures murales du xie siècle dans l'ancien choeur occidental de l'église abbatiale de Lambach (Autriche)', *Monumentum*, 1 (1967), pp. 10–23.

'Die Freilegungsarbeiten im ehemaligen Westchor der Stiftskirche von Lambach', *Österreichische Zeitschrift für Kunst und Denkmalpflege*, 14 (1960), pp. 1–24.

'Die Fresken im ehemaligen Westchor der Stiftskirche von Lambach', in *Romanische Kunst in Österreich, Ausstellungskatalog, Krems an der Donau* (Krems, 1964), pp. 94–104.

'Die frühromanischen Fresken und der ehemalige Westchor der Stiftskirche von Lambach', *14. Mitteilungsblatt des Vereines für Denkmalpflege in Oberösterreich* (1960), pp. 2–6.

'Die Grabungen und Freilegungen in Lambach und ihre Probleme', *Christliche Kunstblätter*, 99 (1961), pp. 84–6.

'Die Lambacher Fresken', *Die Furche*, 22 (11 January 1964), p. 18.

'Neue Funde in Lambach', *Österreichische Zeitschrift für Kunst und Denkmalpflege*, 16 (1962), pp. 91–94.

'Neue romanische Freskenfunde in Lambach', *Linzer Kirchenblatt*, 13 (1 September 1957), no. 35.

'Die neuentdeckten romanischen Fresken in Lambach', *Christliche Kunstblätter*, 97 (1959), pp. 54–6.

'Romanische Freskenfunde in Lambach', *Die Furche*, 15 (21 March 1959), p. 12.

'Die Wandmalereien des XI. Jahrhunderts im ehemaligen Westchor der Klosterkirche von Lambach', *Oberösterreich. Landschaft- Kultur- Wirtschaft- Fremdenverkehr*, 17 (1967), H.3/4 (reprinted in *Alte und moderne Kunst*, 13 (1968), pp. 2–13).

Wies, E., *Kaiser Heinrich IV* (Munich, 1996).

Young, K., *The Drama of the Medieval Church* (Oxford, 1933).

Zappert, G., 'Epiphania', *Sitzungsberichte der philosophisch-historische Klasse der Kaiserliche Akadamie der Wissenschaften*, 21 (1857), pp. 291–372.

Liturgical indices

The following indices were all created using the dBase files of the CANTUS index of the Gottschalk Antiphonary. I am particularly indebted to Charles Downey for his time and effort in creating the dBase files. The following abbreviations are used throughout the indices:

Office column:

V First Vespers
M Matins
L Lauds
P Prime
T Terce
S Sext
N None
V2 Second Vespers
E Stock antiphons 'in evangelio'

Genre column:

A Antiphon
R Responsory
V Verse
H Hymn
I Invitatory Antiphon
P Psalm
M Sequence
v Versicle

Position column:

B *Benedictus* antiphon
M *Magnificat* antiphon

Mode/*Differentia* columns:

? No mode and/or *differentia* are given in the manuscript
* Mode and/or *differentia* trimmed away or otherwise illegible

If a figure appears in the mode column and an asterisk [*] appears in the *differentia* column, the mode was not determinable from the Gottschalk Antiphonary and has instead been drawn from the Engelberg Directorium (or *Gr 29/30*, if the chant is not found in *Eng102*). Chants not in *CAO* have been assigned CANTUS reference numbers beginning with [Q]. The number '9999' is used for chants whose *CAO* number is uncertain.

INDEX I CHANTS IN MANUSCRIPT ORDER

Folio	Feast	Office	Genre	Pos.	Incipit	CAO	Mode	Differentia
11r	Dom. 4 Adventus	M	R	1.1	Canite tuba in Sion vocate	6265	1	a
11r	Dom. 4 Adventus	M	V	1	Annuntiate in finibus terrae	6265b	1	a
11r	Dom. 4 Adventus	M	R	1.2	Vicesima quarta die decimi	7886	7	yc
11r	Dom. 4 Adventus	M	V	1	Ego sum dominus deus vester	7886a	7	yc
11r	Dom. 4 Adventus	M	R	1.3	Non auferetur sceptrum de	7224	2	e
11r	Dom. 4 Adventus	M	V	1	Pulchriores sunt oculi ejus	7224a	2	e
11r	Dom. 4 Adventus	M	R	1.4	Me oportet minui illum autem	7137	3	i
11r	Dom. 4 Adventus	M	V	1	Hoc est testimonium quod	7137a	3	i
11r	Dom. 4 Adventus	M	A	2	Bethleem non*	1737	4	*
11r	Dom. 4 Adventus	M	R	2.1	Ecce jam veniet plenitudo	6596	5	vb
11r	Dom. 4 Adventus	M	V	1	Prope est ut veniat tempus	6596a	5	vb
11r	Dom. 4 Adventus	M	R	2.2	Virgo Israel revertere in	7903	8	w
11r	Dom. 4 Adventus	M	V	1	A solis ortu*	7903a	8	w
11r	Dom. 4 Adventus	M	R	2.3	Juravi dicit dominus ut ultra	7045	8	w
11r	Dom. 4 Adventus	M	V	1	Juxta est salus mea ut veniat	7045b	8	w
11r	Dom. 4 Adventus	M	V	2	A solis ortu*	7045a	8	w
11r	Dom. 4 Adventus	M	R	2.4	Non discedimus a te	7227	8	w
11r	Dom. 4 Adventus	M	V	1	Domine deus virtutum converte	7227a	8	w
11v	Dom. 4 Adventus	M	A	3	Ecce in nubibus caeli filius	2516	1	*
11v	Dom. 4 Adventus	M	R	3.1	Intuemini quantus sit iste	6983	3	*
11v	Dom. 4 Adventus	M	V	1	Et dominabitur a mari usque	6983a	3	*
11v	Dom. 4 Adventus	M	R	3.2	Radix Jesse qui exsurget	7508	8	w
11v	Dom. 4 Adventus	M	V	1	Deus a Libano*	7508z	8	w
11v	Dom. 4 Adventus	M	R	3.3	Egredietur virga de radice	6641	1	a
11v	Dom. 4 Adventus	M	V	1	Et requiescet super eum	6641a	1	a
11v	Dom. 4 Adventus	M	R	3.4	Nascetur nobis parvulus et	7195	7	yb
11v	Dom. 4 Adventus	M	V	1	Ecce advenit dominator	7195a	7	yb
11v	Dom. 4 Adventus	L	A	1	Canite tuba in Sion quia	1757	1	a
11v	Dom. 4 Adventus	L	A	2	Ecce veniet desideratus	2548	1	a
11v	Dom. 4 Adventus	L	A	3	Erunt prava in directa et	2676	1	ag
11v	Dom. 4 Adventus	L	A	4	Dominus veniet occurrite illi	2423	1	a
11v	Dom. 4 Adventus	L	A	5	Omnipotens sermo tuus domine	4144	2	e
11v	Dom. 4 Adventus	L	R		Ostende nobis*	7343	r	*
11v	Dom. 4 Adventus	L	A	B	Dixerunt pharisaei ad Joannem	2264	1	a
11v	Dom. 4 Adventus	P	A		Canite tuba*	1757	1	*
11v	Dom. 4 Adventus	T	A		Ecce veniet*	2548	1	*
11v	Dom. 4 Adventus	S	A		Erunt prava*	2676	1	*
11v	Dom. 4 Adventus	N	A		Omnipotens sermo*	4144	2	*
11v	Dom. 4 Adventus	V2	R		Tu exsurgens*	7790	r	*
11v	Dom. 4 Adventus	V2	A	M	O*	9999	2	*
11v	Hebd. 4 Adventus	M	I		Surgite vigilemus quia veniet	1164	2	e
11v	Hebd. 4 Adventus	M	R	1	Clama in fortitudine qui	6292	6	H
12r	Hebd. 4 Adventus	M	V	1	Super montem excelsum ascende	6292a	6	H
12r	Hebd. 4 Adventus	M	R	2	Orietur stella ex Jacob et	7338	8	w
12r	Hebd. 4 Adventus	M	V	1	A solis ortu*	7338a	8	w
12r	Hebd. 4 Adventus	M	R	3	Modo veniet dominator dominus	7172	6	H
12r	Hebd. 4 Adventus	M	V	1	Ecce dominator*	7172a	6	H
12r	Hebd. 4 Adventus	M	R	4	Egredietur dominus et proeli-	6640	3	i
12r	Hebd. 4 Adventus	M	V	1	Ex Sion species*	6640a	3	i
12r	Hebd. 4 Adventus	M	R	5	Praecursor pro nobis	7421	7	y-
12r	Hebd. 4 Adventus	M	V	1	Ecce dominator*	7421a	7	y-

Folio	Feast	Office	Genre	Pos.	Incipit	*CAO*	Mode	*Differentia*
12r	Hebd. 4 Adventus	M	R	6	Videbunt gentes justum tuum	7854	4	o-
12r	Hebd. 4 Adventus	M	V	1	Et eris corona gloriae in	7854a	4	o-
12r	Hebd. 4 Adventus	M	R	7	Emitte agnum domine	6656	2	e
12r	Hebd. 4 Adventus	M	V	1	Ex Sion species*	6656a	2	e
12r	Hebd. 4 Adventus	M	R	8	Rorate caeli desuper et nubes	7553	2	e
12r	Hebd. 4 Adventus	M	V	1	Emitte agnum domine	7553a	2	e
12r	Hebd. 4 Adventus	M	R	9	Germinaverunt campi eremi	6772	1	a
12r	Hebd. 4 Adventus	M	V	1	Ecce dominator*	6772a	1	a
12r	Hebd. 4 Adventus	M	R	10	Radix Jesse*	7508	8	*
12r	Hebd. 4 Adventus	M	R	11	Egredietur virga*	6641	1	*
12r	Hebd. 4 Adventus	M	R	12	Annuntiatum est*	6103	?	*
12r	Hebd. 4 Adventus	M	I		Prope est jam dominus venite	1120	6	H
12r	Fer. 2 Hebd. 4 Adv.	L	A	1	Ecce veniet dominus princeps	2550	4	o-
12r	Fer. 2 Hebd. 4 Adv.	L	A	2	Dum venerit filius hominis	2476	8	w-
12r	Fer. 2 Hebd. 4 Adv.	L	A	3	Ecce jam veniet plenitudo	2519	5	v-
12r	Fer. 2 Hebd. 4 Adv.	L	A	4	Haurietis aquas in gaudio de	3020	5	v-
12r	Fer. 2 Hebd. 4 Adv.	L	A	5	Egredietur dominus de loco	2612	4	o-
12r	Fer. 2 Hebd. 4 Adv.	L	A	B	Egredietur virga de radice	2613	1	a-
12v	Fer. 3 Hebd. 4 Adv.	L	A	1	Rorate caeli desuper et nubes	4668	4	oc
12v	Fer. 3 Hebd. 4 Adv.	L	A	2	Emitte agnum domine	2642	4	oc
12v	Fer. 3 Hebd. 4 Adv.	L	A	3	Ut cognoscamus domine in	5290	4	oc
12v	Fer. 3 Hebd. 4 Adv.	L	A	4	Da mercedem domine	2087	4	o
12v	Fer. 3 Hebd. 4 Adv.	L	A	5	Lex per Moysen data est gra-	3613	1	a
12v	Fer. 3 Hebd. 4 Adv.	L	A	B	Tu Bethleem terra Juda non	5195	3	i
12v	Fer. 4 Hebd. 4 Adv.	L	A	1	Prophetae praedicaverunt	4392	1	a
12v	Fer. 4 Hebd. 4 Adv.	L	A	2	Spiritus domini super me	4999	2	e
12v	Fer. 4 Hebd. 4 Adv.	L	A	3	Annuntiate populis et dicite	1428	4	*
12v	Fer. 4 Hebd. 4 Adv.	L	A	4	Ecce veniet dominus ut sedeat	2551	4	o
12v	Fer. 4 Hebd. 4 Adv.	L	A	5	Propter Sion non tacebo donec	4400	4	o
12v	Fer. 4 Hebd. 4 Adv.	L	A	B	Quomodo fiet istud angele dei	4563	7	yc
12v	Fer. 4 Hebd. 4 Adv.	P	A		Missus est Gabriel*	3794	8	*
12v	Fer. 4 Hebd. 4 Adv.	T	A		Ave Maria gratia plena	1539	1	a
12v	Fer. 4 Hebd. 4 Adv.	S	A		Dabit illi dominus sedem	2092	1	a
12v	Fer. 4 Hebd. 4 Adv.	N	A		Ecce ancilla domini fiat mihi	2491	8	wd
12v	Fer. 5 Hebd. 4 Adv.	L	A	1	De Sion veniet dominus	2120	1	ap
12v	Fer. 5 Hebd. 4 Adv.	L	A	2	De Sion veniet qui regnaturus	2121	1	ap
12v	Fer. 5 Hebd. 4 Adv.	L	A	3	Convertere domine aliquantu-	1920	8	w
12v	Fer. 5 Hebd. 4 Adv.	L	A	4	Ecce deus meus et honorabo	2503	8	w
12v	Fer. 5 Hebd. 4 Adv.	L	A	5	Dominus legifer noster	2415	3	i
12v	Fer. 5 Hebd. 4 Adv.	L	A	1B	Intuemini quantus sit	3391	4	o
12v	Fer. 5 Hebd. 4 Adv.	L	A	2B	Vigilate animo in proximo est	5418	4	oc
12v	Fer. 6 Hebd. 4 Adv.	L	A	1	Constantes estote videbitis	1899	2	e
12v	Fer. 6 Hebd. 4 Adv.	L	A	2	Ecce rex veniet dominus	2543	4	*
12v	Fer. 6 Hebd. 4 Adv.	L	A	3	Veni domine et noli tardare	5320	4	o
12v	Fer. 6 Hebd. 4 Adv.	L	A	4	Deus a Libano veniet et*	2163	1	a
12v	LACUNA							
21r	S. Stephani	L	A	B	Patefactae sunt januae caeli	4229	8	*
21r	S. Stephani	L	A	R	Ecce advenit*	2489	8	*
21r	S. Stephani	L	A	R	Sancta et immaculata*	4700	6	*
21r	S. Stephani	P	A		Cum autem esset*	1987	1	*
21r	S. Stephani	T	A		Lapidabant*	3575	1	*
21r	S. Stephani	S	A		Stephanus vidit*	5028	8	*
21r	S. Stephani	N	A		Sepelierunt*	4866	8	*

Folio	Feast	Office	Genre	Pos.	Incipit	*CAO*	Mode	*Differentia*
21r	S. Stephani	V2	A	1	Jucundus homo qui miseretur	3510	1	*
21r	S. Stephani	V2	A	2	Quid retribuam domino pro	4530	1	*
21r	S. Stephani	V2	A	3	Domine libera animam meam a	2357	7	*
21r	S. Stephani	V2	A	4	Sustinuit anima mea in verbo	5094	8	*
21r	S. Stephani	V2	R		Sancte Stephane protomartyr*	7584	?	*
21r	S. Stephani	V2	A	1M	Intuens in caelum*	3392	4	*
21r	S. Stephani	V2	A	2M	Stephanus autem*	5025	8	*
21r	S. Stephani	V2	A	R	Verbum caro*	5363	8	*
21r	S. Stephani	V2	A	R	Nesciens mater*	3877	6	*
21r	S. Joannis Evang.	V	R		Vox tonitrui tui deus in rota	7921	6	*
21r	S. Joannis Evang.	V	V	1	Victo senatu cum Caesare	7921a	6S	*
21r	S. Joannis Evang.	V	V	2	Gloria patri et filio et	9000	6S	*
21r	S. Joannis Evang.	V	R		Apparuit caro*	6113	?	*
21r	S. Joannis Evang.	V	v		Annuntiaverunt opera dei	7950	*	
21r	S. Joannis Evang.	V	A	1M	Domine suscipe me*	2391	4	*
21r	S. Joannis Evang.	V	A	2M	Valde honorandus est beatus	5309	8	*
21r	S. Joannis Evang.	M	I		Adoremus regem apostolorum	1013	4	*
21r	S. Joannis Evang.	M	A	1.1	Joannes apostolus et	3494	1	*
21r	S. Joannis Evang.	M	A	1.2	Supra pectus domini Jesu	5068	2	*
21r	S. Joannis Evang.	M	A	1.3	Quasi unum de paradisi	4451	3	*
21r	S. Joannis Evang.	M	A	1.4	In ferventis olei dolium	3234	4	*
21r	S. Joannis Evang.	M	A	1.5	Propter insuperabilem	4397	5	*
21r	S. Joannis Evang.	M	A	1.6	Occurrit beato Joanni ab	4105	6	*
21v	S. Joannis Evang.	M	v	1	In omnem terram exivit sonus*	8097	r	
21v	S. Joannis Evang.	M	A	1.1	Qui vicerit faciam illum	4505	1	*
21v	S. Joannis Evang.	M	A	1.2	Hic est discipulus ille qui	3051	3	*
21v	S. Joannis Evang.	M	A	1.3	Sic eum volo manere donec	4923	3	*
21v	S. Joannis Evang.	M	A	1.4	Cibavit eum dominus pane	1802	7	*
21v	S. Joannis Evang.	M	A	1.5	Spiritu sapientiae salutaris	4995	2	*
21v	S. Joannis Evang.	M	A	1.6	Dedit illi dominus claritatem	2134	1	*
21v	S. Joannis Evang.	M	R	1.1	Valde honorandus est beatus	7817	2	*
21v	S. Joannis Evang.	M	V	1	Mulier ecce filius tuus ad	7817a	2	*
21v	S. Joannis Evang.	M	R	1.2	Hic est beatissimus	6819	8	*
21v	S. Joannis Evang.	M	V	1	Hic est discipulus ille quem	6819a	8	*
21v	S. Joannis Evang.	M	R	1.3	In illo die suscipiam te	6906	8	*
21v	S. Joannis Evang.	M	V	1	In tribulatione invocasti me	6906a	8	*
21v	S. Joannis Evang.	M	V	2	Esto fidelis usque ad mortem	6906b	8	*
21v	S. Joannis Evang.	M	R	1.4	Qui vicerit faciam illum	7486	2	*
21v	S. Joannis Evang.	M	V	1	Vincenti dabo edere de ligno	7486b	2	*
21v	S. Joannis Evang.	M	A	2.1	Apparuit caro suo Joanni	1458	7	*
21v	S. Joannis Evang.	M	A	2.2	Expandens manus suas ad deum	2795	8	*
21v	S. Joannis Evang.	M	A	2.3	Domine suscipe me ut cum	2391	4	*
22r	S. Joannis Evang.	M	A	2.4	Dixit dominus matri suae	2286	1	*
22r	S. Joannis Evang.	M	A	2.5	Exiit sermo inter fratres	2791	1	*
22r	S. Joannis Evang.	M	A	2.6	Iste est Joannes cui Christus	3423	1	*
22r	S. Joannis Evang.	M	v	2	Constitues eos principes*	7994	r	
22r	S. Joannis Evang.	M	A	2.1	Tu es discipulus meus in te	5204	1	*
22r	S. Joannis Evang.	M	A	2.2	Ponam te signaculum dicit	4303	8	*
22r	S. Joannis Evang.	M	A	2.3	Dixit dominus matri suae*	2286	1	*
22r	S. Joannis Evang.	M	A	2.4	Exiit sermo inter fratres*	2791	1	*
22r	S. Joannis Evang.	M	A	2.5	Iste est Joannes cui*	3423	1	*
22r	S. Joannis Evang.	M	A	2.6	Cum reverteretur Joannes ab	2031	1	*
22r	S. Joannis Evang.	M	R	2.1	Ecce puer meus quem elegi	6603	7	*

Folio	Feast	Office	Genre	Pos.	Incipit	CAO	Mode	Differentia
22r	S. Joannis Evang.	M	V	1	Iste est Joannes qui supra	6603a	7	*
22r	S. Joannis Evang.	M	R	2.2	Hic est discipulus qui	6822	7	*
22r	S. Joannis Evang.	M	V	1	Quanta audivimus et	6822a	7	*
22r	S. Joannis Evang.	M	R	2.3	Iste est Joannes cui Christus	7000	8	*
22r	S. Joannis Evang.	M	V	1	Mulier ecce filius tuus ad	7000z	8	*
22r	S. Joannis Evang.	M	R	2.4	Apparuit caro suo Joanni	6113	?	*
22r	S. Joannis Evang.	M	V	1	Cumque complesset apostolus	6113a	?	*
22r	S. Joannis Evang.	M	V	2	Gloria patri et filio et	9000	?	*
22r	S. Joannis Evang.	M	A	3	Iste est Joannes qui supra	3425	1	*
22r	S. Joannis Evang.	M	v	3	Nimis honorati sunt amici tui	8148	r	
22v	S. Joannis Evang.	M	R	3.1	Iste est Joannes qui supra	7001	1	*
22v	S. Joannis Evang.	M	V	1	Valde honorandus est beatus	7001a	1	*
22v	S. Joannis Evang.	M	R	3.2	Diligebat autem eum Jesus	6454	3	*
22v	S. Joannis Evang.	M	V	1	In cruce denique moriturus	6454a	3	*
22v	S. Joannis Evang.	M	R	3.3	Cibavit eum dominus pane	6281	7	*
22v	S. Joannis Evang.	M	V	1	In medio ecclesiae aperuit	6281a	7	*
22v	S. Joannis Evang.	M	R	3.4	In medio ecclesiae aperuit os	6913	1	*
22v	S. Joannis Evang.	M	V	1	Misit dominus manum suam et	6913a	1	*
22v	S. Joannis Evang.	L	A	1	Ecce puer meus electus quem	2536	1	*
22v	S. Joannis Evang.	L	A	2	Hic est discipulus meus sic	3052	3	*
22v	S. Joannis Evang.	L	A	3	Misit dominus manum suam et	3786	7	*
22v	S. Joannis Evang.	L	A	4	Sunt de hic stantibus qui non	5056	1	*
22v	S. Joannis Evang.	L	A	5	Joannes autem apostolus virgo	3495	1	*
22v	S. Joannis Evang.	L	R		Sancte Joannes dilecte	7579	r	*
22v	S. Joannis Evang.	L	V	1	Et impetratam nobis*	7579a	r	*
22v	S. Joannis Evang.	L	v		Annuntiaverunt*	7950	r	
22v	S. Joannis Evang.	L	A	B	In medio ecclesiae aperuit	3255	1	*
22v	S. Joannis Evang.	L	A	R	Pastores loquebantur*	4225	7	*
22v	S. Joannis Evang.	L	A	R	Continet in*	1905	1	*
22v	S. Joannis Evang.	L	A	R	Stephanus vidit*	5028	8	*
22v	S. Joannis Evang.	P	A		Joannes apostolus*	3494	1	*
22v	S. Joannis Evang.	T	A		Supra pectus*	5068	2	*
22v	S. Joannis Evang.	S	A		Quasi unum*	4451	3	*
22v	S. Joannis Evang.	N	A		In ferventis olei*	3234	4	*
22v	S. Joannis Evang.	V2	A	1	Juravit dominus et*	3522	7	*
22v	S. Joannis Evang.	V2	R		Sancte Joannes dilecte*	7579	r	*
22v	S. Joannis Evang.	V2	v		Annuntiaverunt opera dei	7950	r	
22v	S. Joannis Evang.	V2	A	1M	Exiit sermo inter fratres*	2791	1	*
22v	S. Joannis Evang.	V2	A	2M	Domine suscipe*	2391	4	*
22v	S. Joannis Evang.	V2	A	3M	Iste est discipulus qui	3421	?	*
22v	S. Joannis Evang.	V2	A	R	O regem caeli*	4077	4	*
22v	S. Joannis Evang.	V2	A	R	Beatus venter*	1668	8	*
22v	LACUNA							
32r	Epiphania	M	A	2.3	Adorate dominum alleluia in	1288	6	*
32r	Epiphania	M	A	2.4	Adorate dominum alleluia om-	1289	6	H
32r	Epiphania	M	A	2.5	Notum fecit dominus alleluia	3964	6	H
32r	Epiphania	M	A	2.6	Ecce advenit dominator*	2489	8	wb
32r	Epiphania	M	v	2	Omnes gentes quascumque	8160	r	
32r	Epiphania	M	R	2.1	Magi veniunt ab oriente	7112	8	w
32r	Epiphania	M	V	1	Vidimus enim stellam ejus in	7112a	8	w
32r	Epiphania	M	R	2.2	Interrogabat magos Herodes	6981	4	oc
32r	Epiphania	M	V	1	Magi veniunt ab oriente	6981a	4	oc
32r	Epiphania	M	R	2.3	Stella quam viderunt magi in	7701	8	w

179

Folio	Feast	Office	Genre	Pos.	Incipit	CAO	Mode	Differentia
32r	Epiphania	M	V	1	Et intrantes domum invenerunt	7701a	8	w
32r	Epiphania	M	R	2.4	Videntes stellam magi gavisi	7864	4	oc
32r	Epiphania	M	V	1	Reges Tharsis et insulae*	7864a	4	oc
32r	Epiphania	M	A	3	Tria sunt munera quae	5181	4	oc
32r	Epiphania	M	v	3	Adorate dominum	7937	r	
32r	Epiphania	M	R	3.1	Tria sunt munera pretiosa	7777	1	a
32r	Epiphania	M	V	1	Reges Tharsis et insulae	7777a	1	a
32r	Epiphania	M	R	3.2	Dies sanctificatus illuxit	6444	8	w
32r	Epiphania	M	V	1	Venite adoremus eum quia ipse	6444a	8	w
32v	Epiphania	M	R	3.3	Hic est dies praeclarus in	6821	7	yc
32v	Epiphania	M	V	1	Et intrantes domum invenerunt	6821a	7	yc
32v	Epiphania	M	R	3.4	In columbae specie spiritus	6892	2	e
32v	Epiphania	M	V	1	Caeli aperti sunt super eum	6892a	2	e
32v	Epiphania	M	M		Quem non praevalent propria	6892P	2	
32v	Epiphania	L	A	1	Ante luciferum genitus et	1434	2	e
32v	Epiphania	L	A	2	Venit lumen tuum Jerusalem et	5344	1	ag
32v	Epiphania	L	A	3	Apertis thesauris suis	1447	1	ap
32v	Epiphania	L	A	4	Maria et flumina benedicite	3700	4	oc
32v	Epiphania	L	A	5	Magi videntes stellam obtule-	3655	1	a
33r	Epiphania	L	R		Surge illuminare Jerusalem	7729	1	a
33r	Epiphania	L	V	1	Quia venit lumen tuum	7729a	1	a
33r	Epiphania	L	V	2	Gloria patri et filio et	9000	1	a
33r	Epiphania	L	v		Omnes de Saba venient	8159	r	
33r	Epiphania	L	A	B	Hodie caelesti sponso juncta	3095	8	wd
33r	Epiphania	P	A		Lux de luce apparuisti	3649	8	wb
33r	Epiphania	T	A		Tria sunt munera*	5181	4	*
33r	Epiphania	T	v		Venient ad te qui detrahebant	8233	r	
33r	Epiphania	S	A		Vidimus stellam ejus in	5411	4	oc
33r	Epiphania	S	v		Adorate dominum	7937	r	
33r	Epiphania	N	A		Salutis nostrae auctorem magi	4685	1	ah
33r	Epiphania	N	v		Tria sunt munera pretiosa	8223	r	
33r	Epiphania	V2	A	1	Tecum principium*	5127	1	*
33r	Epiphania	V2	R		Omnes de Saba venient aurum	Q614	6	H
33r	Epiphania	V2	V	1	Et laudem domino annuntiantes	Q614	6	H
33r	Epiphania	V2	v		Reges Tharsis et insulae*	8180	r	
33r	Epiphania	V2	A	M	Tribus miraculis ornatum diem	5184	1	a
33r	Epiphania,8	M	I		Christus apparuit*	1054	6	H
33r	Epiphania,8	M	A	1.1	Stella nobis visa est rex	5023	4	oc
33r	Epiphania,8	M	A	1.2	Venient ad te qui detrahebant	5331	8	w
33r	Epiphania,8	M	A	1.3	Stella ista sicut flamma	5022	7	yg
33r	Epiphania,8	M	A	1.4	Videntes stellam magi gavisi	5391	7	yc
33r	Epiphania,8	M	A	1.5	Omnis terra*	4155	4	*
33r	Epiphania,8	M	v	1	Omnes gentes quascumque	8160	r	
33r	Epiphania,8	M	A	2.1	Omnes gentes*	4125	4	*
33r	Epiphania,8	M	v	2	Adorate dominum	7937	r	
33r	Epiphania,8	M	v	2	Omnis terra adoret te deus*	8161	r	
33r	Epiphania,8	M	R	1	Omnes de Saba*	7314	?	*
33r	Epiphania,8	M	R	2	Venit lumen tuum Jerusalem et	7833	8	w
33v	Epiphania,8	M	V	1	Filii tui de longe venient et	7833a	8	w
33v	Epiphania,8	M	R	3	Videbis o Jerusalem et	7853	3	ik
33v	Epiphania,8	M	V	1	Inundatio camelorum operiet	7853a	3	ik
33v	Epiphania,8	M	R	4	Pastores prae claritate	7357	4	oc
33v	Epiphania,8	M	V	1	Annuntio vobis gaudium magnum	7357a	4	oc

Folio	Feast	Office	Genre	Pos.	Incipit	CAO	Mode	Differentia
33v	Epiphania,8	L	A	I	Ante luciferum*	1434	2	*
33v	Epiphania,8	L	A	4	Maria et flumina*	3700	4	*
33v	Epiphania,8	L	R		Reges Tharsis et insulae	7522	6	H
33v	Epiphania,8	L	V	I	Reges Arabum et Saba dona	7522a	6	H
33v	Epiphania,8	L	v		Omnes de Saba venient	8159	r	
33v	Epiphania,8	E	A	I	Vox de caelis sonuit et vox	5507	4	oc
33v	Epiphania,8	E	A	2	Caeli aperti sunt super eum	1835	5	v
33v	Epiphania,8	E	A	3	Joannes quidem clamabat	3503	I	a
33v	Epiphania,8	E	A	4	Aqua comburit peccatum hodie	1467	7	yb
33v	Epiphania,8	E	A	5	Pater de caelis filium	4232	7	yb
33v	Epiphania,8	E	A	6	Baptizatur Christus et	1554	7	yc
33v	Epiphania,8	E	A	7	Super ripam Jordanis stabat	5062	8	w
33v	Epiphania,8	E	A	8	Baptizat miles regem servus	1553	8	w
34r	Epiphania,8	V2	A	I	Tecum principium*	5127	*	
34r	Epiphania,8	V2	R		Omnes de Saba*	Q614	6	*
34r	Epiphania,8	V2	v		Reges Tharsis et insulae*	8180	r	
34r	Dom. I p. Epiph.	V	A	I	Tecum principium*	5127	*	
34r	Dom. I p. Epiph.	V	R		Omnes de Saba*	Q614	6	*
34r	Dom. I p. Epiph.	V	v		Reges Tharsis et insulae*	8180	r	
34r	Dom. I p. Epiph.	V	A	M	Ab oriente venerunt magi in	1205	8	w
34r	Dom. I p. Epiph.	M	I		Christus apparuit*	1054	6	*
34r	Dom. I p. Epiph.	M	A	1.1	Stella nobis visa*	5023	4	oc
34r	Dom. I p. Epiph.	M	R	1.1	Hodie in Jordane*	6849	*	
34r	Dom. I p. Epiph.	M	A	2.1	Afferte domino*	1303	7	*
34r	Dom. I p. Epiph.	L	A	p	Ante luciferum*	1434	*	
34r	Dom. I p. Epiph.	L	R		Reges Tharsis*	7522	*	
34r	Dom. I p. Epiph.	L	v		Omnes de Saba venient	8159	r	
34r	Dom. I p. Epiph.	L	A	B	Cum factus esset Jesus	2006	4	og
34r	Epiphania,8	L	A	R	Vidimus stellam*	5411	4	*
34r	Dom. I p. Epiph.	V2	A	I	Tecum principium*	5127	*	
34r	Dom. I p. Epiph.	V2	A	M	Fili quid fecisti nobis sic	2872	8	wd
34r	Epiphania,8	V2	A	R	Videntes stellam*	5391	7	*
34r	Epiphania,8	E	A	I	Quid est quod me quaerebatis	4521	8	w
34r	Epiphania,8	E	A	2	Maria autem conservabat omnia	3696	8	w
34r	Epiphania,8	E	A	3	Puer Jesus proficiebat aetate	4410	6	H
34r	S. Pauli Heremitae	V	R		Justum deduxit*	9999	*	
34r	S. Pauli Heremitae	V	v		Os justi*	8165	r	
34r	S. Pauli Heremitae	V	A	M	Similabo eum*	4952	I	ab
34r	S. Pauli Heremitae	M	I		Regem confessorum*	1129	*	*
34r	S. Pauli Heremitae	M	v		Justum deduxit dominus*	8115	r	
34r	S. Pauli Heremitae	M	R	I	Euge serve bone*	6677	*	
34r	S. Pauli Heremitae	M	R	2	Justus germinabit*	7060	*	
34r	S. Pauli Heremitae	M	R	3	Iste homo perfecit*	7008	*	
34r	S. Pauli Heremitae	L	A	I	Euge serve bone*	2734	*	
34r	S. Pauli Heremitae	L	R		Amavit eum dominus*	9999	?	*
34r	S. Pauli Heremitae	L	A	B	Justus cor suum*	3544	3	i
34r	S. Pauli Heremitae	L	A	R	Vidimus stellam*	5411	*	
34r	S. Pauli Heremitae	P	A		Justum deduxit*	3541	7	yd
34r	S. Pauli Heremitae	T	A		Domine quinque talenta*	2370	I	ap
34r	Octava Epiphaniae	V	A	I	Tecum principium*	5127	*	
34r	Octava Epiphaniae	V	R		Omnes de Saba*	Q614	*	
34r	Octava Epiphaniae	V	v		Reges Tharsis et insulae*	8180	r	
34r	Octava Epiphaniae	V	A	M	Fontes aquarum sanctificati	2888	8	w

Folio	Feast	Office	Genre	Pos.	Incipit	*CAO*	Mode	*Differentia*
34r	S. Hilarii	V	A	R	Sacerdos et pontifex*	4673	1	a
34v	Octava Epiphaniae	M	I		Christus apparuit*	1054	*	*
34v	Octava Epiphaniae	M	A	3	In columbae specie spiritus	3213	2	e
34v	Octava Epiphaniae	M	v	3	Adorate dominum	7937	r	
34v	Octava Epiphaniae	L	A	1	Veterem hominem renovans	5373	7	yb
34v	Octava Epiphaniae	L	A	2	Te qui in spiritu et igne	5122	7	yb
34v	Octava Epiphaniae	L	A	3	Baptista contremuit et non	1552	7	yb
34v	Octava Epiphaniae	L	A	4	Caput draconis salvator	1768	7	yb
34v	Octava Epiphaniae	L	A	5	Magnum mysterium declaratur	3678	7	yb
34v	Octava Epiphaniae	L	R		Reges Tharsis*	7522	6	*
34v	Octava Epiphaniae	L	v		Omnes de Saba venient	8159	r	
34v	Octava Epiphaniae	L	A	B	Praecursor Joannes exsultat	4358	7	yb
34v	S. Hilarii	L	A	R	Euge serve*	2732	1	a
34v	Octava Epiphaniae	P	A		Veterem hominem*	5373	7	*
34v	Octava Epiphaniae	T	A		Te qui in spiritu*	5122	*	
34v	Octava Epiphaniae	T	v		Venient ad te*	8233	r	
34v	Octava Epiphaniae	S	A		Baptista contremuit*	1552	*	
34v	Octava Epiphaniae	S	v		Adorate dominum	7937	r	
34v	Octava Epiphaniae	N	A		Magnum mysterium*	3678	*	
34v	Octava Epiphaniae	N	v		Tria sunt munera pretiosa	8223	r	
34v	Octava Epiphaniae	V2	A	1	Tecum principium*	5127	*	
34v	Octava Epiphaniae	V2	R		Omnes de Saba*	Q614	6	*
34v	Octava Epiphaniae	V2	R		Vox domini super aquas deus	7918	4	oc
34v	Octava Epiphaniae	V2	V	1	Intonuit dominus super aquas	7918a	4	oc
34v	Octava Epiphaniae	V2	V	2	Gloria patri et filio et	9000	4	oc
34v	Octava Epiphaniae	V2	A	M	Christo datus est principatus	1788	8	w
34v	Dom. per annum	V	A	1	Custodit dominus omnes	2085	4	oh
34v	Dom. per annum	V	A	2	Laudabo deum meum in vita mea	3583	4	oc
34v	Dom. per annum	V	A	3	Deo nostro jucunda sit	2148	8	wb
34v	Dom. per annum	V	A	4	Benedixit filiis tuis in te	1734	6	H
34v	Dom. per annum	V	R		Deus qui sedes*	6433	4	*
34v	Dom. per annum	V	v		Vespertina oratio ascendat ad	8240	r	
34v	Dom. 2 p. Epiph.	V	A	M	Puer Jesus proficiebat*	4410	6	H
34v	Dom. per annum	M	I		Praeoccupemus faciem domini	1115	7	yc
34v	Dom. per annum	M	A	1.1	Domine in virtute tua	2349	8	wd
34v	Dom. per annum	M	A	1.3	Dominus regit me et nihil	2420	4	oc
34v	Dom. per annum	M	A	1.5	Oculi mei semper ad dominum	4109	4	oc
35r	Dom. per annum	M	v	1	Memor fui in nocte nominis*	8138	r	
35r	Dom. per annum	M	R	1.1	Domine ne in ira tua arguas	6501	1	a
35r	Dom. per annum	M	V	1	Timor et tremor venerunt	6501a	1	a
35r	Dom. per annum	M	R	1.2	Deus qui sedes super thronum	6433	4	oc
35r	Dom. per annum	M	V	1	Tibi enim derelictus est	6433a	4	oc
35r	Dom. per annum	M	R	1.3	A dextris est mihi dominus ne	6002	8	w
35r	Dom. per annum	M	V	1	Conserva me domine quoniam in	6002a	8	w
35r	Dom. per annum	M	V	2	Dominus pars hereditatis meae	6002b	8	w
35r	Dom. per annum	M	R	1.4	Notas mihi fecisti domine	7240	8	w
35r	Dom. per annum	M	V	1	Conserva me domine quoniam in	7240a	8	w
35r	Dom. per annum	M	V	2	Gloria patri*	9000	8	w
35r	Dom. per annum	M	A	2.1	Dominus defensor vitae meae	2404	1	aq
35r	Dom. per annum	M	A	2.3	Adorate dominum in aula	1290	8	wd
35r	Dom. per annum	M	A	2.5	In tua justitia libera me	3300	8	wg
35r	Dom. per annum	M	v	2	Media nocte surgebam ad	8136	r	
35r	Dom. per annum	M	R	2.1	Diligam te domine virtus mea	6453	4	oc

Folio	Feast	Office	Genre	Pos.	Incipit	CAO	Mode	Differentia
35r	Dom. per annum	M	V	1	Laudans invocabo dominum et	6453a	4	oc
35r	Dom. per annum	M	R	2.2	Domini est terra et plenitudo	6517	8	w
35r	Dom. per annum	M	V	1	Ipse super maria fundavit eum	6517a	8	w
35r	Dom. per annum	M	R	2.3	Ad te domine levavi animam	6026	2	e
35r	Dom. per annum	M	V	1	Neque irrideant me inimici	6026a	2	e
35r	Dom. per annum	M	R	2.4	Audiam domine vocem laudis	6144	7	yc
35r	Dom. per annum	M	V	1	Domine dilexi decorem domus	6144a	7	yc
35v	Dom. per annum	M	A	3	Alleluia iv (De Sion exibit)	1329	2	e
35v	Dom. per annum	M	v	3	Exaltare domine in virtute	8061	r	
35v	Dom. per annum	M	R	3.1	Quam magna multitudo	7459	1	a
35v	Dom. per annum	M	V	1	Perfecisti eis qui sperant in	7459a	1	a
35v	Dom. per annum	M	R	3.2	Afflicti pro peccatis nostris	6060	8	w
35v	Dom. per annum	M	V	1	Domine deus Israel exaudi	6060a	8	w
35v	Dom. per annum	M	R	3.3	Peccata mea domine sicut	7370	1	a
35v	Dom. per annum	M	V	1	Quoniam iniquitatem meam ego	7370a	1	a
35v	Dom. per annum	M	R	3.4	Fiat manus tua ut salvum me	6731	4	oc
35v	Dom. per annum	M	V	1	Erravi sicut ovis quae	6731a	4	oc
35v	Dom. per annum	M	V	2	Gloria patri et filio et	9000	4	oc
35v	Dom. per annum	M	R	13	Abscondi tamquam aurum	6011	6	H
35v	Dom. per annum	M	V	1	Quoniam iniquitatem meam ego	6011a	6	H
35v	Dom. per annum	L	A	p	Alleluia vii (Dico vobis)	1332	4	od
35v	Dom. per annum	L	A	4	Hymnum dicamus alleluia	3153	8	w
35v	Dom. per annum	L	A	5	Alleluia vi (In domino)	1331	6	H
35v	Dom. per annum	L	R		Haec est dies quam fecit	6799	r	*
35v	Dom. per annum	L	V	1	Exsultemus et laetemur in ea	6799a	r	*
35v	Dom. per annum	L	v		Dominus regnavit decorem	8034	r	
35v	Dom. 2 p. Epiph.	L	A	B	Nuptiae factae sunt in Cana	3979	8	wd
35v	Dom. per annum	P	A		Alleluia vi (Ortus conclusus)	1331	2	e
36r	Dom. per annum	P	v		Exsurge domine adjuva nos	8072	r	
36r	Dom. per annum	T	A		Alleluia viii (Praebe fili)	1333	4	oc
36r	Dom. per annum	T	v		Ego dixi domine miserere mei	8042	r	
36r	Dom. per annum	S	A		Alleluia v (Inter natos mu-)	1330	3	i
36r	Dom. per annum	S	v		Dominus regit me et nihil	8032	r	
36r	Dom. per annum	N	A		Alleluia vii (Innuebant pa-)	1332	4	od
36r	Dom. per annum	N	v		Ab occultis meis munda me	7928	r	
36r	Dom. per annum	V2	A	1	Dixit dominus domino meo sede	2285	7	yg
36r	Dom. per annum	V2	A	2	Fidelia omnia mandata ejus	2865	4	oh
36r	Dom. per annum	V2	A	3	In mandatis ejus volet nimis	3251	4	oh
36r	Dom. per annum	V2	A	4	Sit nomen domini benedictum	4971	7	yd
36r	Dom. per annum	V2	R		Quam magnificata sunt opera	7460	6	H
36r	Dom. per annum	V2	V	1	Omnia in sapientia fecisti	7460a	6	H
36r	Dom. per annum	V2	v		Dirigatur domine oratio mea	8018	r	
36r	Dom. 2 p. Epiph.	V2	A	1M	Quid mihi et tibi est mulier	4526	7	yc
36r	Dom. 2 p. Epiph.	V2	A	2M	Deficiente vino jussit Jesus	2138	1	a
36r	Feria 2 per annum	M	I		Venite exsultemus domino	1179	4	oc
36r	Feria 2 per annum	M	A	1.1	Rectos decet collaudatio	4580	4	oh
36r	Feria 2 per annum	M	A	1.3	Expugna impugnantes me	2801	4	oh
36r	Feria 2 per annum	M	A	1.4	Revela domino viam tuam	4643	6	H
36r	Feria 2 per annum	M	A	1.6	Ne in ira tua arguas me	3859	6	H
36r	Feria 2 per annum	M	v	1	Delectare in domino	Q790	r	
36r	Feria 2 per annum	M	R	1.1	Benedicam domino in omni	6237	5	vb
36r	Feria 2 per annum	M	V	1	In domino laudabitur anima	6237a	5	vb
36r	Feria 2 per annum	M	R	1.2	Delectare in domino et dabit	6404	5	v-

Folio	Feast	Office	Genre	Pos.	Incipit	CAO	Mode	Differentia
36r	Feria 2 per annum	M	V	1	Spera in domino et fac	6404a	5	v-
36r	Feria 2 per annum	M	R	1.3	Cum ceciderit justus non	6359	7	yc
36r	Feria 2 per annum	M	V	1	Junior fui etenim senui et	6359a	7	yc
36v	Feria 2 per annum	M	R	1.4	Auribus percipe domine	6154	2	e
36v	Feria 2 per annum	M	V	1	Dixi custodiam vias meas ut	6154a	2	e
36v	Feria 2 per annum	M	R	1.1	Statuit dominus supra petram	7698	1	ag
36v	Feria 2 per annum	M	V	1	Exspectans exspectavi dominum	7698a	1	ag
36v	Feria 2 per annum	M	R	1.2	Ego dixi domine miserere mei	6627	4	oc
36v	Feria 2 per annum	M	V	1	Domine ne in ira tua arguas	6627a	4	oc
36v	Feria 2 per annum	M	R	1.3	Sedes tua deus in saeculum	7634	1	ag
36v	Feria 2 per annum	M	V	1	Dilexisti justitiam et odisti	7634a	1	ag
36v	Feria 2 per annum	M	R	1.4	Benedicam domino in omni	6236	6	H
36v	Feria 2 per annum	M	V	1	Semper laus ejus in ore meo	6236a	6	H
36v	Feria 2 per annum	M	V	2	Gloria patri*	9000	6	H
36v	Feria 2 per annum	M	A	2.1	Alleluia ii (Ut non delin-)	1327	5	v
36v	Feria 2 per annum	M	A	2.1	Ut non delinquam in lingua	5294	5	v
36v	Feria 2 per annum	M	A	2.3	Sana domine animam meam quia	4696	2	e
36v	Feria 2 per annum	M	A	2.5	Eructavit cor meum verbum	2673	6	H
36v	Feria 2 per annum	M	v	2	Sedes tua deus in saeculum	8194	*	
36v	Feria 2 per annum	L	A	1	Miserere mei deus	3773	6	H
36v	Feria 2 per annum	L	A	2	Intellege clamorem meum	3359	8	wb
36v	Feria 2 per annum	L	A	3	Domine in caelo misericordia	2348	8	wg
36v	Feria 2 per annum	L	A	4	Conversus est furor tuus	1918	8	w
36v	Feria 2 per annum	L	A	5	In excelsis laudate deum	3232	6	H
36v	Feria 2 per annum	L	R		Domine in caelo misericordia	6496	6	H
36v	Feria 2 per annum	L	V	1	Et veritas tua usque ad nubes	6496a	6	H
36v	Feria 2 per annum	L	v		In matutinis domine meditabor	8095	r	
36v	Feria 2 per annum	L	A	B	Benedictus deus Israel	1717	6	H
36v	Feria 2 per annum	P	A		Servite domino in timore et	4876	7	yc
36v	Feria 2 per annum	P	v		Exsurge domine adjuva*	8072	r	
37r	Feria 2 per annum	T	A		Adjuva me et salvus ero	1281	8	w
37r	Feria 2 per annum	T	v		Adjutor meus esto domine	7932	r	
37r	Feria 2 per annum	S	A		Aspice in me et miserere mei	1498	8	wb
37r	Feria 2 per annum	S	v		Dominus regit me et nihil	8032	r	
37r	Feria 2 per annum	N	A		Vide humilitatem meam domine	5380	4	oc
37r	Feria 2 per annum	N	v		Ab occultis meis munda me	7928	r	
37r	Feria 2 per annum	V2	A	1	Domus Jacob de populo barbaro	2427	8	wb
37r	Feria 2 per annum	V2	A	2	Inclinavit dominus aurem suam	3319	1	*
37r	Feria 2 per annum	V2	A	3	Laudate dominum omnes gentes	3586	3	i
37r	Feria 2 per annum	V2	A	4	Benediximus vobis in nomine	1732	8	wg
37r	Feria 2 per annum	V2	R		Adjutorium nostrum in nomine	6039	6	H
37r	Feria 2 per annum	V2	V	1	Qui fecit caelum et terram	6039a	6	H
37r	Feria 2 per annum	V2	v		Dirigatur domine oratio*	8018	r	
37r	Feria 2 per annum	V2	A	M	Magnificat anima mea dominum	3667	8	w
37r	Feria 3 per annum	M	I		Jubilemus deo salutari nostro	1095	6	H
37r	Feria 3 per annum	M	A	1.1	Adjutor in tribulationibus	1278	4	oh
37r	Feria 3 per annum	M	A	1.3	Magnus dominus et laudabilis	3680	4	o-
37r	Feria 3 per annum	M	A	1.5	Deus deorum dominus locutus	2168	8	wb
37r	Feria 3 per annum	M	v	1	Immola deo sacrificium laudis	8091	r	
37r	Feria 3 per annum	M	R	1.1	Ne perdideris me domine cum	7208	6	H
37r	Feria 3 per annum	M	V	1	Miserere mei deus miserere	7208a	6	H
37r	Feria 3 per annum	M	R	1.2	Paratum cor meum deus paratum	7350	5	v
37r	Feria 3 per annum	M	V	1	Exsurge gloria mea exsurge	7350a	5	v

Folio	Feast	Office	Genre	Pos.	Incipit	*CAO*	Mode	*Differentia*
37r	Feria 3 per annum	M	R	1.3	Adjutor meus tibi psallam	6038	7	yc
37r	Feria 3 per annum	M	V	1	Eripe me de inimicis meis	6038a	7	yc
37r	Feria 3 per annum	M	R	1.4	Deus in nomine tuo salvum me	6421	6	H
37r	Feria 3 per annum	M	V	1	Et in virtute tua libera me	6421a	6	H
37r	Feria 3 per annum	M	V	2	Gloria patri*	9000	6	H
37r	Feria 3 per annum	M	A	2.1	Alleluia iii (Juste judicate)	1328	8	wg
37r	Feria 3 per annum	M	A	2.2	Avertit dominus captivitatem	1549	8	w
37r	Feria 3 per annum	M	A	2.4	Intende in me et exaudi me	3363	6	H
37v	Feria 3 per annum	M	A	2.6	Juste judicate filii hominum	3533	8	wg
37v	Feria 3 per annum	M	v	2	Deus vitam meam annuntiavi	8011	r	
37v	Feria 3 per annum	L	A	1	Secundum magnam misericordiam	4845	1	ap
37v	Feria 3 per annum	L	A	2	Salutare vultus mei deus meus	4683	6	H
37v	Feria 3 per annum	L	A	3	Quoniam in te confidit anima	4568	8	wd
37v	Feria 3 per annum	L	A	4	Cunctis diebus vitae nostrae	2079	3	ib
37v	Feria 3 per annum	L	A	5	Omnes angeli ejus laudate	4116	6	H
37v	Feria 3 per annum	L	R		Miserere mei deus miserere	7160	6	H
37v	Feria 3 per annum	L	V	1	Quoniam in te confidit anima	7160a	6	H
37v	Feria 3 per annum	L	v		In matutinis domine meditabor	8095	*	
37v	Feria 3 per annum	L	A	B	Erexit dominus nobis cornu	2664	7	yc
37v	Feria 3 per annum	P	A		Domine deus meus in te	2333	1	aq
37v	Feria 3 per annum	T	A		Clamavi et exaudivit me	1824	4	oc
37v	Feria 3 per annum	S	A		Qui habitas in caelis	4473	8	w
37v	Feria 3 per annum	N	A		Facti sumus sicut consolati	2839	5	v
37v	Feria 3 per annum	V2	A	1	De profundis clamavi ad te	2116	8	wb
37v	Feria 3 per annum	V2	A	2	Speret Israel in domino	4990	4	oc
37v	Feria 3 per annum	V2	A	3	Et omnis mansuetudinis ejus	2713	4	oc
37v	Feria 3 per annum	V2	A	4	Ecce quam bonum et quam	2537	1	ah
37v	Feria 3 per annum	V2	A	M	Quia fecit mihi dominus magna	4510	1	ab
37v	Feria 4 per annum	M	I		In manu tua domine omnes	1087	6	H
37v	Feria 4 per annum	M	A	1.1	Da nobis domine auxilium de	2089	2	e
37v	Feria 4 per annum	M	A	1.3	Benedicite gentes deo nostro	1701	6	H
37v	Feria 4 per annum	M	A	1.5	In ecclesiis benedicite	3230	8	wd
37v	Feria 4 per annum	M	v	1	Benedicite gentes deo nostro	7969	r	
37v	Feria 4 per annum	M	R	1.1	Exaudi deus deprecationem	6685	7	yc
37v	Feria 4 per annum	M	V	1	Dum anxiaretur cor meum in	6685a	7	yc
37v	Feria 4 per annum	M	R	1.2	Deus in te speravi domine ut	6423	3	i
37v	Feria 4 per annum	M	V	1	Esto mihi domine in deum	6423a	3	i
37v	LACUNA							
42r	S. Agathae	M	R	1.1	Dum ingrederetur beata Agatha	6546	7	*
42r	S. Agathae	M	V	1	Ego autem habeo mamillas	6546a	7	*
42r	S. Agathae	M	R	1.2	Vidisti domine et exspectasti	7883	5	v
42r	S. Agathae	M	V	1	Propter veritatem et	7883a	5	v
42r	S. Agathae	M	R	1.3	Quis es tu qui venisti ad me	7499	8	wb
42r	S. Agathae	M	V	1	Nam et ego apostolus ejus sum	7499a	8	wb
42r	S. Agathae	M	R	1.4	Medicinam carnalem corpori	7140	8	wd
42r	S. Agathae	M	V	1	Ego autem adjuta a domino	7140a	8	wd
42r	S. Agathae	M	A	2.1	Nisi diligenter perfeceris	3881	4	oh
42r	S. Agathae	M	A	2.2	Mens mea solidata est et a	3744	7	yd
42r	S. Agathae	M	A	2.3	Ego Christum confiteor labiis	2568	7	yd
42r	S. Agathae	M	A	2.4	Beata Agatha ingressa	1557	1	ab
42r	S. Agathae	M	A	2.5	Vidisti domine agonem meum	5412	7	yd
42r	S. Agathae	M	A	2.6	Propter fidem castitatis	4396	7	yd
42r	S. Agathae	M	v	2	Specie tua*	8201	r	

Folio	Feast	Office	Genre	Pos.	Incipit	CAO	Mode	Differentia
42r	S. Agathae	M	R	2.1	Ipse me coronavit qui per	6990	8	wd
42r	S. Agathae	M	V	1	Vidisti domine agonem meum	6990a	8	wd
42v	S. Agathae	M	R	2.2	Agatha laetissima et	6061	7	yc
42v	S. Agathae	M	V	1	Beata Agatha ingressa	6061z	7	yc
42v	S. Agathae	M	R	2.3	Propter veritatem*	7441	8	*
42v	S. Agathae	M	V	1	Dilexisti justitiam et odisti	7441b	8	*
42v	S. Agathae	M	R	2.4	Ego autem adjuta a domino	6625	4	oc
42v	S. Agathae	M	V	1	Medicinam carnalem corpori	6625b	4	oc
42v	S. Agathae	M	A	3	Mentem sanctam spontaneam	3746	4	oc
42v	S. Agathae	M	R	3.1	Induit me dominus*	6955	6	*
42v	S. Agathae	M	R	3.2	Qui me dignatus est ab omni	7479	7	yc
42v	S. Agathae	M	V	1	Medicinam carnalem corpori*	7479a	7	yc
42v	S. Agathae	M	R	3.3	Beata Agatha ingressa	6160	1	a
42v	S. Agathae	M	V	1	Agatha ingressa carcerem	6160a	1	a
42v	S. Agathae	M	R	3.4	Gaudeamus omnes in domino	6760	1	a
42v	S. Agathae	M	V	1	Immaculatus dominus	6760a	1	a
42v	S. Agathae	L	A	1	Quis es tu qui venisti ad me	4547	7	yd
42v	S. Agathae	L	A	2	Medicinam carnalem corpori	3733	1	a
42v	S. Agathae	L	A	3	Gratias tibi ago domine quia	2975	7	yd
42v	S. Agathae	L	A	4	Benedico te pater domini mei	1702	8	w
42v	S. Agathae	L	A	5	Qui me dignatus est ab omni	4480	7	yh
43r	S. Agathae	L	R		Specie tua et pulchritudine*	7679	r	*
43r	S. Agathae	L	v		Audi filia et vide*	7955	r	
43r	S. Agathae	L	A	B	Paganorum multitudo fugiens	4208	5	vb
43r	S. Agathae	P	A		Agatha sancta dixit*	1308	7	*
43r	S. Agathae	T	A		Agatha laetissima*	1306	7	*
43r	S. Agathae	S	A		Beata Agatha*	1557	1	*
43r	S. Agathae	N	A		Mentem sanctam*	3746	4	*
43r	S. Agathae	V2	A	1	Quis es tu qui venisti*	4547	7	*
43r	S. Agathae	V2	A	2	Medicinam carnalem*	3733	1	*
43r	S. Agathae	V2	A	3	Gratias tibi ago*	2975	7	*
43r	S. Agathae	V2	A	4	Qui me dignatus*	4480	7	*
43r	S. Agathae	V2	A	M	Beata Agatha ingressa	1558	7	yc
43r	S. Scholasticae	V	R		Benedictus quam devotas*	Q603	6	*
43r	S. Scholasticae	V	A	M	Sanctimonialis autem femina	4749	6	H
43r	S. Scholasticae	M	I		Regem virginum*	9999	4	*
43r	S. Scholasticae	M	A	3	Veni sponsa*	5328	8	*
43r	S. Scholasticae	M	R		Benedictus*	Q603	6	*
43r	S. Scholasticae	M	V	1	Uterque*	Q603	6S	*
43r	S. Scholasticae	M	V	2	Gloria patri*	9000	6S	*
43r	Cathedra S. Petri	V	R		Tu es Petrus*	7788	?	*
43r	Cathedra S. Petri	V	v		Annuntiaverunt opera dei	7950	r	
43r	Cathedra S. Petri	V	A	M	Tu es pastor ovium princeps	5207	1	a
43r	Cathedra S. Petri	M	I		Tu es pastor ovium princeps	1167	2	e
43r	Cathedra S. Petri	M	A	1.1	In omnem terram*	3262	2	*
43r	Cathedra S. Petri	M	v	1	In omnem terram*	8097	r	
43r	Cathedra S. Petri	M	R	1.1	Simon Petre*	7674	?	*
43r	Cathedra S. Petri	M	R	1.2	Si diligis me*	7649	?	*
43r	Cathedra S. Petri	M	R	1.3	Tu es Petrus*	7788	?	*
43r	Cathedra S. Petri	M	R	1.4	Quodcumque ligaveris*	7503	?	*
43r	Cathedra S. Petri	M	A	2.1	Exaltabuntur cornua*	2757	6	*
43r	Cathedra S. Petri	M	A	2.2	Tollite jugum*	5158	3	*
43r	Cathedra S. Petri	M	A	2.3	Qui diligitis dominum	4466	1	ag

Folio	Feast	Office	Genre	Pos.	Incipit	*CAO*	Mode	*Differentia*
43r	Cathedra S. Petri	M	A	2.4	Jugum enim*	3520	7	*
43r	Cathedra S. Petri	M	A	2.5	Custodiebant*	2083	4	*
43r	Cathedra S. Petri	M	A	2.6	Manete*	3693	8	*
43r	Cathedra S. Petri	M	v	2	Constitues eos principes*	7994	r	
43r	Cathedra S. Petri	M	R	2.1	Posui adjutorium*	7411	?	*
43r	Cathedra S. Petri	M	R	2.2	Ecce vere Israelita*	6615	?	*
43r	Cathedra S. Petri	M	R	2.3	Solve jubente*	7678	?	*
43r	Cathedra S. Petri	M	R	2.4	Tu es pastor ovium*	7787	?	*
43r	Cathedra S. Petri	M	A	3	Solve jubente*	4981	*	
43r	Cathedra S. Petri	M	R	3.1	Quem dicunt*	7467	?	*
43r	Cathedra S. Petri	M	R	3.2	Qui regni claves*	7483	?	*
43r	Cathedra S. Petri	M	R	3.3	Ego pro te rogavi*	6630	?	*
43r	Cathedra S. Petri	M	R	3.4	Petre amas*	7382	?	*
43r	Cathedra S. Petri	L	A	1	Petre amas me*	4281	4	*
43r	Cathedra S. Petri	L	R		Exaltent eum in ecclesia	Q607	6	H
43r	Cathedra S. Petri	L	V	1	Et in cathedra seniorum	Q607	6	H
43r	Cathedra S. Petri	L	v		Annuntiaverunt opera dei	7950	r	
43r	Cathedra S. Petri	L	A	B	Quodcumque ligaveris super	4561	8	w
43r	Cathedra S. Petri	P	A		Petre amas*	4281	4	*
43r	Cathedra S. Petri	T	A		Tu es pastor ovium*	5207	1	*
43r	Cathedra S. Petri	S	A		Tu es Petrus et*	5208	7	*
43v	Cathedra S. Petri	N	A		Solve jubente*	4981	7	yd
43v	Cathedra S. Petri	V2	A	1	Juravit dominus*	3522	7	*
43v	Cathedra S. Petri	V2	A	2	Potens in terra*	4348	8	*
43v	Cathedra S. Petri	V2	A	3	Collocet eum*	1854	8	*
43v	Cathedra S. Petri	V2	A	4	Confortatus*	1881	7	*
43v	Cathedra S. Petri	V2	H		Jam bone pastor*	8268	*	
43v	Cathedra S. Petri	V2	v		Annuntiaverunt opera dei	7950	r	
43v	Cathedra S. Petri	V2	A	M	Simon Bar Jona*	4958	4	*
43v	Cathedra S. Petri	V2	V	1	Parce tuis ovibus quos raptor	4958	4	oc
43v	Cathedra S. Petri	V2	A	M	Simon Bar Jona tu vocaberis	4958	4	oc
43v	S. Gregorii	V	R		O pastor apostolice*	7279	?	*
43v	S. Gregorii	V	A	M	Gloriosa sanctissimi	2956	1	a
43v	S. Gregorii	M	I		Ad dominum vigiles cuncti	1001	4	og
43v	S. Gregorii	M	H		Confessor dei*	Q820	*	
43v	S. Gregorii	M	A	1.1	Gregorius ortus Romae ex	2981	1	ag
43v	S. Gregorii	M	A	1.2	Lineam sui generis factis et	3629	2	e
43v	S. Gregorii	M	A	1.3	Adhaerebat moralibus seniorum	1270	3	ik
43v	S. Gregorii	M	A	1.4	Gregorius ut creditur	2983	4	oc
43v	S. Gregorii	M	A	1.5	Studiis liberalibus nulli	5036	5	v
43v	S. Gregorii	M	A	1.6	Hic ab adolescentia divina	3046	6	H
43v	S. Gregorii	M	v	1	Justum deduxit dominus per	8115	r	
43v	S. Gregorii	M	R	1.1	Fulgebat in venerando duplex	6752	1	a
43v	S. Gregorii	M	V	1	Beatus vir qui timet dominum	6752a	1	a
43v	S. Gregorii	M	R	1.2	Videns Romae vir beatus	7862	2	e
43v	S. Gregorii	M	V	1	Quoniam domini est*	7862a	2	e
43v	LACUNA							
45r	S. Gregorii	L	A	5	Virginum tria milia Romae	5444	6	*
45r	S. Gregorii	L	R		Amavit eum dominus*	9999	?	*
45r	S. Gregorii	L	v		Ecce sacerdos*	8040	*	
45r	S. Gregorii	L	A	B	Christi fidelis famulus	1785	7	*
45r	S. Gregorii	P	A		Gregorius ortus*	2981	1	*
45r	S. Gregorii	T	A		Lineam sui generis*	3629	2	*

Folio	Feast	Office	Genre	Pos.	Incipit	CAO	Mode	Differentia
45r	S. Gregorii	S	A		Adhaerebat moralibus*	1270	3	*
45r	S. Gregorii	N	A		Gregorius ut creditur*	2983	4	*
45r	S. Gregorii	V2	A	1	Gregorius vigiliis*	2984	2	*
45r	S. Gregorii	V2	A	2	Lentis quidem*	3605	3	*
45r	S. Gregorii	V2	A	3	Caelesti cinctus*	1833	4	*
45r	S. Gregorii	V2	A	4	Bissenos nummos*	1740	5	*
45r	S. Gregorii	V2	R		Justus ut palma*	9999	*	
45r	S. Gregorii	V2	v		Ecce sacerdos magnus*	8040	r	
45r	S. Gregorii	V2	A	M	O Gregori dulcissime sancti	4031	4	*
45r	S. Benedicti	V	A	p	Sanctissime confessor domini	4752	?	*
45r	S. Benedicti	V	R		Alme pater*	Q602	*	
45r	S. Benedicti	V	v		Os justi*	8165	r	
45r	S. Benedicti	V	A	M	Magna semper et praeclara	Q222	1	*
45r	S. Benedicti	M	I		Ut Christo celebri jubilemus	Q102	4	*
45r	S. Benedicti	M	A	1.1	Benedictus tam nomine quam	Q209	1	*
45r	S. Benedicti	M	A	1.2	Hic ergo Romae traditus	Q214	2	*
45r	S. Benedicti	M	A	1.3	Mundum suis cum floribus	Q225	3	*
45r	S. Benedicti	M	A	1.4	Sanctum Romanus habitum dans	Q232	4	*
45r	S. Benedicti	M	A	1.5	In specu sub quo latitat dei	Q218	5	*
45r	S. Benedicti	M	A	1.6	Athleta dei gravibus poenis	Q205	6	*
45r	S. Benedicti	M	v	1	Justum deduxit dominus*	8115	r	
45r	S. Benedicti	M	R	1.1	Florem mundi periturum	Q608	1	*
45r	S. Benedicti	M	V	1	Pennas sumens ut columbae	Q608a	1S	*
45v	S. Benedicti	M	R	1.2	Puer fletum subsecutae	Q616	2	*
45v	S. Benedicti	M	V	1	Elongatus a nutrice mansit in	Q616a	2S	*
45v	S. Benedicti	M	R	1.3	Agnosce dei famule surrexit	Q601	3	*
45v	S. Benedicti	M	V	1	Haec dies quam fecit deus in	Q601a	3S	*
45v	S. Benedicti	M	R	1.4	Electo grex mortiferum patri	Q606	4	*
45v	S. Benedicti	M	V	1	Intenderunt arcum suum ut	Q606a	4S	*
45v	S. Benedicti	M	V	2	Gloria patri et filio et	9000	4S	*
45v	S. Benedicti	M	A	2.1	Jam latius innotuit quasi	Q220	7	*
45v	S. Benedicti	M	A	2.2	Ejus ergo sub tramite multi	Q211	8	*
45v	S. Benedicti	M	A	2.3	Hic non impar Eliseo ciet	Q215	1	*
45v	S. Benedicti	M	A	2.4	Maurus verbo currens patris	Q223	4	*
45v	S. Benedicti	M	A	2.5	Favent cuncta Benedicto vas	Q213	5	*
45v	S. Benedicti	M	A	2.6	O quanta plenus gratia qui	Q228	6	*
45v	S. Benedicti	M	R	2.1	Servus dei Benedictus stetit	Q617	5	*
45v	S. Benedicti	M	V	1	Orans jacentem suscitat	Q617a	5S	*
45v	S. Benedicti	M	R	2.2	Benedictus quam devotas deo	Q603	6	*
45v	S. Benedicti	M	V	1	Uterque duxit gaudia soror	Q603a	6S	*
45v	S. Benedicti	M	R	2.3	O Israelita verus cor in deum	Q613	7	*
45v	S. Benedicti	M	V	1	Caelo quoque ferri sanctam	Q613a	7S	*
45v	S. Benedicti	M	R	2.4	Alme pater qui praescius tui	Q602	8	*
46r	S. Benedicti	M	V	1	Per te ducem clarissimum ut	Q602a	8S	*
46r	S. Benedicti	M	V	2	Gloria patri et filio et	9000	8S	*
46r	S. Benedicti	M	A	3	Benedictum propheticis	Q207	1	aq
46r	S. Benedicti	M	R	3.1	Grandi pater fiducia morte	Q611	1	ab
46r	S. Benedicti	M	V	1	Fecit Christe quod jussisti	Q611a	1	ab
46r	S. Benedicti	M	R	3.2	Fratribus illuxit Benedictum	Q609	2	e
46r	S. Benedicti	M	V	1	Virque super candens micuit	Q609a	2	e
46r	S. Benedicti	M	R	3.3	Ecce jam cari noscite quam	Q605	4	oc
46r	S. Benedicti	M	V	1	Accepit ergo centuplum et	Q605a	4	oc
46r	S. Benedicti	M	R	3.4	Gloria Christe tuo tibi	Q610	2	e

Folio	Feast	Office	Genre	Pos.	Incipit	*CAO*	Mode	*Differentia*
46r	S. Benedicti	M	V	1	Nos ejus norma rege serva	Q610a	2	e
46r	S. Benedicti	M	V	2	Gloria patri et filio et	9000	2	e
46r	S. Benedicti	L	A	1	Armis praecinctus verae fidei	Q204	2	e
46r	S. Benedicti	L	A	2	Huic jubilate quo pater iste	Q217	3	ik
46r	S. Benedicti	L	A	3	Quemquam non laesit post te	Q231	4	oc
46r	S. Benedicti	L	A	4	Laus puerilis hunc benedicit	Q221	5	v
46r	S. Benedicti	L	A	5	Tympana laeta chori mens	Q236	6	H
46r	S. Benedicti	L	R		Amavit eum*	9999	*	
46r	S. Benedicti	L	H		Christe sanctorum*	8280	*	
46r	S. Benedicti	L	v		Os justi*	8165	r	
46r	S. Benedicti	L	A	B	Benedictus es domine qui	Q208	7	yc
46r	S. Benedicti	P	A		Benedictus tam nomine*	Q209	1	*
46r	S. Benedicti	T	A		Hic non impar*	Q215	1	*
46r	S. Benedicti	S	A		Favent cuncta*	Q213	5	*
46r	S. Benedicti	N	A		O quanta plenus*	Q228	6	*
46r	S. Benedicti	V2	A	1	Praeclarum late tibi vir sine	Q230	1	a
46r	S. Benedicti	V2	A	2	Membra specu claudis quo	Q224	2	e
46v	S. Benedicti	V2	A	3	Instar tu Christi patiens ad	Q219	3	ik
46v	S. Benedicti	V2	A	4	Hic probris actus tumidisque	Q216	4	oc
46v	S. Benedicti	V2	R		Justus ut palma*	9999	?	*
46v	S. Benedicti	V2	H		Rex benedicte*	Q822	*	
46v	S. Benedicti	V2	v		Os justi meditabitur	8165	r	
46v	S. Benedicti	V2	A	M	O caelestis norma vitae	Q226	1	a
46v	Annuntiatio Mariae	V	A	p	Ingressus angelus ad Mariam	3339	4	oc
46v	Annuntiatio Mariae	V	R		Christi virgo dilectissima*	6278	2	*
46v	Annuntiatio Mariae	V	v		Audi filia et vide*	7955	*	
46v	Annuntiatio Mariae	V	A	M	Ave spes nostra dei genetrix	1546	8	wd
46v	Annuntiatio Mariae	M	I		Ave Maria gratia plena	1041	7	yc
46v	Annuntiatio Mariae	M	A	1.1	Benedicta tu in mulieribus*	1709	4	*
46v	Annuntiatio Mariae	M	A	1.1	Missus est angelus Gabriel a	3793	1	ab
46v	Annuntiatio Mariae	M	A	1.2	Ingressus angelus ad Mariam	3339	2	e
46v	Annuntiatio Mariae	M	A	1.3	Maria turbatur in sermone	3706	3	ik
46v	Annuntiatio Mariae	M	A	1.4	Respondens angelus dixit ad	4629	4	oc
46v	Annuntiatio Mariae	M	A	1.5	Ecce concipies et paries	2499	5	vb
46v	Annuntiatio Mariae	M	A	1.6	Dabit illi deus sedem David	2093	6	H
46v	Annuntiatio Mariae	M	v	1	Ave Maria gratia plena	7958	r	
46v	Annuntiatio Mariae	M	R	1.1	Ingressus angelus ad Mariam	6963	1	ab
46v	Annuntiatio Mariae	M	V	1	Benedicta tu in mulieribus et	6963a	1	ab
46v	Annuntiatio Mariae	M	R	1.2	Benedicta tu in mulieribus et	6244	4	oc
47r	Annuntiatio Mariae	M	V	1	Ave Maria gratia plena	6244a	4	oc
47r	Annuntiatio Mariae	M	R	1.3	Maria ut audivit turbata est	7130	7	*
47r	Annuntiatio Mariae	M	V	1	Quomodo fiet istud quia virum	7130c	7	*
47r	Annuntiatio Mariae	M	R	1.4	Posuit Moyses bissenas virgas	Q615	1	*
47r	Annuntiatio Mariae	M	V	1	Scientes hoc signum in beatae	Q615a	1S	*
47r	Annuntiatio Mariae	M	V	2	Gloria patri et filio et	9000	1S	*
47r	Annuntiatio Mariae	M	A	2.1	Haec est quae*	3001	3	*
47r	Annuntiatio Mariae	M	A	2.1	Dixit autem Maria ad angelum	2279	7	*
47r	Annuntiatio Mariae	M	A	2.2	Ideoque et quod nascetur ex	3164	8	*
47r	Annuntiatio Mariae	M	A	2.3	Dixit autem Maria ad angelum	2278	1	*
47r	Annuntiatio Mariae	M	A	2.4	Post abscessum angeli Maria	Q229	2	*
47r	Annuntiatio Mariae	M	A	2.5	Spiritu sancto repleta	Q235	3	*
47r	Annuntiatio Mariae	M	A	2.6	Beata quae credidit quoniam	Q206	4	*
47r	Annuntiatio Mariae	M	R	2.1	Dixit angelus ad Mariam ne	6466	1	*

189

Folio	Feast	Office	Genre	Pos.	Incipit	CAO	Mode	Differentia
47r	Annuntiatio Mariae	M	V	I	Ecce concipies et paries	6466a	I	*
47r	Annuntiatio Mariae	M	R	2.2	Ecce concipies et paries	6579	8	*
47r	Annuntiatio Mariae	M	V	I	Hic erit magnus et filius	6579a	8	*
47r	Annuntiatio Mariae	M	R	2.3	Dabit illi dominus deus sedem	6390	4	*
47r	Annuntiatio Mariae	M	V	I	Et regni ejus non erit finis	6390a	4	*
47r	Annuntiatio Mariae	M	R	2.4	Salve nobilis virga Jesse	7564	I	*
47r	Annuntiatio Mariae	M	V	I	Odor tuus super cuncta	7564a	IS	*
47v	Annuntiatio Mariae	M	V	2	Gloria patri parilique proli	7564z	IS	*
47v	Annuntiatio Mariae	M	A	3	O gloriosa femina non solum	Q227	?	*
47v	Annuntiatio Mariae	M	A	3	Dabit illi dominus*	2092	I	*
47v	Annuntiatio Mariae	M	v	3	Speciosa facta es et suavis*	8202	r	
47v	Annuntiatio Mariae	M	R	3.1	Quomodo fiet istud respondens	7505	I	*
47v	Annuntiatio Mariae	M	V	I	Ideoque et quod nascetur ex	7505a	I	*
47v	Annuntiatio Mariae	M	R	3.2	Conversus Ezechiel ad	Q604	7	*
47v	Annuntiatio Mariae	M	V	I	Hinc evidenter ostensum est	Q604a	7S	*
47v	Annuntiatio Mariae	M	R	3.3	Dixit autem Maria ad angelum	6469	I	*
47v	Annuntiatio Mariae	M	V	I	Spiritus sanctus superveniet	6469b	I	*
47v	Annuntiatio Mariae	M	R	3.4	Christi virgo dilectissima	6278	2	*
47v	Annuntiatio Mariae	M	V	I	Quoniam peccatorum mole	6278a	2S	*
47v	Annuntiatio Mariae	M	V	2	Gloria patri et filio et	9000	2S	*
47v	Annuntiatio Mariae	L	A	I	Missus est Gabriel*	3794	8	*
47v	Annuntiatio Mariae	L	A	2	Ave Maria gratia*	1539	I	*
47v	Annuntiatio Mariae	L	A	3	Spiritus sanctus*	5006	8	*
47v	Annuntiatio Mariae	L	A	4	Ne timeas Maria invenisti*	3863	8	*
47v	Annuntiatio Mariae	L	A	5	Ecce ancilla domini fiat*	2491	8	*
47v	Annuntiatio Mariae	L	A	I	Quando venit ergo sacri	4443	2	*
47v	Annuntiatio Mariae	L	A	2	Verbum supernum a patre ante	5364	3	*
47v	Annuntiatio Mariae	L	A	3	Beatus auctor saeculi servile	1613	4	*
47v	Annuntiatio Mariae	L	A	4	Clausa parentis viscera*	1776	5	*
47v	LACUNA							
52r	Dom. Sexagesimae	L	A	B	Cum turba plurima conveniret	2040	*	
52r	Dom. Sexagesimae	P	A		Exiit qui seminat seminare	2789	4	*
52r	Dom. Sexagesimae	T	A		Jesus haec dicens*	3490	I	*
52r	Dom. Sexagesimae	S	A		Si vere fratres divites esse	4915	7	yd
52r	Dom. Sexagesimae	N	A		Si culmen veri honoris	4882	7	yd
52r	Dom. Sexagesimae	V2	R		Spes mea domine*	7687	?	*
52r	Dom. Sexagesimae	V2	A	M	Vobis datum est nosse	5483	6	H
52r	Hebd. Sexagesimae	E	A	I	Exiit qui seminat*	2789	4	*
52r	Hebd. Sexagesimae	E	A	2	Jesus haec dicens*	3490	I	*
52r	Hebd. Sexagesimae	E	A	3	Semen cecidit in terram bonam	4860	8	wg
52r	Hebd. Sexagesimae	E	A	4	Semen cecidit in terram bonam	4859	8	wg
52r	Hebd. Sexagesimae	E	A	5	Si vere fratres*	4915	7	*
52r	Hebd. Sexagesimae	E	A	6	Si culmen*	4882	7	*
52r	Hebd. Sexagesimae	E	A	7	Si gloriam dignitatum	4895	7	yd
52r	Hebd. Sexagesimae	E	A	8	Qui verbum dei retinent corde	4503	I	a
52r	Dom. Quinquagesimae	V	R		Angelus domini*	6098	2	*
52r	Dom. Quinquagesimae	V	H		Dies absoluti*	Q821	*	
52r	Dom. Quinquagesimae	V	v		Vespertina oratio*	8240	r	
52r	Dom. Quinquagesimae	V	A	M	Quod autem cecidit in terram	4557	4	og
52r	Dom. Quinquagesimae	M	I		Adoremus deum quia ipse fecit	1007	4	oc
52r	Dom. Quinquagesimae	M	A	1.1	Domine in virtute*	2349	8	*
52r	Dom. Quinquagesimae	M	R	1.1	Quadraginta dies et noctes	7454	5	vb
52r	Dom. Quinquagesimae	M	V	I	Noe vero et uxor ejus filii	7454a	5	vb

Folio	Feast	Office	Genre	Pos.	Incipit	CAO	Mode	Differentia
52r	Dom. Quinquagesimae	M	R	1.2	Ponam arcum meum in nubibus	7391	1	a
52r	Dom. Quinquagesimae	M	V	1	Cumque obduxero nubibus	7391a	1	a
52r	Dom. Quinquagesimae	M	R	1.3	Per memetipsum juravi dicit	7375	6	H
52r	Dom. Quinquagesimae	M	V	1	Ponam arcum meum in nubibus	7375a	6	H
52v	Dom. Quinquagesimae	M	R	1.4	Aedificavit Noe altare domino	6055	*	
52v	Dom. Quinquagesimae	M	V	1	Ecce ego statuam pactum meum	6055a	?	*
52v	Dom. Quinquagesimae	M	R	2.1	Locutus est dominus ad Abra-	7097	2	e
52v	Dom. Quinquagesimae	M	V	1	Benedicens benedicam tibi et	7097a	2	e
52v	Dom. Quinquagesimae	M	R	2.2	Dum staret Abraham ad radicem	6563	1	a
52v	Dom. Quinquagesimae	M	V	1	Dixit dominus ad Abraham ecce	6563a	1	a
52v	Dom. Quinquagesimae	M	R	2.3	Temptavit deus Abraham et	7762	2	e
52v	Dom. Quinquagesimae	M	V	1	Immola deo sacrificium laudis	7762a	2	e
52v	Dom. Quinquagesimae	M	R	2.4	Angelus domini vocavit	6098	2	e
52v	Dom. Quinquagesimae	M	V	1	Et benedicentur in te omnes	6098a	2	e
52v	Dom. Quinquagesimae	M	A	3	Miserere mei fili David quid	3776	8	w
52v	Dom. Quinquagesimae	M	R	3.1	Vocavit angelus domini	7911	8	w
52v	Dom. Quinquagesimae	M	V	1	Et benedicentur in te omnes	7911a	8	w
52v	Dom. Quinquagesimae	M	R	3.2	Deus domini mei Abraham	6420	8	w
52v	Dom. Quinquagesimae	M	V	1	Obsecro domine fac	6420b	8	w
52v	Dom. Quinquagesimae	M	V	2	Deus in cujus conspectu	6420a	8	w
52v	Dom. Quinquagesimae	M	R	3.3	Veni hodie ad fontem aquae et	7827	1	a
52v	Dom. Quinquagesimae	M	V	1	Igitur puella cui dixero da	7827a	1	a
52v	Dom. Quinquagesimae	M	R	3.4	Caecus sedebat secus viam	6260	8	w
53r	Dom. Quinquagesimae	M	V	1	Et qui praeibant increpabant	6260a	*	
53r	Dom. Quinquagesimae	L	A	1	Secundum multitudinem*	4846	*	
53r	LACUNA							
53v	Fer. 6 post Cineres	L	A	B	Cum facis eleemosynam nesciat	2005	*	
53v	Fer. 6 post Cineres	P	A		Nesciat sinistra tua quid	3876	*	
53v	Fer. 6 post Cineres	T	A		Tu autem cum oraveris intra*	5193	*	
53v	LACUNA							
55r	Dom. 1 Quadragesimae	V2	A	1	Dixit dominus*	2285	7	*
55r	Dom. 1 Quadragesimae	V2	R		Bonum mihi domine quod	6257	2	e
55r	Dom. 1 Quadragesimae	V2	V	1	Manus tuae domine fecerunt me	6257a	2	e
55r	Dom. 1 Quadragesimae	V2	A	M	Non in solo pane vivit homo	3919	1	ab
55r	Fer. 2 Hebd. 1 Quad.	M	I		Non sit vobis vanum surgere	Q101	6	H
55r	Fer. 2 Hebd. 1 Quad.	M	A	1.1	Rectos decet*	4580	4	*
55r	Fer. 2 Hebd. 1 Quad.	L	A	1	Miserere mei deus*	3773	6	*
55r	Fer. 2 Hebd. 1 Quad.	L	R		Participem me*	7353	?	*
55r	Fer. 2 Hebd. 1 Quad.	L	A	B	Cum venerit filius hominis in	Q210	7	yc
55r	Fer. 2 Hebd. 1 Quad.	P	A		Venite benedicti patris mei	5350	8	w
55r	Fer. 2 Hebd. 1 Quad.	P	A		Vivo ego dicit dominus nolo	5481	3	id
55r	Fer. 2 Hebd. 1 Quad.	T	A		Advenerunt nobis dies	1294	8	w
55r	Fer. 2 Hebd. 1 Quad.	S	A		Commendemus nosmetipsos in	1857	4	o
55r	Fer. 2 Hebd. 1 Quad.	N	A		Per arma justitiae virtutis	4261	1	a
55r	Fer. 2 Hebd. 1 Quad.	V2	A	M	Quod uni ex minimis meis	4560	1	a
55r	Fer. 3 Hebd. 1 Quad.	L	A	B	Domus mea domus orationis	2428	1	ab
55r	Fer. 3 Hebd. 1 Quad.	P	A		Hosanna filio David	3141	7	*
55r	Fer. 3 Hebd. 1 Quad.	V2	A	M	Scriptum est enim quia domus	4836	8	wd
55r	Fer. 4 Hebd. 1 Quad.	L	A	B	Generatio haec prava et	2935	8	w
55r	Fer. 4 Hebd. 1 Quad.	P	A		Sicut fuit Jonas in ventre	4934	4	o
55r	Fer. 4 Hebd. 1 Quad.	T	A		Si quis fecerit voluntatem	4908	1	ab
55r	Fer. 4 Hebd. 1 Quad.	V2	A	M	Dixit quidam ad Jesum ecce	2306	1	ab
55r	Fer. 5 Hebd. 1 Quad.	L	A	B	Si manseritis in sermone meo	Q233	8	w

Folio	Feast	Office	Genre	Pos.	Incipit	CAO	Mode	Differentia
55v	Fer. 5 Hebd. 1 Quad.	V2	A	M	Si veritatem dico quare non	Q234	3	ik
55v	Fer. 6 Hebd. 1 Quad.	L	A	B	Angelus domini descendebat de	1412	4	oc
55v	Fer. 6 Hebd. 1 Quad.	P	A		Domine non habeo hominem ut	2362	7	yb
55v	Fer. 6 Hebd. 1 Quad.	T	A		Qui me sanum fecit ille mihi	4483	1	a
55v	Fer. 6 Hebd. 1 Quad.	V2	A	M	Vade jam et noli peccare ne	5301	4	oh
55v	Sabb. Hebd. 1 Quad.	L	A	B	Assumpsit Jesus discipulos	1501	2	e
55v	Sabb. Hebd. 1 Quad.	P	A		Domine bonum est nos hic esse	2327	1	aq
55v	Sabb. Hebd. 1 Quad.	T	A		Faciamus hic tria tabernacula	2832	4	o
55v	Sabb. Hebd. 1 Quad.	S	A		Descendentibus illis de monte	2153	1	a
55v	Sabb. Hebd. 1 Quad.	N	A		Visionem quam vidistis nemini	5465	1	a
55v	Dom. 2 Quadragesimae	V	A	M	Nemini dixeritis visionem	3869	1	a
55v	Dom. 2 Quadragesimae	M	I		Quoniam deus magnus dominus	1124	7	yc
55v	Dom. 2 Quadragesimae	M	A	1	Advenerunt nobis*	1294	8	*
55v	Dom. 2 Quadragesimae	M	R	1.1	Tolle arma tua pharetram et	7767	7	yc
55v	Dom. 2 Quadragesimae	M	V	1	Cumque venatu aliquid	7767a	7	yc
55v	Dom. 2 Quadragesimae	M	R	1.2	Ecce odor filii mei sicut	6601	7	yc
55v	Dom. 2 Quadragesimae	M	V	1	Qui maledixerit tibi sit ille	6601a	7	yc
55v	Dom. 2 Quadragesimae	M	R	1.3	Det tibi deus de rore caeli	6415	7	yc
55v	Dom. 2 Quadragesimae	M	V	1	Et incurventur ante te filii	6415a	7	yc
55v	Dom. 2 Quadragesimae	M	R	1.4	Quis igitur ille est qui	7500	1	a
56r	Dom. 2 Quadragesimae	M	V	1	Dominum tuum illum constitui*	7500a	*	
56r	LACUNA							
56v	Dom. 2 Quadragesimae	M	R	3.2	Minor sum cunctis	7156	*	
56v	Dom. 2 Quadragesimae	M	V	1	Tu locutus es quod mihi bene	7156b	*	
56v	LACUNA							
57r	Fer. 2 Hebd. 2 Quad.	V2	A	M	Qui me misit mecum est et non	4482	1	*
57r	Fer. 3 Hebd. 2 Quad.	L	A	B	Unus est enim magister vester	5278	2	*
57r	Fer. 3 Hebd. 2 Quad.	V2	A	M	Qui major est vestrum erit	4477	8	*
57r	Fer. 4 Hebd. 2 Quad.	L	A	B	Ecce ascendimus Jerusalem et	2496	7	*
57r	Fer. 4 Hebd. 2 Quad.	P	A		Tradetur enim gentibus ad	5165	1	*
57r	Fer. 4 Hebd. 2 Quad.	V2	A	M	Sedere autem mecum non est	4857	7	*
57r	Fer. 5 Hebd. 2 Quad.	E	A	1	Non possum ego a meipso	3927	?	*
57r	Fer. 5 Hebd. 2 Quad.	E	A	2	[Quia non quaero] voluntatem	Q202	?	*
57r	Fer. 5 Hebd. 2 Quad.	E	A	3	[Ego veni in nomi]ne patris	Q201	?	*
57r	Fer. 5 Hebd. 2 Quad.	E	A	4	Pater Abraham*	4231	8	*
57r	Fer. 5 Hebd. 2 Quad.	E	A	5	Fili recordare*	2873	8	*
57r	Fer. 6 Hebd. 2 Quad.	L	A	B	Malos male perdet et vineam	3687	8	*
57r	Fer. 6 Hebd. 2 Quad.	P	A		Malos male perdet et vineam	3686	8	*
57r	Fer. 6 Hebd. 2 Quad.	V2	A	M	Quaerentes eum tenere	4428	3	*
57r	Sabb. Hebd. 2 Quad.	X	R		Pater peccavi in caelum et	7362	7	*
57r	Sabb. Hebd. 2 Quad.	X	V	1	Quanti mercennarii in domo	7362a	7	*
57r	Sabb. Hebd. 2 Quad.	L	A	B	Vado ad patrem meum et dicam	5299	1	*
57r	Sabb. Hebd. 2 Quad.	P	A		Dixit autem pater ad servos	2280	8	*
57r	Sabb. Hebd. 2 Quad.	T	A		Fili tu semper mecum fuisti	2875	7	*
57r	Dom. 3 Quadragesimae	V	R		Igitur Joseph ductus est in	6878	?	*
57v	Dom. 3 Quadragesimae	V	V	1	Misertus enim est deus illius	6878a	?	*
57v	Dom. 3 Quadragesimae	V	V	2	Gloria patri et filio et	9000	?	*
57v	Dom. 3 Quadragesimae	V	A	M	Fili tu semper mecum es et	2874	3	*
57v	Dom. 3 Quadragesimae	M	I		Deus magnus dominus et rex	1062	7	*
57v	Dom. 3 Quadragesimae	M	R	1.1	Videntes Joseph a longe	7863	8	*
57v	Dom. 3 Quadragesimae	M	V	1	Cumque vidissent Joseph	7863a	8	*
57v	Dom. 3 Quadragesimae	M	R	1.2	Dixit Judas fratribus suis	6477	7	*
57v	Dom. 3 Quadragesimae	M	V	1	Cumque abisset Ruben ad	6477a	7	*

Folio	Feast	Office	Genre	Pos.	Incipit	CAO	Mode	*Differentia*
57v	Dom. 3 Quadragesimae	M	R	1.3	Videns Jacob vestimenta	7858	6	*
57v	Dom. 3 Quadragesimae	M	V	1	Vide si tunica filii tui sit	7858a	6	*
57v	Dom. 3 Quadragesimae	M	R	1.4	Joseph dum intraret in terram	7037	5	*
57v	Dom. 3 Quadragesimae	M	V	1	Divertit ab oneribus dorsum	7037a	5	*
57v	Dom. 3 Quadragesimae	M	R	2.1	Memento mei dum bene tibi	7144	7	*
57v	Dom. 3 Quadragesimae	M	V	1	Tres enim adhuc dies sunt	7144a	7	*
57v	LACUNA							
61r	Fer. 5 in Cena Dom.	C	v		Custodi nos domine*	8001	*	
61r	Fer. 5 in Cena Dom.	C	v		In pace in idipsum*	8099	*	
61r	Fer. 6 in Parasceve	M	A	1.1	Astiterunt reges terrae et	1506	8	*
61r	Fer. 6 in Parasceve	M	A	1.2	Diviserunt sibi vestimenta	2260	8	*
61r	Fer. 6 in Parasceve	M	A	1.3	Insurrexerunt in me testes	3358	8	*
61r	Fer. 6 in Parasceve	M	v	1	Diviserunt sibi vestimenta	8020	*	
61r	Fer. 6 in Parasceve	M	R	1.1	Omnes amici mei dereliquerunt	7313	3	*
61r	Fer. 6 in Parasceve	M	V	1	Et dederunt in escam meam fel	7313a	3	*
61r	Fer. 6 in Parasceve	M	R	1.2	Velum templi scissum est et	7821	2	*
61r	Fer. 6 in Parasceve	M	V	1	Amen dico tibi hodie mecum	7821a	2	*
61r	Fer. 6 in Parasceve	M	R	1.3	Vinea mea electa ego te	7887	8	*
61r	Fer. 6 in Parasceve	M	V	1	Ego quidem plantavi te vineam	7887a	8	*
61r	Fer. 6 in Parasceve	M	A	2.1	Vim faciebant qui quaerebant	5423	8	*
61r	Fer. 6 in Parasceve	M	A	2.2	Confundantur et revereantur	1883	4	*
61r	Fer. 6 in Parasceve	M	A	2.3	Alieni insurrexerunt in me et	1321	4	*
61r	Fer. 6 in Parasceve	M	v	2	Insurrexerunt in me testes	8102	1	
61r	Fer. 6 in Parasceve	M	R	2.1	Tamquam ad latronem existis	7748	8	*
61r	Fer. 6 in Parasceve	M	V	1	Filius quidem hominis vadit	7748a	8	*
61r	Fer. 6 in Parasceve	M	R	2.2	Tenebrae factae sunt dum	7760	7	*
61v	Fer. 6 in Parasceve	M	V	1	Et velum templi scissum est a	7760a	7	*
61v	Fer. 6 in Parasceve	M	R	2.3	Barabbas latro dimittitur et	6159	2	*
61v	Fer. 6 in Parasceve	M	V	1	Verax datur fallacibus pium	6159b	2	*
61v	Fer. 6 in Parasceve	M	A	3.1	Ab insurgentibus in me libera	1201	1	*
61v	Fer. 6 in Parasceve	M	A	3.2	Longe fecisti notos meos a me	3632	8	*
61v	Fer. 6 in Parasceve	M	A	3.3	Captabant in animam justi et	1767	8	*
61v	Fer. 6 in Parasceve	M	v	3	Locuti sunt adversum me	8124	1	
61v	Fer. 6 in Parasceve	M	R	3.1	Tradiderunt me in manus	7773	6	*
61v	Fer. 6 in Parasceve	M	V	1	Astiterunt reges terrae et	7773a	6	*
61v	Fer. 6 in Parasceve	M	R	3.2	Jesum tradidit impius summis	7035	8	*
61v	Fer. 6 in Parasceve	M	V	1	Et ingressus Petrus in atrium	7035a	8	*
61v	Fer. 6 in Parasceve	M	R	3.3	Caligaverunt oculi mei a	6261	5	*
61v	Fer. 6 in Parasceve	M	V	1	O vos omnes qui transitis per	6261a	5	*
61v	Fer. 6 in Parasceve	L	A	1	Proprio filio suo non	4395	7	*
61v	Fer. 6 in Parasceve	L	A	2	Anxiatus est in me spiritus	1442	4	*
61v	Fer. 6 in Parasceve	L	A	3	Ait latro ad latronem nos	1316	1	*
61v	Fer. 6 in Parasceve	L	A	4	Dum conturbata fuerit anima	2444	1	*
61v	Fer. 6 in Parasceve	L	A	5	Memento mei domine deus dum	3736	8	*
61v	Fer. 6 in Parasceve	L	v		Proprio filio suo non	8174	1	
61v	Fer. 6 in Parasceve	L	A	B	Posuerunt super*	4343	1	*
61v	LACUNA							
72r	Dom. Resurrectionis	L	A	B	...alleluia	9999	?	*
72r	Dom. Resurrectionis	L	A	R	Crucem sanctam subiit qui	1951	2	*
72r	Dom. Resurrectionis	L	A	R	Alleluia sancta dei genetrix	Q203	5	*
72r	Dom. Resurrectionis	L	A	R	Fulgebunt justi sicut*	2908	2	*
72r	Dom. Resurrectionis	V2	A	R	In tabernaculis justorum*	3289	1	*
72r	Dom. Resurrectionis	P	A		Surgens Jesus mane prima	5075	8	w-

Folio	Feast	Office	Genre	Pos.	Incipit	*CAO*	Mode	*Differentia*
72r	Dom. Resurrectionis	T	A		Et dicebant ad invicem quis	2697	8	wd
72r	Dom. Resurrectionis	D	v		Haec est dies quam fecit	8085	r	
72r	Dom. Resurrectionis	T	v		In resurrectione tua Christe	8100	r	
72r	Dom. Resurrectionis	S	A		Et respicientes viderunt	2718	8	w-
72r	Dom. Resurrectionis	S	v		Surrexit dominus vere	8213	r	
72r	Dom. Resurrectionis	N	A		Nolite expavescere Jesum	3893	8	w-
72r	Dom. Resurrectionis	N	v		Surrexit dominus de sepulcro	8212	r	
72r	Dom. Resurrectionis	V2	A	p	Alleluia vi (Crucifixus)	1331	6	H
72r	Dom. Resurrectionis	V2	R		Surrexit dominus de sepulcro	7738	6	H
72r	Dom. Resurrectionis	V2	V	1	Qui pro nobis pependit in	7738a	6	H
72r	Dom. Resurrectionis	V2	V	2	Gloria patri et filio et	9000	6	H
72r	Dom. Resurrectionis	V2	v		Gavisi sunt discipuli	8080	r	
72r	Dom. Resurrectionis	V2	A	M	Surrexit enim sicut dixit	5081	4	o-
72r	Dom. Resurrectionis	V2	A	R	Crucem sanctam subiit*	1951	2	*
72r	Dom. Resurrectionis	X	A	P	Christus resurgens ex mortuis	1796	2	*
72r	Dom. Resurrectionis	X	V	1	Dicant nunc Judaei quomodo	1796a	2	e-
72v	In tempore Paschae	E	A	1	Post passionem domini factus	4333	1	a
72v	In tempore Paschae	E	A	2	Surgens Jesus*	5075	8	*
72v	In tempore Paschae	E	A	3	Nolite expavescere*	3893	8	*
72v	In tempore Paschae	E	A	4	Scio quod Jesum quaeritis	4833	7	yb
72v	In tempore Paschae	E	A	5	Jesum qui crucifixus est	3484	8	*
72v	In tempore Paschae	E	A	6	Cito euntes dicite discipulis	1813	7	yc
72v	In tempore Paschae	E	A	7	Et recordatae sunt verborum	2717	8	w
72v	In tempore Paschae	E	A	8	Oportebat pati Christum et	4163	8	wd
72v	In tempore Paschae	E	A	9	Nonne cor nostrum ardens erat	3943	1	ab
72v	In tempore Paschae	E	A	10	Cognoverunt discipuli dominum	1848	6	H
72v	In tempore Paschae	E	A	11	Inclinavit se Maria prospexit	3321	1	*
72v	In tempore Paschae	E	A	12	Ardens est cor meum desidero	1479	8	wd
72v	In tempore Paschae	E	A	13	Ite nuntiate fratribus meis	3462	4	oc
72v	In tempore Paschae	E	A	14	In Galilaea Jesum videbitis	3237	7	yc
72v	In tempore Paschae	E	A	15	Alleluia resurrexit dominus	1352	5	v
72v	In tempore Paschae	E	A	16	Alleluia quem quaeris*	1350	5	*
72v	In tempore Paschae	E	A	17	Alleluia noli flere Maria	1348	5	v
72v	In tempore Paschae	E	A	18	Ego sum alpha et o. primus et	2588	8	w
72v	In tempore Paschae	E	A	19	Surrexit dominus de sepulcro	5079	4	oc
72v	In tempore Paschae	E	A	20	Surrexit dominus de sepulcro	5079	8	w
72v	In tempore Paschae	E	A	21	Surrexit Christus et illuxit	5077	4	-C
72v	In tempore Paschae	E	A	22	Crucifixus surrexit a mortuis	1957	6	H
72v	In tempore Paschae	E	A	23	Crucem sanctam subiit*	1951	2	*
72v	In tempore Paschae	E	A	24	Jesum quem quaeritis non est	3483	8	w
72v	In tempore Paschae	E	A	25	Crucifixus resurrexit	1956	6	H
72v	Fer. 2 p. Pascha	M	I		Surrexit dominus vere	1166	6	H
72v	Fer. 2 p. Pascha	M	A	1	Nolite expavescere*	3893	8	*
72v	LACUNA							
77r	Dom. Resurrect.,8	M	v	1	Resurrexit dominus	8185	r	
77r	Dom. Resurrect.,8	M	v	2	Surrexit dominus vere	8213	r	
77r	Dom. Resurrect.,8	M	v	3	Surrexit dominus de sepulcro	8212	r	
77r	Dom. Resurrect.,8	L	v		Surrexit Christus	8211	r	
77r	Dom. Resurrect.,8	V2	v		Gavisi sunt discipuli	8080	r	
77r	Dom. Resurrect.,8	M	v	1	Quem quaeris mulier	8176	r	
77r	Dom. Resurrect.,8	M	v	2	Tulerunt dominum meum	8228	r	
77r	Dom. Resurrect.,8	M	v	3	Noli flere Maria	8149	r	
77r	Dom. Resurrect.,8	L	v		Resurrexit dominus	8185	r	

Folio	Feast	Office	Genre	Pos.	Incipit	CAO	Mode	Differentia
77r	Dom. Resurrect.,8	V2	v		Gavisi sunt discipuli*	8080	r	
77r	Fer. 2 p. Pascha	M	R	1.1	Maria Magdalena et altera	7128	7	yc
77r	Fer. 2 p. Pascha	M	V	1	Cito euntes dicite discipulis	7128a	7	yc
77r	Fer. 2 p. Pascha	M	R	1.2	Surgens Jesus dominus noster	7734	7	yc
77r	Fer. 2 p. Pascha	M	V	1	Surrexit dominus de sepulcro	7734a	7	yc
77r	Fer. 2 p. Pascha	M	R	1.3	Congratulamini mihi omnes qui	6323	3	i
77r	Fer. 2 p. Pascha	M	V	1	Tulerunt dominum meum et	6323a	3	i
77r	Fer. 2 p. Pascha	M	A	2	Scio quod Jesum quaeritis*	4833	7	*
77r	Fer. 2 p. Pascha	L	A		Angelus autem domini*	1408	8	w
77r	Fer. 2 p. Pascha	L	R		Surrexit dominus vere*	7740	6	*
77r	Fer. 2 p. Pascha	L	A	B	Jesus junxit se discipulis	3491	8	w
77r	Fer. 2 p. Pascha	P	A		Tu solus peregrinus es et non	5222	1	ag
77r	Fer. 2 p. Pascha	T	A		Nonne sic oportuit pati	3950	3	i
77r	Fer. 2 p. Pascha	T	v		In resurrectione tua Christe	8100	r	
77r	Fer. 2 p. Pascha	S	A		Et incipiens a Moyse et	2706	1	ag
77r	Fer. 2 p. Pascha	S	v		Surrexit dominus vere	8213	r	
77r	Fer. 2 p. Pascha	N	A		Et coegerunt illum dicentes	2692	2	e
77v	Fer. 2 p. Pascha	N	v		Surrexit dominus de sepulcro	8212	r	
77v	Fer. 2 p. Pascha	V2	A	p	Alleluia viii (Surrexit)	1333	4	oc
77v	Fer. 2 p. Pascha	V2	R		Surrexit dominus de sepulcro	7738	6	H
77v	Fer. 2 p. Pascha	V2	V	1	Qui pro nobis pependit in	7738a	6	H
77v	Fer. 2 p. Pascha	V2	V	2	Gloria patri et filio et	9000	6	H
77v	Fer. 2 p. Pascha	V2	R		Surrexit dominus de sepulcro	7738	r	*
77v	Fer. 2 p. Pascha	V2	V	1	Qui pro nobis pependit in	7738a	r	*
77v	Fer. 2 p. Pascha	V2	A	M	Qui sunt hi sermones quos	4500	8	wd
77v	Fer. 3 p. Pascha	M	I		Surrexit dominus vere*	1166	6	*
77v	Fer. 3 p. Pascha	M	A	1	Jesum qui crucifixus est*	3484	8	w
77v	Fer. 3 p. Pascha	M	v	1	Resurrexit dominus	8185	r	
77v	Fer. 3 p. Pascha	M	R	1.1	Virtute magna reddebant	7907	3	i
77v	Fer. 3 p. Pascha	M	V	1	In omnem terram exivit sonus	7907a	3	i
77v	Fer. 3 p. Pascha	M	R	1.2	Tulerunt dominum meum et	7797	8	w
77v	Fer. 3 p. Pascha	M	V	1	Cito euntes dicite discipulis	7797a	8	w
77v	Fer. 3 p. Pascha	M	R	1.3	Expurgate vetus fermentum ut	6699	1	ab
77v	Fer. 3 p. Pascha	M	V	1	Non in fermento malitiae et	6699a	1	ab
77v	Fer. 3 p. Pascha	M	A	2	Venite et videte*	5352	8	w
77v	Fer. 3 p. Pascha	L	A		Et ecce terraemotus*	2699	7	yd
77v	Fer. 3 p. Pascha	L	R		Surrexit dominus vere	7740	6	H
77v	Fer. 3 p. Pascha	L	V	1	Et apparuit Simoni	7740a	6	H
77v	Fer. 3 p. Pascha	L	A	B	Stetit Jesus in medio	5032	8	w
77v	LACUNA							
81r	Dom. 3 p. Pascha	E	A	1	Modicum et non videbitis me	3803	6	*
81r	Dom. 3 p. Pascha	E	A	2	Quid est hoc quod dicit nobis	4519	3	i
81r	Dom. 3 p. Pascha	E	A	3	Amen amen dico vobis quia	1375	8	w
81r	Dom. 3 p. Pascha	E	A	4	Mulier cum parit tristitiam	3819	1	a
81r	Dom. 3 p. Pascha	E	A	5	Tristitia implebit cor	5189	8	w
81r	Dom. 3 p. Pascha	E	A	6	Tristitia vestra alleluia	5190	6	H
81r	Dom. 3 p. Pascha	E	A	7	Iterum autem videbo vos et	3465	8	wd
81r	Dom. 3 p. Pascha	E	A	8	Iterum autem videbo vos et	3465	4	oc
81r	Dom. 4 p. Pascha	E	A	1	Vado ad eum qui misit me sed	5306	1	a
81r	Dom. 4 p. Pascha	E	A	2	Ego veritatem dico vobis	2607	7	yc
81r	Dom. 4 p. Pascha	E	A	3	Dum venerit paraclitus spiri-	2478	8	w
81r	Dom. 4 p. Pascha	E	A	4	Adhuc multa habeo vobis	1276	5	vb
81r	Dom. 4 p. Pascha	E	A	5	Cum autem venerit ille	1990	7	yc

Folio	Feast	Office	Genre	Pos.	Incipit	*CAO*	Mode	*Differentia*
81r	Dom. 4 p. Pascha	E	A	6	Non enim loquetur a semetipso	3909	8	w
81r	Dom. 4 p. Pascha	E	A	7	Ille me clarificabit quia de	3172	1	a
81r	Dom. 5 p. Pascha	E	A	1	Usque modo non petistis	5284	2	e
81r	Dom. 5 p. Pascha	E	A	2	Petite et accipietis ut	4279	8	w
81r	Dom. 5 p. Pascha	E	A	3	Exivi a patre et veni in	2793	4	oc
81r	Dom. 5 p. Pascha	E	A	4	Exivi a patre meo et veni in	Q212	6	H
81r	Dom. 5 p. Pascha	E	A	5	Ecce nunc palam loqueris et	2530	8	wd
81v	In Letaniis	E	A	1	Petite et dabitur vobis	4280	2	e
81v	In Letaniis	E	A	2	Omnis qui petit accipit et	4151	1	a
81v	In Letaniis	E	A	3	Si ergo vos cum sitis mali	4893	8	w
81v	Dom. 2 p. Pascha	V	R		Audivi voces in caelo*	6152	1	*
81v	Dom. 2 p. Pascha	M	I		Alleluia ii	1022	7	*
81v	Dom. 2 p. Pascha	M	R	1.1	Dignus es domine accipere	6448	7	yc
81v	Dom. 2 p. Pascha	M	V	1	Parce domine parce populo tuo	6448a	7	yc
81v	Dom. 2 p. Pascha	M	R	1.2	Ego sicut vitis fructificavi	6633	3	i
81v	Dom. 2 p. Pascha	M	V	1	Ego diligentes me diligo et	6633a	3	i
81v	Dom. 2 p. Pascha	M	R	1.3	Audivi vocem de caelo tamquam	6153	7	yc
81v	Dom. 2 p. Pascha	M	V	1	Vidi angelum dei fortem	6153a	7	yc
81v	Dom. 2 p. Pascha	M	R	1.4	Resurrexit dominus alleluia	7540	6	H
81v	Dom. 2 p. Pascha	M	V	1	Sicut dixit vobis	7540a	6	H
81v	Dom. 2 p. Pascha	M	R	2.1	Locutus est ad me unus ex	7096	2	e
81v	Dom. 2 p. Pascha	M	V	1	Et sustulit me in spiritu in	7096b	2	e
81v	Dom. 2 p. Pascha	M	V	2	Ego diligentes*	7096a	2	e
81v	Dom. 2 p. Pascha	M	R	2.2	Audivi voces in caelo angelo-	6152	1	a
81v	Dom. 2 p. Pascha	M	V	1	Vidi angelum dei fortem	6152a	1	a
81v	Dom. 2 p. Pascha	M	R	2.3	Decantabat populus in Israel	6400	6	H
81v	Dom. 2 p. Pascha	M	V	1	Moyses et Aaron in	6400a	6	H
81v	LACUNA							
91r	S. Afrae	M	A	1.2	In qua civitate cum puellis	3275	2	*
91r	S. Afrae	M	A	1.3	Cujus prostibulum cum Felice	1967	3	*
91r	S. Afrae	M	A	1.4	Cum psalmis deo et hymnis	2026	4	*
91r	S. Afrae	M	A	1.5	Audiens vero beatum virum	1517	5	*
91r	S. Afrae	M	A	1.6	Quam vir sanctus verbis	4437	6	*
91r	S. Afrae	M	v	1	Justorum animae*	8114	r	
91r	S. Afrae	M	R	1.1	Beatus pontifex Narcissus cum	6223	1	*
91r	S. Afrae	M	V	1	Domino pro ipsis supplicans	6223a	1S	*
91r	S. Afrae	M	R	1.2	Sancto praesule precibus	7604	2	*
91r	S. Afrae	M	V	1	Mundi cordis amatorem nil in	7604a	2S	*
91r	S. Afrae	M	R	1.3	Hostis antiquus caelesti	6871	3	*
91r	S. Afrae	M	V	1	Coactus a sancto pontifice	6871a	3S	*
91r	S. Afrae	M	R	1.4	Justorum animae*	9999	?	*
91r	S. Afrae	M	A	2.1	Sancto pontifice in divinis	4760	7	*
91r	S. Afrae	M	A	2.2	Cumque dulcem sanae doctrinae	2059	8	*
91r	S. Afrae	M	A	2.3	Afra priscam Rahab	1304	1	*
91r	S. Afrae	M	A	2.4	Imbuta verae fidei rudimentis	3189	4	*
91r	S. Afrae	M	A	2.5	Quae beatum virum noctu ad se	4423	5	*
91r	S. Afrae	M	A	2.6	Auditis praesul sanctus	1524	7	*
91v	S. Afrae	M	R	2.1	Propulso post longum	7442	4	*
91v	S. Afrae	M	V	1	Familiam totam cognatos	7442a	4S	*
91v	S. Afrae	M	R	2.2	Cum fontem vitae sitientes et	6365	5	*
91v	S. Afrae	M	V	1	Vasa prius irae in vasa	6365a	5S	*
91v	S. Afrae	M	R	2.3	Mox omnibus in fide Christi	7181	6	*
91v	S. Afrae	M	V	1	Ut ubi spurca pridem	7181a	6S	*

Folio	Feast	Office	Genre	Pos.	Incipit	*CAO*	Mode	*Differentia*
91v	S. Afrae	M	R	2.4	Justi autem in perpetuum*	9999	?	*
91v	S. Afrae	M	A	3	Gratias tibi domine Jesu	2978	8	*
91v	S. Afrae	M	R	3.1	Postquam novellam conversa	7409	7	*
91v	S. Afrae	M	V	1	Ubi cum Felice diacono suo	7409a	7S	*
91v	S. Afrae	M	R	3.2	Fervente interim immani	6727	8	*
91v	S. Afrae	M	V	1	Gaudens et tripudians	6727a	8S	*
91v	S. Afrae	M	R	3.3	Multis hinc inde sermonum	7189	1	*
91v	S. Afrae	M	V	1	Christum libere confitens	7189a	1S	*
91v	S. Afrae	M	R	3.4	Martyr sancta dei quae	7135	3	*
91v	S. Afrae	M	V	1	Crescat ut in nobis divini	7135a	3S	*
91v	S. Afrae	M	V	2	Gloria patri et filio et	9000	3S	*
91v	S. Afrae	L	A	1	Invicta Christi testis Afra	3397	1	*
91v	LACUNA							
101v	Nativitas Mariae	M	R	1.1	Hodie nata est beata virgo	6854	*	
101v	Nativitas Mariae	M	V	1	Beatissimae virginis Mariae	6854a	*	
101v	Nativitas Mariae	M	R	1.2	Beatissimae virginis Mariae	6184	*	
101v	Nativitas Mariae	M	V	1	Hodie nata est beata virgo	6184a	*	
101v	Nativitas Mariae	M	R	1.3	Gloriosae virginis Mariae	6781	*	
101v	Nativitas Mariae	M	V	1	Beatissimae virginis Mariae	6781a	*	
101v	Nativitas Mariae	M	R	1.4	Solem justitiae regem	7677	*	
101v	Nativitas Mariae	M	V	1	Cernere divinum lumen gaudete	7677a	*	
101v	Nativitas Mariae	M	R	2.1	Diem festum praecelsae	6441	*	
102r	Nativitas Mariae	M	V	1	Nativitatem hodiernam*	6441a	?	*
102r	Nativitas Mariae	M	R	2.2	Corde et animo Christo	6339	8	w
102r	Nativitas Mariae	M	V	1	Cum jucunditate nativitatem	6339a	8	w
102r	Nativitas Mariae	M	R	2.3	Regali ex progenie Maria	7519	1	a
102r	Nativitas Mariae	M	V	1	Corde et animo Christo	7519a	1	a
102r	Nativitas Mariae	M	R	2.4	Stirps Jesse virgam produxit	7709	2	e
102r	Nativitas Mariae	M	V	1	Virgo dei genetrix virga est	7709a	2	e
102r	Nativitas Mariae	M	V	2	Gloria patri et filio et	9000	2	e
102r	Nativitas Mariae	M	A	3	Beatissimae virginis Mariae	1596	7	yc
102r	Nativitas Mariae	M	v	3	Speciosa facta es et suavis	8202	r	
102r	Nativitas Mariae	M	R	3.1	Nativitas tua dei genetrix	7199	1	a
102r	Nativitas Mariae	M	V	1	Ave Maria gratia plena*	7199a	1	a
102r	Nativitas Mariae	M	R	3.2	Nativitas gloriosae virginis	7198	1	a
102r	Nativitas Mariae	M	V	1	Gloriosae virginis Mariae	7198a	1	a
102r	Nativitas Mariae	M	R	3.3	Felix namque es*	6725	1	ab
102r	Nativitas Mariae	M	V	1	Ora pro populo interveni pro	6725a	1	ab
102r	Nativitas Mariae	M	R	3.4	Ad nutum domini nostrum	6024	3	?
102r	Nativitas Mariae	M	V	1	Ut vitium virtus operiret	6024a	3S	?
102r	Nativitas Mariae	M	V	2	Gloria patri et filio et	9000	3S	?
102r	Nativitas Mariae	L	A	1	Nativitas gloriosae virginis	3850	8	w
102r	Nativitas Mariae	L	A	2	Nativitas est hodie sanctae	3849	7	yd
102r	Nativitas Mariae	L	A	3	Regali ex progenie Maria	4591	6	H
102r	Nativitas Mariae	L	A	4	Corde et animo Christo	1931	8	w
102v	Nativitas Mariae	L	A	5	Cum jucunditate nativitatem	2016	7	yd
102v	Nativitas Mariae	L	R		Adjuva nos tuis precibus	6041	4	og
102v	Nativitas Mariae	L	V	1	Oraculum aeternae vitae	6041a	4	og
102v	Nativitas Mariae	L	V	2	Gloria patri et filio et	9000	4	og
102v	Nativitas Mariae	L	v		Egredietur virga de radice	8044	r	
102v	Nativitas Mariae	L	A	B	Nativitatem hodiernam	3853	8	w
102v	Nativitas Mariae	P	A		Nativitas gloriosae*	3850	8	*
102v	Nativitas Mariae	P	A		Hodie nata est beata virgo	3108	4	og

Folio	Feast	Office	Genre	Pos.	Incipit	*CAO*	Mode	*Differentia*
102v	Nativitas Mariae	T	A		Adest namque*	1266	4	*
102v	Nativitas Mariae	S	A		Regali ex progenie*	4591	6	*
102v	Nativitas Mariae	N	A		Beatissimae virginis*	1596	7	*
102v	Nativitas Mariae	V2	A	1	Nativitas est hodie*	3849	7	*
102v	Nativitas Mariae	V2	R		Adjuva nos tuis*	6041	4	*
102v	Nativitas Mariae	V2	v		Egredietur virga*	8044	r	
102v	Nativitas Mariae	V2	A	M	Quando nata est virgo	4440	3	ik
102v	Exaltatio S. Crucis	V	R		Hoc signum crucis*	6845	6	*
102v	Exaltatio S. Crucis	V	v		Adoramus te Christe et	7936	r	
102v	Exaltatio S. Crucis	V	A	M	Sanctifica nos domine	4744	4	oc
102v	Exaltatio S. Crucis	V	A	R	Isti sunt sancti qui pro*	3444	2	*
102v	Exaltatio S. Crucis	M	I		Adoremus regem*	1015	4	*
102v	Exaltatio S. Crucis	M	A	3	Dulce lignum*	2432	1	*
102v	Exaltatio S. Crucis	M	v	3	Salva nos Christe salvator	8189	r	
102v	Exaltatio S. Crucis	M	R	3.1	Dulce lignum*	6530	?	*
102v	Exaltatio S. Crucis	M	R	3.2	Hoc signum crucis*	6845	6	*
102v	Exaltatio S. Crucis	M	R	3.3	O crux gloriosa*	7266	?	*
102v	Exaltatio S. Crucis	M	R	3.4	O crux benedicta*	7265	?	*
102v	Exaltatio S. Crucis	L	A	1	O magnum pietatis opus mors	4035	7	yd
102v	Exaltatio S. Crucis	L	A	2	Salva nos Christe salvator	4686	3	i
102v	Exaltatio S. Crucis	L	A	3	O crux admirabilis evacuatio	4014	1	aq
102v	Exaltatio S. Crucis	L	A	4	Nos autem gloriari oportet in	3953	7	yd
102v	Exaltatio S. Crucis	L	A	5	Crux benedicta nitet dominus	1961	8	w
102v	Exaltatio S. Crucis	L	R		Hoc signum crucis erit in	Q612	6	H
102v	Exaltatio S. Crucis	L	V	1	Cum dominus ad judicandum	Q612a	6	H
102v	Exaltatio S. Crucis	L	v		Adoramus te Christe et	7936	r	
102v	Exaltatio S. Crucis	L	A	B	Super omnia ligna cedrorum tu	5061	1	ab
102v	Exaltatio S. Crucis	P	A		Nos autem gloriari*	3953	7	*
102v	Exaltatio S. Crucis	T	A		Lignum vitae*	3628	3	*
102v	Exaltatio S. Crucis	T	v		Hoc signum crucis*	8088	r	
102v	Exaltatio S. Crucis	S	A		Salvator mundi salva*	9999	7	*
102v	Exaltatio S. Crucis	S	v		Per signum crucis*	8168	r	
102v	Exaltatio S. Crucis	N	A		Dulce lignum*	2432	1	*
102v	Exaltatio S. Crucis	N	v		Salva nos Christe salvator	8189	r	
102v	Exaltatio S. Crucis	V2	A	1	O magnum pietatis*	4035	7	*
102v	Exaltatio S. Crucis	V2	A	2	Salva nos Christe*	4686	3	*
102v	LACUNA							
111r	S. Andreae	M	R	1.1	Dum deambularet dominus juxta	6554	4	*
111r	S. Andreae	M	V	1	Erant enim piscatores et ait	6554a	4	*
111r	S. Andreae	M	R	1.2	Venite post me faciam vos	7835	8	w
111r	S. Andreae	M	V	1	Dum deambularet dominus supra	7835a	8	w
111r	S. Andreae	M	R	1.3	Mox ut vocem domini	7182	3	ik
111r	S. Andreae	M	V	1	Ad unius jussionis vocem	7182a	3	ik
111r	S. Andreae	M	R	1.4	Homo dei ducebatur ut	6868	2	e
111r	S. Andreae	M	V	1	Cumque carnifices ducerent	6868a	2	e
111r	S. Andreae	M	A	2.1	Salve crux quae in corpore	4694	8	wb
111r	S. Andreae	M	A	2.2	Recipe me ab hominibus et	4575	8	w
111r	S. Andreae	M	A	2.3	Biduo vivens pendebat in	1739	1	a
111r	S. Andreae	M	A	2.4	Andreas Christi famulus	1396	8	w
111r	S. Andreae	M	A	2.5	Dignum sibi dominus	2221	7	yd
111r	S. Andreae	M	A	2.6	Dilexit Andream dominus in	2229	8	w
111r	S. Andreae	M	R	2.1	Cum vidisset beatus Andreas	6378	1	ag
111r	S. Andreae	M	V	1	Exspecta me sancta crux	6378a	1	ag

Folio	Feast	Office	Genre	Pos.	Incipit	CAO	Mode	Differentia
111r	S. Andreae	M	R	2.2	Salve crux quae in corpore	7563	7	yc
111r	S. Andreae	M	V	1	O bona crux quam diu	7563a	7	yc
111r	S. Andreae	M	R	2.3	O bona crux quae decorem et	7260	8	w
111v	S. Andreae	M	V	1	Salve crux quae in corpore	7260a	8	w
111v	S. Andreae	M	R	2.4	Doctor bonus et amicus dei	6484	3	*
111v	S. Andreae	M	V	1	Salve crux quae in corpore	6484a	3	*
111v	S. Andreae	M	V	2	Cum vero pervenisset ad locum	6484b	3	*
111v	S. Andreae	M	A	3	Concede nobis hominem justum	1863	7	yc
111v	S. Andreae	M	R	3.1	Oravit sanctus Andreas dum	7335	8	wd
111v	S. Andreae	M	V	1	Tu es magister meus Christe	7335a	8	wd
111v	S. Andreae	M	R	3.2	Expandi manus meas tota die	6698	4	oc
111v	S. Andreae	M	V	1	Deus ultionum dominus deus	6698a	4	oc
111v	S. Andreae	M	R	3.3	Vir iste in populo suo	7899	3	i
111v	S. Andreae	M	V	1	Pro eo ut me diligerent	7899a	3	i
111v	S. Andreae	M	R	3.4	Dilexit Andream dominus in	6451	4	oc
111v	S. Andreae	M	V	1	Elegit eum dominus et	6451b	4	oc
111v	S. Andreae	L	A	1	Salve crux pretiosa suscipe	4693	7	yd
111v	S. Andreae	L	A	2	Non me permittas domine	3923	8	w
111v	S. Andreae	L	A	3	Beatus Andreas orabat dicens	1610	8	w
111v	S. Andreae	L	A	4	Qui persequebatur justum	4492	7	yc
111v	S. Andreae	L	A	5	Maximilla Christo amabilis*	3722	8	w
111v	LACUNA							
121r	S. Luciae	M	R	3.4	Grata facta est a domino in	6789	5	*
121r	S. Luciae	M	V	1	Adjuvabit eam deus vultu suo	6789a	5	*
121r	S. Luciae	L	A	1	Orante sancta Lucia apparuit	4178	7	*
121r	S. Luciae	L	A	2	Lucia virgo quid a me petis	3639	7	*
121r	S. Luciae	L	A	3	Per te Lucia virgo civitas	4267	8	*
121r	S. Luciae	L	A	4	Benedico te pater domini mei	1703	8	*
121r	S. Luciae	L	A	5	Tanto pondere eam fixit	5110	7	*
121r	S. Luciae	L	A	B	Columna es immobilis Lucia	1855	1	*
121r	S. Luciae	P	A		Orante sancta Lucia*	4178	7	*
121r	S. Luciae	T	A		Lucia virgo*	3639	7	*
121r	S. Luciae	S	A		Per te Lucia virgo*	4267	8	*
121r	S. Luciae	N	A		Tanto pondere*	5110	7	*
121r	S. Luciae	V2	A	1	Vidi speciosam*	5407	3	*
121r	S. Luciae	V2	A	2	Veni electa*	5323	3	*
121r	S. Luciae	V2	A	3	Ista est speciosa*	3416	2	*
121r	S. Luciae	V2	A	4	Ornatam*	4197	4	*
121r	S. Luciae	V2	A	M	In tua patientia possedisti	3301	1	*
121r	Antiphonae Majores	V	A	M	O sapientia*	4081	2	*
121r	S. Thomae Apost.	V	A	M	O Thoma Didyme per Christum	4083	2	*
121r	S. Thomae Apost.	L	A	B	Thomas qui dicitur*	5145	1	*
121r	S. Thomae Apost.	L	A	R	Nolite timere quinta*	3898	8	*
121r	S. Thomae Apost.	V2	A	M	Quia vidisti me*	4513	8	*
121r	Comm. Evangelistarum	V	R		Qui sunt hi qui ut nubes	7484	1	*
121r	Comm. Evangelistarum	V	V	1	Dorsa eorum plena sunt oculis	7484z	1S	*
121r	Comm. Evangelistarum	V	V	2	Gloria patri et filio et	9000	1S	*
121r	Comm. Evangelistarum	V	A	M	Ecce ego Joannes vidi ostium	2511	1	*
121r	Comm. Apostolorum	V	R		In omnem terram*	6919	1	*
121r	Comm. Apostolorum	V	R		Tollite jugum*	7770	7	*
121r	Comm. Apostolorum	V	v		Annuntiaverunt opera dei	7950	r	
121r	Comm. Apostolorum	V	v		Nimis honorati sunt*	8148	r	
121r	Comm. Apostolorum	V	A	1M	Isti sunt viri sancti quos	3449	4	*

Folio	Feast	Office	Genre	Pos.	Incipit	CAO	Mode	Differentia
121v	Comm. Apostolorum	V	A	2M	Ecce ego mitto vos sicut oves	2512	1	*
121v	Comm. Apostolorum	V	A	3M	Dum steteritis ante reges et	2470	2	*
121v	Comm. Apostolorum	M	I		Regem apostolorum dominum	1125	4	*
121v	Comm. Apostolorum	M	I		Regem apostolorum dominum	1125	3	ik
121v	Comm. Apostolorum	M	A	1.1	In omnem terram exivit sonus	3262	2	*
121v	Comm. Apostolorum	M	A	1.2	Clamaverunt justi et dominus	1823	7	*
121v	Comm. Apostolorum	M	A	1.3	Constitues eos principes	1902	7	*
121v	Comm. Apostolorum	M	A	1.4	Principes populorum	4379	8	*
121v	Comm. Apostolorum	M	A	1.5	Dedisti hereditatem	2133	8	*
121v	Comm. Apostolorum	M	A	1.6	Annuntiaverunt opera dei et	1429	8	*
121v	Comm. Apostolorum	M	A	1.1	In omnem terram*	3262	2	*
121v	Comm. Apostolorum	M	A	1.2	Haec est generatio	2999	3	*
121v	Comm. Apostolorum	M	A	1.3	Exsultate justi in domino	2815	8	*
121v	Comm. Apostolorum	M	A	1.4	Clamaverunt justi*	1823	7	*
121v	Comm. Apostolorum	M	A	1.5	Constitues eos principes*	1902	7	*
121v	Comm. Apostolorum	M	A	1.6	Principes populorum*	4379	8	*
121v	Comm. Apostolorum	M	R	1.1	Ecce ego mitto vos sicut oves	6588	7	*
121v	Comm. Apostolorum	M	V	1	Dum lucem habetis credite in	6588a	7	*
121v	Comm. Apostolorum	M	V	2	...ut filii lucis sitis	6588a	7	*
121v	Comm. Apostolorum	M	R	1.2	Tollite jugum meum super vos	7770	7	*
121v	Comm. Apostolorum	M	V	1	Et invenietis requiem	7770a	7	*
121v	Comm. Apostolorum	M	R	1.3	Dum steteritis ante reges et	6564	3	*
121v	Comm. Apostolorum	M	V	1	Non enim vos estis qui	6564a	3	*
121v	Comm. Apostolorum	M	R	1.4	In omnem terram exivit sonus	6919	1	*
121v	Comm. Apostolorum	M	V	1	Non sunt loquelae neque*	6919a	1	*
121v	LACUNA							
131r	Comm. Virginum	V	A	M	Simile est regnum caelorum	4953	4	*
131r	Comm. Virginum	M	I		Regem virginum*	9999	4	o-
131r	Comm. Virginum	M	A	1.1	Ante torum hujus virginis	1438	4	*
131r	Comm. Virginum	M	A	1.2	Unguentum effusum nomen tuum	5273	1	*
131r	Comm. Virginum	M	A	1.3	O quam pulchra est casta	4069	7	y-
131r	Comm. Virginum	M	A	1.4	Specie tua et pulchritudine	4987	7	y-
131r	Comm. Virginum	M	A	1.5	Adjuvabit eam deus vultu suo	1282	7	y-
131r	Comm. Virginum	M	A	1.6	Laeva ejus sub capite meo et	3574	4	*
131r	Comm. Virginum	M	v	1	Diffusa est gratia*	8014	r	
131r	Comm. Virginum	M	A	1.1	Dextram meam*	2186	7	*
131r	Comm. Virginum	M	A	1.2	Posuit signum*	4346	7	*
131r	Comm. Virginum	M	A	1.3	Induit me*	3328	7	*
131r	Comm. Virginum	M	A	1.4	Specie tua*	4987	7	*
131r	Comm. Virginum	M	A	1.5	Adjuvabit eam*	1282	7	*
131r	Comm. Virginum	M	A	1.6	O quam pulchra es*	4069	7	*
131r	Comm. Virginum	M	v	1	Diffusa est gratia in labiis*	8014	r	
131r	Comm. Virginum	M	R	1.1	Veni sponsa Christi accipe	7828	3	*
131r	Comm. Virginum	M	V	1	Veni electa mea et ponam in	7828a	3	*
131r	Comm. Virginum	M	R	1.2	Haec est virgo sapiens quam	6809	7	*
131r	Comm. Virginum	M	V	1	Media autem nocte clamor	6809a	7	*
131r	Comm. Virginum	M	R	1.3	Specie tua et pulchritudine	7680	7	*
131r	Comm. Virginum	M	V	1	Diffusa est gratia in labiis	7680a	7	*
131r	Comm. Virginum	M	R	1.4	Dilexisti justitiam et odisti	6450	4	*
131r	Comm. Virginum	M	V	1	Specie tua et pulchritudine	6450b	4	*
131r	Comm. Virginum	M	R	1.5	Propter veritatem et	7441	8	*
131r	Comm. Virginum	M	V	1	Dilexisti justitiam et odisti	7441b	8	*
131r	Comm. Virginum	M	R	1.6	Diffusa est gratia in labiis	6445	r	*

Folio	Feast	Office	Genre	Pos.	Incipit	*CAO*	Mode	*Differentia*
131r	Comm. Virginum	M	V	1	Propterea benedixit te deus	6445a	r	*
131v	Comm. Virginum	M	A	2.1	Cum esset rex in accubitu suo	2450	3	*
131v	Comm. Virginum	M	A	2.2	Pulchra es et decora filia	4418	1	?
131v	Comm. Virginum	M	A	2.3	Jam hiems transiit imber	3470	8	?
131v	Comm. Virginum	M	A	2.4	Surge aquilo et veni auster	5070	7	?
131v	Comm. Virginum	M	A	2.5	Nigra sum sed formosa filia	3878	3	?
131v	Comm. Virginum	M	A	2.6	Aquae multae non potuerunt	1470	8	-G
131v	Comm. Virginum	M	v	2	Specie tua et pulchritudine	8201	r	
131v	Comm. Virginum	M	A	2.1	Ipsi sum desponsata*	3407	7	*
131v	Comm. Virginum	M	A	2.2	Christus circumdedit me*	1790	7	*
131v	Comm. Virginum	M	A	2.3	Ista est speciosa inter	3415	?	-D
131v	Comm. Virginum	M	A	2.4	Mel et lac ex*	3734	1	*
131v	Comm. Virginum	M	A	2.5	Cujus pulchritudinem*	1968	2	*
131v	Comm. Virginum	M	A	2.6	Ipsi soli*	3406	1	*
131v	Comm. Virginum	M	v	2	Specie tua et pulchritudine*	8201	r	
131v	Comm. Virginum	M	R	2.1	Diffusa est gratia in labiis	6446	4	?
131v	Comm. Virginum	M	V	1	Dilexisti justitiam et odisti	6446b	4	?
131v	Comm. Virginum	M	R	2.2	Concupivit rex speciem tuam	6308	5	-B
131v	Comm. Virginum	M	V	1	Specie tua et pulchritudine	6308a	5	-B
131v	Comm. Virginum	M	R	2.3	Pulchra facie sed pulchrior	7452	5	?
131v	Comm. Virginum	M	V	1	Specie tua et pulchritudine*	7452a	5	?
131v	Comm. Virginum	M	R	2.4	Ornatam in monilibus filiam*	7340	8	-D
131v	Comm. Virginum	M	V	1	Astitit regina a dextris*	7340a	8	-D
131v	Comm. Virginum	M	R	2.5	Specie tua et pulchritudine	7679	r	?
131v	Comm. Virginum	M	V	1	Intende prospere procede et	7679a	r	?
131v	Comm. Virginum	M	A	3	Inventa bona margarita dedit	3396	8	w
131v	Comm. Virginum	M	v	3	Adjuvabit eam*	7934	r	
131v	Comm. Virginum	M	A	3	Veni sponsa Christi accipe	5328	8	w
131v	Comm. Virginum	M	v	3	Dilexisti justitiam*	8017	r	
131v	Comm. Virginum	M	R	3.1	Induit me dominus vestimento	6955	6	H
131v	Comm. Virginum	M	V	1	Induit me dominus cyclade	6955a	6	H
131v	Comm. Virginum	M	R	3.2	Ista est speciosa inter	6994	2	e
131v	Comm. Virginum	M	V	1	Specie tua et pulchritudine	6994a	2	e
131v	Comm. Virginum	M	R	3.3	Veni electa mea et ponam in*	7826	2	e?

INDEX 2 CHANTS IN THE GOTTSCHALK ANTIPHONARY THAT DO NOT APPEAR IN *CAO*

Folio	Feast	Office	Pos.	Incipit	CANTUS ref.	Mode	*Differentia*
Invitatories							
55r	Fer. 2 Hebd. 1 Quad.	M		Non sit vobis vanum surgere	Q101	6	H
45r	S. Benedicti	M		Ut Christo celebri jubilemus	Q102	4	*
Antiphons							
72r	Dom. Resurrectionis	L	R	Alleluia sancta dei genetrix	Q203	5	*
46r	S. Benedicti	L	1	Armis praecinctus verae fidei	Q204	2	e
45r	S. Benedicti	M	1.6	Athleta dei gravibus poenis	Q205	6	*
47r	Annuntiatio Mariae	M	2.6	Beata quae credidit quoniam	Q206	4	*
46r	S. Benedicti	M	3	Benedictum propheticis	Q207	1	aq
46r	S. Benedicti	L	B	Benedictus es domine qui	Q208	7	yc
46r	S. Benedicti	P		Benedictus tam nomine*	Q209	1	*
45r	S. Benedicti	M	1.1	Benedictus tam nomine quam	Q209	1	*
55r	Fer. 2 Hebd. 1 Quad.	L	B	Cum venerit filius hominis in	Q210	7	yc
57r	Fer. 5 Hebd. 2 Quad.	E	3	[Ego veni in nomi]ne patris	Q201	?	*
45v	S. Benedicti	M	2.2	Ejus ergo sub tramite multi	Q211	8	*
81r	Dom. 5 p. Pascha	E	4	Exivi a patre meo et veni in	Q212	6	H
45v	S. Benedicti	M	2.5	Favent cuncta Benedicto vas	Q213	5	*
46r	S. Benedicti	S		Favent cuncta*	Q213	5	*
45r	S. Benedicti	M	1.2	Hic ergo Romae traditus	Q214	2	*
45v	S. Benedicti	M	2.3	Hic non impar Eliseo ciet	Q215	1	*
46r	S. Benedicti	T		Hic non impar*	Q215	1	*
46v	S. Benedicti	V2	4	Hic probris actus tumidisque	Q216	4	oc
46r	S. Benedicti	L	2	Huic jubilate quo pater iste	Q217	3	ik
45r	S. Benedicti	M	1.5	In specu sub quo latitat dei	Q218	5	*
46v	S. Benedicti	V2	3	Instar tu Christi patiens ad	Q219	3	ik
45v	S. Benedicti	M	2.1	Jam latius innotuit quasi	Q220	7	*
46r	S. Benedicti	L	4	Laus puerilis hunc benedicit	Q221	5	v
45r	S. Benedicti	V	M	Magna semper et praeclara	Q222	1	*
45v	S. Benedicti	M	2.4	Maurus verbo currens patris	Q223	4	*
46r	S. Benedicti	V2	2	Membra specu claudis quo	Q224	2	e
45r	S. Benedicti	M	1.3	Mundum suis cum floribus	Q225	3	*
46v	S. Benedicti	V2	M	O caelestis norma vitae	Q226	1	a
47v	Annuntiatio Mariae	M	3	O gloriosa femina non solum	Q227	?	*
45v	S. Benedicti	M	2.6	O quanta plenus gratia qui	Q228	6	*
46r	S. Benedicti	N		O quanta plenus*	Q228	6	*
47r	Annuntiatio Mariae	M	2.4	Post abscessum angeli Maria	Q229	2	*
46r	S. Benedicti	V2	1	Praeclarum late tibi vir sine	Q230	1	a
46r	S. Benedicti	L	3	Quemquam non laesit post te	Q231	4	oc
57r	Fer. 5 Hebd. 2 Quad.	E	2	[Quia non quaero] voluntatem	Q202	?	*
45r	S. Benedicti	M	1.4	Sanctum Romanus habitum dans	Q232	4	*
55r	Fer. 5 Hebd. 1 Quad.	L	B	Si manseritis in sermone meo	Q233	8	w
55v	Fer. 5 Hebd. 1 Quad.	V2	M	Si veritatem dico quare non	Q234	3	ik
47r	Annuntiatio Mariae	M	2.5	Spiritu sancto repleta	Q235	3	*
46r	S. Benedicti	L	5	Tympana laeta chori mens	Q236	6	H
Responsories							
45v	S. Benedicti	M	1	Haec dies quam fecit deus in	Q601	3S	*
45v	S. Benedicti	M	1.3	Agnosce dei famule surrexit	Q601	3	*
45r	S. Benedicti	V		Alme pater*	Q602		*

Folio	Feast	Office	Pos.	Incipit	CANTUS ref.	Mode	*Differentia*
46r	S. Benedicti	M	1	Per te ducem clarissimum ut	Q602	8S	*
45v	S. Benedicti	M	2.4	Alme pater qui praescius tui	Q602	8	*
43r	S. Scholasticae	V		Benedictus quam devotas*	Q603	6	*
43r	S. Scholasticae	M	1	Uterque*	Q603	6S	*
45v	S. Benedicti	M	2.2	Benedictus quam devotas deo	Q603	6	*
45v	S. Benedicti	M	1	Uterque duxit gaudia soror	Q603	6S	*
43r	S. Scholasticae	M		Benedictus*	Q603	6	*
47v	Annuntiatio Mariae	M	3.2	Conversus Ezechiel ad	Q604	7	*
47v	Annuntiatio Mariae	M	1	Hinc evidenter ostensum est	Q604	7S	*
46r	S. Benedicti	M	3.3	Ecce jam cari noscite quam	Q605	4	oc
46r	S. Benedicti	M	1	Accepit ergo centuplum et	Q605	4	oc
45v	S. Benedicti	M	1	Intenderunt arcum suum ut	Q606	4S	*
45v	S. Benedicti	M	1.4	Electo grex mortiferum patri	Q606	4	*
43r	Cathedra S. Petri	L		Exaltent eum in ecclesia	Q607	6	H
43r	Cathedra S. Petri	L	1	Et in cathedra seniorum	Q607	6	H
45r	S. Benedicti	M	1.1	Florem mundi periturum	Q608	1	*
45r	S. Benedicti	M	1	Pennas sumens ut columbae	Q608	1S	*
46r	S. Benedicti	M	1	Virque super candens micuit	Q609	2	e
46r	S. Benedicti	M	3.2	Fratribus illuxit Benedictum	Q609	2	e
46r	S. Benedicti	M	3.4	Gloria Christe tuo tibi	Q610	2	e
46r	S. Benedicti	M	1	Nos ejus norma rege serva	Q610	2	e
46r	S. Benedicti	M	1	Fecit Christe quod jussisti	Q611	1	ab
46r	S. Benedicti	M	3.1	Grandi pater fiducia morte	Q611	1	ab
98v	Exaltatio S. Crucis	L	1	Cum dominus ad judicandum	Q612	6	H
98v	Exaltatio S. Crucis	L		Hoc signum crucis erit in	Q612	6	H
45v	S. Benedicti	M	2.3	O Israelita verus cor in deum	Q613	7	*
45v	S. Benedicti	M	1	Caelo quoque ferri sanctam	Q613	7S	*
34r	Epiphania,8	V2		Omnes de Saba*	Q614	6	*
34r	Dom. 1 p. Epiph.	V		Omnes de Saba*	Q614	6	*
34v	Octava Epiphaniae	V2		Omnes de Saba*	Q614	6	*
33r	Epiphania	V2		Omnes de Saba venient aurum	Q614	6	H
33r	Epiphania	V2	1	Et laudem domino annuntiantes	Q614	6	H
34v	Octava Epiphaniae	V		Omnes de Saba*	Q614	*	
47r	Annuntiatio Mariae	M	1	Scientes hoc signum in beatae	Q615	1S	*
47r	Annuntiatio Mariae	M	1.4	Posuit Moyses bissenas virgas	Q615	1	*
45v	S. Benedicti	M	1	Elongatus a nutrice mansit in	Q616	2S	*
45v	S. Benedicti	M	1.2	Puer fletum subsecutae	Q616	2	*
45v	S. Benedicti	M	1	Orans jacentem suscitat	Q617	5S	*
45v	S. Benedicti	M	2.1	Servus dei Benedictus stetit	Q617	5	*

Versicles

36r	Feria 2 per annum	M	1	Delectare in domino	Q790	r	

Hymns

43v	S. Gregorii	M		Confessor dei*	Q820	*	
52r	Dom. Quinquagesimae	V		Dies absoluti*	Q821	*	
46v	S. Benedicti	V2		Rex benedicte*	Q822	*	

INDEX 3 CHANTS IN ALPHABETICAL ORDER

Incipit	Feast	CAO	Folio
Invitatories			
Ad dominum vigiles cuncti	S. Gregorii	1001	43v
Adoremus deum quia ipse fecit	Dom. Quinquagesimae	1007	52r
Adoremus regem apostolorum	S. Joannis Evang.	1013	21r
Adoremus regem*	Exaltatio S. Crucis	1015	102v
Alleluia ii	Dom. 2 p. Pascha	1022	81v
Ave Maria gratia plena	Annuntiatio Mariae	1041	46v
Christus apparuit*	Dom. 1 p. Epiph.	1054	34r
Christus apparuit*	Epiphania,8	1054	33r
Christus apparuit*	Octava Epiphaniae	1054	34v
Deus magnus dominus et rex	Dom. 3 Quadragesimae	1062	57v
In manu tua domine omnes	Feria 4 per annum	1087	37v
Jubilemus deo salutari nostro	Feria 3 per annum	1095	37r
Non sit vobis vanum surgere	Fer. 2 Hebd. 1 Quad.	Q101	55r
Praeoccupemus faciem domini	Dom. per annum	1115	34v
Prope est jam dominus venite	Hebd. 4 Adventus	1120	12r
Quoniam deus magnus dominus	Dom. 2 Quadragesimae	1124	55v
Regem apostolorum dominum	Comm. Apostolorum	1125	121v
Regem apostolorum dominum	Comm. Apostolorum	1125	121v
Regem confessorum*	S. Pauli Heremitae	1129	34r
Regem virginum*	S. Scholasticae	9999	43r
Regem virginum*	Comm. Virginum	9999	131r
Surgite vigilemus quia veniet	Hebd. 4 Adventus	1164	11v
Surrexit dominus vere*	Fer. 3 p. Pascha	1166	77v
Surrexit dominus vere	Fer. 2 p. Pascha	1166	72v
Tu es pastor ovium princeps	Cathedra S. Petri	1167	43r
Ut Christo celebri jubilemus	S. Benedicti	Q102	45r
Venite exsultemus domino	Feria 2 per annum	1179	36r
Antiphons			
...alleluia	Dom. Resurrectionis	9999	72r
...-ne patris mei et non	Fer. 5 Hebd. 2 Quad.	Q201	57r
...voluntatem meam sed	Fer. 5 Hebd. 2 Quad.	Q202	57r
Ab insurgentibus in me libera	Fer. 6 in Parasceve	1201	61v
Ab oriente venerunt magi in	Dom. 1 p. Epiph.	1205	34r7
Adest namque*	Nativitas Mariae	1266	102v
Adhaerebat moralibus seniorum	S. Gregorii	1270	43v
Adhaerebat moralibus*	S. Gregorii	1270	45r
Adhuc multa habeo vobis	Dom. 4 p. Pascha	1276	81r
Adjutor in tribulationibus	Feria 3 per annum	1278	37r
Adjuva me et salvus ero	Feria 2 per annum	1281	37r
Adjuvabit eam deus vultu suo	Comm. Virginum	1282	131r
Adjuvabit eam*	Comm. Virginum	1282	131r
Adorate dominum alleluia in	Epiphania	1288	32r
Adorate dominum alleluia om-	Epiphania	1289	32r
Adorate dominum in aula	Dom. per annum	1290	35r
Advenerunt nobis dies	Fer. 2 Hebd. 1 Quad.	1294	55r
Advenerunt nobis*	Dom. 2 Quadragesimae	1294	55v
Afferte domino*	Dom. 1 p. Epiph.	1303	34r
Afra priscam Rahab	S. Afrae	1304	91r
Agatha laetissima*	S. Agathae	1306	43r

Incipit	Feast	*CAO*	Folio
Agatha sancta dixit*	S. Agathae	1308	43r
Ait latro ad latronem nos	Fer. 6 in Parasceve	1316	61v
Alieni insurrexerunt in me et	Fer. 6 in Parasceve	1321	61r
Alleluia x 2 (Ut non delin-)	Feria 2 per annum	1327	36v
Alleluia x 3 (Juste judicate)	Feria 3 per annum	1328	37r
Alleluia x 4 (De Sion exibit)	Dom. per annum	1329	35v
Alleluia x 5 (Inter natos mu-)	Dom. per annum	1330	36r
Alleluia x 6 (In domino)	Dom. per annum	1331	35v
Alleluia x 6 (Ortus conclusus)	Dom. per annum	1331	35v
Alleluia x 7 (Dico vobis)	Dom. per annum	1332	35v
Alleluia x 7 (Innuebant pa-)	Dom. per annum	1332	36r
Alleluia x 8 (Praebe fili)	Dom. per annum	1333	36r
Alleluia noli flere Maria	In tempore Pascha	1348	72v
Alleluia quem quaeris*	In tempore Pascha	1350	72v
Alleluia resurrexit dominus	In tempore Pascha	1352	72v
Alleluia sancta dei genetrix	Dom. Resurrectionis	Q203	72r
Amen amen dico vobis quia	Dom. 3 p. Pascha	1375	81r
Andreas Christi famulus	S. Andreae	1396	111r
Angelus autem domini*	Fer. 2 p. Pascha	1408	77r
Angelus domini descendebat de	Fer. 6 Hebd. 1 Quad.	1412	55v
Annuntiate populis et dicite	Fer. 4 Hebd. 4 Adv.	1428	12v
Annuntiaverunt opera dei et	Comm. Apostolorum	1429	121v
Ante luciferum genitus et	Epiphania	1434	32v
Ante luciferum*	Epiphania,8	1434	33v
Ante luciferum*	Dom. 1 p. Epiph.	1434	34r
Ante torum hujus virginis	Comm. Virginum	1438	131r
Anxiatus est in me spiritus	Fer. 6 in Parasceve	1442	61v
Apertis thesauris suis	Epiphania	1447	32v
Apparuit caro suo Joanni	S. Joannis Evang.	1458	21v
Aqua comburit peccatum hodie	Epiphania,8	1467	33v
Aquae multae non potuerunt	Comm. Virginum	1470	131v
Ardens est cor meum desidero	In tempore Pascha	1479	72v
Armis praecinctus verae fidei	S. Benedicti	Q204	46r
Aspice in me et miserere mei	Feria 2 per annum	1498	37r
Assumpsit Jesus discipulos	Sabb. Hebd. 1 Quad.	1501	55v
Astiterunt reges terrae et	Fer. 6 in Parasceve	1506	61r
Athleta dei gravibus poenis	S. Benedicti	Q205	45r
Audiens vero beatum virum	S. Afrae	1517	91r
Auditis praesul sanctus	S. Afrae	1524	91r
Ave Maria gratia plena	Fer. 4 Hebd. 4 Adv.	1539	12v
Ave Maria gratia*	Annuntiatio Maria	1539	47v
Ave spes nostra dei genetrix	Annuntiatio Maria	1546	46v
Avertit dominus captivitatem	Feria 3 per annum	1549	37r
Baptista contremuit et non	Octava Epiphaniae	1552	34v
Baptista contremuit*	Octava Epiphaniae	1552	34v
Baptizat miles regem servus	Epiphania,8	1553	33v
Baptizatur Christus et	Epiphania,8	1554	33v
Beata Agatha ingressa	S. Agathae	1557	42r
Beata Agatha*	S. Agathae	1557	43r
Beata quae credidit quoniam	Annuntiatio Mariae	Q206	47r
Beatissimae virginis Mariae	Nativitas Mariae	1596	102r
Beatissimae virginis*	Nativitas Mariae	1596	102v
Beatus Andreas orabat dicens	S. Andreae	1610	111v

Incipit	Feast	*CAO*	Folio
Beatus auctor saeculi servile	Annuntiatio Mariae	1613	47v
Beatus venter*	S. Joannis Evang.	1668	22v
Benedicite gentes deo nostro	Feria 4 per annum	1701	37v
Benedico te pater domini mei	S. Agathae	1702	42v
Benedico te pater domini mei	S. Luciae	1703	121r
Benedicta tu in mulieribus*	Annuntiatio Mariae	1709	46v
Benedictum propheticis	S. Benedicti	Q207	46r
Benedictus deus Israel	Feria 2 per annum	1717	36v
Benedictus es domine qui	S. Benedicti	Q208	46r
Benedictus tam nomine quam	S. Benedicti	Q209	45r
Benedictus tam nomine*	S. Benedicti	Q209	46r
Benediximus vobis in nomine	Feria 2 per annum	1732	37r
Benedixit filiis tuis in te	Dom. per annum	1734	34v
Bethleem non*	Dom. 4 Adventus	1737	11r
Biduo vivens pendebat in	S. Andreae	1739	111r
Bissenos nummos*	S. Gregorii	1740	45r
Caelesti cinctus*	S. Gregorii	1833	45r
Caeli aperti sunt super eum	Epiphania,8	1835	33v
Canite tuba in Sion quia	Dom. 4 Adventus	1757	11v
Canite tuba*	Dom. 4 Adventus	1757	11v
Captabant in animam justi et	Fer. 6 in Parasceve	1767	61v
Caput draconis salvator	Octava Epiphaniae	1768	34v
Christi fidelis famulus	S. Gregorii	1785	45r
Christo datus est principatus	Octava Epiphaniae	1788	34v
Christus circumdedit me*	Comm. Virginum	1790	131v
Christus resurgens ex mortuis	Dom. Resurrectionis	1796	72r
Cibavit eum dominus pane	S. Joannis Evang.	1802	21v
Cito euntes dicite discipulis	In tempore Paschae	1813	72v
Clamaverunt justi et dominus	Comm. Apostolorum	1823	121v
Clamaverunt justi*	Comm. Apostolorum	1823	121v
Clamavi et exaudivit me	Feria 3 per annum	1824	37v
Clausa parentis viscera*	Annuntiatio Mariae	1776	47v
Cognoverunt discipuli dominum	In tempore Paschae	1848	72v
Collocet eum*	Cathedra S. Petri	1854	43v
Columna es immobilis Lucia	S. Luciae	1855	121r
Commendemus nosmetipsos in	Fer. 2 Hebd. 1 Quad.	1857	55r
Concede nobis hominem justum	S. Andreae	1863	111v
Confortatus*	Cathedra S. Petri	1881	43v
Confundantur et revereantur	Fer. 6 in Parasceve	1883	61r
Constantes estote videbitis	Fer. 6 Hebd. 4 Adv.	1899	12v
Constitues eos principes	Comm. Apostolorum	1902	121v
Constitues eos principes*	Comm. Apostolorum	1902	121v
Continet in*	S. Joannis Evang.	1905	22v
Conversus est furor tuus	Feria 2 per annum	1918	36v
Convertere domine aliquantu-	Fer. 5 Hebd. 4 Adv.	1920	12v
Corde et animo Christo	Nativitas Mariae	1931	102r
Crucem sanctam subiit qui	Dom. Resurrectionis	1951	72r
Crucem sanctam subiit*	Dom. Resurrectionis	1951	72r
Crucem sanctam subiit*	In tempore Paschae	1951	72v
Crucifixus resurrexit	In tempore Paschae	1956	72v
Crucifixus surrexit a mortuis	In tempore Paschae	1957	72v
Crux benedicta nitet dominus	Exaltatio S. Crucis	1961	102v
Cujus prostibulum cum Felice	S. Afrae	1967	91r

Incipit	Feast	*CAO*	Folio
Cujus pulchritudinem*	Comm. Virginum	1968	131v
Cum autem esset*	S. Stephani	1987	21r
Cum autem venerit ille	Dom. 4 p. Pascha	1990	81r
Cum esset rex in accubitu suo	Comm. Virginum	2450	131v
Cum facis eleemosynam nesciat	Fer. 6 post Cineres	2005	53v
Cum factus esset Jesus	Dom. 1 p. Epiph.	2006	34r
Cum jucunditate nativitatem	Nativitas Mariae	2016	102v
Cum psalmis deo et hymnis	S. Afrae	2026	91r
Cum revereretur Joannes ab	S. Joannis Evang.	2031	22r
Cum turba plurima conveniret	Dom. Sexagesimae	2040	52r
Cum venerit filius hominis in	Fer. 2 Hebd. 1 Quad.	Q210	55r
Cumque dulcem sanae doctrinae	S. Afrae	2059	91r
Cunctis diebus vitae nostrae	Feria 3 per annum	2079	37v
Custodiebant*	Cathedra S. Petri	2083	43r
Custodit dominus omnes	Dom. per annum	2085	34v
Da mercedem domine	Fer. 3 Hebd. 4 Adv.	2087	12v
Da nobis domine auxilium de	Feria 4 per annum	2089	37v
Dabit illi deus sedem David	Annuntiatio Mariae	2093	46v
Dabit illi dominus sedem	Fer. 4 Hebd. 4 Adv.	2092	12v
Dabit illi dominus*	Annuntiatio Mariae	2092	47v
De profundis clamavi ad te	Feria 3 per annum	2116	37v
De Sion veniet dominus	Fer. 5 Hebd. 4 Adv.	2120	12v
De Sion veniet qui regnaturus	Fer. 5 Hebd. 4 Adv.	2121	12v
Dedisti hereditatem	Comm. Apostolorum	2133	121v
Dedit illi dominus claritatem	S. Joannis Evang.	2134	21v
Deficiente vino jussit Jesus	Dom. 2 p. Epiph.	2138	36r
Deo nostro jucunda sit	Dom. per annum	2148	34v
Descendentibus illis de monte	Sabb. Hebd. 1 Quad.	2153	55v
Deus a Libano veniet et*	Fer. 6 Hebd. 4 Adv.	2163	12v
Deus deorum dominus locutus	Feria 3 per annum	2168	37r
Dextram meam*	Comm. Virginum	2186	131r
Dicant nunc Judaei quomodo	Dom. Resurrectionis	1796	72r
Dignum sibi dominus	S. Andreae	2221	111r
Dilexit Andream dominus in	S. Andreae	2229	111r
Diviserunt sibi vestimenta	Fer. 6 in Parasceve	2260	61r
Dixerunt pharisaei ad Joannem	Dom. 4 Adventus	2264	11v
Dixit autem Maria ad angelum	Annuntiatio Mariae	2279	47r
Dixit autem Maria ad angelum	Annuntiatio Mariae	2278	47r
Dixit autem pater ad servos	Sabb. Hebd. 2 Quad.	2280	57r
Dixit dominus domino meo sede	Dom. per annum	2285	36r
Dixit dominus matri suae	S. Joannis Evang.	2286	22r
Dixit dominus matri suae*	S. Joannis Evang.	2286	22r
Dixit dominus*	Dom. 1 Quadragesimae	2285	55r
Dixit quidam ad Jesum ecce	Fer. 4 Hebd. 1 Quad.	2306	55r
Domine bonum est nos hic esse	Sabb. Hebd. 1 Quad.	2327	55v
Domine deus meus in te	Feria 3 per annum	2333	37v
Domine in caelo misericordia	Feria 2 per annum	2348	36v
Domine in virtute tua	Dom. per annum	2349	34v
Domine in virtute*	Dom. Quinquagesimae	2349	52r
Domine libera animam meam a	S. Stephani	2357	21r
Domine non habeo hominem ut	Fer. 6 Hebd. 1 Quad.	2362	55v
Domine quinque talenta*	S. Pauli Heremitae	2370	34r
Domine suscipe me ut cum	S. Joannis Evang.	2391	21v

Incipit	Feast	*CAO*	Folio
Domine suscipe me*	S. Joannis Evang.	2391	21r
Domine suscipe*	S. Joannis Evang.	2391	22v
Dominus defensor vitae meae	Dom. per annum	2404	35r
Dominus legifer noster	Fer. 5 Hebd. 4 Adv.	2415	12v
Dominus regit me et nihil	Dom. per annum	2420	34v
Dominus veniet occurrite illi	Dom. 4 Adventus	2423	11v
Domus Jacob de populo barbaro	Feria 2 per annum	2427	37r
Domus mea domus orationis	Fer. 3 Hebd. 1 Quad.	2428	55r
Dulce lignum*	Exaltatio S. Crucis	2432	102v
Dulce lignum*	Exaltatio S. Crucis	2432	102v
Dum conturbata fuerit anima	Fer. 6 in Parasceve	2444	61v
Dum steteritis ante reges et	Comm. Apostolorum	2470	121v
Dum venerit filius hominis	Fer. 2 Hebd. 4 Adv.	2476	12r
Dum venerit paraclitus spiri-	Dom. 4 p. Pascha	2478	81r
Ecce advenit dominator*	Epiphania	2489	32r
Ecce advenit*	S. Stephani	2489	21r
Ecce ancilla domini fiat mihi	Fer. 4 Hebd. 4 Adv.	2491	12v
Ecce ancilla domini fiat*	Annuntiatio Mariae	2491	47v
Ecce ascendimus Jerusalem et	Fer. 4 Hebd. 2 Quad.	2496	57r
Ecce concipies et paries	Annuntiatio Mariae	2499	46v
Ecce deus meus et honorabo	Fer. 5 Hebd. 4 Adv.	2503	12v
Ecce ego Joannes vidi ostium	Comm. Evangelistarum	2511	121r
Ecce ego mitto vos sicut oves	Comm. Apostolorum	2512	121v
Ecce in nubibus caeli filius	Dom. 4 Adventus	2516	11v
Ecce jam veniet plenitudo	Fer. 2 Hebd. 4 Adv.	2519	12r
Ecce nunc palam loqueris et	Dom. 5 p. Pascha	2530	81r
Ecce puer meus electus quem	S. Joannis Evang.	2536	22v
Ecce quam bonum et quam	Feria 3 per annum	2537	37v
Ecce rex veniet dominus	Fer. 6 Hebd. 4 Adv.	2543	12v
Ecce veniet desideratus	Dom. 4 Adventus	2548	11v
Ecce veniet dominus princeps	Fer. 2 Hebd. 4 Adv.	2550	12r
Ecce veniet dominus ut sedeat	Fer. 4 Hebd. 4 Adv.	2551	12v
Ecce veniet*	Dom. 4 Adventus	2548	11v
Ego Christum confiteor labiis	S. Agathae	2568	42r
Ego sum alpha et o. primus et	In tempore Paschae	2588	72v
[Ego veni in nomi]ne patris	Fer. 5 Hebd. 2 Quad.	Q201	57r
Ego veritatem dico vobis	Dom. 4 p. Pascha	2607	81r
Egredietur dominus de loco	Fer. 2 Hebd. 4 Adv.	2612	12r
Egredietur virga de radice	Fer. 2 Hebd. 4 Adv.	2613	12r
Ejus ergo sub tramite multi	S. Benedicti	Q211	45v
Emitte agnum domine	Fer. 3 Hebd. 4 Adv.	2642	12v
Erexit dominus nobis cornu	Feria 3 per annum	2664	37v
Eructavit cor meum verbum	Feria 2 per annum	2673	36v
Erunt prava in directa et	Dom. 4 Adventus	2676	11v
Erunt prava*	Dom. 4 Adventus	2676	11v
Et coegerunt illum dicentes	Fer. 2 p. Pascha	2692	77r
Et dicebant ad invicem quis	Dom. Resurrectionis	2697	72r
Et ecce terraemotus*	Fer. 3 p. Pascha	2699	77v
Et incipiens a Moyse et	Fer. 2 p. Pascha	2706	77r
Et omnis mansuetudinis ejus	Feria 3 per annum	2713	37v
Et recordatae sunt verborum	In tempore Paschae	2717	72v
Et respicientes viderunt	Dom. Resurrectionis	2718	72r
Euge serve bone*	S. Pauli Heremitae	2734	34r

Incipit	Feast	*CAO*	Folio
Euge serve*	S. Hilarii	2732	34v
Exaltabuntur cornua*	Cathedra S. Petri	2757	43r
Exiit qui seminat seminare	Dom. Sexagesimae	2789	52r
Exiit qui seminat*	Hebd. Sexagesimae	2789	52r
Exiit sermo inter fratres	S. Joannis Evang.	2791	22r
Exiit sermo inter fratres*	S. Joannis Evang.	2791	22v
Exiit sermo inter fratres*	S. Joannis Evang.	2791	22r
Exivi a patre et veni in	Dom. 5 p. Pascha	2793	81r
Exivi a patre meo et veni in	Dom. 5 p. Pascha	Q212	81r
Expandens manus suas ad deum	S. Joannis Evang.	2795	21v
Expugna impugnantes me	Feria 2 per annum	2801	36r
Exsultate justi in domino	Comm. Apostolorum	2815	121v
Faciamus hic tria tabernacula	Sabb. Hebd. 1 Quad.	2832	55v
Facti sumus sicut consolati	Feria 3 per annum	2839	37v
Favent cuncta Benedicto vas	S. Benedicti	Q213	45v
Favent cuncta*	S. Benedicti	Q213	46r
Fidelia omnia mandata ejus	Dom. per annum	2865	36r
Fili quid fecisti nobis sic	Dom. 1 p. Epiph.	2872	34r
Fili recordare*	Fer. 5 Hebd. 2 Quad.	2873	57r
Fili tu semper mecum es et	Dom. 3 Quadragesimae	2874	57v
Fili tu semper mecum fuisti	Sabb. Hebd. 2 Quad.	2875	57r
Fontes aquarum sanctificati	Octava Epiphaniae	2888	34r
Fulgebunt justi sicut*	Dom. Resurrectionis	2908	72r
Generatio haec prava et	Fer. 4 Hebd. 1 Quad.	2935	55r
Gloriosa sanctissimi	S. Gregorii	2956	43v
Gratias tibi ago domine quia	S. Agathae	2975	42v
Gratias tibi ago*	S. Agathae	2975	43r
Gratias tibi domine Jesu	S. Afrae	2978	91v
Gregorius ortus Romae ex	S. Gregorii	2981	43v
Gregorius ortus*	S. Gregorii	2981	45r
Gregorius ut creditur	S. Gregorii	2983	43v
Gregorius ut creditur*	S. Gregorii	2983	45r
Gregorius vigiliis*	S. Gregorii	2984	45r
Haec est generatio	Comm. Apostolorum	2999	121v
Haec est quae*	Annuntiatio Mariae	3001	47r
Haurietis aquas in gaudio de	Fer. 2 Hebd. 4 Adv.	3020	12r
Hic ab adolescentia divina	S. Gregorii	3046	43v
Hic ergo Romae traditus	S. Benedicti	Q214	45r
Hic est discipulus ille qui	S. Joannis Evang.	3051	21v
Hic est discipulus meus sic	S. Joannis Evang.	3052	22v
Hic non impar Eliseo ciet	S. Benedicti	Q215	45v
Hic non impar*	S. Benedicti	Q215	46r
Hic probris actus tumidisque	S. Benedicti	Q216	46v
Hodie caelesti sponso juncta	Epiphania	3095	33r
Hodie nata est beata virgo	Nativitas Mariae	3108	102v
Hosanna filio David	Fer. 3 Hebd. 1 Quad.	3141	55r
Huic jubilate quo pater iste	S. Benedicti	Q217	46r
Hymnum dicamus alleluia	Dom. per annum	3153	35v
Ideoque et quod nascetur ex	Annuntiatio Mariae	3164	47r
Ille me clarificabit quia de	Dom. 4 p. Pascha	3172	81r
Imbuta verae fidei rudimentis	S. Afrae	3189	91r
In columbae specie spiritus	Octava Epiphaniae	3213	34v
In ecclesiis benedicite	Feria 4 per annum	3230	37v

Incipit	Feast	*CAO*	Folio
In excelsis laudate deum	Feria 2 per annum	3232	36v
In ferventis olei dolium	S. Joannis Evang.	3234	21r
In ferventis olei*	S. Joannis Evang.	3234	22v
In Galilaea Jesum videbitis	In tempore Paschae	3237	72v
In mandatis ejus volet nimis	Dom. per annum	3251	36r
In medio ecclesiae aperuit	S. Joannis Evang.	3255	22v
In omnem terram exivit sonus	Comm. Apostolorum	3262	121v
In omnem terram*	Cathedra S. Petri	3262	43r
In omnem terram*	Comm. Apostolorum	3262	121v
In qua civitate cum puellis	S. Afrae	3275	91r
In specu sub quo latitat dei	S. Benedicti	Q218	45r
In tabernaculis justorum*	Dom. Resurrectionis	3289	72r
In tua justitia libera me	Dom. per annum	3300	35r
In tua patientia possedisti	S. Luciae	3301	121r
Inclinavit dominus aurem suam	Feria 2 per annum	3319	37r
Inclinavit se Maria prospexit	In tempore Paschae	3321	72v
Induit me*	Comm. Virginum	3328	131r
Ingressus angelus ad Mariam	Annuntiatio Mariae	3339	46v
Ingressus angelus ad Mariam	Annuntiatio Mariae	3339	46v
Instar tu Christi patiens ad	S. Benedicti	Q219	46v
Insurrexerunt in me testes	Fer. 6 in Parasceve	3358	61r
Intellege clamorem meum	Feria 2 per annum	3359	36v
Intende in me et exaudi me	Feria 3 per annum	3363	37r
Intuemini quantus sit	Fer. 5 Hebd. 4 Adv.	3391	12v
Intuens in caelum*	S. Stephani	3392	21r
Inventa bona margarita dedit	Comm. Virginum	3396	131v
Invicta Christi testis Afra	S. Afrae	3397	91r
Ipsi soli*	Comm. Virginum	3406	131v
Ipsi sum desponsata*	Comm. Virginum	3407	131v
Ista est speciosa inter	Comm. Virginum	3415	131v
Ista est speciosa*	S. Luciae	3416	121r
Iste est discipulus qui	S. Joannis Evang.	3421	22v
Iste est Joannes cui Christus	S. Joannis Evang.	3423	22r
Iste est Joannes cui*	S. Joannis Evang.	3423	22r
Iste est Joannes qui supra	S. Joannis Evang.	3425	22r
Isti sunt sancti qui pro*	Exaltatio S. Crucis	3444	102v
Isti sunt viri sancti quos	Comm. Apostolorum	3449	121r
Ite nuntiate fratribus meis	In tempore Paschae	3462	72v
Iterum autem videbo vos et	Dom. 3 p. Pascha	3465	81r
Iterum autem videbo vos et	Dom. 3 p. Pascha	3465	81r
Jam hiems transiit imber	Comm. Virginum	3470	131v
Jam latius innotuit quasi	S. Benedicti	Q220	45v
Jesum quem quaeritis non est	In tempore Paschae	3483	72v
Jesum qui crucifixus est	In tempore Paschae	3484	72v
Jesum qui crucifixus est*	Fer. 3 p. Pascha	3484	77v
Jesus haec dicens*	Dom. Sexagesimae	3490	52r
Jesus haec dicens*	Hebd. Sexagesimae	3490	52r
Jesus junxit se discipulis	Fer. 2 p. Pascha	3491	77v
Joannes apostolus et	S. Joannis Evang.	3494	21r
Joannes apostolus*	S. Joannis Evang.	3494	22v
Joannes autem apostolus virgo	S. Joannis Evang.	3495	22v
Joannes quidem clamabat	Epiphania,8	3503	33v
Jucundus homo qui miseretur	S. Stephani	3510	21r

Incipit	Feast	*CAO*	Folio
Nativitas est hodie sanctae	Nativitas Mariae	3849	102r
Nativitas est hodie*	Nativitas Mariae	3849	102v
Nativitas gloriosae virginis	Nativitas Mariae	3850	102r
Nativitas gloriosae*	Nativitas Mariae	3850	102v
Nativitatem hodiernam	Nativitas Mariae	3853	102v
Ne in ira tua arguas me	Feria 2 per annum	3859	36r
Ne timeas Maria invenisti*	Annuntiatio Mariae	3863	47v
Nemini dixeritis visionem	Dom. 2 Quadragesimae	3869	55v
Nesciat sinistra tua quid	Fer. 6 post Cineres	3876	53v
Nesciens mater*	S. Stephani	3877	21r
Nigra sum sed formosa filia	Comm. Virginum	3878	131v
Nisi diligenter perfeceris	S. Agathae	3881	42r
Nolite expavescere Jesum	Dom. Resurrectionis	3893	72r
Nolite expavescere*	In tempore Paschae	3893	72v
Nolite expavescere*	Fer. 2 p. Pascha	3893	72v
Nolite timere quinta*	S. Thomae Apost.	3898	121r
Non enim loquetur a semetipso	Dom. 4 p. Pascha	3909	81r
Non in solo pane vivit homo	Dom. 1 Quadragesimae	3919	55r
Non me permittas domine	S. Andreae	3923	111v
Non possum ego a meipso	Fer. 5 Hebd. 2 Quad.	3927	57r
Nonne cor nostrum ardens erat	In tempore Paschae	3943	72v
Nonne sic oportuit pati	Fer. 2 p. Pascha	3950	77r
Nos autem gloriari oportet in	Exaltatio S. Crucis	3953	102v
Nos autem gloriari*	Exaltatio S. Crucis	3953	102v
Notum fecit dominus alleluia	Epiphania	3964	32r
Nuptiae factae sunt in Cana	Dom. 2 p. Epiph.	3979	35v
O*	Dom. 4 Adventus	9999	11v
O caelestis norma vitae	S. Benedicti	Q226	46v
O crux admirabilis evacuatio	Exaltatio S. Crucis	4014	102v
O gloriosa femina non solum	Annuntiatio Mariae	Q227	47v
O Gregori dulcissime sancti	S. Gregorii	4031	45r
O magnum pietatis opus mors	Exaltatio S. Crucis	4035	102v
O magnum pietatis*	Exaltatio S. Crucis	4035	102v
O quam pulchra est casta	Comm. Virginum	4069	131r
O quam pulchra es*	Comm. Virginum	4069	131r
O quanta plenus gratia qui	S. Benedicti	Q228	45v
O quanta plenus*	S. Benedicti	Q228	46r
O regem caeli*	S. Joannis Evang.	4077	22v
O sapientia*	Antiphonae Majores	4081	121r
O Thoma Didyme per Christum	S. Thomae Apost.	4083	121r
Occurrit beato Joanni ab	S. Joannis Evang.	4105	21r
Oculi mei semper ad dominum	Dom. per annum	4109	34v
Omnes angeli ejus laudate	Feria 3 per annum	4116	37v
Omnes gentes*	Epiphania,8	4125	33r
Omnipotens sermo tuus domine	Dom. 4 Adventus	4144	11v
Omnipotens sermo*	Dom. 4 Adventus	4144	11v
Omnis qui petit accipit et	In Letaniis	4151	81v
Omnis terra*	Epiphania,8	4155	33r
Oportebat pati Christum et	In tempore Paschae	4163	72v
Orante sancta Lucia apparuit	S. Luciae	4178	121r
Orante sancta Lucia*	S. Luciae	4178	121r
Ornatam*	S. Luciae	4197	121r
Paganorum multitudo fugiens	S. Agathae	4208	43r

Incipit	Feast	*CAO*	Folio
Quid est quod me quaerebatis	Epiphania,8	4521	34r
Quid mihi et tibi est mulier	Dom. 2 p. Epiph.	4526	36r
Quid retribuam domino pro	S. Stephani	4530	21r
Quis es tu qui venisti ad me	S. Agathae	4547	42v
Quis es tu qui venisti*	S. Agathae	4547	43r
Quod autem cecidit in terram	Dom. Quinquagesimae	4557	52r
Quod uni ex minimis meis	Fer. 2 Hebd. 1 Quad.	4560	55r
Quodcumque ligaveris super	Cathedra S. Petri	4561	43r
Quomodo fiet istud angele dei	Fer. 4 Hebd. 4 Adv.	4563	12v
Quoniam in te confidit anima	Feria 3 per annum	4568	37v
Recipe me ab hominibus et	S. Andreae	4575	111r
Rectos decet collaudatio	Feria 2 per annum	4580	36r
Rectos decet*	Fer. 2 Hebd. 1 Quad.	4580	55r
Regali ex progenie Maria	Nativitas Mariae	4591	102r
Regali ex progenie*	Nativitas Mariae	4591	102v
Respondens angelus dixit ad	Annuntiatio Mariae	4629	46v
Revela domino viam tuam	Feria 2 per annum	4643	36r
Rorate caeli desuper et nubes	Fer. 3 Hebd. 4 Adv.	4668	12v
Sacerdos et pontifex*	S. Hilarii	4673	34r
Salutare vultus mei deus meus	Feria 3 per annum	4683	37v
Salutis nostrae auctorem magi	Epiphania	4685	33r
Salva nos Christe salvator	Exaltatio S. Crucis	4686	102v
Salva nos Christe*	Exaltatio S. Crucis	4686	102v
Salvator mundi salva*	Exaltatio S. Crucis	9999	102v
Salve crux pretiosa suscipe	S. Andreae	4693	111v
Salve crux quae in corpore	S. Andreae	4694	111r
Sana domine animam meam quia	Feria 2 per annum	4696	36v
Sancta et immaculata*	S. Stephani	4700	21r
Sanctifica nos domine	Exaltatio S. Crucis	4744	102v
Sanctimonialis autem femina	S. Scholasticae	4749	43r
Sanctissime confessor domini	S. Benedicti	4752	45r
Sancto pontifice in divinis	S. Afrae	4760	91r
Sanctum Romanus habitum dans	S. Benedicti	Q232	45r
Scio quod Jesum quaeritis	In tempore Paschae	4833	72v
Scio quod Jesum quaeritis*	Fer. 2 p. Pascha	4833	77r
Scriptum est enim quia domus	Fer. 3 Hebd. 1 Quad.	4836	55r
Secundum magnam misericordiam	Feria 3 per annum	4845	37v
Secundum multitudinem*	Dom. Quinquagesimae	4846	53r
Sedere autem mecum non est	Fer. 4 Hebd. 2 Quad.	4857	57r
Semen cecidit in terram bonam	Hebd. Sexagesimae	4859	52r
Semen cecidit in terram bonam	Hebd. Sexagesimae	4860	52r
Sepelierunt*	S. Stephani	4866	21r
Servite domino in timore et	Feria 2 per annum	4876	36v
Si culmen veri honoris	Dom. Sexagesimae	4882	52r
Si culmen*	Hebd. Sexagesimae	4882	52r
Si ergo vos cum sitis mali	In Letaniis	4893	81v
Si gloriam dignitatum	Hebd. Sexagesimae	4895	52r
Si manseritis in sermone meo	Fer. 5 Hebd. 1 Quad.	Q233	55r
Si quis fecerit voluntatem	Fer. 4 Hebd. 1 Quad.	4908	55r
Si vere fratres divites esse	Dom. Sexagesimae	4915	52r
Si vere fratres*	Hebd. Sexagesimae	4915	52r
Si veritatem dico quare non	Fer. 5 Hebd. 1 Quad.	Q234	55v
Sic eum volo manere donec	S. Joannis Evang.	4923	21v

Incipit	Feast	*CAO*	Folio
Sicut fuit Jonas in ventre	Fer. 4 Hebd. 1 Quad.	4934	55r
Similabo eum*	S. Pauli Heremitae	4952	34r
Simile est regnum caelorum	Comm. Virginum	4953	131r
Simon Bar Jona tu vocaberis	Cathedra S. Petri	4958	43v
Simon Bar Jona*	Cathedra S. Petri	4958	43v
Sit nomen domini benedictum	Dom. per annum	4971	36r
Solve jubente*	Cathedra S. Petri	4981	43r
Solve jubente*	Cathedra S. Petri	4981	43v
Specie tua et pulchritudine	Comm. Virginum	4987	131r
Specie tua*	Comm. Virginum	4987	131r
Speret Israel in domino	Feria 3 per annum	4990	37v
Spiritu sancto repleta	Annuntiatio Mariae	Q235	47r
Spiritu sapientiae salutaris	S. Joannis Evang.	4995	21v
Spiritus domini super me	Fer. 4 Hebd. 4 Adv.	4999	12v
Spiritus sanctus*	Annuntiatio Mariae	5006	47v
Stella ista sicut flamma	Epiphania,8	5022	33r
Stella nobis visa est rex	Epiphania,8	5023	33r
Stella nobis visa*	Dom. 1 p. Epiph.	5023	34r
Stephanus autem*	S. Stephani	5025	21r
Stephanus vidit*	S. Joannis Evang.	5028	22v
Stephanus vidit*	S. Stephani	5028	21r
Stetit Jesus in medio	Fer. 3 p. Pascha	5032	77v
Studiis liberalibus nulli	S. Gregorii	5036	43v
Sunt de hic stantibus qui non	S. Joannis Evang.	5056	22v
Super omnia ligna cedrorum tu	Exaltatio S. Crucis	5061	102v
Super ripam Jordanis stabat	Epiphania,8	5062	33v
Supra pectus domini Jesu	S. Joannis Evang.	5068	21r
Supra pectus*	S. Joannis Evang.	5068	22v
Surge aquilo et veni auster	Comm. Virginum	5070	131v
Surgens Jesus mane prima	Dom. Resurrectionis	5075	72r
Surgens Jesus*	In tempore Paschae	5075	72v
Surrexit Christus et illuxit	In tempore Paschae	5077	72v
Surrexit dominus de sepulcro	In tempore Paschae	5079	72v
Surrexit dominus de sepulcro	In tempore Paschae	5079	72v
Surrexit enim sicut dixit	Dom. Resurrectionis	5081	72r
Sustinuit anima mea in verbo	S. Stephani	5094	21r
Tanto pondere eam fixit	S. Luciae	5110	121r
Tanto pondere*	S. Luciae	5110	121r
Te qui in spiritu et igne	Octava Epiphaniae	5122	34v
Te qui in spiritu*	Octava Epiphaniae	5122	34v
Tecum principium*	Octava Epiphaniae	5127	34r
Tecum principium*	Dom. 1 p. Epiph.	5127	34r
Tecum principium*	Epiphania,8	5127	34r
Tecum principium*	Epiphania	5127	33r
Tecum principium*	Dom. 1 p. Epiph.	5127	34r
Tecum principium*	Octava Epiphaniae	5127	34v
Thomas qui dicitur*	S. Thomae Apost.	5145	121r
Tollite jugum*	Cathedra S. Petri	5158	43r
Tradetur enim gentibus ad	Fer. 4 Hebd. 2 Quad.	5165	57r
Tria sunt munera quae	Epiphania	5181	32r
Tria sunt munera*	Epiphania	5181	33r
Tribus miraculis ornatum diem	Epiphania	5184	33r
Tristitia implebit cor	Dom. 3 p. Pascha	5189	81r

Incipit	Feast	*CAO*	Folio
Tristitia vestra alleluia	Dom. 3 p. Pascha	5190	81r
Tu autem cum oraveris intra*	Fer. 6 post Cineres	5193	53v
Tu Bethleem terra Juda non	Fer. 3 Hebd. 4 Adv.	5195	12v
Tu es discipulus meus in te	S. Joannis Evang.	5204	22r
Tu es pastor ovium princeps	Cathedra S. Petri	5207	43r
Tu es pastor ovium*	Cathedra S. Petri	5207	43r
Tu es Petrus et*	Cathedra S. Petri	5208	43r
Tu solus peregrinus es et non	Fer. 2 p. Pascha	5222	77r
Tympana laeta chori mens	S. Benedicti	Q236	46r
Unguentum effusum nomen tuum	Comm. Virginum	5273	131r
Unus est enim magister vester	Fer. 3 Hebd. 2 Quad.	5278	57r
Usque modo non petistis	Dom. 5 p. Pascha	5284	81r
Ut cognoscamus domine in	Fer. 3 Hebd. 4 Adv.	5290	12v
Ut non delinquam in lingua	Feria 2 per annum	5294	36v
Vade jam et noli peccare ne	Fer. 6 Hebd. 1 Quad.	5301	55v
Vado ad eum qui misit me sed	Dom. 4 p. Pascha	5306	81r
Vado ad patrem meum et dicam	Sabb. Hebd. 2 Quad.	5299	57r
Valde honorandus est beatus	S. Joannis Evang.	5309	21r
Veni domine et noli tardare	Fer. 6 Hebd. 4 Adv.	5320	12v
Veni electa*	S. Luciae	5323	121r
Veni sponsa Christi accipe	Comm. Virginum	5328	131v
Veni sponsa*	S. Scholasticae	5328	43r
Venient ad te qui detrahebant	Epiphania,8	5331	33r
Venit lumen tuum Jerusalem et	Epiphania	5344	32v
Venite benedicti patris mei	Fer. 2 Hebd. 1 Quad.	5350	55r
Venite et videte*	Fer. 3 p. Pascha	5352	77v
Verbum caro*	S. Stephani	5363	21r
Verbum supernum a patre ante	Annuntiatio Mariae	5364	47v
Veterem hominem renovans	Octava Epiphaniae	5373	34v
Veterem hominem*	Octava Epiphaniae	5373	34v
Vide humilitatem meam domine	Feria 2 per annum	5380	37r
Videntes stellam magi gavisi	Epiphania,8	5391	33r
Videntes stellam*	Epiphania,8	5391	34r
Vidi speciosam*	S. Luciae	5407	121r
Vidimus stellam ejus in	Epiphania	5411	33r
Vidimus stellam*	Epiphania,8	5411	34r
Vidimus stellam*	S. Pauli Heremitae	5411	34r
Vidisti domine agonem meum	S. Agathae	5412	42r
Vigilate animo in proximo est	Fer. 5 Hebd. 4 Adv.	5418	12v
Vim faciebant qui quaerebant	Fer. 6 in Parasceve	5423	61r
Virginum tria milia Romae	S. Gregorii	5444	45r
Visionem quam vidistis nemini	Sabb. Hebd. 1 Quad.	5465	55v
Vivo ego dicit dominus nolo	Fer. 2 Hebd. 1 Quad.	5481	55r
Vobis datum est nosse	Dom. Sexagesimae	5483	52r
Vox de caelis sonuit et vox	Epiphania,8	5507	33v

Responsories

Agnosce dei famule surrexit	S. Benedicti	Q601	45v
Alme pater qui praescius tui	S. Benedicti	Q602	45v
Alme pater*	S. Benedicti	Q602	45r
Amavit eum*	S. Benedicti	9999	46r
Amavit eum dominus*	S. Pauli Heremitae	9999	34r
Amavit eum dominus*	S. Gregorii	9999	45r

Incipit	Feast	*CAO*	Folio
Ecce concipies et paries	Annuntiatio Mariae	6579	47r
Ecce ego mitto vos sicut oves	Comm. Apostolorum	6588	121v
Ecce jam cari noscite quam	S. Benedicti	Q605	46r
Ecce jam veniet plenitudo	Dom. 4 Adventus	6596	11r
Ecce odor filii mei sicut	Dom. 2 Quadragesimae	6601	55v
Ecce puer meus quem elegi	S. Joannis Evang.	6603	22r
Ecce vere Israelita*	Cathedra S. Petri	6615	43r
Ego autem adjuta a domino	S. Agathae	6625	42v
Ego dixi domine miserere mei	Feria 2 per annum	6627	36v
Ego pro te rogavi*	Cathedra S. Petri	6630	43r
Ego sicut vitis fructificavi	Dom. 2 p. Pascha	6633	81v
Egredietur dominus et proeli-	Hebd. 4 Adventus	6640	12r
Egredietur virga de radice	Dom. 4 Adventus	6641	11v
Egredietur virga*	Hebd. 4 Adventus	6641	12r
Electo grex mortiferum patri	S. Benedicti	Q606	45v
Emitte agnum domine	Hebd. 4 Adventus	6656	12r
Euge serve bone*	S. Pauli Heremitae	6677	34r
Exaltent eum in ecclesia	Cathedra S. Petri	Q607	43r
Exaudi deus deprecationem	Feria 4 per annum	6685	37v
Expandi manus meas tota die	S. Andreae	6698	111v
Expurgate vetus fermentum ut	Fer. 3 p. Pascha	6699	77v
Felix namque es*	Nativitas Mariae	6725	102r
Fervente interim immani	S. Afrae	6727	91v
Fiat manus tua ut salvum me	Dom. per annum	6731	35v
Florem mundi periturum	S. Benedicti	Q608	45r
Fratribus illuxit Benedictum	S. Benedicti	Q609	46r
Fulgebat in venerando duplex	S. Gregorii	6752	43v
Gaudeamus omnes in domino	S. Agathae	6760	42v
Germinaverunt campi eremi	Hebd. 4 Adventus	6772	12r
Gloria Christe tuo tibi	S. Benedicti	Q610	46r
Gloriosae virginis Mariae	Nativitas Mariae	6781	101v
Grandi pater fiducia morte	S. Benedicti	Q611	46r
Grata facta est a domino in	S. Luciae	6789	121r
Haec est dies quam fecit	Dom. per annum	6799	35v
Haec est virgo sapiens quam	Comm. Virginum	6809	131r
Hic est beatissimus	S. Joannis Evang.	6819	21v
Hic est dies praeclarus in	Epiphania	6821	32v
Hic est discipulus qui	S. Joannis Evang.	6822	22r
Hoc signum crucis erit in	Exaltatio S. Crucis	Q612	102v
Hoc signum crucis*	Exaltatio S. Crucis	6845	102v
Hoc signum crucis*	Exaltatio S. Crucis	6845	102v
Hodie in Jordane*	Dom. 1 p. Epiph.	6849	34r
Hodie nata est beata virgo	Nativitas Mariae	6854	101v
Homo dei ducebatur ut	S. Andreae	6868	111r
Hostis antiquus caelesti	S. Afrae	6871	91r
Igitur Joseph ductus est in	Dom. 3 Quadragesimae	6878	57r
In columbae specie spiritus	Epiphania	6892	32v
In illo die suscipiam te	S. Joannis Evang.	6906	21v
In medio ecclesiae aperuit os	S. Joannis Evang.	6913	22v
In omnem terram exivit sonus	Comm. Apostolorum	6919	121v
In omnem terram*	Comm. Apostolorum	6919	121r
Induit me dominus vestimento	Comm. Virginum	6955	131v
Induit me dominus*	S. Agathae	6955	42v

Incipit	Feast	*CAO*	Folio
Ingressus angelus ad Mariam	Annuntiatio Mariae	6963	46v
Interrogabat magos Herodes	Epiphania	6981	32r
Intuemini quantus sit iste	Dom. 4 Adventus	6983	11v
Ipse me coronavit qui per	S. Agathae	6990	42r
Ista est speciosa inter	Comm. Virginum	6994	131v
Iste est Joannes cui Christus	S. Joannis Evang.	7000	22r
Iste est Joannes qui supra	S. Joannis Evang.	7001	22v
Iste homo perfecit*	S. Pauli Heremitae	7008	34r
Jesum tradidit impius summis	Fer. 6 in Parasceve	7035	61v
Joseph dum intraret in terram	Dom. 3 Quadragesimae	7037	57v
Juravi dicit dominus ut ultra	Dom. 4 Adventus	7045	11r
Justi autem in perpetuum*	S. Afrae	9999	91v
Justorum animae*	S. Afrae	9999	91r
Justum deduxit*	S. Pauli Heremitae	9999	34r
Justus germinabit*	S. Pauli Heremitae	7060	34r
Justus ut palma*	S. Gregorii	9999	45r
Justus ut palma*	S. Benedicti	9999	46v
Locutus est ad me unus ex	Dom. 2 p. Pascha	7096	81v
Locutus est dominus ad Abra-	Dom. Quinquagesimae	7097	52v
Magi veniunt ab oriente	Epiphania	7112	32r
Maria Magdalena et altera	Fer. 2 p. Pascha	7128	77r
Maria ut audivit turbata est	Annuntiatio Mariae	7130	47r
Martyr sancta dei quae	S. Afrae	7135	91v
Me oportet minui illum autem	Dom. 4 Adventus	7137	11r
Medicinam carnalem corpori	S. Agathae	7140	42r
Memento mei dum bene tibi	Dom. 3 Quadragesimae	7144	57v
Minor sum cunctis	Dom. 2 Quadragesimae	7156	56v
Miserere mei deus miserere	Feria 3 per annum	7160	37v
Modo veniet dominator dominus	Hebd. 4 Adventus	7172	12r
Mox omnibus in fide Christi	S. Afrae	7181	91v
Mox ut vocem domini	S. Andreae	7182	IIIIr
Multis hinc inde sermonum	S. Afrae	7189	91v
Nascetur nobis parvulus et	Dom. 4 Adventus	7195	11v
Nativitas gloriosae virginis	Nativitas Mariae	7198	102r
Nativitas tua dei genetrix	Nativitas Mariae	7199	102r
Ne perdideris me domine cum	Feria 3 per annum	7208	37r
Non auferetur sceptrum de	Dom. 4 Adventus	7224	11r
Non discedimus a te	Dom. 4 Adventus	7227	11r
Notas mihi fecisti domine	Dom. per annum	7240	35r
O bona crux quae decorem et	S. Andreae	7260	IIIIr
O crux benedicta*	Exaltatio S. Crucis	7265	102v
O crux gloriosa*	Exaltatio S. Crucis	7266	102v
O Israelita verus cor in deum	S. Benedicti	Q613	45v
O pastor apostolice*	S. Gregorii	7279	43v
Omnes amici mei dereliquerunt	Fer. 6 in Parasceve	7313	61r
Omnes de Saba venient aurum	Epiphania	Q614	33r
Omnes de Saba*	Octava Epiphaniae	Q614	34r
Omnes de Saba*	Epiphania,8	7314	33r
Omnes de Saba*	Octava Epiphaniae	Q614	34v
Omnes de Saba*	Dom. 1 p. Epiph.	Q614	34r
Omnes de Saba*	Epiphania,8	Q614	34r
Oravit sanctus Andreas dum	S. Andreae	7335	IIIIv
Orietur stella ex Jacob et	Hebd. 4 Adventus	7338	12r

Incipit	Feast	*CAO*	Folio
Ornatam in monilibus filiam*	Comm. Virginum	7340	131v
Ostende nobis*	Dom. 4 Adventus	7343	11v
Paratum cor meum deus paratum	Feria 3 per annum	7350	37r
Participem me*	Fer. 2 Hebd. 1 Quad.	7353	55r
Pastores prae claritate	Epiphania,8	7357	33v
Pater peccavi in caelum et	Sabb. Hebd. 2 Quad.	7362	57r
Peccata mea domine sicut	Dom. per annum	7370	35v
Per memetipsum juravi dicit	Dom. Quinquagesimae	7375	52r
Petre amas*	Cathedra S. Petri	7382	43r
Ponam arcum meum in nubibus	Dom. Quinquagesimae	7391	52r
Postquam novellam conversa	S. Afrae	7409	91v
Posui adjutorium*	Cathedra S. Petri	7411	43r
Posuit Moyses bissenas virgas	Annuntiatio Mariae	Q615	47r
Praecursor pro nobis	Hebd. 4 Adventus	7421	12r
Propter veritatem et	Comm. Virginum	7441	131r
Propter veritatem*	S. Agathae	7441	42v
Propulso post longum	S. Afrae	7442	91v
Puer fletum subsecutae	S. Benedicti	Q616	45v
Pulchra facie sed pulchrior	Comm. Virginum	7452	131v
Quadraginta dies et noctes	Dom. Quinquagesimae	7454	52r
Quam magna multitudo	Dom. per annum	7459	35v
Quam magnificata sunt opera	Dom. per annum	7460	36r
Quem dicunt*	Cathedra S. Petri	7467	43r
Qui me dignatus est ab omni	S. Agathae	7479	42v
Qui regni claves*	Cathedra S. Petri	7483	43r
Qui sunt hi qui ut nubes	Comm. Evangelistarum	7484	121r
Qui vicerit faciam illum	S. Joannis Evang.	7486	21v
Quis es tu qui venisti ad me	S. Agathae	7499	42r
Quis igitur ille est qui	Dom. 2 Quadragesimae	7500	55v
Quodcumque ligaveris*	Cathedra S. Petri	7503	43r
Quomodo fiet istud respondens	Annuntiatio Mariae	7505	47v
Radix Jesse qui exsurget	Dom. 4 Adventus	7508	11v
Radix Jesse*	Hebd. 4 Adventus	7508	12r
Regali ex progenie Maria	Nativitas Mariae	7519	102r
Reges Tharsis et insulae	Epiphania,8	7522	33v
Reges Tharsis*	Octava Epiphaniae	7522	34v
Reges Tharsis*	Dom. 1 p. Epiph.	7522	34r
Resurrexit dominus alleluia	Dom. 2 p. Pascha	7540	81v
Rorate caeli desuper et nubes	Hebd. 4 Adventus	7553	12r
Salve crux quae in corpore	S. Andreae	7563	111r
Salve nobilis virga Jesse	Annuntiatio Mariae	7564	47r
Sancte Joannes dilecte	S. Joannis Evang.	7579	22v
Sancte Joannes dilecte*	S. Joannis Evang.	7579	22v
Sancte Stephane protomartyr*	S. Stephani	7584	21r
Sancto praesule precibus	S. Afrae	7604	91r
Sedes tua deus in saeculum	Feria 2 per annum	7634	36v
Servus dei Benedictus stetit	S. Benedicti	Q617	45v
Si diligis me*	Cathedra S. Petri	7649	43r
Simon Petre*	Cathedra S. Petri	7674	43r
Solem justitiae regem	Nativitas Mariae	7677	101v
Solve jubente*	Cathedra S. Petri	7678	43r
Specie tua et pulchritudine	Comm. Virginum	7679	131v
Specie tua et pulchritudine	Comm. Virginum	7680	131r

Incipit	Feast	*CAO*	Folio
Specie tua et pulchritudine*	S. Agathae	7679	43r
Spes mea domine*	Dom. Sexagesimae	7687	52r
Statuit dominus supra petram	Feria 2 per annum	7698	36v
Stella quam viderunt magi in	Epiphania	7701	32r
Stirps Jesse virgam produxit	Nativitas Mariae	7709	102r
Surge illuminare Jerusalem	Epiphania	7729	33r
Surgens Jesus dominus noster	Fer. 2 p. Pascha	7734	77r
Surrexit dominus de sepulcro	Dom. Resurrectionis	7738	72r
Surrexit dominus de sepulcro	Fer. 2 p. Pascha	7738	77v
Surrexit dominus de sepulcro	Fer. 2 p. Pascha	7738	77v
Surrexit dominus vere	Fer. 3 p. Pascha	7740	77v
Surrexit dominus vere*	Fer. 2 p. Pascha	7740	77r
Tamquam ad latronem existis	Fer. 6 in Parasceve	7748	61r
Temptavit deus Abraham et	Dom. Quinquagesimae	7762	52v
Tenebrae factae sunt dum	Fer. 6 in Parasceve	7760	61r
Tolle arma tua pharetram et	Dom. 2 Quadragesimae	7767	55v
Tollite jugum meum super vos	Comm. Apostolorum	7770	121v
Tollite jugum*	Comm. Apostolorum	7770	121r
Tradiderunt me in manus	Fer. 6 in Parasceve	7773	61v
Tria sunt munera pretiosa	Epiphania	7777	32r
Tu es pastor ovium*	Cathedra S. Petri	7787	43r
Tu es Petrus*	Cathedra S. Petri	7788	43r
Tu es Petrus*	Cathedra S. Petri	7788	43r
Tu exsurgens*	Dom. 4 Adventus	7790	11v
Tulerunt dominum meum et	Fer. 3 p. Pascha	7797	77v
Valde honorandus est beatus	S. Joannis Evang.	7817	21v
Velum templi scissum est et	Fer. 6 in Parasceve	7821	61r
Veni electa mea et ponam in*	Comm. Virginum	7826	131v
Veni hodie ad fontem aquae et	Dom. Quinquagesimae	7827	52v
Veni sponsa Christi accipe	Comm. Virginum	7828	131r
Venit lumen tuum Jerusalem et	Epiphania,8	7833	33r
Venite post me faciam vos	S. Andreae	7835	111r
Vicesima quarta die decimi	Dom. 4 Adventus	7886	11r
Videbis o Jerusalem et	Epiphania,8	7853	33v
Videbunt gentes justum tuum	Hebd. 4 Adventus	7854	12r
Videns Jacob vestimenta	Dom. 3 Quadragesimae	7858	57v
Videns Romae vir beatus	S. Gregorii	7862	43v
Videntes Joseph a longe	Dom. 3 Quadragesimae	7863	57v
Videntes stellam magi gavisi	Epiphania	7864	32r
Vidisti domine et exspectasti	S. Agathae	7883	42r
Vinea mea electa ego te	Fer. 6 in Parasceve	7887	61r
Vir iste in populo suo	S. Andreae	7899	111v
Virgo Israel revertere in	Dom. 4 Adventus	7903	11r
Virtute magna reddebant	Fer. 3 p. Pascha	7907	77v
Vocavit angelus domini	Dom. Quinquagesimae	7911	52v
Vox domini super aquas deus	Octava Epiphaniae	7918	34v
Vox tonitrui tui deus in rota	S. Joannis Evang.	7921	21r

Versicles

Ab occultis meis munda me	Feria 2 per annum	7928	37r
Ab occultis meis munda me	Dom. per annum	7928	36r
Adjutor meus esto domine	Feria 2 per annum	7932	37r
Adjuvabit eam*	Comm. Virginum	7934	131v

Incipit	Feast	*CAO*	Folio
Adoramus te Christe et	Exaltatio S. Crucis	7936	102v
Adoramus te Christe et	Exaltatio S. Crucis	7936	102v
Adorate dominum	Epiphania	7937	32r
Adorate dominum	Epiphania	7937	33r
Adorate dominum	Octava Epiphaniae	7937	34v
Adorate dominum	Octava Epiphaniae	7937	34v
Adorate dominum	Epiphania,8	7937	33r
Annuntiaverunt opera dei	S. Joannis Evang.	7950	21r
Annuntiaverunt opera dei	Cathedra S. Petri	7950	43v
Annuntiaverunt opera dei	Comm. Apostolorum	7950	121r
Annuntiaverunt opera dei	Cathedra S. Petri	7950	43r
Annuntiaverunt opera dei	S. Joannis Evang.	7950	22v
Annuntiaverunt*	S. Joannis Evang.	7950	22v
Annuntiaverunt opera dei	Cathedra S. Petri	7950	43r
Audi filia et vide*	S. Agathae	7955	43r
Audi filia et vide*	Annuntiatio Mariae	7955	46v
Ave Maria gratia plena	Annuntiatio Mariae	7958	46v
Benedicite gentes deo nostro	Feria 4 per annum	7969	37v
Constitues eos principes*	S. Joannis Evang.	7994	22r
Constitues eos principes*	Cathedra S. Petri	7994	43r
Custodi nos domine*	Fer. 5 in Cena Dom.	8001	61r
Delectare in domino	Feria 2 per annum	Q790	36r
Deus vitam meam annuntiavi	Feria 3 per annum	8011	37v
Diffusa est gratia in labiis*	Comm. Virginum	8014	131r
Diffusa est gratia*	Comm. Virginum	8014	131r
Dilexisti justitiam*	Comm. Virginum	8017	131v
Dirigatur domine oratio*	Feria 2 per annum	8018	37r
Dirigatur domine oratio mea	Dom. per annum	8018	36r
Diviserunt sibi vestimenta	Fer. 6 in Parasceve	8020	61r
Dominus regit me et nihil	Feria 2 per annum	8032	37r
Dominus regit me et nihil	Dom. per annum	8032	36r
Dominus regnavit decorem	Dom. per annum	8034	35v
Ecce sacerdos magnus*	S. Gregorii	8040	45r
Ecce sacerdos*	S. Gregorii	8040	45r
Ego dixi domine miserere mei	Dom. per annum	8042	36r
Egredietur virga*	Nativitas Mariae	8044	102v
Egredietur virga de radice	Nativitas Mariae	8044	102v
Exaltare domine in virtute	Dom. per annum	8061	35v
Exsurge domine adjuva*	Feria 2 per annum	8072	36v
Exsurge domine adjuva nos	Dom. per annum	8072	36r
Gavisi sunt discipuli	Dom. Resurrect.,8	8080	77r
Gavisi sunt discipuli	Dom. Resurrectionis	8080	72r
Gavisi sunt discipuli*	Dom. Resurrect.,8	8080	77r
Haec est dies quam fecit	Dom. Resurrectionis	8085	72r
Hoc signum crucis*	Exaltatio S. Crucis	8088	102v
Immola deo sacrificium laudis	Feria 3 per annum	8091	37r
In matutinis domine meditabor	Feria 3 per annum	8095	37v
In matutinis domine meditabor	Feria 2 per annum	8095	36v
In omnem terram*	Cathedra S. Petri	8097	43r
In omnem terram exivit sonus*	S. Joannis Evang.	8097	21v
In pace in idipsum*	Fer. 5 in Cena Dom.	8099	61r
In resurrectione tua Christe	Fer. 2 p. Pascha	8100	77r

Incipit	Feast	*CAO*	Folio
In resurrectione tua Christe	Dom. Resurrectionis	8100	72r
Insurrexerunt in me testes	Fer. 6 in Parasceve	8102	61r
Justorum animae*	S. Afrae	8114	91r
Justum deduxit dominus*	S. Pauli Heremitae	8115	34r
Justum deduxit dominus per	S. Gregorii	8115	43v
Justum deduxit dominus*	S. Benedicti	8115	45r
Locuti sunt adversum me	Fer. 6 in Parasceve	8124	61v
Media nocte surgebam ad	Dom. per annum	8136	35r
Memor fui in nocte nominis*	Dom. per annum	8138	35r
Nimis honorati sunt amici tui	S. Joannis Evang.	8148	22r
Nimis honorati sunt*	Comm. Apostolorum	8148	121r
Noli flere Maria	Dom. Resurrect.,8	8149	77r
Omnes de Saba venient	Octava Epiphaniae	8159	34v
Omnes de Saba venient	Dom. 1 p. Epiph.	8159	34r
Omnes de Saba venient	Epiphania	8159	33r
Omnes de Saba venient	Epiphania,8	8159	33v
Omnes gentes quascumque	Epiphania,8	8160	33r
Omnes gentes quascumque	Epiphania	8160	32r
Omnis terra adoret te deus*	Epiphania,8	8161	33r
Os justi*	S. Benedicti	8165	45r
Os justi*	S. Pauli Heremitae	8165	34r
Os justi meditabitur	S. Benedicti	8165	46v
Os justi*	S. Benedicti	8165	46r
Per signum crucis*	Exaltatio S. Crucis	8168	102v
Proprio filio suo non	Fer. 6 in Parasceve	8174	61v
Quem quaeris mulier	Dom. Resurrect.,8	8176	77r
Reges Tharsis et insulae*	Epiphania,8	8180	34r
Reges Tharsis et insulae*	Epiphania	8180	33r
Reges Tharsis et insulae*	Dom. 1 p. Epiph.	8180	34r
Reges Tharsis et insulae*	Octava Epiphaniae	8180	34r
Resurrexit dominus	Dom. Resurrect.,8	8185	77r
Resurrexit dominus	Fer. 3 p. Pascha	8185	77v
Resurrexit dominus	Dom. Resurrect.,8	8185	77r
Salva nos Christe salvator	Exaltatio S. Crucis	8189	102v
Salva nos Christe salvator	Exaltatio S. Crucis	8189	102v
Sedes tua deus in saeculum	Feria 2 per annum	8194	36v
Specie tua et pulchritudine	Comm. Virginum	8201	131v
Specie tua et pulchritudine*	Comm. Virginum	8201	131v
Specie tua*	S. Agathae	8201	42r
Speciosa facta es et suavis	Nativitas Mariae	8202	102r
Speciosa facta es et suavis*	Annuntiatio Mariae	8202	47v
Surrexit Christus	Dom. Resurrect.,8	8211	77r
Surrexit dominus de sepulcro	Fer. 2 p. Pascha	8212	77v
Surrexit dominus de sepulcro	Dom. Resurrect.,8	8212	77r
Surrexit dominus de sepulcro	Dom. Resurrectionis	8212	72r
Surrexit dominus vere	Fer. 2 p. Pascha	8213	77r
Surrexit dominus vere	Dom. Resurrectionis	8213	72r
Surrexit dominus vere	Dom. Resurrect.,8	8213	77r
Tria sunt munera pretiosa	Octava Epiphaniae	8223	34v
Tria sunt munera pretiosa	Epiphania	8223	33r
Tulerunt dominum meum	Dom. Resurrect.,8	8228	77r
Venient ad te qui detrahebant	Epiphania	8233	33r

Incipit	Feast	*CAO*	Folio
Venient ad te*	Octava Epiphaniae	8233	34v
Vespertina oratio ascendat ad	Dom. per annum	8240	34v
Vespertina oratio*	Dom. Quinquagesimae	8240	52r
Hymns			
Confessor dei*	S. Gregorii	Q820	43v
Dies absoluti*	Dom. Quinquagesimae	Q821	52r
Rex benedicte*	S. Benedicti	Q822	46v
Sequence			
Quem non praevalent propria	Epiphania		32v

Index of manuscripts cited

General index

Facsimiles

11 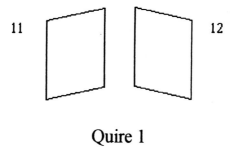 12

Quire 1

CANITE TVBA INSYON uocate gentes annunciate populis et dicite
ecce deus saluator noster ad uenit et v. Annunciate infinibus
terre et ininsulis que procul sunt dicite ecce ds.

Vicesima quarta die decimi mensis ieiuna bitis dicit dominus
et mittam uobis saluatorem et propugnatorem prouobis qui uos pre
cedat et introducat interram quam iuraui patribus
uestris. v. Ego sum dominus deus uester qui eduxi uos deterra egypti. Init.

Non auferetur sceptrum deiuda et dux defemore eius donec ueniat
qui mittendus est et ipse erit expectatio gentium. v. Pulchriores
sunt oculi eius uino et dentes eius lacte candidiores. et ipse

Me oportet minui illum autem crescere qui post me uenit ante
me factus est cuius non sum dignus corrigiam calciamenti
eius soluere v. Hoc est testimonium quod phibuit iohannes. Quip? I u. ii.

Ecce iam ueniet plenitudo temporis inquo Bethlehem non
misit deus filium suum in terris natum deuirgine factum suble ge
ut eos qui sublege erant re dimeret v. Prope est ut ueniat tempus
eius et dies eius non elongabuntur. Ut eos qui sublege erant red.

Virgo israhel reuertere inciuitates tuas usque quo dolens auerteris gene
rabis dominum saluatorem oblationem nouam interra ambulabunt ho
mines insaluatione nem. v. A solis ortu. Ambul... tur. v. A solis ortu et est

Iuraui dicit dominus ut ultra iam non irascar super terram montes enim
et colles suscipient iustitiam me am et testamentum pacis erit inhie
rusalem. v. Iuxta est salus mea ut ueniat et iusticia mea ut reuele

Non discedimus ate uiuificabis nos domine et nomen tuum in
uoca bimus ostende nobis faciem tuam et salui erimus.

Domine deus uirtitum conuerte nos. Ostende nobis faciem tuam

Ã Ecce innubibus celi filius hominis ueniet aeuia. Ad cantica.

℟ Intue mini quantus sit iste qui ingreditur adsaluandas gen tes ipse est rex iusti cie e euius generatio non habet finem.

℣ Et domina bi tur amari usq; admare sui gn̄i.

℟ Radix iesse qui exurget iudicare gentes ineum gentes spa bunt & erit nomen eius benedictum in secu la. ℣ Deus a lybano. Egre

℟ Egredietur uirga de radice iesse & flos de germine eius ascendet & erit iusti cia cingulum lumborum ei us & fides cinctorium re num eius. ℣ Et re quiescet super eum spiritus domini spiritus sapientie & intel lectus. Et er

℟ Nascetur nobis paruu lus & uoca bi tur deus for tis ipse sede bit super thronum dauid pa tris sui & impera bit cui us potes tas su per humerum ei us. ℣ Ec ce aduenit domi nator dominus & regnum inmanu eius & potestas & impe ri um. Cuius po.

Ã Canite tuba insyon quia prope est dies do mi ni ecce ueniet Ad laud adsaluandum nos aeuia aeuia. Ã Ecce ueniet desideratus cunctis gentibus & replebitur gloria domus domini a euia. Ã Erunt praua indirecta & aspera inuias planas ueni domine & noli tardare aeuia. Ã Dominus ueniet occur rite illi dicentes magnum principium & regni eius non erit finis deus fortis dominator princeps pacis aeuia aeuia. Ã Omnipotens sermo tuus domine aregalibus sedibus ueniet aeuia. ℟ Ostende nobis. ℣ Ã Dixerunt pha risei adiohannem. Quis ergo es ut responsum demus his qui miserunt nos Et ait illis. Ego uox clamantis indeserto. Parate uiam domi ni sicut dixit esayas propheta. Ã Canite tuba. Ã Ecce ueniet. ℣. Erunt praua. ℣.

Ã Omnipotens sermo. ℣℟ Lux urgens. ℣ Ã Ohauit. Surgite uigile my qui a labia infortitudine qui annuncias pa cem in Que ueniet rex hierusa lem dicciuitatibus iuda & habitatoribus sy on ecce deus

noster quem expectabamus ad ueniet. Super montem excelsum ascen
de tu qui euangelizas syon exalta infortitudine uocem tu am. Die ciuita.

Orietur stella exiacob & consurget homo de isr rahel & confringet omnes
duces alienige narum & erit omnis terra possessio ei us. A solis ortu. et

Vodo ueniet dominator dominus & nomen eius emmanuel uo cabi tur.

Egredietur dominus & preliabitur contra gen tes. Ecce dominator. et nom
& stabunt pedes eius sup montes oliuarum adorientem. Ex syon species. et stab.

Precursor pnobis ingredi tur agnus si ne macu la secundum ordi
nem melchisedech pontifex factus est ineternum & inseculum seculi.

Videbunt gentes iustum tuum & cuncti reges incli. Ecce dominator. et pontifex
tum tiuum & uocabitur tibi nomen nouum quod os domi ni no mi nauit.

Eteris corona glorie inmanu domini & diadema regni inmanu dei tui. et uoc
Emitte agnum domine dominatorem ter re de petra deserti admontem filie
sy on. Ex syon species. ad monte V serti admontem fi lie syon. Aperiat

Rorate celi de super & nubes plu ant iustum ape riatur ter ra & germi
net saluato rem. Emitte agnum domine dominatorem terre de petra de

Germinauerunt campi here mi germen odoris is ra hel quia ecce deus no
ster cum uirtute ueni et & splendor eius cum e o. Ecce dinator. et spl

Radix iesse. Egredietur uirga. Annunciatum est. Prope est iam dns uenite

Ecce ueniet dominus princeps regum terre beati qui Adlaud. Adoremus.
parati sunt occurrere illi. Dum uenerit filius hominis putas inueniet fidem
sup terram. Ecce iam ueniet plenitudo temporis inquo misit deus filium
suum interris. Haurietis aquas ingaudio defontibus saluatoris.

Egredietur dominus de loco sco suo ueniet ut saluet populum suum. Rex
Egredietur uirga deradice iesse & replebi tur omnis terra gloria domini
& uidebit omnis caro salutare dei. FERIA III.

145 B

oc	ã Rorate celi de super· æ nubes pluant iustum aperiatur· terra æ germinet salua
oc	ã E mitte agnum dne dominatorem terre de petra deserti ad montē filie syon· torcal
oc	ã Vt cognoscamus domine interra uiam tuam inomibus gentibus salutare tuum·
o.	ã Da mercedem domine sustinentibus te ut prophete tui fideles inueniantur·
a.	ã Lex per moysen data est gratia æ ueritas per ihm xpm facta est ·
1	ã Tu bethlem terra iuda non eris minima inprincipibus iuda exte enim exiet
	dux qui regat populum meum istahel · egrediatur ut splendor iustus eius ·
a.	ã Prophete predicauerunt nasci saluatorem de uirgine MARIA ·
e	ã Spiritus domini super· me euangelizare pauperibus misit me· Annuniate
o.	populis æ dicite ecce deus saluator noster ueniet ã Ecce ueniet dominus ut sede
o.	at cum principibus æ solium glorie teneat ã Propter syon non tacebo donec
ye	ã Quomodo fiet istud angele dei quia uirum inconcipiendo non pertuli ·
	audi MARIA uirgo xpi spiritus sanctus super ueniet inte æ uirtus altissimi
a.	obumbrabit tibi · ã Missus est g̃ · Aue MARIA gratia plena dominus tecum
· a.	benedicta tu inmulieribus æ uia · Dabit illi dominus sedem dauid patris
wd	sui æ regnabit ineternum · Ecce ancilla domini fiat mihi sedm uerbu tuum
ap.	ã De syon ueniet dns omnipotens ut saluum faciat populum suum·
ap.	ã De syon ueniet qui regnaturus est dominus emmanuel magnum nomen eius·
w.	ã Conuertere domine aliquantulum æ ne tardes uenire ad seruos tuos·
w.	ã Ecce deus meus æ honorabo eum deus patris mei æ exaltabo eum·
1.	ã Dominus legifer noster· dominus rex noster· ipse ueniet æ saluabit nos·
o.	ã Inuenimini quantus sit gloriosus iste qui ingreditur ad saluandas gentes ·
oc ·	Alia ã Vigilate animo inproximo est dominus deus noster·
e	ã Constantes estote uidebitis auxilium domini super uos · Ecce rex ueniet do
o.	minus terre æ ipse auferet iugum captiuitatis nostre ã Veni domine æ noli
a.	tardare relaxa facinora plebis tue istahel ã Deus a lybano ueniet æ splendor

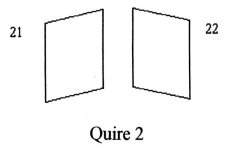

21   22

Quire 2

torum inuentus est primus & ideo triumphat incelis coronatus aeuia.

fece aduenit. Sca & immaculata. Cum aut eet. Lapidabant

Stephanus uidit. Sepelierunt R̃. in. ii. a̧. Beatus uir q̃ ti.

Iocundus homo qui miseretur indomino non commouebitur ineternum.

Quid retribuam domino pomnibus que retribuit mihi calicem salutari accipiam.

Credidi. Domine libera animam meam alabiis iniquis & alingua dolosa. Addnac.

Sustinuit anima mea inuerbo domini sperauit anima mea inipso. Deprofundis.

Scē Stephane pro. Intuens incelū. vt. Stephanus aut. Uerbu ca. S. maria.

Uox tonitrui tui deus inro ta. Ad processione S. Iohannis Euge. Nesciens mat.

Iohannes est eu angelista mundi per ambitum predicans lumen eclicumqui

triumphans rome lauit imui no stolam suam & insangui ne o

li ue pallium suum. Victo senatu cum cesare uirgineo corpore tri pu

diat inigne. Lauit. Gloria patri & filio & spiritui sancto si cut erat inprin

cipio. Cinsang. Sive. Apparuit caro. Annuntiauerᵘ opa di. Eĩ.

Domine suscipe me. Sive. Ualde honorandus est beatus iohannes qui supra

pectus domini incena recubuit. Adoremus regem apostolo rum

qui priuilegio amoris iohannem dilexit apostolum. Iohannes apo

tolus & euangelista uirgo est electus adomino atq; inter ceteros magis dile

ctus. Ceti eri. Supra pectus domini iesu recumbens euangelii fluenta deipso

sacro dominei pectoris fonte potauit. Benedicit d. Quasi unum deparadysi

fluminibus euangelista iohannes uerbi dei gratiam intoto terrarum orbe

diffudit. Fructant. Inferuentis olei dolium missus iohannes apostolus

diuina se pregente gratia illesus exiuit. Uñs oñis. Propter insuperabilem

euangelilandi constantiam exilio relegatus diuine uisionis & allocutionis

meruit crebra consolatione releuari. Exaudi dñs depe. Occurrit beato iohan

ni abexilio reuertenti omnis populus uirorum acmulierum clamantium

Frag. 54/8, no. 1ʳ
Stiftsbibliothek St-Paul-im-Lavanttal

ᴂ dicentium benedictus qui uenit innomine domini. Inomnē terrā exiuit.

ᴀ Qui uicerit faciam illum columnam meam intemplo meo dicit dominus.

ᴀ Hic est discipulus ille qui testimonium phibuit seipsu quia uerum est testimonium eius. Sic eum uolo manere donec ueniam tu me sequere.

ᴀ Cibauit eum dominus pane uite ᴂ aqua sapientie potauit eum.

ᴀ Spiritu sapientie salutaris repleuit eum dominus ᴂ intellectus.

Dedit illi dns claritatem eternam ᴂ nomine eterno hereditabit illum.

ALDE HONORANDVS EST BE ATVS IOHANNES QVI SVPRA pectus domi ni incena recu buit eui xpe meruce matrem uirginem uirgi ni commendauit. Mulier ecce filius tuus addiscipulum autem ecce

Hic est beatissimus euangelista ᴂ apostolus IOHANNES mater tu a. cui x qui priuilegi o amoris prei pu i ceteris altius adomino me ruit bono ra ri. Hic est discipulus ille quem diligebat iesus qui su pra pectus domini incena recubu it. Qui p. S me i. Et scribam.

I nillo di e suscipiam te seruum me um ᴂ ponam te sicut signaculum inconspectu me o quoni am ego ele gi te dicit domi nus. Intri bulatione inuocasti me ᴂ exaudiui te ᴂ li berabo te. Quo ego. E sto fidelis usq; admortem ᴂ dabo tibi co ronam ui te. Quoe.

Qui uicerit faciam illum columnam intemplo me o dicit domi nus ᴂ scri bam sup e um no men me um ᴂ nomen ciuitatis noue ie ru sa lem. Vincenti dabo edere delligno uite qd est inparadyso dei

A pparuit caro suo iohanni dominus ihe xpe cum discipulis suis ᴂ ait illi. veni dilecte mi abme quia tempus est ut epuleri inconuiuio meo cum fratribus tuis.

Confi..... Expandens manus suas addeum dixit inuitatus adconuiuium tuum uenio gratias agens quia me dignatus es domine ihu xpe adtuas epulas inuitare sciens quod extoto corde meo desiderabam te. Iam tei Domine suscipe me ut cum fratribus meis sim cum quibus ueniens inuitasti me aperi mihi ianuam

unte & pduc me ad conuiuium epularum tuarum tu es enim xpe filius dei uiui

qui precepto patris mundum saluasti tibi gratias referimus p in finita seculorum

secula. Dns regit eas. Dixit dominus matri sue mulier ecce filius tuus ad disci

pulum autem ecce mater tua aeuia. Euouae. Exiit sermo inter frrs qd discipu

lus ille non moritur & non dixit ihe non moritur sed sic eum uolo manere

donec ueniam. Dns regit uase. Iste est iohannes cui xpe in cruce matrem

uirginem uirgini commendauit. Oriim uirud. Constitues eos pnc sup oem

Tu es discipulus meus unte complacuit anime mee dicit dominus. Alle

Ponam te signaculum dicit dominus in conspectu meo semper quoniam elegi te:

Dixit dns matri s. Exiit sermo int frs. Iste est iohannes cui xpe. Cum reuertere

tur iohannes ab exilio uiduam suscitauit & iuueni uitam restituit

Ec ce puer me us quem e le gi dicit do mi nus electus me us

complacuit si bi in illo anime me e. Iste est iohannes qui supra pectus

Hic est discipulus qui testimonium perhibet domim in cena recu bu it. Cõpl.

de his & scripsit hec & scimus quia uerum est testimonium

eius. Quanta audiuimus & cognouimus e a & patres nri narra uerint no bis. Tes

Iste est iohannes cui xpe in cruce matrem uirgi nem uirgini commen

da uit. Mulier ecce filius tuus ad discipulum autem ecce mater tu a Virg.

Apparuit caro suo iohanni do minus cum discipulis su is & dixit e i

ueni dilecte m in ad me quia tempus est ut epule ris in conuiuio me o

cum fratribus tu is. Cumq; compleset apostolus cursum unte presentis in se

nectute bona apparuit ei saluator mundi & dixit ad e um. Veni dilecte.

Gloria patri & filio & spiritui sancto sicut erat in principio & nunc & semp. Veni.

Iste est iohannes qui supra pectus domini recubuit beatus apostolus cui reuelata

sunt secreta celestia. Vos sci dni uocab. Himis honorati s. Amici t ds.

℟ Iste est iohannes qui supra pectus domini in cena recubuit beatus apostolus cui in revelata sunt secreta celestia. Ualde honorandus est beatus iohannes qui supra pectus domini in cena recubuit. Beatus ap. commendauit ea

℟ Diligebat autem eum iesus suis quoniam specialis prerogatiue casti tatis ampliori dilectione fecerat dignum quia uirgo electus abipso uirgo in euum permansit. Incruce denique moriturus matrem huic suam uirginem uirgini

℟ Cibauit eum dominus pane uite et intellectus et aqua sapientie salutaris potauit illum et exaltauit eum apud proximos su os.

℣ In medio ecclesie aperuit dominus os eius et impleuit eum spiritu sapientie et

℟ In medio eccle sie aperuit os eius et impleuit eum intellectus lex dominus spiritu sapientie et intel lectus. Uisit dominus manum suam et tetigit os me um. Compl. Ec

A Ecce puer meus electus quem elegi posui super eum spiri in telle intellectus tum meum. Hic est discipulus meus sic eum uolo manere donec ueniam.

A Uisit dominus manum suam et tetigit os meum et reple uit eum suo.

A Sunt de hic stantibus qui non gustabunt mortem donec uideant filium hominis in regno

A Iohannes autem apostolus uirgo dei electus cui uirgineam matrem domini uirgi ni commendauit. Sce Iohes dilecte xpi a.u.r: s. Et imperatam nob. Annunciauer.

A In medio ecclesie aperuit dominus os eius et impleuit eum spiritu sapi entie et intellectus a e u i a. Pastores loq. Continet in. S s Stephi.

A Stephanus uidit. Iohannes apls. Supra pectus. Quasi unum.

A Inferuentis o. Iurauit dns et cu ret R DE aplis. Sce Iohs dilecte xpi.

℣ Annunciauer o di. Exiit sermo int frs R Jy il s. Siue. Domine suscipe

A Iste est discipulus qui dignus fuit esse inter secreta celi iste solus meruit diuina in oratione dicere in principio erat uerbum et uerbum erat apud deum et deus erat uerbum hoc erat in principio apud deum. U rege celi.

Beatus uenit

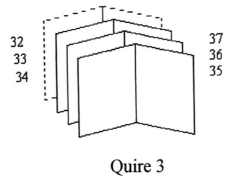

32
33
34

37
36
35

Quire 3

Adorate dominum aeuia. in aula sancta eius aeuia. Cantate d̄ . Adorate dn̄m
aeuia omnes angeli eius aeuia. Dn̄s r̄ ex. Notum fecit dn̄s aeuia salutare
suum aeuia. Cantate d̄ . Ecce aduenit dn̄ator. Dn̄s r̄ iñe. Om̄s ḡm̄s q̄scūq. fec. ve.

Magi ueniunt ab oriente ierosolimam querentes ₇ dicentes ubi est qui
natus est cuius stellam ui dimus ₇ uenimus adorare domi num.

Uidimus enim stellam eius in orien te. Et uenimus.

Interrogabat magos herodes quod signum uidistis sup natum regem:
stellam magnam fulgentem cuius splendor illuminat mundum ₇ nos cogno
uimus ₇ uenimus adorare dominum. Magi ueniunt ab oriente in
quirentes faciem domini ₇ dicentes. Et nos cogn.

Stella quam uiderunt magi in oriente antecedebat eos donec ueni
rent ad locum ubi pu er erat uidentes autem eam gauisi sunt gaudio
magno. Et intrantes domum inuenerunt puerum cum maria matre eius

Uidentes stellam ma gi gaui si sunt gaudi o et pcidentes adora uerunt e um ba.
o magno ₇ intrantes domum inuenerunt pue rum cum maria matre eius
₇ pcidentes adorauerunt e um ₇ apertis thesauris su is obtule runt ei
mune ra aurum thus ₇ myrram. Reges tharsis ₇ insule. Capit ad. can.

Tria sunt munera que obtulerunt magi domino aurum thus ₇ myrram filio dei
regi magno aeuia. Can. Ppl̄s q̄ amb̄. Adorate dn̄m. In aula scā eius.

Tria sunt munera precio sa que obtulerunt magi domino indie istae
habent inse diuina myste ri a. in auro ut ostendatur regis poten ti a
in thu re sacerdotem magnum considera ₇ in myrra dominicam sepulturam.

Reges tharsis ₇ insule munera offerent reges arabum ₇ saba do na addu cent na.

Di es sanctificatus illuxit no bis uenite gentes ₇ adorate dominum quia
hodie apparuit lux magna in terra. Uenite adoremus e um
quia ipse est dominus de us no ster. Quia hodie

Hic est dies precla rus inquo saluator mun di apparu it quem prophete
predixerunt angeli adora ue runt cuius stellam magi uidentes
ga uisi sunt et munera e i obtu le runt. Et intrantes domum
inuenerunt puerum cum MARIA matre eius et pcidentes ado i uerunt e um. Im.

Incolumbe spei e spiritus sanctus uisus est paterna uox audita est hic est
filius meus dilectus inquo mihi bene complacui ipsum audi te

Ce li aperti sunt super e um et uox patris audi ta est. Hic est. Esap.
Quem non preualent ppria magnitudine.
Celi terre atq; maria amphisepere.
De uirgineo natus utero ponitur inpresepio.
Vt ppheticus sermo nunciat stat simul bos et asinus.
Sed oritur stella lucida prebitura domino obsequia.
Quam balaam extudiuca orituram dixerat prosapia.
Hec magorum oculos fulgurant lumine pstrinxit puidos.
Atq; ipsos preuia xpi adcunabula pduxit uilia.
Illi exiguis adorant obstium pannulis.
Offerentes regia aurum thus et myrram munera.
Ipsa sed tamen mysticis non carent munera figuris.
Aurum ut regi thus deo et magno offerunt sacerdoti.
Atq; myrram insepulturam. AD LAVDES do apparuit
Ante luciferum genitus et ante secula dominus saluator noster hodie mun
Venit lumen tuum ierusa lem et gloria domini sup te orta est et ambula
bunt gentes inlumine tuo a e u i a. Apertis thesauris suis obtulerunt
magi domino aurum thus et myrram a e u i a. Maria et flumina bene
dicite domino ymnum dicite fontes domino a e u i a. Magi uidentes stellam

obtulerunt domino aurum thus & myrram. ℟ Surge illuminare ieru salem

ⱴ Quia uenit lumen tuum. ier̄l̄m. ⱴ Gloria patri & filio & spiritui sancto. Surge

ⱴ Omnes de saba uenient auru & thus deferentes & laude dno annunc̄.

A Hodie celesti sponso iuncta est ecclesia quoniam in iordane lauit xpe eius cri

mina currunt cum muneribus magi ad regales nuptias & ex aqua facto uino

letantur conuiue AEVIA. Lux de luce apparuisti xpe cui magi munera

offerunt aeuia aeuia aeuia. Tria sunt munera. ⱴ Veniunt adte qui de

A Vidimus stellam eius in oriente & uenimus cum muneribus adorare dominum.

ⱴ Adorate dnm. In aula sca cc̄. Salutis nostre auctorem magi uenerati

sunt incunabulis & de thesauris suis mysticas ei rerum species obtulerunt.

ⱴ Tria sunt munera preciosa. Que obtuler̄t magi dno. a. thus & myrrā.

A Tecum principium cum rel̄. Omnes de saba uenient aurum &

thus deferentes. ⱴ Et laudem dno annunciantes. ⱴ Reges tharsis & insule.

A Tribus miraculis ornatum diem sanctum colimus. hodie stella magos

duxit ad presepium. hodie uinum ex aqua factum est ad nuptias. hodie

a iohanne xpe baptizari uoluit ut saluaret nos aeuia. Xpe apparuit

A nuptiis adh. siq. si q. de psalmi. si aut nulla habet de psalmi. alinati cantent singlis

noctib. duc. ea istis. A Stella nobis uisa est rex celorum natus est uenite adoremus.

A Venient adte qui detrahebant tibi & adorabunt uestigia pedum tuorum.

A Stella ista sicut flamma coruscat & regem regum deum demonstrat mā gi

eam uiderunt & xpo regi munera obtulerunt. A Videntes stellam magi gauisi

sunt gaudio magno & intrantes domum obtulerunt domino auru thus & myrram.

Vsus de epiph. Ad mat. & ad Horas. Jn die. ℣ō. Si tangit diez. A Omnis tra. m. i. ℟.

dica̅t usus. ꝺ. ii. ℟. scilicet. ⱴ Omnis gentes q seq̅q. f. Similit si diza̅t. A. Omnes gentes.

sit usus. Adorate dnm. ut. Omnis tra adoret te ꝺs. & psall. ℟ Omnes de saba uenient

℟ Venit lumen tuum ierusalem & gloria domi ni super te orta est

& ambulabunt gentes inlumine tuo & reges insplendore ortus tui L.

℣ Fili tui delonge uenient & filie tue dela tere sur gent & amb.

℟ Uide bis o me rusa lem & afflues & mirabitur & dilata bitur cor

tuum quando conuersa fuerit adte multitu do maris for titu do

gen tium ue nerit ti bi. ℣ Inundatio camelorum operiet te dro

medarii madi an & e pha Quando.

℟ Pasto res preclaritate lumi nis non permittebantur uide re ange luon

magis turbabantur & facta est uox decelo dicens nolite timere pax uobis

cum ego sum gabri el angelus aduirginem missus ℣ Annuncio uobis

gaudium magnum quod erit om ni po pulo. Ego sum. Aᴅ ʟᴀᴠᴅᴇs.

Ā Ante luciferii. Singulis noctib' una. Ā Maria & flumina. ñ cantu ℟ Reges

tharsis & insule munera offerent. ℣ Reges arabum & saba dona adducent.

℣ Omnis desaba uenient aurũ & thus def. Iɴ ᴇ ᴠɢ Ɩ o. ℣ placuit ipsum audire.

Ā Uox decelis sonuit & uox patris audita est hic est filius meus inquo mihi com

Ā Celi aperti sunt super eum & uox facta est decelo dicens hic est filius meus

dilectus inquo mihi complacui. Ā Iohannes quidem clamabat dicens ego ñ sum

dignus baptihare dominum respondit ihc & dixit sine modo sic enim decet

nos adimplere omnem iustitiam accui a. Ā Aqua comburit peccatum hodie

apparens liberator & rorat omnem mundum diuinitatis ope. Ā Pater dece

lis filium testificans spiritus sancti presentia aduenit unum edocens qui

baptihatur xpe. Ā Baptihatur xpe & sanctificatur omnis mundus & tri

buens nobis remissionem peccatorum aqua & spiritu omnes purificans.

Ā Sup ripam iordanis stabat beatus iohannes indutus est splendore baptihans

saluatorem baptiha me Iohannes baptiha me benedico te & tu iordanis con

gaudens suscipe me. Ā Baptihat miles regem seruus dominum suum

iohannes saluatorem aqua iordanis stupuit columba prestatur paterna

Ink. II/ı/i, flyleaf ıᵛ
Stiftsbibliothek Lambach

248

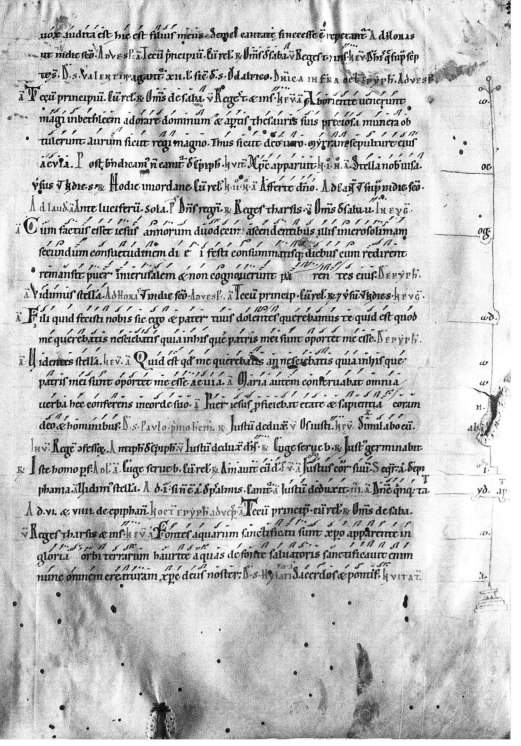

Ink. II/1/i, flyleaf 2r
Stiftsbibliothek Lambach

L2v

f.34v

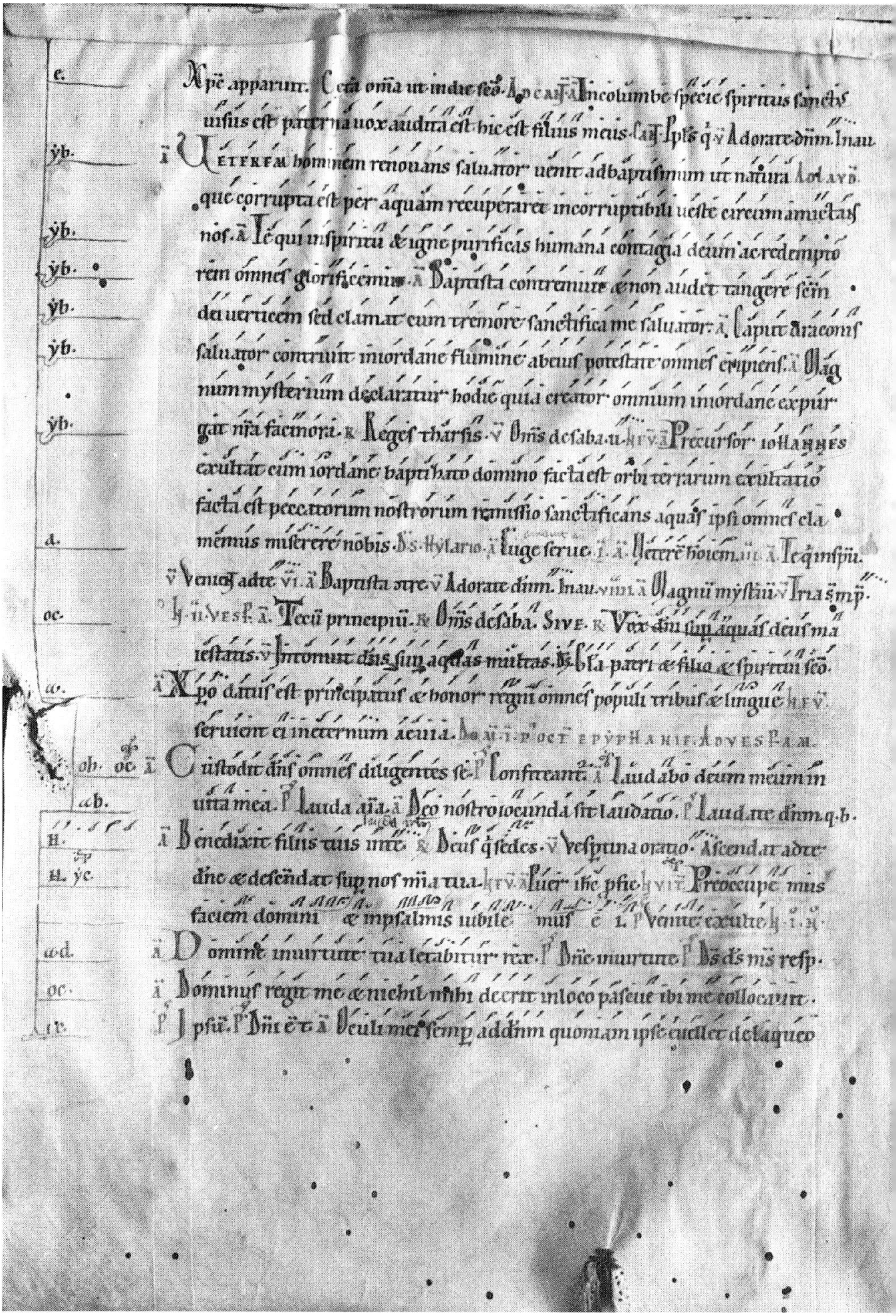

Ink. II/1/i, flyleaf 2v
Stiftsbibliothek Lambach

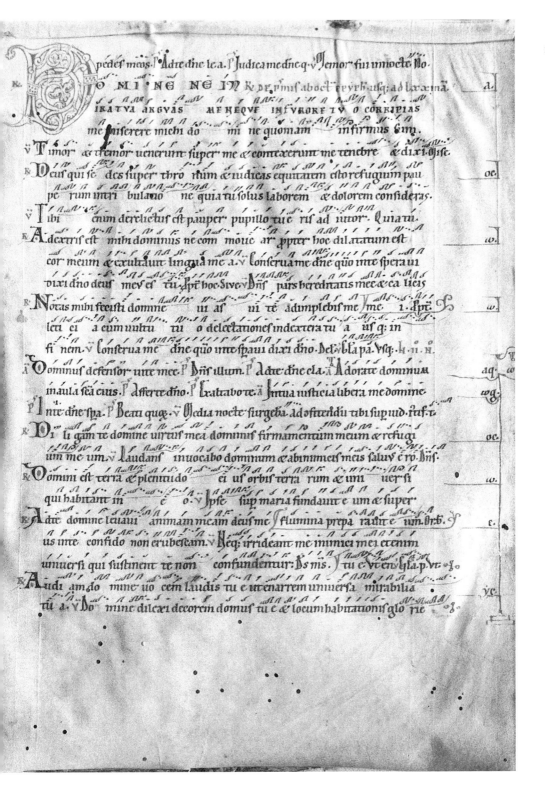

pedes meos. P Adte dne le.a. P Judica me dne q. V Memor sui innocte No

DO MI NE NG IM R pe pmis aboel er yrt atg; ad lxx ina a

IRATVA ARGVAS ME NEQVE INSVRORE IV O CORRIPIAS

me miserere michi do mi ne quoniam infirmus sum.

V Timor ac tremor uenerunt super me ec contexerunt me tenebre ec dixi dise

R Deus qui se des super thro num ec iudicas equitatem esto refugium pau

pe rum intri bulatio ne quia tu solus laborem ec dolorem consideras.

V Tibi enim derelictus est pauper pupillo tue ris ad iutor. Quia tu

R A dextris est mihi dominus ne com moue ar ppter hoc dilatatum est

cor meum ec exultauit lingua me a. V Conserua me dne quo inte speraui

dixi dno deus meus es tu. pt hoc. Sive V Dns pars hereditatis mee ec ca licis

R Notas mihi fecisti domine iu as ni te adimplebis me sme. I pt

leti ei a cum uultu tu o delectationes in dextera tu a us q; in

fi nem. V Conserua me dne quo inte spaui dixi dno. Det vbl a pa. Vsq; 4. ii. n.

A Dominus defensor uite mee. P Dns illum. P Adte dne cla. A Adorate dominum

in aula sea eius. P Afferte dno. P Exatta bote. A Intua iusticia libera me domine

P Inte dne spa. P Beati quoe. V Media nocte surgeba ad ostendu tibi sup iud. fus. t.

R Di li gam te domine uirtus mea dominus firmamentum meum ec refugi

um me um. V Laudans inuocabo dominum ec ab inimicis meis saluus e ro. Dns

R Domini est terra ec plenitudo ei us orbis terra rum ec uni uersi

qui habitant in e o. V Ipse sup maria fundauit e um ec super

R Adte domine leuaui animam meam deus me P flumina prepa rauit e um. Or t. S

us inte confido non erubescam. V Neq; irrideant me inimici mei etenim

unuersi qui sustinent te non confundentur. Ds mis. P tu e vt en ysia p vt. 0.

R Audi am do mine uo cem laudis tu e ut enarrem uniuersa mirabilia

tu a. V Do mine dilexi decorem domus tu e ec locum habitationis glo ne

Ink. II/1/i, flyleaf 3r
Stiftsbibliothek Lambach

Alleluia alleuia aeuia acuia aeuia. Itē ā Defyore caribuſ.ſ.b ūe miſerere ñi.

C Audire q̄ longe. C Miſerere dñe ple. v̄ Crattare dñe inuirtute tua cantabimꝰ yp̄.ut.

Quare magna multitu. uo dulcedinꝭ tue do mi ne quam abſcondiſti rimentibus te v̄ Perfeciſti eis qui ſpant unte inconſpectu ſuo rum ho mi nū luā.

Afflicti propeccatis noſtris cottidie eum lacrimiſ expectamus finem noſtrum dolor cordis noſtri aſcendat adte domi ne ut eruaſ noſ ama lis que innouan tur in nobis v̄ Domine deuſ iſrahel exaudi preces noſtras auribuſ percipe dolorem cordis noſ tri. Vt eruaſ noſ ama.

Peccata mea domi ne ſicut ſā gr̄ te infixa ſunt inme ſed ante quam uulnera generent inme ſana me domine medicamento penitentie de uſ. v̄ Quoniam iniquitatem meam ego agnoſco æ de lictum meum coram me eſt ſemper tibi ſoli pec ca ui. Sana me do.

Fi at manuſ tu a ut ſaluum me faciaſ quia mandata tuæ te gi concupi ui ſalutare tu um do mine. v̄ Grraui ſicut ouiſ que pierat require ſeruum tuum domine quia mandata tua non ſum obli tuſ. Concupiui. v̄ Gloria patri æ filio æ ſpirituu ſancto. Concu.

Abſcondi tamquam aurum peccata me a æ cela ui inſinu me o iniquitatem me am miſerere mei deuſ ſecundum magnam miſe ricordiam tu am. v̄ Quoniam iniquitatem meam ego agnoſco æ deli ctum meum coram me eſt ſemper tibi ſoli pecca ui. Miſerere mei. Ad L.

ā Alleuia acuia acuia aeuia aeuia aeuia. v̄ā Dico uob. P Miſerere m̄ōs.f.

P Confitemini. P Bż ōs m̄s. ā Ymnum dicamuſ aeuia domino deonr̄o aeuia. P Bñdicite.

ā Aleuia acuia acuia acuia aeuia. acuia. v̄ā Indño. ꝶ Hec eſt dieſ quā ſfecit dñs. v̄ Exultemuſ æ letemur mea. v̄ Dñſ regnauit decorē induit indur̄ē dñſ.f. yp̄ ſe iui.

ā Nuptie facte ſunt inchana galylee æ erat ibi ih̄c cum maria matr̄e eiuſ. Ineuē.

ā Aleuia acuia aeuia aeuia aeuia aeuia. v̄ā Ortuſ ſeluſuſ. Ad Primā.

Ink. II/1/i, flyleaf 3ᵛ
Stiftsbibliothek Lambach

P In quo corrig. P Retribue s. P Adhesit p.a. V Exurge dne adiuua nos & lib. n. ppt n. nu.
Sext. P Quicumq: uult. iii. A A evia acuia acuia acuia acuia acuia acuia acuia
acuia. vt. A Prebe fili. P lege pone. P Et ueniat. P Memor esto. V Ego dixi dne.
Miserere m. s. a. m. q. p. t. vi. A A euia acuia acuia acuia acuia acuia. Va In timato m.

P Portio mea. P Bonitate fec. P Manu tue. V Dns regit me & nichil m derit inl p. i me e.
Ad viii. A A evia acuia acuia acuia acuia acuia acuia. Va Innuebant pat ei.
P Deter insat. P Inctinu dne. P Quomodo dilexi. V Ab occultis meis. Mundam d. raba.

A Dixit dominus domino meo sede adextris meis. P Dix dns dno. h. ii. VESP.
A f idelia omnia mandata eius confirmata inseculum seculi. P Confitebor t. d.
A I n mandatis eius uolet nimis. P Beat uir: q. v. A Sit nomen dni benedictum in
secula. P Laudate p. R. Quam magnificata sunt opa tua dne. V Omnia in sa
pientia fecisti replata est terra. Cui m. V Dirigat dne orationem s. i. inesp. t. e. m. m. s. v.

A Quid mihi & tibi est mulier nondum uenit hora mea & conuertit IN EV.
aquam in uinum & crediderunt in eum discipuli eius hoc in ieium signorum
fecit iesus & manifestauit gloriam suam. A Deficiente uino iussit iesu e
implere hydrias aqua que in uinum conuerse sunt acuia. FER. II. IN V I T.

P Venite exultemus domino. P Iubilemus do. i. n. R. Rectos decet collaudatio.
P Exultate iu. P Benedica. A Expugna impugnantes me. P Iudica dne nocentes.
A R euela domino uiam tuam. P Noli emulari. P Declina a malo. A Reuinia tua
arguas me domine. P Domine ne in f. V Delectare in dno. C dab t pet e tui.

R Benedicam do mino in omni tempore semp laus ei iis in ore me o.
V In domino laudabitur anima me a audiay mansueti & le
R Delectare in domi no & da bit ti bi peticio nes cor Ten tur. Semp
Dis tu LV Spera in dno & fac bo nita tem inhabita terram & pasceris in di

R Cum cecide rit iustus non conturbabi tur quia domi nus tiis ei us t da
nus firmat manum eius. V Iunior fui & enim senui i & non uidi iustum

derelictum nee semen eius querens pa nem. Quia do.

Auribus percipe do mi ne lacrimas me as ne sileas a me remitte mihi quoniam incola ego sum apud te & pe gri nus. Dixi custodiam uias meas ut non delinquam in lingua me a. Quoniam incola ego.

Statuit dominus supra pe tram pe des me os & direx it gressus meos deus me us & immi sit inos meum canticum nouum. Expectans expectaui dominum & respexit me & exaudiuit deprecati onem me am & inmisit.

Ego dixi domi ne mi se rere mei sana animam me am quia peca ui tibi. Domine ne in ira tua arguas me neque in furore tuo corripi.

Sedes tua deus in seculum seculi uirga equitatis uirga regni tui as me. Sana a. Dilexisti iusticiam & odisti iniquitatem ppterea unxit te deus deus

Consurge lauda in nocte in principio testate tui us uirga uigilarii & effunde sic aquã cor tuii ante conspectũ dni di tui. Leua ad eũ manus tuas & miserebitur tui. Tu aut

Benedicã domino in omni tempore. Semp laus eius in ore meo. Gl ap.

Alleluia alleluia. Vt non delinquam in lingua mea. Dixi custodiã. Expectas.

Sana domine animam meam quia peccaui tibi. Bea q um. Que ad modũ.

Eructauit cor meum uerbum bonum. Ds aurib. Eructauit. Sedes tua ds. in sclm scli uirga directionis uirga regni tui. Miserere mei deus. Ipsũ.

Intellege clamorem meum domine. Herba mea. Domine in celo misericordia tua. Dixi in iust. Conuersus est furor tuus domine & ꝯsolatus es me. Confitebor t dne quo. In ex celsis laudare deum. Laudate d. s.

Domine in celo misericordia tua. ueritas tua usq ad nubes.

In mandatis dne meditabor ut me q f. a. mis. Benedictus deus israhel

Seruite domino in timore & exultate ei cum tremore. Bea uir qn.

Quare frem. Dne ne in furore. Cuncũq uult. Exurge dne. Aduui. A d iii.

Ink. II/1/i, flyleaf 4^v
Stiftsbibliothek Lambach

254

Adiuua me æ saluus ero domine. Luena ped. Iniqs odio. feci iudicium. Adiu
tor ns esto dñe. Ne derel neq; despicia me ds sal ms. Aspice in me æ misere
re mei domine. Ostabilia t. Iust es dñe. Clamaui inuo. Dñs regit me. Et nichil m. d.
in loco pascue ibi me collocauit. Vide humilitatem meam domine æ
eripe me. Ipsu. Principes ps. Apppinquet deo. Ab occulti mei. Mundam. d. æ
Domus iacob de populo barbaro. In exitu isrl. Inclinauit dominus
aurem suam mihi. Dilexi quo. Laudate dominum omnes gentes. Credidi ppt
laudare dñm o. g. Benediximus uobis in nomine domini. Sepe expugnauert.
Adiutorium nostrum in nomine domini. Qui fec celu æ terram. Dirigat dñe. o.
Magnificat anima mea dominum. Ipsu. Iubilemus deo salutari nro.
Venite ex. Adiutor in tribulationibus. Ds nr r. Omes gentes. Magnus
dominus æ laudabilis nimis. Ipsu. Audite hec. Deus deorum dominus
locutus est. Ipsu. Qd gloriaris. Immola do. sacrificiu laudis æ r. alt. uota tua.
Ne perdideris me domi ne cum iniquitatibus meis neq; infinem ira
tus restr ues mala me a. Misere re me i deus miserere
me i quoniam in te sfidit anima me a. Neq; inf. Exurgam diluculo. Con.
Paratum cor meum de us paratum cor meum cantabo æ psalmum di
cam domino. Exurge gloria mea exurge psalterium æ cythara
Adiutor meus tibi psallam quia deus susceptor meus es deus meus mise
ricordia me a. sri pe me de inimicis meis deus meus æ ab insurgenti
bus in me libe ra me. Ds meus esto. Dns sapientia fun
dauit terram. stabiliuit celos prudentia. Sapientia illius
eruperunt abyssi. æ nubes rore concrescunt. Deus in no
mine tuo saluum me fac domine. Et inuirtute tua libera me. Gl a pa.
Leuia acuta acuta. Ta iuste iudicate. Auertit dominus capti
uitatem plebis sue. Dixit insip. Ds in noie. Intende in me æ exaudi

me domine · Exaudi ds depc · Miserere mn̄ ds q oeul̄ Iuste iudicate filii ho
minum · Si uere utiq; · Eripe me dnim v Ds̄ uita mea · dnn̄ t pos·la·m·mes·tuo·

S ecundum magnam misericordiam tuam domine miserere mei· Miser Ad lav̄.

S alutare uultus mei des mes · Iudica me ds̄ Quoniam inte ofidit anima
mea · Miserere m·ds mis·m· Cunetis diebus uit̄ nr̄e saluos nos fac domine

E go dixi m· Omnes angeli eius laudate dn̄m· Laud̄ d de Miserere mei des
miserere mei· Quonia inte ofidit anima mea· v Inmatutini dn̄e Med HEV.

E rexit dn̄s nobis cornu salutis indomo dauid pueri sui· B̄ndicī dīs Ad i·

D omine deus meus inte spaui· Ipsū· Dn̄e dn̄s nr̄· Confitebor· Quicūq; uult·

Clamaui ad exaudiuit me· Ad dn̄m cū tb· Leuauio· Letat sum Ad vI·

C ui habitas incelis miserere nobis· Ad te leuaui· Nisi qa dīs· Q ofidit Ad viii·

F acti sumus sicut consolati· In iuitendo· Nisi dn̄s e· Beati oms q̄ Ad vesp̄·

D eprofundis clamaui ad te dn̄e· Ipsū Speret istahel indomino· Dn̄e n̄ e ex·

E t omnis mansuetudinis eius· Oestto dn̄e Ecce quam bonum & quam io
cundum· Ipsū &· uisū Prota ebdam v in pori die HEV· Quia fecit mihi domi
nus magna quia potens est & sanctum nomen eius· FR QVARTA INVIT·

In manu tua domine omnes fines terre · i, n, a, D a nobis dn̄e auxilium de
tribulatione · Ds repulisti · Exaudi depc Benedicite gentes deo nostro·

Nonne do sub· Iubilate do Inecclesiis benedicite domino · Exurgat ds·

Benedicī dn̄s die· v Benedicite gente do nr̄o & obaudite uocī laudi eius·

Exaudi de us deprecationem me am intende orationi me e afinibus
ter re ad te clama ui do mi ne v Dum anxiare tur cor meum
impetra exaltasti me deduxisti me quia factus ad uttor me us ofinib·

De us inte spaui domi ne ut non ofun dar ineternum intua iusti cia
libera me & e ri pe me v Esto mihi domine indeum pro
tectorem & inlocum munitum ut saluum me faci as· Intua iusti

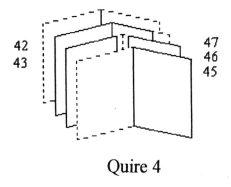

Quire 4

iudi cem impie crudelis & dei tyranne non es ofusus amputare infemina

quod ipse inmatre sux . iſ ti. v̄ Ego autem habeo mamillas integras

intus inanima me a quas abinfantia domino conse cra ui. Impie crud.

℟ Uidisti domine & expectas ti agonem me um quomodo pug

naui insta di o Sed quia nolui obedire mandatis princi pum iussa

sum inmamillas tor que ti.v̄ ppter ueritatem & mansuetudinem

℟ Quis esti qui uenisti admee curare uulnera me a et iustici am iussa

ego sum apostolus xpie ti nichil inme dubites fili a ipse me misit ad

te quem dilexisti mente & puro cor de Nam & ego apostolus

eius sum & noui medici nam. Ipse me misit.

℟ Medicinam carnalem corpori meo numquam ex hibui sed habeo domi

num iesum xpm qui solo sermone restaurat uni uer sa.

v̄ f Ego autem adiuta adomino perseuerabo inofessi one me a. Qui sc. ius.

Ã Nisi diligenter pfeceris corpus meum acarnificibus atrectari non

potest anima mea inparadysum domini cum palma intrare martyri.

Ã Mens mea solidata est & a xpo fundata. Ã Ego xpm ofiteor labiis & corde

non cessabo inuocare dominu. Ã Beata agathes ingressa carcerem bene

dicebat dominum ihm xpm. Ã Uidisti domine agonem meum quomodo

pugnaui instadio sed quia nolui obedire m andatis principum iussa sua

inmamillas torqueri. Ã Propter fidem castitatis iussa sum suspendi inecu

leo adiuua me domine deus meus intortura mamillarum mearua v̄ Spe ti

℟ Ipse me coronauit qui p apostolum PE TRVM incustodia me conforta

uit. pco quod iussa sum suspendi ine cule o ppter fidem castitatis ad

iuua me domine deus me us intortu ra mamilla rum me a rum.

v̄ Uidisti domine agonem meum quomodo pugnaui instadi o sed quia

nolui obedire manda tis princi pum ppter fidem castitatis

v.

ob.

cod.

cod.

ius.

ob.

ẏd. ẏd.

ab.

ẏd.

ẏd.

cod.

℟ Agathes letissi ma & gloriancer i bat ad carcerem & quasi adepulas
inuita ta agonem suum domino pre cibus commen da bat.
℣ Bea ta Agathes ingressa carce rem benedice bat do mi num et qsi.
℟ Propter ueritatem. ℣ Dilexisti iusticiam & odisti iniq. ppterea unxit te ds ds. t. et de
℟ Ego autem adiuta a domino pseuera bo inofessio ne ei us
qui me saluam fe cit & consolatus est me. Medicinam carnalem
corpori meo numquam exhibui sed habeo dominum ihm xpm. Qui me.
ã Ostentem sanctam spontaneam honorem deo & patrie liberationem. Locau
℟ Induit me dns. ℟ Qui me dignatus est ab omni pla ga cu ra re
& mamillas meas meo pectori restitue re ipsum inuo co deuia
ui uium. ℣ Medici nam carnalem corp. m. numqua exhib. Ipsu.
℟ Beata Agathes ingressa carcerem expan dit ma nus su as ad deum
& dixit do mi ne qui me fecisti uincere tormenta carnifi cum
iube me domine adtu am misericordiam per uem re ℣ Agathes
ingressa carcerem benedicebat dominum iesum xpietum. Iube me do.
℟ Gaudeamus omnes in domi no diem festum cele brantes in honore agathe
martyris decuius passione gaudent ange li & collau dant
fi lium de i. ℣ Immaculatus dominus inmaculatam sibi famu
lam inhoc fragilitatis corpore positam misericorditer conse cra uit. Decui.
ã Quis es tu qui uenisti ad me curare uulnera mea ego sum apostolus Laud
xpi nichil in me dubites filia. Medicinam carnalem corpori meo num
quam exhibui sed habeo dominum ihm xpm qui solo sermone restaurat
uniuersa. ã Gratias tibi ago domine quia memor es mei & misisti ad me
apostolum tuum curare uulnera mea. ã Benedico te pater domini mei
ihu xpi quia p apostolum tuum mamillas meas meo pectori restituisti.
ã Qui me dignatus est ab omni plaga curare & mamillas meas meo pectori

restituere ipsum inuoco deum uiuia. Specie tua. & p. Audi filia & u.

Paganorum multitudo fugiens adsepulchrum uirginis tulerunt uelum
eius contra ignem ut comparet dominus quod apiculis incendii meritis
agathe martyris sue eos liberaret. Agatha sca dix. Agathes leuissima.

Beata agathes. Ostentem scam. Quis estu que dix dns.

O medicina carn. Laud p. Gratias t a. Letat sū. Qui me dignat. Nisi dns ed.

Beata agathes ingressa carcerem expandit manus suas add eum & dixit
domine qui me fecisti uincere tormenta carnificum iube me domi ne adu
am misericordiam puenire. Benedictus quam. duo.

Sancti monialis autem femina cum negantis uerba audisset orationem fu
dit & inundatio pluuie erupit. Rege uirg. Et cetera oma ut de uginib.

Veni sponsa. ñ cantt. Tu es petrus. Annunciauer o di.

Tu es pastor ouiu n princeps apostolorum tibi tradite sunt claues regni celorum

Tu es pastor ouiu n princeps apostolorum tibi tra dite sunt claues
regni celorum. Venite. In omne terra. Cū religs. In omne terra.

Symon petre. Si diligis me Tues pe trus. Qdcumq ligaueris.

Exaltabunt cornua Confitebun cu ret. Tollite iugu. Qui diligitis dominū
letamini in domino & ostemini memorie sanctitatis eius. Dns regnauit.

Iugum eni. Custodiebant Sanete Constitues eos. p. Posui adiutoriū

Ecce uere isrlita. Solue iubente. Tues pastor o. Solue iubente.

Quem dicunt. Qui regni cla. Ego pte rog. Petre amas. AD LAUD.

Petre amas me cum ret. Exaltent eum in ecclesia plebis. Et in cathedra
seniorum laudent eum. Annunciauer o di. Quodcumq ligaueris
sup terram erit ligatum & in celis & quodcumq solueris super terram
erit solutum & in celis dicit dominus symoni PETRO. Petre amas.

Tu es pastor o. Tu es pe trus &. AD VIII.

De sco Scolastica Aduent. Benedictus. O. Tertia. Sext. Gloria pater

Solue uibente ḯ-ii̯ṷrs Ea Iurauit dns. P̃otens inīta Collocet eū. Consortat

Iam bone p. Sit inītati   Annunciauer o di Symon bariona.

Parce tuis ouibus quos raptor uexat iniquus . a Symon bariona tu uoca

beris cephas quod interpretatur petrus ianitor celi pulsantibus aperi

supra modum peccauimus omnes dimitte septuagies septies . GREGORII PP

O   pastoraplice ẽuā Gloriosa sanctissimi sollempnia GREGORII

toto corde catholica suscipiat ecclesia cuius doctrina aurea per mundi

splend et climata quam meritis & precibus xpicto commende quesumus.

Ad do minum uigiles cuncti uertite mentes GREGO RIVM uigi INVIT.

lem celi qui uexit ad arcem P Venite . i-ña Gregorius ortus rome

ex senatorum sanguine fulsit mundo uelut gemma auro sup addita

dum preclarior preclaris hic accessit attauis. Beat uir. cū reliqs.

Lineam sui generis factis a dictis extulit bibens inpueritia quod ructua

uit postea . a Adherebat moralibus seniorum relatibus quos tenaci me

morie non cessabat committere . Gregorius ut creditur diuinitus sic

dicitur qui sibi & ecclesie uigilauit catholice . a Studiis liberalibus

nulli secundus habitus pretor urbanus extitit adolescens spectabilis.

a Hic abadolescentia diuina fretus gratia anhelare non desiit adregnum

uite perpetis. P Indno sido . Iustū deduxit dns. Euias recta

VI GEBAT INVENERANDO DVPLEX DECVS GREGORI O SENATO

ria   dignitas secundum genus se culi uoluntaria paup

tas iuxta preceptum do   mi mi. v Beatus uir qui

timet do minum inmandatis eius cupit ni mis. Iuxta preceptū

Uidens ro me uir be atus anglo rum forte pueros bene inquit

bene angli uultu nitent ut an geli oportet il lis monstrari itur

salu tis eter   ne. v Quo niam domini est

exceptis dei famulis longe uci ppe positus & Amauit eu dns & cecosac..

X picti fidelis famulus prudens quoq; gregorius post quam sua intempore
uixit eius familie celo reddidit animam terre carnis materiam. A d Horas.

Gregorius ort a lineam surg a Adherebat morta Gregorius ut e h. ii. Vesp.

Gregorius uigil P Dix d a lenius qde P Beat uir a celesti cinct P Laud pueri.

Bissenos num P credidi ppe & Iust ut palma. v cece sacdos magn li Eu.

O Gregori dulcissime sancti spiritus organum atq; uirtutum speculum
posce nobis suffragium ut hoc possimus asequi quo te gaudens perfrui.

Sanctissime confessor domini mo In nat s. Benedicti ofess. sup P fr
nachorum pater e dux benedicte intercede pnostra omnium salute: Adue pa.
ad Dilect do e ho. & Aime pater: v Os iusti, h Ev a Magna semp ce preclara
deum decent preconia cuius igne spernens mundu sui ges inturba ce li
tum o ofessor Benedicte uota seruo rum suscipe, h vit Ut x picto
celebri iubilemus laude uenite qui dedit eterne Benedicto gaudia uite P Uenite
Benedictus tam nomine quam gratiarum munere enursia pgenituis claris h. i. h
fulsit parentibus P Beat uir a Hic ergo rome traditus disciplinis scolaribus
nil scire duxit commodum nisi crucis mysterium P quare f. a Mundum
suis cum floribus sciciter spreuit nescius iesus sacris stigmata spelunce
petit abdita P su inuoc a Sanctum romanus habitum dans illi fert sub
sidium sed magister inuidie seuit in illum Lip de P Hei da.m. a In spelu sub
quo latitat dei miles se cruciat sed rex mundi cui militat hunc sacerdote
uisitat P Dne dns. n. a Athleta dei gaiubus penis ardens exterius hostis in
mente iacula igne restrinxit ignea P Indno ofido. v Iusti ded ð.

Floreo Mundi pecc rituvrum
Despexit tamquam aridum ut flo reat in eter
num Benedictus an —————— te deum. v Pennas sumens

Private collection, recto

263

...olumbe recessit gaudens requie vt floreat. Tone Ne laude pe

Puer sic tum subsecit consolatus nutricule uas ubi prece solidat fu
git ne laude per
e at v. Llongatus a nutrice mansit insolita

R Agnosce de i sa mule surrexit xpietus hac die assunt quas misit epule su
amo re percipe v. Hec dies quam fecit deus in qua iubet exultemus.

R Electo grex mor tiferum patri fere bat po culum sed uir dei si
ui te uas rupit tam quam la pide v. Intende runt arcum
suum ut pderent innoxium. Sed uir. Gloria pa tri et fi lio et spiritui

a Iam latius innotuit quasi lampas emicuit fit benedictus celebris In ii.
frequentatur a populis P. Dne qs ha. a Cuius ergo subtramite multi dum
certant uiuere locis florent duodenis fulget ipse miraculis P. Dne munit

a Hic non impar helyseo eicet ferrum de pfundo sensus et corda pspicit
presens absentes arguit P. Dne et a Maurus uerbo currens patris petri
fertur uestigiis sup liquens elementum mersumq: trahit placidum.

P Edecet y. a Fauent cuncta benedicto uas sponte manat oleo fugit uita spiritu
terra eius priuatim gratia P. Bonum e sit a U quanta plenus gratia qui res
pectu rumpit uincla sedens curuat impia Benedictus p seculа P. Dns regnaui

R Seruus de i BENEDICTVS stetit misertus illius qui clamita bat o
me um o redde redde filium v. Orans iacentem suscitat reddit patri

R Benedictus uam deuotas de o solue bat gra tias I qui cla mitat O mei
ire uidens ut columbam celo so ro ris a nimam. v Vterq:
duxit gau uia soror celo hic in cella ire J cernens a nimam. Q in

R O issabe lita uerus cor in deum dila tatus qui infra se angustatam
uidit omnem cre a turam v. Celo quoq: ferri sanctam Germani

R Alme pa ter qui pres eius tu i sacrati trans tuus hunc preno
tasti fia tribus tue re nos tros ex i tus.

erte ducem clarissimum ut transeamus ad deum. Tuere ᵛ Glori a

patri æ filio æ spiritu i sanc to. Tuere ʌoᶜ ā Benedictum ppheticis

condecoremus canticis qui tam fulsit ppheria quam æ doctrine gratia.

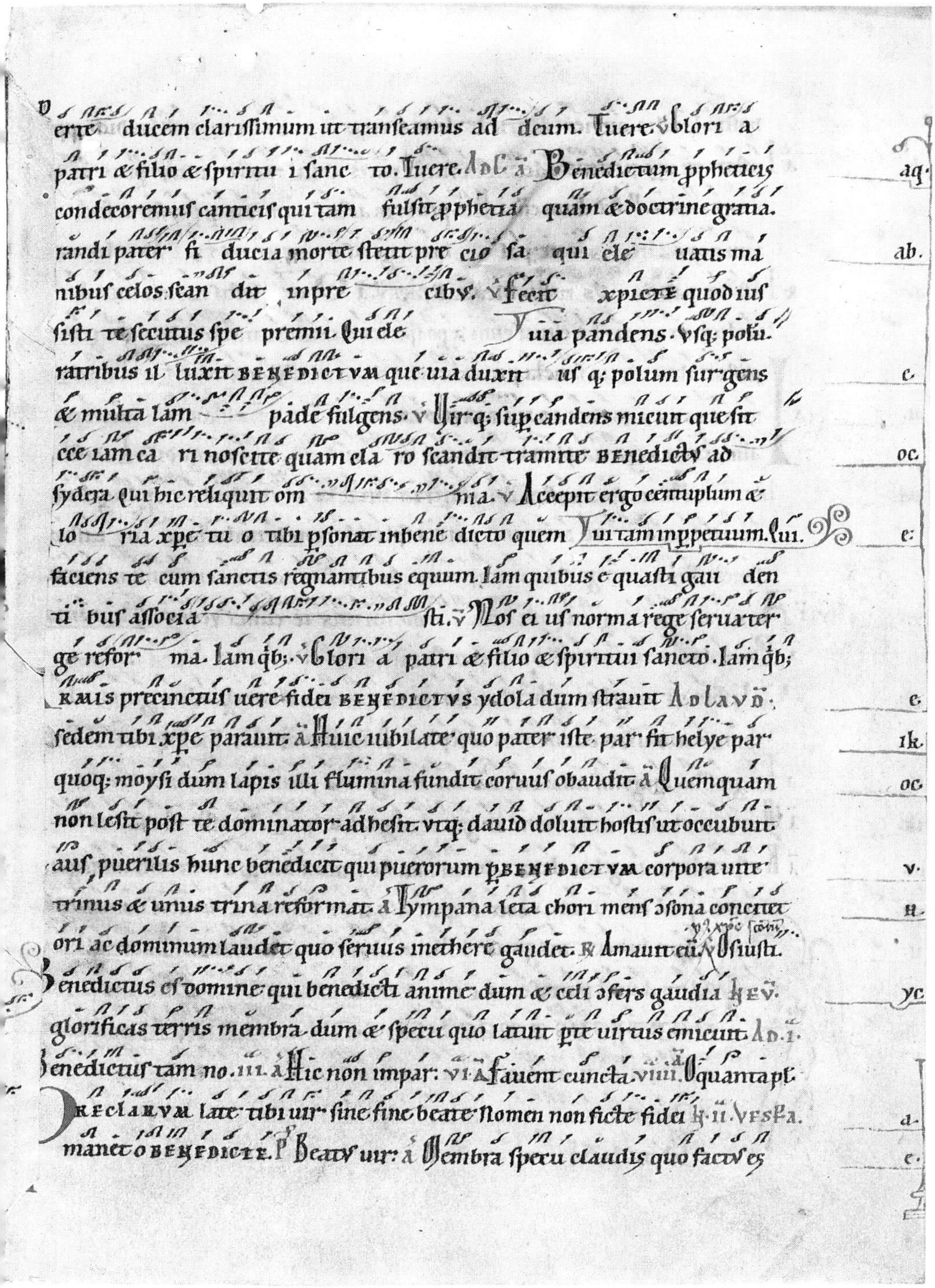

randi pater fi ducia morte stetit pre eio sa qui ele uatis ma

nibus celos scan dit in pre cibᵤ ᵛ fecit xpiere quod ius

sisti te secutus spe premii. Qui ele Tuia pandens ᵛ∫�q poli.

ratribus il luxit Benedictum que uia duxit us q polum surgens

æ multa iam pade fulgens ᵛ Uir�q ∫up eandens micuit que sit

ece iam ca ri noseite quam ela ro scandit tramite Benediceᵗuᶠ ad

sydera qui hic reliquit om mia ᵛ Accepit ergo eentuplum æ

lo ria xpe tu o tibi psonat inbene dieto quem Tuitam inppetuum. Cui

faciens te cum sanctis regnantibus equum. Iam quibus e quasti gau den

ti buſ associa sti ᵛ Nos ei uſ norma rege seruater

ge refor ma. Iam qb, ᵛ Glori a patri æ filio æ spiritui sancto. Iam qb,

Rais precinctus uere fidei Benedictus ydola dum strauit ʌoLauᴅ

sedem tibi xpe parauit ā Huie iubilate quo pater iste par fit helye par

quoq, moyſi dum lapis illi flumina fundit coruuſ obaudit ā Quemquam

non lefit post te dominator adhefit vtq, dauid doluit hoſtis ut occubuit

auſ puerilis hunc benedicat qui puerorum pBenedictum corpora uite

trinus æ unus trina reformat ā Tympana leta chori mens psona eoneitet

ori ac dominum laudet quo seruuſ inethere gaudet ℟ Amauit eü Ɔſiuſti.

Benedictuſ eſ domine qui benedicti anime dum æ celi ofers gaudia Heᵛ.

glorificas terris membra dum æ specu quo latuit pie uirtus emicuit ʌᴅⁱ.

Benedictuſ tam no.III. ā Hic non impar; VI ʌ fauent cuncta VIIII. O quanta pt.

Reclaruꝟ late tibi uir sine fine beate Nomen non ficte fidei H.II VESPA.

manet o Benedicte.P Beatuſ uir: ā Qembra specu claudis quo factuſ eſ hostia laudis carnem districte dum frenas o BENEDICTE credidi ppi

Instar tui xpi patiens adcuncta fuisti pacis æ in uicte cultor pius o

BENEDICTE. Ad dnm cu Hic probris actus tumidisq pipsima factus

iam noys in uie te pal mam geris o BENEDICTE. Adte leuauioci

Iust ut palma. Os iusti meditab. f. O ce lestis norma uite doctor

æ dux BENEDICTE cuius cum xpo spiritus exultat incelestibus gregem

pastor alme serua sancta prece corrobora uia celos clarescere fac te duce pe

INGRESSVS ANGELVS ADMARIAM DIXIT super psfr. intrare.

Aue MARIA gratia plena dominus te cum. Xpi uirgo dil Audi filia yu

Aue spes nostra dei genitrix intacta a ve illud ave pangelum

accipiens. ve decipiens patris splendorem benedicta a ue casta

sanctissima uirgo sola innupta te glo rificat omnis creatura matrem

Aue MARI a gratia ple na do minus te cum. Venite luminis.

Benedicta tu inmul. sie sup inPurifie eius. In p mo n. Alie.

Missus est angelus gabriel adeo inciuitatem nazareth aduirginem de

sponsatam uiro cui nomen ioseph. Dne dns nr surel inpurif uldiuirg

Ingressus angelus admari am ait aue gratia plena do minus tecum.

Maria turbatur insermone angeli æ cogitabat qua lis esset ista salutatio.

Respondens angelus dixit admariam ne timeas MARIA inuenisti enim gra

tiam apud dominum. Ecce decipies æ paries fi lium æ uocabis nomen eius

iesum hic erit magnus æ filius altissimi uocabitur. Dabit illi des

sedem dauid patris eius æ regnabit indomo iacob ineternum æ regni

INGRESSVS ANGELVS ADMA eius n erit finis. uue m.q.p

RI AMA si aue MARIA GRATIA PLENA DOMINVS TE CVM.

Benedicta tu inmulieribus æ benedictus fructus uentris tui i. Aue

Benedicta tu inmulie ribus æ benedictus fructus uentris tui

Ⅱ 8841

MS 481.51.7   7

Aue maria gratia plena dominus te cum. Et bened

Mari a ut audiuit turbata est insermo ne angeli & | cogitabit

qualis esset ista salu tati o. Quomodo fiet istud qua | [unknown]

Posuit moyses bis senas uirgas de singulis tribubus fili co ar | [unknown]

orum israhel intabnaculum testimonii gaudete fratres gaud | ete

inter ipsas uirga aaron arida floruit fronduit & nuces | cecedit

Scientes hoc signum inbea te uirginis MARIE partu fuisse c | ompletum

Gloria patri & filio & spiritui sancto. Gaudete i | i. Hec e qu | i

Dixit autem maria ad angelum quomodo fiet istud quoniam | virum non

cognosco & respondit angelus spiritus sanctus sup ueniet in | e et virtus

atissimi obumbrabit tibi. Ideoque & quod nascetur ex te sanc | tum vocabitur

filius dei. Dixit autem MARIA ad angelum ecce ancilla de | i fiat mihi

secundum uerbum tuum. Post abscessium angeli MARIA asc | endit in mon

tana & ingressa domum hacharie salutauit elisabeth incuius | s utero exulta

uit infans ingaudio aduocem MARIE. Spiritu sancto reple | ta elisabet

dixit ad MARIAM benedicta tu inter mulieres & benedictu | fructus ven

tris tui. Beata que credidit quoniam perfici entur que du | ta sunt ei

Dixit ange lus ad MARI am ne timeas MARI a inue ac | domino

nisti gra tiam apud domi num. Ecce scipies & paries filiu | m et vocabilis

Ecce scipies & pari es fi lium & uoca bi tur nomen ei | us iesum

nomen eius ie suc. Hic erit magnus & filius atissimi | vocabitur ut

dabit illi dominus deus sedem dauid patris su i. Et vocabitur

Dabit illi dominus deus sedem dauid patris su i & regnabit i | in domo ia

cob ine ternum. Et regni ei us non erit finis. Et reg

Salue nobilis uirga iesse salue flos campi MARIA ja | ia ex te ortum

est lilium conualli um. Odor tuus sup cuncta pre | ciosa unguenta

favus distill	ans labia tua mel & lac sublingua tua. Ceteror: Gloria patri
[unknown]	& tibi compar utriusq; semp spiritus al me. Ceteror: Ad can
O gloriosa fe	mina non solum benedicta inter mulieres sed inter mulieres
[unknown]	maiori benedictione specialiter insignis. Sive a Gabri illi dns
quomodo	fiet istud respondens Cant Audite me v Speciosa f. e. s:
R.Quomod fiet istud	angele dei quia uirum non cognosco angelus ad hec
spiritus	sanctus sup ue niet inte & uirtus atius simi ob umbra
bit	t a bi. v Ideoq; & quod nascetur ecte sanctum uocabitur
R.Conversus e	hechiel adorientem portam aspexerat fi liius de 1. Spe
clavisum di	ctumq; est ei porta hec quam uides clau sa erit &
vir non tr	ansibit pc am sed semp e rit clausa. v Hinc euiden
ter ostensu	m est quod maria semper uirgo fuerit uirgo permanserit
virgo ante	partum uirgo inpartu uirgo post partum. Et uir non
R.Dixit aut	em maria ad angelum ecce ancil la do mini fiat
mihi secun	dum uerbum tuum. v Spc scs sup ueniet inte & uirtisatussi
R.Christi virgo	o dilec tissima uir tu mi obumbrabit ti bi. Ecce
tum op	e ra trix magni fica opem fer miseris subueni domna
clamantibu	s ad te iugiter: Quo ni am peccato rum
mole premi	l mur ob hoc te depre camur: Subue v Glo ri a patri & filio
A.Missus est g	ab Aue maria g a Spiritus scs Ad laud Ve spiritui sco Subve
A.Ne timeas m	maria inuen a Ecce ancilla dni fiat m. Ad laudes alie
A. Quando v	enit ergo sacri plenitudo temporis missus est abarce patris
natus orbis	s oditor interris a Uerbum supnum apatre ante tempora ge
nitum hod	ie pnobis factus homo exinaniuit semetipsum. Beatus auctor
seculi servi	te corpus induit ut carne carnem liberans ne perderet
quod cond	idit a Clausa parentis uiscera celestis intrat gratia uenter

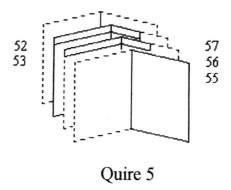

52
53

57
56
55

Quire 5

[unknown] [A Cum turba plurima conveniret ad jesum et de
civitatibus properarent ad eum dixit per similitudinem Exiit]
qui seminat seminare semen suum **Ad 1ᵃ A** Exiit qui seminat seminare semen

B8ʳ
I/95/1ʳ
f.52r

Ink. I/95, flyleaf 1ʳ
Stiftsbibliothek Lambach

[holocaustum odoratus est domi]nus odorem [suavitatis et
benedixit eis Crescite et multiplicatamini et replete terram
E[cce ego] statuam pactum meum vobiscum vestra post

Ink. I/95, flyleaf 1v
Stiftsbibliothek Lambach

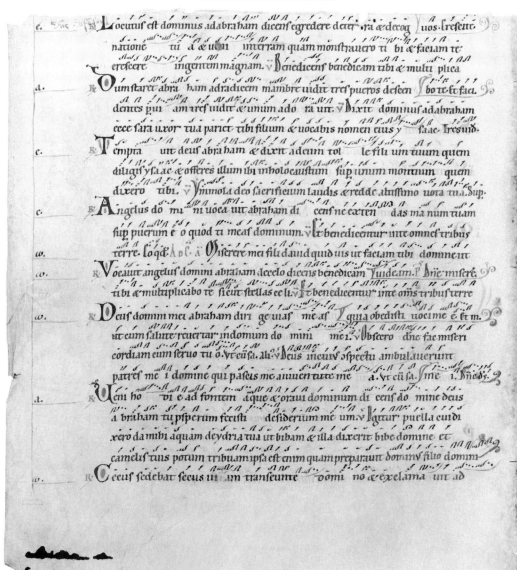

men. v Et qui pr[eibant increpavit eum ut [taceret at ille ma]
ecundum multitudinem] miserationem tuarum. **Ad laud**/gis clamabat. Rab

I/95/2ᵛ a Cum facis [elemosynam nesciat sinistra tua] quid faciat dextra tua **f.vi**

f.53v a Nesciat sinistra tua quid faciat dextura tua. iii * **a** Tu autem cuɪ
[ora]veris intra

Dixit dns. R Bonum michi domine quod humiliasti me bonum mihi lex oris
tui sup milia auri & argenti. V Manus tue domine fecerunt me & plas
mauerunt me da mihi intellectum ut discam mandata tua. Bonum m. Euuan.

on in solo pane uiuit homo sed inomni uerbo dei. F R ii invit.

on sit uobis uanum surgere ante lucem. P Venite. H I N R Rectos decet A D L A U D

iserere mi ds. Cur reliqs. R Participem me Euuan. A. Cum uenerit filius hominis
in maiestate sua & omnes angeli cum eo tunc sedebit sup sedem maiestatis sue
& congregabuntur ante eum omnes gentes & separabit eos sic pastor segregat
oues ab hedis A D i. Venite benedicti patris mei percipite regnum quod uobis para
tum est aborigine mundi. Privatis dieb ad i eun e ppa. A. Uiuo ego dicit dns
nolo mortem peccatoris sed ut magis ouertatur & uiuat iii. A. Aduenerunt
nobis dies penitentie ad redimenda peccata ad saluandas animas. A D vi.
ommendemus nosmetipsos inmulta pacientia par ma iusticie uirtutis dei.
erarma iusticie uirtutis dei commendemus nosmetipsos inmulta A D viiii.
pacientia. A D V E S P A. A. Quod uni ex minimis meis fecistis mihi fecistis
dicit dominus. F R i. A. Domus mea domus orationis uocabitur: i. A. Osanna
filio dauid benedictus qui uenit in nomine domini. Vesp. A. Scriptum est enim
quia domus mea domus orationis est cunctis gentibus uos autem fecistis illam
spelumcam latronum & erat cottidie do cens intemplo. F R . numione ppheta iiii
eneratio hec praua & puersa signum querit & signum non dabitur ei nisi sig
Sicut fuit ionas inuentre ceti tribus diebus & tribus noctibus ita erit A D i.
filius hominis incorde terre iii. A. Siquis fecerit uoluntatem patris mei
ipse meus frater soror & mater est. A. Dixit quidam adiesum ecce mater A D V E S P.
tua & fratres tui foris stant querentes loqui tecum at ille respondens dicens
sibi ait que est mater mea & fratres mei & extendens manum indiscipulos
suos dixit ecce mater mea & fratres mei. Euuan. A. Si manseritis insermone

meo uere discipuli mei eritis & cognoscetis ueritatem & ueritas liberabit uos

Si ueritatem dico quare non creditis mihi qui est ex deo uerba dei audit

Angelus domini descendebat de celo mouebatur aqua & sanabatur unus

Domine non habeo hominem ut cum mota fuerit aqua mittat me in piscinam.

Qui me sanum fecit ille mihi precepit tolle grabbatum tuum & ambula in pac

Vade iam & noli peccare ne deterius tibi aliquid contingat. SABBATO

Assumpsit ihc discipulos suos & ascendit in montem & transfiguratus est ante

Domine bonum est nos hic esse si uis faciamus hic tria tabernacula tibi unum

moysi unum & helye unum. III. faciamus hic tria tabnacula tibi unum

moysi unum & helye unum. VI. Descendentibus illis de monte precepit

eis dicens nemini dixeritis uisionem. VIII. Uisionem quam uidistis nemini

dixeritis donec a mortuis resurgat filius hominis

Nemini dixeritis uisionem donec filius hominis

a mortuis resurgat. IN VII. Quoniam de us magnus dominus & rex mag

nus super om nes de os. Uenite ex. Aduenerunt nob. Isur.

tol le arma tu a pharetram et arcum et affer

de uenatione tua ut co me dam & benedicat ti bi anima

me a sume; uenatu aliquid adtuleris fac mihi inde pulmentum ut

Ecce odor filii me i sicut o dor a gri pleni co me dam et

quem benedixit domi nus crescere te fa ci at de us me us

sicut are nam ma ris & donet tibi de rore celi benedicti

o nem. Qui maledi xerit tibi sit ille maledictus & qui benedixerit tibi b

Det tibi de us de rore celi & depin benedictionibus reple a tur si

quedine terre habun danti am seruiant tibi tribus popu li esto domi

nus fratrum tu o rum. Et incuruentur ante te filii matris tui estu

Quis igitur ille est qui dudum captam uena tio nem attulit mi hi et

152

comedi ex omnibus priusquam tu venires Benedixique ei et erit bene]
dictus v Dominum tuum illum constitui et o **vl r** D

[Esau quia valde contremit cor meum illum timens **v** Tu locutus es quod mih
bene faceres et dilatares sem]en meum sicut arenam maris Libera me **Sive**

[unknown]. A.Qui me misit mecum est et
ei facio semper
t christus dominus A.Tui maior
i se exaltat humiliabitur
s traditur ut /dicit dominus
d illudendum et flagellandum
m non est meum dare vobis sed
possum ego a meipso facere
um iustum est. A Non quaero
misit me A.Ego veni in nomi
venerit in nomini suo illum
dare A.[unknown]/fructum temporibus suis
liis agricolis qui reddunt ei
t agricolas A.Querentes eum
m eum habebant
te iam non sum dignis vocari
rcennarus tuis
undant panius ego autem
meum et dicam ei fac me
fac me sicut unum
pater ad servos suos cito pro
ate anulum in manu eius et
mper mecum fuisti et omnia mea
oseph ductus est in egyptum

[fuitque dominus cum eo per quem erat vir in cunctis prospere agens
V. Misertus enim est deus illius, et omnia eius opera dirigebat.
Per quem. Gloria] patri et filio et spiritui sancto. P[er qu]em

Ink. I/95, flyleaf 4ᵛ
Stiftsbibliothek Lambach

Fili tu semper mecum es omn | ia mea tua sunt epulari autem & gaudere opor
tebat quia frater tuus mortu | us fuerat & reuixit perierat & inuentus est.
Invit. Deus mag | nus domi nus & rex magnus sup omnes deos.
V identes IOSEPH ALONGE LOQVEBAHTVR.
fratres dicen | tes ecce somniator uenit venite occidamus
eum et vida | imus si psint il li som nia sua.
V.Cumque vidissent ioseph fratres | sui quod apatre cunctis fratribus plus ama
retur oderant eum nec poteran | t ei quicquam pacifice lo qui unde & dicc bai. ven.
R.Dixit iudas fratribus su | is ecce ismahelite trans eunt venite
venumdetur et manus nos | tre non pollu antur earo e nim & frater nr. est
V.Cumque abisset ruben ad puteum | & non inuenisset e um scissis uestibus pgens
ad fratres ait puer non c | omparet & e go quo i bo caro eni.
R.Videns iacob vestimenta io | seph sci dit uestimenta sii a eum fieri
et dixit fera pessima devo | rauit filium meum ioseph. V Vide
si tunica filii tui sit an no | n & cum uidisset pater a it. fera pessi.
R.Ioseph dum | intraret interram e gypti linguam quam
non novit audivit man | us eius inlaboribus seru erunt & lin
gua eius inter principies l | oquebatur sapienti am. V Diuertit aboneribus
R.Memento mei dum bene t | ibi fue rit ut sugge J dorsum eius. Man.
ras pharoni ut educat m | e de isto carcc re quia furtim subla
tus sum et hic innocens in | lacum missus sum. V Ires e nim adhuc
dies sunt post quos recorda | bitur pharao ministerii tui & reuocat te
in gradum pristinum tunc | me memto me i. Vt suggeras.

MS 481.51.10ᵛ
The Beinecke Rare Book and Manuscript Library, Yale University

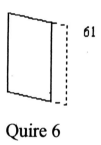

61

Quire 6

equiescam
[unknown]
rasceve
eius
t sortem
sibi
eam miserunt sortem
me et prevaluer
bam et terribilibus
v. Et dederunt in secam
am fel et in siti mea Aceto
ine dum veneris
paradiso memento
es in amaritudinem
uidem plantavi
modo. In ii° n°
in furore A. Confundantur
t eam
meam
tas sibi
dere me cotidie
et ecce flagella
minis vadit sicut
etur Ad crucifigendum
circa horam nonam
ne dereliquisti

et inclinato capite

perforavit et continu

est a summo usque dec

R.Barrabos latro dim

tor sceleris qu

minum iesum xp

A.Ab insurgentibus in

A.Lo

A.Captaba

v.Locuti

R.Tradiderunt me in

proiecerunt m

versum me forte

reges terre et pri

R.Iesum tradidit

populi petrus autem

R.Caligaverunt ocul

batur me videte

v.O vos omnes qui t

A.Proprio filio suo

A.Anxiatus est in m

A.Ait latro ad lotronem

memento mei dom

A.Dum conturbata fuer

A.Memento mei domi

v. Proprio filio suo non per

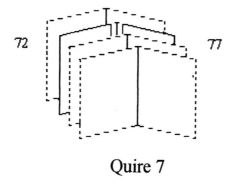

Quire 7

poeta Omnia sunt hominum tenui pendentia filo et subito
casu que valuere ruunt.

MS 481.51.12

AEVIA. Benedictus dns ſ.ſ.crucē. a. Crucem ſanctam ſubiit qui infernum
ſfregit accinctus eſt potentia ſurrexit die tercia ae VIA. S. MARIA.

AEVIA Sancta dei genitrix MARIA intercede pnobis AEVIA AEVIA. S. KYLIANO.

Fulgebunt iuſti ſic Ad veſp. a. In tabernaculis iuſtis. Suffragia ſcō 7 oīnb̄ ſcīs

Surgens ieſuſ mane prima ſabbati apparuit primo ... In binario ſepul eſt

MARIE magdalene dequa eiecerat ſeptem demonia AEVIA. III. a. Et dicebant
adinuicem quis reuoluet nobis lapidem abhoſtio monumenti AEVIA AEVIA.

v Hec e dies quā fec dns ... crucem 7 ... mea. alla. alla. alla. Iste uir̄ poī̄ſ hora
dicend e n tantū adcompletoriū 7 ad matut Siue v Inreſurrectione tua xpe celu 7 tra l. alla.

Et reſpicientes uiderunt reuolutum lapidem erat quippe magnus ualde Ad vi.

AEVIA. v Surrexit dns uere et apparuit ſymoni AEVIA. alla alla. Ad viiii.

Nolite expaueſcere ieſum nazarenum queritis crucifixum non eſt hic ſurrexit

AEVIA v Surrexit dns deſepulchro. Qui pnob pependit inligno alla. a. a. In ii.

AEVIA AEVIA AE VIA AEVIA AEVIA AEVIA. vt a Crucifixus reſ. VESPA.

Laudate p. Laud d. o. gītē Laudate d. q. b. pſ. Lauda ierlm Una dicat uq̄ adſabbm.

urrexit dominus deſepulchro AEVIA AE VIA. v Qui pnobis pependit inligno

AEVIA AE VIA. v Gloria pat et filio et ſui Ao Sicut erat ino et u et ō et ieua euouae

AEVIA. a. Surrex v gauiſi ſ diſcipli. viſo dno. AEVIA. alla alleluia. In evg.

urrexit enim ſicut dixit dominus et precedet uos ingalyleam aeuia ibi
eum uidebitis AEVIA AEVIA AE VIA. S. cruce. Crucem ſcām ſub Ad pceſſionē

Xpc reſurgens exmortuis iam non moritur mors illi ultra non domina
bitur quod e nim ui uit ui uit deo ae VIA AEVIA ITEM.

Dicant nunc iudei quomodo milites cuſtodientes ſepulchrum pdiderunt
regem adlapidis poſitionem quare non ſeruabant petram iuſti e aut ſe
pul tum reddant aut re ſurgentem ado rent nobis cum
di centes. Quod enim uiuit uiuit deo ae VIA. AEVIA.

Senta. Summa phyloſophia eſt ſuipſius notitia
Bernardus: Siquis calet ingenio et uiget arte, inſtrumenta hec
ſunt tam uitiorum quam virtutum

In [...] libidine hec perfinito compleduntur
[...] pulsa abuslarene, oluu in sonitus

A DE RESVRRECTIOHE DNI IN EVGLO ADLAVDES·

Post passionem domini factus est conuentus quia non est inuentum corpus inmo
numerito lapis sustinuit ppetuam uitam monumentum reddidit celestem marga
ritam aeuia. ꞇ Surgens ihc. Nolite expauescere. ꞇ in die sco ad pmā ʒad·viii.

A Scio quod iesum queritis crucifixum surrexit aeuia. Iesum qui crucifixus est
queritis aeuia non est hic surrexit enim sicut dixit uobis aeuia. Ito euntes
dicite discipulis quia surrexit dominus aeuia. ꞇ Et recordate sunt uerborum
eius & regresse amonumento nunciauerunt hec omnia illis undecim & ceteris
omnibus aeuia. ꞇ Oportebat pa ti xpm & intrare ingloriam suam aeuia.

A Nonne cor nrm ardens erat innobis de iesu dum loqueretur nob milia aeuia.

A Cognouerunt discipuli dominum aeuia infractione panis aeuia. Inclinauit
se MARIA pspexit inmonumentum uidit duos angelos inalbis sedentes aeuia.

A Ardens est cor me um desidero uidere dominum meum quero & non inuenio
ubi posuerunt eum aeuia. ꞇ Ite nunciate fratribus meis aeuia ut eant ingaly
leamibi me uidebunt aeuia aeuia ac via. Ingalylea ihm uidebitis
sicut dixit uobis aeuia. ꞇ Aeuia Resurrexit dominus aeuia sicut dixit no
bis aeuia aeuia. ꞇ Aeuia Quem queris mu. ꞇ m.s. nocte adcompl· alleluia
Noli flere MARIA aeuia resurrexit dominus aeuia aeuia. ꞇ Ego sum alpha
& w primus & nouissimus & stella matutina ego clauis dauid aeuia.

A Surrexit dominus desepulchro qui pnobis pependit inligno aeuia aeuia aeuia.

A Surrexit dominus desepulchro qui pnobis pependit inligno A E V I A.

A Surrexit xpe & illuxit populo suo quem redemit sanguine suo aeuia aeuia.

A Crucifixus surrexit amortuis & redemit nos AE V IA AEVIA.

A Crucem sciam subiit ꞇ Iesum quem queritis non est hic sed surrexit recor
dami m qualiter locutus est uobis dum adhuc ingalylea esset A E V I A.

A Crucifixus resurrexit AEVIA. FERIA Seda INVITATORIV·
Surrexit dominus uere AE V IA Venite exultem. H IN A Nolite expa

Beat⁹ uir q̅ n̅. Quare frem̅. Cū inuocarē. Uerbam. Dn̅e dn̅s n̅r. Inchio oſtdo.

In i N. Reſurrexit dn̅s· ſic dix̅ h̅ u̅ i̅ N̅ Surrex̅ dn̅s uere· & apparuit ſymoni. a.

h̅ u̅ i̅ N̅ Surrexit dn̅s deſepulchro· Qui pn̅· p·inl· acuia. a. a. Ad lau̅d· v̅ Surrexit xp̅e

& illuxit pp̅lo ſuo· a cuia. a. a. Ad veſſu v̅ Gauiſi ſ diſepli· viſo dn̅o acuia. a. a.

Cū quers mulier· viu. Tulert̅ dn̅m meū. & neſcio ubi po. h̅ u̅ i̅ N̅ Koli flere maria·

I̅resurrex̅ dn̅s· alla· Ad lau̅d· v̅ Reſurrex̅ dn̅s· ſic d̅. Ad veſſu v̅ Gauiſi ſ diſepli·

ARIA MAGDALENA ET ALTERA MARIA IBANT DILV ye.

culo admonumentum iesum quem querit̅ non est hic ſurrexit

ſicut locutus est precedet uos ingalyle· am ibi eum uidebitis acuia

AE Y IA· v̅ Ci̅ to cuntes dicite diſcipulis eius & petro quia ſurrext̅

Surgens iesus do minus noster· ſtans inmedi o diſcipulo do mi nus· Peedit ye.

rum ſuo rum· dixit pax uobis acuia gaui ſi ſunt diſcipu li ui ſo

domi no AE vi IA· Surrexit dominus deſepulchro qui pnobis

Congratulamini mihi om̅ nes qui diligitis domi pependit in lig no· Gauiſi 1.

num quia quem querebam apparuit mic hi & dum flerem admonumentum

uidi dominum me um AE VIA· v̅ Tulerunt dominum meum &

neſcio ubi poſuerunt e um ſi tu ſuſtulisti eum di cito mic hi· & diſfle h̅ i̅ N̅

Scio quod itm̅ que· P Saluū me fac· b· q· df· Vſq· q· P Dix̅ inſipiens· P Dn̅e qs hab·

Conſerua me d· P Exaudi dn̅e iuſtciā Ad lau̅d· a̅ Angelus aute do· Surrex̅ dn̅s uere· h̅ r̅ v̅ w.

Iesus iunxit ſe diſcipulis ſuis inui a· & ibat cum illis oculi eorum tenebatur w.

ne eum agnoſcerent & increpabat cos dicens o ſtulti & tardi corde ad credendum

mihis que locuti ſunt pphete acuia· Ad i̅ a̅ Tu ſolus pegrinus es & non audisti de ag.

iesu quomodo tradiderunt e um in dampnationem mortis acuia. iii a̅ Honne 1.

ſic opor f tuit pati xp̅m & intra ingloriam ſuam acuia· v̅ In reſurroe t· x·

Et incipiens a moyse & omnibus pphetis interpretabatur illis ſcripturas vi ag.

de omnibus que de ipſo erant acuia. v̅ Surrex̅ d· ue· viii a̅ Et coegerunt illum e·

Quando ueneris iudicare noli me ō domine condemnare.
ne gaudeat inimicus meus super me.

dicentes mane nobiscum domine quia aduesperascit ε cua. ℣ Surrex̄ dn̄s desep.

A EVIA AEVIA AEVIA AEVIA AEVIA AEVIA AEVIA. AEVIA Vt̄ Surrexit Uᵈⱽeſp.

P laudate p. Vt ſup. ℟ Surrexit dominus desepulchro AEVIA. AEVIA. Qui p

nobis pependit inligno AEVIA AEVIA. ℣. Gloria patri æ filio æ ſpīritui ſc̄o ſic

erat inprincipio æ nunc æ ſemp æ inſecula ſeculorum amen. AEVIA AE VIA. ℣.

P ſanodieb. ℟. Surrex̄ dn̄s deſepulch̄. AEVIA AEVIA. ℣. Qui pnob pepend inligno AEVIA alla

Q ui ſunt hi ſermones quos oſfertis adinuicem ambulantes æ eſtis triſtes ℟ ℣.

AEVIA AEVIA. Reſpondens unus cui nomen cleopas dixit ei tuſolus pegrinuſeſ

inierusalem æ non cognouiſti que facta ſunt inilla his diebus AEVIA. Quibꝰ ille

dixit Que æ dixerunt deieſu na̅hareno qui fuit uir ꝓpheta potens inopere

æ ſermone coram deo æ omni populo AEVIA AEVIA. ℟ ℣. ℟ ℣ Surrexit dn̄s uere

i̅h̅m̅ quicrucifixꝰ eſt. P̄ Dn̄e dn̄s nr̄. P̄ Dn̄e q̄s hab. P̄ Celi enar. P̄ Laudati t.d.

Dn̄e inuirtut̄ P̄ Dn̄s regit me. ℣ Resurrexit dn̄s. Sic dix̄ uob. AEVIA.

IRTVTE MAG NA REDDEBANT APOSTO LI TESTIMO

ni um Resurrecti o nis ieſu xp̄i ⁊ domini noſtri AEVIA AE VIA.

I nomnem terram exiuit ſonꝰ eorum æ infines orbis trē uer̄ba eo ruā. Teſt

T ulerunt dominum meum æ neſcio ubi poſuerunt ⁊ um. Dixit ei ange

lus noli flere MA RI A ſurrexit ſicut dixit precedet uos ingalyleam ibi

eum uidebitis AEVIA AEVIA. ℣ Cito euntes dicite diſcipulis eius æ petro quia

E xpurgate uetus fermentum ut ſitis noua con ſp̄i o Surrexit domi nꝰ. Pced

æ enim paſcha noſtrum ymmolatus eſt xp̄ietus ita q̄ epulemur indomino

AE VIA. ℣ Non infermento malicie æ nequitie ſed in a̅z̅imis ſinceritatis

æ uerita tis Itaq̄. i̅h̅m̅ A Venite æ uidete. P̄ Dn̄e ira. P̄ Iu dica me dn̄e.

P̄ Adte dn̄e clamabo. P̄ Afferte dn̄o. P̄ Exaltabo te dn̄e. P̄ Exultate ſti. X. Ad lauᵈ

E t ecce terre motꝰ. ℟. Surrexit dn̄s uere AEVIA alla. ℣ Et apparuit ſymoni AEVIA.

S tetit ieſuſ inmedio diſcipulorum ſuorum æ dixit eis pax uob AEVIA alla

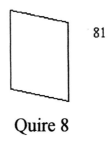
81

Quire 8

Sene. Ebrius est omnium uitiorum seruus.
Hic Ebrietas est omnium uitiorum mater, genitrix omnium culparum
et radix criminum.

me quia uado adpatrem aeua aeua. Quid est hoc quod dicit nobis modicum nescimus

quid loquitur aeua. Amen amen dico uobis quia plorabitis & flebitis uos mundus

autem gaudebit uos autem contristabimini sed tristicia uestra uertetur ingaudium aeua.

Mulier cum parit tristiciam habet quia uenit hora eius cu aut peperit puerum iam non meminit

pressure ppter gaudium quia natus est homo in mundum aeua. Tristicia imple

bit cor uestrum aeua & gaudium uestrum nemo tollet auobis aeua. Tristicia

uestra aeua uertetur ingaudium aeua. Iterum autem uidebo uos & gaudebit

cor uestrum aeua & gaudium uestrum nemo tollet auob ar uia. Iterum autem

uidebo uos & gaudebit cor uestrum aeua & gaudium uestrum nemo tollet auobis

uado adeum qui misit me sed quia hec locutus sim uobis Do.xi. iiii. aeua.

tristicia implebit cor uestrum aeua. Ego ueritatem dico uobis expedit uobis ut

ego uadam si enim non abiero paraclytus non ueniet aeua. Dum uenerit paracly

tus spiritus ueritatis ille arguet mundum de peccato & deiusticia & deiudicio aeua.

Adhuc multa habeo uobis dicere sed non potestis portare modo cum autem uenerit

ille spiritus ueritatis docebit uos omnem ueritatem aeua. Cum autem uenerit

ille spiritus ueritatis docebit uos omnem ueritatem & que uentura sunt annuncia

bit uobis aeua. Non enim loquetur asemetipso sed quecumq audiet loquetur

& que uentura sunt annunciabit uobis aeua. Ille me clarificabit quia demeo

accipiet & annunciabit uobis aeua.

Usq modo non petistis quicquam petite & accipietis aeua. Petite & accipie

tis ut gaudium uestrum plenum sit ipse enim pater amat uos quia uos me amastis

& credidistis aeua. Exiui apatre & ueni in mundum aeua iterum relinquo mun

dum & uado adpatrem aeua aeua aeua. Exiui apatre meo & ue. mi mun

dum iterum relinquo mundum & uado adpatrem dicunt ei discipuli eius ecce

nunc palam loqueris & puerbium nullum dicis aeua aeua aeua. Ecce nunc

palam loqueris & puerbium nullum dicis nunc scimus quia scis omnia & non opus est

Seneca. Si ista dño q nomina meum et tuum toll...
in re medio, omnia essent quieta.

Petite & dabitur uobis querite & inuenietis pulsate & aperietur uobis ROGATIONIB
aeuia. Omnis qui petit accipit & qui querit inuenit & pulsanti aperietur aeuia.

Si ergo uos cum sitis mali nostis bona data dare filiis uestris quantomagis pater
uester decelo dabit bona petentibus se aeuia. DOM PMA. P OCT PASCHE

Audiui uoces in celo. EV Aeuia aeuia. Venite exultem

DIGNUS ES DOMINE ACCIPERE LIBRUM ETAPE
rire signa eius quoniam occisus es & redemisti nos deo in
sanguine tuo ÷ ae VIA. Lar ce domine parce popu
lo tuo o quem rede misti xpie TE. Insanguine tuo ÷ ae

Ego sicut uitis fructifica ui siauitatem odoris ÷ AEVIA transire adme om
nes qui concupiscitis me & agenerationibus meis adimplemini aeuia aeuia.

Ego diligentes me diligo & qui mane uigilauerint admein uenient me. Transite

Audiui uocem de ce lo tamquam uocem tonitrui magni ÷ E VIA regnauit
deus noster ineternum aeuia quia facta est salus & uirtus & potestas
xpi eius aeuia ae uia. Vidi di angelū desfortem uolantem pmedium celi ÷

Resurrexit dñs aeuia aeuia. Sie dixt uobis alia atta. ee magna clamantem & dicentem. Regni

Locutus est adme u nus exseptem angelis di cens ueni ostendam tibi nouam
nuptam sponsam agni & uidi ierusalem descendentem decelo ornatam thoni li
bus suis aeuia ae uia. Et sustulit me inspiritu inmontem magnum &

Audiui uoces in ce lo angelorum multorum dicen Altum. Audi. Ai. V Ego diligente
ti um timete dominum & date claritatem illi & adorate eum qui fecit celum
& terram mare & fontes aquarum aeuia ae VIA. V Vidi angelum
dei fortem uolantem pmedium celi uoce magna clamantem & di centem. Timete

Decantabat populus israhel aeuia & uniuersa multitudo iacob cane bant legem
me & dauid cum cantoribus eytharam percutiebat indomo domi ni & laudes deo
cane bant aeuia ae uia. V Moyses & aaron insacerdotibus eius & samuel in

Fuere os. Et dauid

Crisod. occultum pctm nu publico arguere non nisi corripere sed dissi
man.
Psal. LII Eui hominibus placent confusi sunt, quoniam dñs spreuit illos
Ad Gal. i cap. Si adhuc hominibus placerem serius dei non essem
Bernhard. Detractor et libens aud tor uterq portat diabolum in
in unius illo linqua.

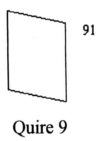

91

Quire 9

Inqua ciuita te cum puellis suis ueneris sacris dedita. tunc turpis sed post
modum sanctissima habitabat afra. Huius pstibulum cum felice diacono suo
sanctius presul ignorans ingressus pacem domui imprecatur· benigneq; quasi pripi
amatore suscipitur. Cum psalmis deo & ymnis sancti uiri uota psolueret. Afra
stupens & tremebun da msoluti quid sibi hospites uelint est amirata. Audi
ens uero beatum uirum xpianorum esse antistitem pedibus eius psternitur se
turpem se peccatricem taliq; indignam hospite psitetur. Quam uir sanctus uer
bis euangelicis isolatur ad penitentiam & conuersionem cohortatur eiq; si credere &
baptisari uelit ueniam & ui tam eternam polli cetur· v Iusta aie

BEATVS PONTIFEX NARCISSVS CVM BEATAS SE MINAS GRATIA
diuina preuen tas capaces uerbi psen sisset toto nisu fructiecs erro
rum exstir pare & ueritatis fru gem studuit in serere·
v Domino pipsis sup plicans &uerbum uite eis annuncians. Veritatis.
R Sancto presule precibus obnixius uisistente demon nigerrimus chor ro
re plenus ap paruit ac se nimiuria suis esedi bus pelli pro cla mabat.
v Mundi cordis amatorem nil mitam sordidis habere uatis pro testatur: de se in.
R Hostis anti quus ecclesti uirtu te & ratio num ueritate confutat v ut vts
tandem au fugit & dedita s iam xpo feminas e nilans reliquit.
v Coactus a sancto pontifice mortiferum in faucibus alpium draconem pimere ded·
R Iustorum inime-k-ii.n.a. Sancto pontifice indnuims laudibus pnoctante lux
cethus emissa & tenebras noctis excussit & cor afre splendore si dei illu
minauit. v Cumq; dulcem sane doctrine saporem pregustasset afra puellas su
is allocuta pmptas eas aduiam uite pedissequas in ueunt. Afra prisca raab
meretronum secuta ueri ihu legatos adsupplicuum apsecutoribus requisitos
sublin fasciculis supne ciuitatis futura ciuis oc cultabat. Imbuta uere fidei
rudimentis afra queq; a sancto hospite salutaria pcepta matri sue hyla pie
fideliter in dicauit. Que beatum uirum noct v adse transmissum gratula
bunda suscipiens pedes eius amplectitur uiteq; prioris miseros errores con
fitetur: Audiens presul sanctis turpissimis abhylaria demonum culturis

gemitus & lacrimas fundens pias cum diacono suo prauo errore dno peccata effudit

℟ Pro pulso post longum oflictum prisci erroris per suaso re uir domini nar
cissus beatas mulie res fide xpi plenius instruxit & saluta ri laua ero
penitentia & ieiuniis prepara ri fecit familiam totam cognatos affi

℟ Cum fontem uite sitien tes & fide alacres prospexisset san ſnes & iam eos fid x
Aus pontifex domino gratias re ferens xpi baptismo qui dentes ab
luit omnes Ṿ Uasa prius ire inuasa emun dans misericor die Xpi bapt

℟ Mox omnibus infide xpie ti oconfortans auunculum afre dyonisium episcopum
eis pre fecit & domum hy larie ecclesiam de diea uir

Ṿ Vt ubi spurca pridem commercia xpi deinceps frequen tarentur mysteria. Domi.

℟ Iusti aute imppetui... ā Gratias tibi domine ihu referimus inmensas quia in
beata martyre afra ubi habundauit iniquitas sup abundauit & gratia tua.

℟ Postquam no uellam conuersa afra beatus narcissus auguste fundauit ec ele
siam nouam domino lucraturus fam liam Hyspaniarum uir bem
adiit ge rundam. Ṿ Ubi cum felice diacono suo feliciter martyr uim con

℟ Fer uente interim inma ni persecutio niseu eia summauit. Hysp
bea ta a fra compre hen ditur & ga i iudicis tribu nalibus pre
sentatur: Gaudens & tripudians coronamq; martyru adipisci de

℟ Dut tus hinc inde ser monum con fluctationibus ha bmus siderans ba rud
mutus blandi eius minis & terroribus meassum consumptus beata mar
tyr interri ta per manens omnia pxpo per pen tor men to
rum genera de fi dicta bat Ṿ Xpm libere confitens
xpm ardenter sitiens dissolui & esse cum xpo tu pciens. Omnia pxpo.

℟ Mar tyr sancta dei que flagrans ig ne fidei flammas spre
uisti tortorum uic tima xpi qui fe dant mo res pre
cibus restingue ea lo res uiscea ut uino
bis diui ni feruor a moris cui se uiori a patri & filio & spiri

ā Inuicta xpi testis afra uariis aiudice gaio modis A o laua ſtui sancto. Efe
ttemptata abagnite ueritatis confessione nulla potuit deterreri ta tione.

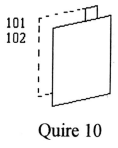

Quire 10

[R H—O-D-I-E N–A-T-A E–S–T beata virgo ma-ria expgenie da–vid pquam
salus mun-di creden-tib ap-paruit cuius vita glorio—sa lucem dedit seculo.
V Beatissime virginis marie nativitatem devotissime   celebre—mus] Cuius
[R Beatissime   virginis ma-rie nativitatem devotissi—me   celebre—
mus   ut   ipsa p   no—bis intercedat ad dominum de ihesum   xp]m
[R Gloriose virginis marie   ortu dignissimu recole—ntes cuius dns/]V Hodie
[humilitatm respici—ens angelo nunciate conce-pit   salvato—re   mun—di/]ipsa
[V Beatissime virginis virginis marie nativitate devotissime celebre—mus] Cuius
[R So—lem iustitie regem paritu—ra spremum stella   maris maris hodie pro
ces——————————————————————————————
——————————sit ad ortum. V Cernere divinum lumen gaude—te fideles.]Stella
[antiphon incipits]
[R Diem festum precelse genetri-cis dei vir-ginis ma-rie]/[antiphon incs. cont.]
[sollempniter celebre—mus quo incoata es eius felix na——tivita]s

nata est beata virgo maria expgenie david. Ut

Nauitatem hodiernã ppet. Quo incho. Solempniter celebre mus. Vt ipsa

Corde & animo xpie to canamus glori am inhac sacra sollempnita te pre

celse gentricis de i uirginis MARIE ut ipsa intercedat pnobis ad

domi num. Cum iocunditate natiuitatem beate uirginis MARIE sol

Regali expgeni e MARIA uirgo exorta refulget cuius precibus nos adiuuari

mente & spiri tu de uotissime poscimus. Corde & animo xpo

canamus gloriam inhac sacra sollempnitate precelse geni tricis de i cui pe

Stirps ies se uir gam p duxit vir gaq; florem & sup hunc

flo rem requies cit spiritus al mus. Uirgo dei

gentrix uirga est flos filius ei us. Et sup. Vbio ria patri &

fili o & spiritui sanc to. Et sup hc Ad cant. Vc suauis. Ind.

Beatissime uirginis MARIE natiuitatem deuotissime celebremus ut ipsa pno

bis intercedat addominum nrm ihm xpm. Ca Audire me. Speciosa facta es

Natiuitas tu a dei gentrix uirgo gaudium annunciauit uniuerso mundo

exte enim ortus est sol iusti ci e xpe deus noster: qui soluens maledictio

nem de dit benedictio nem & confundens mortem donauit no bis uitam

sempi ter nam. Aue MARIA gra p. Qui soluens. Vmus. Cui uita.

Natiuitas glorio se uirgi nis MA RI E exsemine abra he orta de tribu

iu da excela ta stirpe ua uid cuius uita inclita cunc tas illustrat

ec clesi as. Gloriose uirginis MARIE ortum dignissimum rteo la

Felix namq; es. Vra ppopulo mt quicuq; celebrant tuum na talem. Ca ex.

Ad nutum domini nostrum dictantis hono rem. Sicut spina rosam ge

nuit iude a MA RIAM. Vt uicium uirtus operi

ret gratia culpam. Sic spi. Gloria pa tri & filio & spirtui sancto. Sicut.

à Nativitas gloriose uirginis MARIE exsemine abrahe orta de tribu A laun.

iuda clara exstirpe dauid. à Natiuitas est hodie sce MARIE uirginis cuius

uita inclita cunctas illustrat ecclesias. à Regali expgenie MARIA exorta re

fulget cuius precibus nos adiuuari mente & spirtu deuotissime poscimus.

à Corde & animo xpo canamus gloriam inhac sacra sollempnitate precelse geni

149

Exalt. Crucis

tricis dei MARIE. Cum iocunditate natiuitatem beate MARIE celebremus
ut ipsa pro nobis intercedat ad dominum ihm xpm. Adiuua nos tuis precibus
mater xpi MARIA. Oraculum eterne uite claritas celorum. Mater xpi.
Gloria patri & filio & spiritui sancto. Adiuua. Egredietur uirga. Bera dicet iesse

Natiuitatem hodiernam ppetue uirginis genitricis dei MARIE sollempni
ter celebremus qua celsitudo throni pcessit aeuia. Natiuitas glose Alia.

Hodie nata est beata uirgo MARIA ex progenie dauid aeuia aeuia aeuia.

Adest namq. Regali ex pg. Beatissime uirginis. In ii. VESPERA

Natiuitas e hod. Sur rel. Dix dns. Letat fil. Nisi dns. Memento. Adiuua nos.

Egredietur uirga. Quando nata est uirgo sacratissima tunc illuminatus est
mundus stirps beata radix sancta & benedictus fructus eius. In exaltatione cru

Hoc signu crucis. Adoram te xpe & bnd t ca pe tua redimisti mundu. eis adu

Sanctifica nos domine signaculo sancte crucis ut fiat nobis obstaculum
contra seua iacula inimicorum defende nos domine p lignum sanctum.
& ppreciu iusti sanguinis tui cum quo nos redimisti. Scsa isti ii sci q pe

Adoremus rege. Leta ut de myrib. AdCan. Dulce lignu. Inuentioe CANTIC

Dne audiui. Quiqd inflem. Egressus es insal. Salua nos xpe saluator. Invirtu.

Dulce lignu. Hoc signu cru. Verux glosa. Verux benedicta. Inuenem.

O magnum pietatis opus mors mortua tunc est quando in ligno AD LAVDES.
mortua uita fuit. Salua nos xpe saluator. In uirtutem crucis qui saluasti
petrum in mari miserere nobis. Verux ammirabilis euacuatio uulneris.
restitutio sanitatis. Nos autem gloriari oportet inircuce dni nri ihu xpi.

Crux benedicta inter dominus qua morte pependit atq; cruore suo
uulnera nra lauit. Hoc signu crucis erit incelo. cu dns adiudicandu uenerit

Adoram te xpe &c. Super omnia ligna cedrorum tu sola excelsior:
in qua uita mundi pependit in qua xpe triumphauit & mors mortem su
perauit ineternua. Ad. Nos autem gla. Lignum uite. Inuenem. Hoc
signu crucis. Adu. Saluator mundi sy. P signu crucis. Adu. Dulce lignu.
Salua nos xpe saluator. In uespa. O magnu pietatis. Dix d. Salua nos xpe.

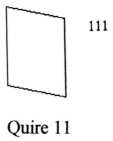

111

Quire 11

& andre am re tia mittentes in ma re uocauit eos dicens. uenite post me
faciam uos piscato res hominum. erant enim piscatores & ait illis. Uenite
uenite post me faciam uos piscatores hominum. at illi relictis reti bus & naui
secuti sunt dominum. Dum deambularet dominus supra mare secus litus
galylee uidit petrum & andream & uo cauit e os. At illi res

Uox ut uocem domini predicantis audi uit beatus andreas relictis retibus.
quorum usu actuq; uiue bat eterne uite secutus est pre miatur eit eam.
Adunius iussionis uocem petrus & andreas relictis retibus secuti sunt redemp

Homo dei duceba tur ut crucifigerent e um populus aute to rem pre
clama bat uoce magna di cens innocens huius sanguis sine causa dampna
tur. Cumq; carnifices ducerent eum ut crucifigere tur factus est concur
sus populorum clamantium & dicen ti um. Innocens huius.

Salue crux quem in corpore xpi dedicata es & ex membris eius tamquam mar
garitis ornata. Recipe me ab hominibus & redde me magistro meo ut
pte me recipiat qui pte redemit me a eua. Biduo uiuens pendebat
in cruce pxpi nomine beatus andreas & docebat populum. Andreas xpi fa
mulus dignus deo apostolus germanus petri & in passione socius. Dignum
in dominus computauit martyrem quem uocauit apostolum dum esset in
mari a eua. Dilexit andream dominus in odorem suauitatis a eua.

Cum uidisset beatus andreas crucem exclamauit & dixit salue crux
quam diu fatiga ris ex pectans me. Sicut expectasti dominum & ma
gistrum me um. Expecta me sancta crux humilem pptur do mi niui. Sic
Salue crux que in corpore xpi de di cata es & ex membris ei us
tamquam margaritis orna ta es suscie pe discipulum eius qui pepen
dit in te. O bo na crux quam diu desiderata & iam concupiscenti anime
O bo na crux que decorem & pulchritudinem de i prepa ra ta. Suscei.
membris do mini susce pisti. Accipe me ab homini bus & redde me.
magistro me o ut pte me recipiat qui pte me re de mit.

Salue crux que incorpore xpi dedicata es & ex membris eius tamquam margari

Doctor bonus & amicus dei andreas ducitur adcrucem. tis orna ta. Acci

aspiciens alonge uidit crucem. Salue crux suscipe discipulum eius qui pepen

dit inte magister meus xpe. Salue crux que incorpe xpi eiaa es & ee i eiv

tamquam a ai i orna ta. Suscipe. Cum ue ro puenisset adlocum ubi crux

parata erat uidens eam alonge exclamauit uoce magna di cens. Salue

Concede nobis hominem iustum redde nobis hominem sanctum. ne inter

ficias hominem deo carum. iustum. mansuetum & pium. of sci dm.

Orauit sanctus ANDREAS dum respiceret celos uoce magna clamauit & dixit

tu es deus meus quem ui dine me patiaris abimpio iudice depo ni. quia ui

uutem sancte crucis ag no ui. Tues magister meus xpe quem

dilexi. quem cognoui. quem confessus sum tantummodo ista uoce exaudi

Expandi manus meas tota di e in cruce adpopulum non me. Pa uit

credentem sed contradi centem michi qui ambulant ui as non bo

nas sed post peccata sua. Deus ultionum dominus deus ultionum liber

egit exaltare qui iudicas terram redde retribucio nem su perbis. Qui amb

Uir iste inpopulo su o mitissimus apparuit. sanctitate autem & grana

plenus iste est qui assidue o rat ppopulo & p ciuitate ista.

Proeo ut me diligerent detrahebant mihi ego autem ora bam. Applo

Dilexit ANDREAM dominus modorem suauita tis dum penderet incruce dig

num sibi computauit marty rem quem uocauit apostolum dum esset inuia ri

& ide o amicus dei appel latus est. elegit eum dominus & excelsum fecit illum. Cui

Salve crux preciosa suscipe discipulum eius qui pependit inte Anlaudes

magister meus xpe. Non me pmittas dne famulum tuum ate separari

tempus est ut commendes terre corpus meum. Beatus andreas orabat di

cens. domine rex eterne glorie suscipe me pendentem inpatibulo. Quipse

quebatur iustum dimer sisti eum domine ininferno & inligno crucis dux

iusti fuisti. Maximilla xpo amabilis tulit corpus apostoli optimo loco cum

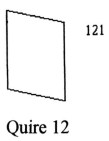

121

Quire 12

mi nes glorificata est inconspectu principum loquebatur sapi enti am

& dominus omni um dilexit e am. Adiuuabit eam deus uultu su o

deus inmedio eius non commouebi tur. Et dominus. Ad laudes.

Orante sancta Lucia apparuit ei beata agathes consolabatur ancilla xpi.

Lucia uirgo quid ame petis quod ipsa poteris prestare continuo matri tue.

Per te lucia uirgo ciuitas siracusana decorabitur adomino ihu xpi e to.

Benedico te pater domini mei ihu xpi quia psilium tuum ignis exstinctus est

alatere meo. Tanto pondere eam fixit spiritus sanctus ut uirgo domini

immobilis per maneret. [ev] Columna es immobilis lucia sponsa xpi quia

omnis plebs te expectat ut accipias coronam uite ae v i a. Ad horas.

Orante sca l. Lucia uirgo. P te lucia uirgo. Tanto ponde. in ii vespa.

Uidi speciosa. Dix d. Usem electa. Laud p. Ista e speciosa. Letat Ornatam.

Nisi dns ed. [eva] Intua patientia possedisti animam tuam Lucia sponsa xpi

odisti que immundo sunt & coruscas cum angelis sanguine pprio inimicum

subisti. Hic incipiat O sapientia. De sco Thoma aplo. Ad vespa in euo.

O Thoma didime p.xpm quem meruisti tangere te precibus rogamus altisonis

succurre nobis miseris ne dampnemur cum impiis inaduentu iudicis. Leta

omia plene hie de aplis. Ad laud [ev] Thomas qui dr. Post bndicam dno canr.

Nolite timere quinta. in vespm ev] Lucia uidisti me. De euangelistis

Qui sunt hii qui ut nubes uo lant & quasi co lumbe ad

fe nestras su as. Dorsa eorum plena sunt oculis a sein

tille ac lampades immedio discurrentes. Et quasi. Gloria patri & filio

spiritui sancto si cut erat inprincipio. Et quasi. Ecce ego iohanne

uidi hostium apertum incelo & ecce sedes posita erat ineo & inmedio sedis &

incircuitu eius quatuor animalia plena oculis ante & retro & dabant gloriam

& honorem & benedictionem sedenti sup thronum uiuenti inseculaseculoru.

Iohan eam ter ram. vel. Tollite iugu. Annunciauer opa di.

vel Nimis honorati s. [ev] Isti sunt uiri sancti quos elegit dominus in caritate non ficta . & dedit illis gloriam sempiternam quo   rum

doctrina fulget ecclesia ut sol & luna etua. Ecce ego mitto uos sicut

oues inmedio luporum estote ergo prudentes sicut serpentes & simplices

sicut columbe. Dum steteritis ante reges & presides nolite premeditari

qualiter respondeatis dabitur enim uobis in illa hora quid loquamini.

Regem apostolorum dominum uenite adoremus. Venite ul. Regem aptox dom. ik.

num uenite   adore mus. Venite.   In omnem terram exiuit sonus eo

rum & in fines orbis terre uerba eorum. Celi enarrant. Clamauerunt iusti

& dominus exaudiuit eos. Benedica Constitues eos principes sup omne

terram memores erunt nominis tui domine. Eructauit Principes populo

rum congregati sunt cum deo abraham. Omnes gentes. Dedisti hereditatem

timentibus nomen tuum domine. Exaudi ds depc. Annunciauerunt opa

dei & facta eius intellexerunt. Exaudi ds. o. m. cu dep. Alt. In omne terram.

Hec est generatio querentium dominum querentium faciem dei iacob. Dñe ira.

Exultate iusti indomino rectos decet collaudatio. Ipsu. Clamauerun iusti.

Constitues eos. p. Principes pplx.

CCE EGO MITTO VOS SICVT O VES INMEDIO LVPO

rum dicit   domi nus estote ergo prudentes   sicut ser

pentes & simplices si cut co   lumbe. Dum lu cem habens

credite inlucem ut filii lucis sitis di cit domi nus. Estote. Vt sit filii

Tollite iugum meum su per uos di cit   domi nus & disci lucis si tis sito

quia mitis sum & humilis corde. iugum enim meum suaue est

& onus me um leue. Et inuenie tis requiem animabus uestris. Iugu.

Dum steteritis ante reges & pre si des nolite cogitare quomodo aut quid

loquamini dabitur enim uo bis in illa ho ra quid loqua mi ni.

Non enim uos estis qui loquimi ni sed spiritus patris uri qui loqui tur

In omnem ter ram exiuit sonus eo rum & infi inuo bis Dabi

nes orbis terre uer ba eo rum. Non sunt loquele neq; ser

In omnes tra \ Celi enarrat E

Hec e gnaco dñi est tra ik

Letatu i dño Et ku ęo

Clamauerunt iudica   ut

148

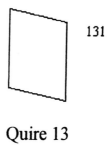

131

Quire 13

accipientes lampades suas exierunt obuiam sponso & sponse quinq; erant
fatue & quinq; prudentes a eua. ae mia. ae mia ae uia h vii Regem uirginu h i n.

à Ante thorum huius uirginis frequentare nobis d ulcia cantica dramatis.
P Dne dns nr. à Vngentum effusum nomen tuum ideo adolescentule dilexerunt
te nimis. P Celi en. à O quam pulchra est easta generatio cum claritate P Dni et.
à Specie tua & pulchritudine tua intende prospere pcede & regna. P Eructauit.
à Adiuuabit eam deus uultu suo deus in medio eius non commouebit P Ds nr. re
à Leua eius sub capite meo & dextera illius amplexabitur me. P agid.
v Diffusa e gra. Alt à Dextram mea. à Posuit signu à Induit me
à Specie tua. à Adiuuabit eā. à O quam pulchra es. v Diffusa e gra. inl.

ENI SPONSA XPI CTI
ACCIPE CORONAM QUAM TI BI DO MINVS PREPARAVIT
procinus amo re sanguinem tu um fudisti & cum
angelis inparadysum intro is tu Ueni electa mea & po
nam inte thronum me um quia concupiuit rex spe ciem tu am. P cui.
R Hec est uirgo sa pi ens quam domi nus uigilan tem in ue nit
que acceptis lampadibus sumpsit se cum o le um & ueniente domi
no introiuit cum e o ad nupti as VlSe dia autem nocte clamor
factus est ec ce sponsus uenit exite ob uiam e i. R ueniente
R Specie tu a & pulchritudine: tu a inten de prospe re pro
cede & regna. v Diffusa est gratia inlabiis tu is ppterea benedixit te dev
R Dilexisti iusti ciam & odisti iniquita tem ppterea uine ter num. P ced.
unxit te deus de us tu us oleo le ticie. v Specie tua & pulchri
tudine tu a intende prospere proce de & regna. ppterea.
R Propter ueritatem & mansuetudinem & iu sticiam & deducet te
mirabi liter dextera tu a. v Dilexisti iusticiam & odisti iniquita
tem ppterea unxit te deus deus tu us. Et deducat inestate. Diffusa
est gratia inlabiis tuis. v Propterea benedixit te deus ineternui. h ii h.

ã Cum esset rex in accubitu suo nardus mea dedit odorem suauitatis. P Benedixisti.

ã Pulchra es & decora filia ierusalem terribilis ut castrorum acies ordinata.

P Fundamta. ã Iam hiemps transiit ymber abiit & recessit surge amica mea & ueni. P Cantate. ã Surge aquilo & ueni auster psla ortum meum &

fluent aromata illius. P Dns r. ex. ã Nigra sum sed formosa filia hierusalem ideo dilexit me rex & introduxit me in cubiculum suum. P Cantate dno.

ã Aque multe non potuerunt exstinguere caritatem. P Dns regn. i ras e.

℣ Specie tua & p t imend psp pe 7 r. Aliu. ã Ipsi sum desp. ã Xpe circumdedit me

℟ mnaus agneus. ã Ista est speciosa inter filias hierusalem. ã Mel & lac ex.

ã Cuius pulchritudine. ã Ipsi soli. ℟ mnaus agneus. ℣ Specie tua & pulchr.

℟ Diffusa est gratia in labiis tuis ppterea benedixit te de us in eternum. ℣ Dilexisti iustitiam & odisti iniquitatem. Ppterea.

℟ Concupiuit rex speciem tuam quia ipse est dns tuus deus & adorabunt eum. ℣ Specie tua & uirtute ua a ice oce peede &

℟ Pulchra facie sed pulchrior fide beata es uirgo Ireg na. et ado respuens mundum letaberis cum angelis intere de pomnibus nobis. ℣ Specie tua & p. intreo. In assumptioe s. MARIE.

℟ Ornatam in monilibus filia. ℣ Astitit regina a dextris tuis. Et beatis. ℟ in In estare. Specie tua & pulchritudine tua. ℣ Inunde psp peede & regina. Adc.

ã Inuenta bona margarita dedit omnia sua & comparauit eam. ℣ Adiuuabit eā.

℣ Veni electa sponsa xpi accipe coronam quam tibi dns preparauit in eternum.

℣ Dilexisti iustitiā ℟ Induit me domi nus uestimento sa luis tus & indumento leticie circumdedit me & tamquam sponsam decorauit me corona ℣ Induit me dominus cyclade auro texta & inmensis

℟ Ista est speciosa inter filias hierusalem In monilibus ornauit me et tāq sicut uidistis eam plenam caritate & dilectio ne in cubilibus & in ortis aro matum. ℣ Specie tua & pulchritudine u a ice oce peede & e a. In cu.

℟ Veni electa me a & ponam inte tronum meum quia concupiuit